CHARLES DICKENS

AND THE BLACKING FACTORY

Also by Michael Allen

Charles Dickens' childhood
1st edition. Macmillan, 1988
2nd revised edition. Oxford-Stockley Publications, 2012

An English Lady in Paris: the diary of Frances Anne Crewe 1786
1st edition, Oxford-Stockley Publications, 2006
2nd edition, 2011
Kindle edition, 2011

As contributor to:

Oxford Reader's Companion to Dickens
edited by Paul Schlicke
Oxford University Press, 1999
Paperback edition, 2000
Anniversary edition 2011

A Blackwell Companion to Dickens
edited by David Paroissien
Blackwell Publishing, 2007
Paperback edition, 2011

Little Charles Dickens at the blacking warehouse
by Fred Barnard

Charles Dickens

and the

Blacking Factory

MICHAEL ALLEN

Oxford-Stockley Publications

Published by
Oxford-Stockley Publications
17 Heather Close, St Leonards BH24 2QJ
United Kingdom
email: oxfordstockley@btinternet.com

First edition 2011
ISBN-13: 978-1463687908
ISBN-10: 1463687907

To the wonders of The National Archives

Acknowledgments

This book would not have been written were it not for The National Archives at Kew in south-west London. Not only do they hold treasures beyond description, which they preserve and care for, but they make them available in a wonderful building, with excellent facilities, expert staff and a willingness to help people to which many other research institutions might well aspire. My thank go to the Bodleian Library, Oxford for its fascinating John Johnson Collection of ephemera and to the collection's librarian, Julie Anne Lambert. Thanks also to the people who carried out the painstaking work for The Adelphi Theatre Project at the University of Eastern Michigan – the lack of similar detailed information about other theatres makes me realise how very special was this excellent piece of work. My appreciation goes to Allan Sutcliffe, who brought the project to my attention. Similarly, the Old Bailey online website is an example of excellence of which all those who contributed should be proud. I'd like to thank Laurence Worms and Ross Milbourne for information relating to their family histories. Some of the information from the research for this book was originally published in *The Dickensian*, Spring 2010. A talk was also given at The National Archives in June 2010 which is now available as a podcast on their website.

Contents

List of illustrations

Introduction

The story of Charles Dickens' childhood is dominated by a single narrative, mostly written down by Dickens himself, then edited, arranged and supplemented by John Forster.[1] Dickens' time spent working at a blacking factory was a pivotal point in that story. The accuracy and truthfulness of his account of his own life was never seriously questioned or tested, reinforced or challenged. Neither of his parents, none of his uncles and aunts, nor any of his brothers and sisters wrote down their own recollections of the childhood of their famous relative. Or if they did, it hasn't survived. Forster claimed a prodigious memory for his friend, but if it frequently failed him we wouldn't know about it. And if Dickens chose to omit particular events or people from his narrative, or to adjust their impact and influence, then we are entirely in his hands – there has been nobody to challenge him. He exercised supreme control over the history of his own childhood and of his time at Warren's Blacking. Yet, inevitably, it was not the complete story: what life story ever is? Dickens knew that to be the case and at the end of that part of his fragment of autobiography relating to the blacking factory he wrote: "It does not seem a tithe of what I might have written, or of what I meant to write".

When Dickens wrote about himself – about his emotions, his observations of the people and events around him – there's little that modern biographers can add to those aspects of the account. Small beer might be found in Dickens' own words elsewhere, other pieces of writing where he adds to, confirms or contradicts his fragment of autobiography; and to *David Copperfield*, if the fact can be sorted from the fiction; otherwise we have to fall back on analysis and dissection of the primary source.

It's rare for a completely new source of information to be found. My heart took a leap when, standing in the research room of The National Archives, I first unrolled the rather large parchments from the Court of Chancery in London, relating to disputes between the people who owned and ran the blacking factory where Dickens was employed. What's more, the events described in the documents took place in the years leading up to, during and just after the period of Dickens' employment at Warren's Blacking. Contained in this first document I

---

[1] *The Life of Charles Dickens*, by John Forster. First published by Chapman and Hall in 3 volumes, 1872-1874, and in many editions since.

found, and in dozens more that flowed from it, was a wealth of information throwing new light on the history, the people, the business practices and the time-line relating to Warren's Blacking. Where Dickens' memory and understanding failed him these documents do, in many instances, correct and enhance the story.

Though they are well worth the effort, the documents are not easy to deal with: they are lengthy, the first item I found, for example, amounting to nearly 20,000 words; they are couched in that stilted, repetitive language that irritated Dickens so much when he worked as a reporter in the courts some years later; they deny the existence of punctuation and the sensible practice of forming sentences and paragraphs: working through the never-ending flow of words is a bit like reading Joyce's *Ulysses* without the imagination, insight and humour – a legal stream of consciousness. These statements, often biased for their own cause and opinionated with regard to the opposition, nevertheless are rich in description of the people who paid Dickens his six or seven shillings a week. It's fascinating to discover that the labels which Dickens assiduously stuck onto the pots of blacking, as described in his fragment of autobiography, were at the very centre of these court cases, described in forensic detail, and the claimed cause of loss and gain.

Three cases were started in the Court of Chancery: Woodd v Lamerte, Warren v Lamerte, and Warren v Woodd. I have seen the Pleadings for each case – that is, the statements laying out their case made by the Complainants, and the opposing Answers giving by the Defendants – and also the Affidavits sworn by the witnesses in two of the three cases. In my narrative I have tried to select from these extensive documents what I consider the most relevant and interesting information, but I recognise that other biographers might choose differently. For that reason I have published in this book the full transcripts I made of the most informative material. These transcripts are not available anywhere else. As a young man the value of primary sources to the researcher and writer was firmly impressed on me. In this instance the reliability of evidence written at a time very close to the events it describes can be deemed greater than that recollected many years later, and not published for about fifty years, in Forster's biography of Dickens. However, I have not included the transcript of the Pleadings in the case of Warren v Woodd, since the contents were so very similar to those in the case of Warren v Lamerte.

The Pleadings are valuable but I found the Affidavits sworn and signed by the witnesses in the two cases of Warren v Lamerte and Warren v Woodd to be more absorbing, bringing us that bit closer to the thoughts, motives and characters of the people involved. I was disappointed, though, not to find the Affidavits in the case of Woodd v

Lamerte. The archive of the Court of Chancery is very extensive, complex in its arrangement, incomplete because of loss and only partially indexed. It is possible the Affidavits exist somewhere among the millions of documents, but they are not in the most obvious places; on the other hand, they may have been lost or discarded at any time over the past 180 years.

We might ascribe a weight of reliability to the court documents, statements truthfully and accurately given, sworn to and signed; yet the many certainties averred to are often edged around with provisos: they "have heard and believe" something to be true; they give evidence "to the best of their knowledge information and belief" or "to the best of their recollection"; and if they don't know something or don't wish to say they know then "they do not have and are unable to set forth as to their belief or otherwise".

All the evidence comprises documents written before the litigants ever step into Court. There is, in The National Archives, no official record of what was said in Court. For this we must turn to the newspapers who, fortunately, judged the cases of Warren v Lamerte and Warren v Woodd to be of interest to their readers. These newspaper reports are also a primary source, written by those present in Court to listen to and watch the proceedings, and while the journalists are not under the same legal obligation to be accurate and, indeed, differ one newspaper from the other, do nevertheless provide the best indication of what the barristers said and how the Lord-Chancellor or the Vice-Chancellor responded. Three of these newspaper reports are given at Appendix 7.

There are four main characters in the story that unfolds in this book: Robert Warren and Jonathan Warren, nephew and uncle, who manufactured blacking in opposition to each other, William Edward Woodd, who bought Jonathan Warren's business from him, and George Lamerte, Woodd's brother in law and cousin by marriage to Charles Dickens. In order to better understand the dynamics between these people some effort has been made to establish their histories and family relationships. One particularly important outcome of this research outside The National Archives has been to correct the assertion by Dickens and Forster that Warren's Blacking was owned by James Lamert and his cousin/brother in law, George Lamert. As will be seen in the body of the book, when Dickens said James Lamert he meant George Lamerte, and when he said George Lamert he meant William Edward Woodd. Another outcome has been to draw attention to the Jewish background of George Lamerte and to his cousins in the Worms family.

In his fragment of autobiography Dickens recognises that Lamerte had some influence on his fascination with theatre, and new information presented here re-inforces Lamerte's involvement with the stage, interestingly during the very years on which this book focuses, and in particular with a theatre, The Adelphi, which was to become a prominent part of Dickens' life. Recognition has to be paid here to the value of the internet in carrying out research. In this particular instance access to The Adelphi Theatre Project, constructed and made available online by the English Department at the University of Eastern Michigan led to information that would have been beyond reach thirty years ago.

Similarly the internet led me to genealogy sites, to digitised newspapers, to bottle and coin collectors, to sites steeped in military history, to the Internet Archive and the Hathi Trust with their digitised rare books, to Australian record offices and to the wonderful John Johnson Collection of ephemera at Oxford's Bodleian Library. Through the internet I have also been able to contact and exchange information with descendents of the Worms, Woodd and Milbourne families; the Lamertes and the Barrows have eluded me. How much more difficult or, indeed, impossible, would this have been without the world-wide-web.

Chapter One

Chatham and the Lamertes

When Charles Dickens was taken to Chatham in 1817, at the age of five, his immediate family comprised not only his mother and father and his two sisters, Fanny and Letitia, but also his Aunt Mary. Mary Barrow, the slightly older sister of Dickens' mother, had been baptised 26th March 1789 at Lambeth in London and had married Thomas Allen, a lieutenant in the Royal Navy, on the 22nd May 1812 at Stoke Damerel, now part of Plymouth, in Devon. Allen was 30 years old and his bride 23. No doubt the wedding took place here because her husband was stationed at the naval dockyard at Devonport; there's a possibility he may also have spent time at the Portsmouth dockyard where John Dickens was located. It's worth considering, too, that Mary Barrow may have been part of the Dickens household as early as February 1810 when her parents fled the country following the discovery of embezzlement by her father, Charles Barrow[2], and that she continued to live with the Dickens family while her husband was at sea. Unfortunately Aunt Mary's marriage was a short one. Lieutenant Allen was the senior officer on board the Cutter Dart, and having married in May 1812 he set sail from England little more than two months later, on 1st August. The Dart was a small ship, two years old, carrying 10 guns and a crew of 40 men. On 2nd August 1813 it was reported to be at Rio de Janeiro and eight weeks later, on 27th October, it sailed for England from Pernambuco, about 1100 miles north of Rio. After that it was never heard of again, officially reported as foundered at sea, with all lives lost.[3] Almost a year later, sufficient time having passed to allow the ship had been lost, John Dickens wrote to the Navy Board on behalf of Mary Allen:

"Navy Pay Office Portsmouth, 17th September 1814. Sir, On behalf of my Sister I have herewith the honor to enclose the papers necessary for the Attainment of her pension (I believe) duly presented. I am Sir, Your most obedient, very humble servt, John Dickens"[4]

---

[2] See Michael Allen: *Charles Dickens' Childhood*. Macmillan, 1988.

[3] *The Naval History of Great Britain from the declaration of war by France in 1793 to the accession of George IV*, by William James, in six volumes, vol 6, 1837.

[4] The National Archives. Admiralty: Service Records, Registers, Returns and Certificates; Certificates and other papers submitted by applicants to the Charity. Ref ADM 6/352/37, ff157-162.

A small batch of five papers in The National Archives record that Lieutenant Allen had paid the "usual allowance of threepence per pound towards the payment of widows pensions" and would seem to indicate that Mary Allen was entitled to a pension of £50 a year. From that time until 1822 she remained part of the family as a live-in aunt for young Charles and his brothers and sisters. This domestic arrangement, it might be suggested, may have had some lasting impact on Dickens, bearing in mind that he adopted exactly the same arrangement in his own married life, first with his wife's sister Mary Hogarth and later with the introduction of Georgina Hogarth. The happiest part of Dickens' childhood was when his Aunt was part of the family and maybe this was a recipe he wished to carry into adulthood – when Aunt Mary left, his life took a turn for the worse and when Mary Hogarth died a great sorrow descended on him; fortunately for him when Georgina Hogarth came to stay she remained by his side for the rest of his life – but that's another story.

At Chatham one of the servants later recalled that Aunt Mary helped with the education of the children and a brief glimpse of her role is given in a few lines from one of Dickens' writings when he recalls being taken to an orrery: "I had expressed a profane wish in the morning that it was a play: for which a serious aunt had probed my conscience deep, and my pocket deeper, by reclaiming a bestowed half-crown".[5]

It was probably through John Dickens' work in the Navy Pay Office that Aunt Mary – or Aunt Fanny as she was known to the family – became acquainted with Matthew Lamerte[6], a half-pay Regimental Surgeon attached to the military hospital at Chatham. His surname was pronounced "Lammer" and some 15 years later Charles Dickens, just embarking on his career as a novelist, caricatured both him and his name as Doctor Slammer in *The Pickwick Papers*:

> "One of the most popular personages, in his own circle, present, was a little fat man, with a ring of upright black hair round his head, and an extensive plain on the top of it – Doctor Slammer, surgeon for the 97th. The Doctor took snuff with every body, chatted with every body, laughed, danced, made jokes, played whist, did everything, and was everywhere. To these pursuits, multifarious as they were, the little Doctor added a more important one than any – he was

---

[5] *Charles Dickens' Childhood*, op cit.
[6] The name of Lamerte has been spelt with and without the final 'e' in a wide variety of documents and to avoid confusion I have chosen to use only the spelling Lamerte, primarily because that is the spelling used in documents from The National Archives that form the backbone of this book.

indefatigable in paying the most unremitting and devoted attention to a little old widow…"

In *Pickwick* Dickens may have mocked the surgeon-soldier but Lamerte had seen serious military action. Starting in 1795 as a Hospital Assistant, at the age of 21, he fought for 16 long years in Britain's wars against Napoleon. Serving first in the West Indies at St. Domingo in 1796-7, where sickness and death from the climate took its toll of the British military, he must have proved his worth since two years later, in 1799, he was promoted to Assistant Surgeon. In 1799 he was in, or passing through, Lisbon, Portugal. Then, serving with the 90th Regiment of Light Infantry, in 1801 he was sent to Egypt where, on the 13th March, he and his comrades were in the forefront of the action at the Battle of Mandora, attacking the strong French positions in the sandhills between Alexandria and Aboukir: "With characteristic élan these devoted regiments advanced eagerly against the foe, and although raked by grape shot, rushed to the mouths of the guns and straightway captured them, cutting down their valiant defenders to a man"[7]. This battle did much towards ousting the French from Egypt but left its mark on Lamerte who, together with seven other officers, was wounded in the action. Nevertheless, he was well rewarded with a gold medal from the Sultan of Egypt and three months later with promotion to Regimental Surgeon with the 50th Foot (West Kent) Regiment[8]. In 1807 he served at Copenhagen and the following year was despatched to the Spanish Peninsula, fighting in the first battle of the campaign at Rolica, where the British lost 500 men, going on to help defeat the French at Vimiera, fighting at Fuentes d'Onora and eventually involved in the retreat to, and battle of, Corunna. In 1809 he was involved in the expedition to Walcheren in Holland and on 4th July 1811 was appointed on half pay to the 7th Royal Veteran Battalion. This veteran status didn't, however, exclude him from the ongoing war against Napoleon since he was given permission, in General Orders from the Adjutant General's Office at Fuente de Guinaldo, dated 13th September 1811, to proceed to join his battalion at Gibraltar. Two years later he was thanked in General Orders for his care of the sick there.[9]

His record shows Matthew Lamerte to have been a seasoned soldier, and as surgeon in those bloody battles he would have seen a great deal of

[7] *Records of the 90th Regiment, Perthshire Light Infantry, with roll of officers from 1795 to 1880,* by Alex. M. Delavoye, London: Richardson & Co., 1880.
[8] Their history is told at the regimental museum in Maidstone: museum.maidstone.gov.uk/queensown/.
[9] Information in this paragraph is taken mostly from *The Peninsula Roll-Call,* by Lionel S. Challis (napoleon-series.org/research/biographies/GreatBritain/Challis/ c_ChallisIntro.html); and from *The New Annual Army List,* with an index, corrected to 7th February 1840, by H.G. Hart, London: John Murray, 1840.

blood and gore, death and painful injury. In his writings Dickens had a way of mocking those with whom he did not empathise and his unsympathetic vignette of Doctor Slammer may be complemented by another of Major Bagstock in *Dombey and Son*, each of them reflecting, perhaps, ambivalence towards Matthew Lamerte:

"He is truly military, and full of anecdote. I have been informed that his valour, when he was in active service, knew no bounds. I am told that he did all sorts of things in the Peninsula, with every description of fire-arm; and in the East and West Indies, my love, I really couldn't undertake to say what he did not do."

Despite serving in such diverse locations as the West Indies, North Africa, Holland and Spain Lamerte also managed to establish a family life. Born in 1774, Matthew Lamerte came from a German Jewish background, his father being Jacob Joseph Lamerte and his first wife the daughter of Isaac Lamert, a Jewish quack-doctor living in the Spitalfields area of East London. The short, odd ways of expressing himself that were later remembered by people in Chatham may have been a throwback to this background. He married a cousin, Sarah Lamert, at the Great Synagogue in London on 5th September 1798 and had seven children, four boys and three girls, of whom one of the boys died young. The first born was Sophia, baptised on 13th October 1799 at the oddly-named British Factory Chaplaincy in Lisbon.[10] The eldest son, George Lamerte, was born in London 2nd September 1802. There must have been an early link with Cork in Ireland since the next son, John Thomas Lamerte, was baptised there on 9th April 1806. The Irish connection was reinforced at a later date. In 1810 the family were living at, or visiting, Hastings in Sussex where another daughter, Hannah, was baptised on 26th May. I don't have a date of birth for the next son, Joseph Richard, but it was probably between 1810 and the birth of a third daughter, Anne, born in 1816. All feature to a greater or lesser extent in this book with Sophia as a lynch-pin, through her marriage, on 18th March 1820, to William Edward Woodd, whose family came from Richmond-upon-Thames; their wedding took place in central London at St Martin in the Fields. We don't have a date for the death of Matthew's first wife, Sarah, but since their daughter Anne was born in 1816 it must have been then or soon after. Matthew Lamerte's religious leanings took a noticeable shift from his Jewish beginnings – although he married within the Jewish faith he and his first wife had at least one of their children baptised into the Church of England; and when arrangements were made for his second marriage, to Mary Allen, he would appear content to put his

---

[10] A 'factory' in this context was an establishment for traders carrying on business in a foreign country or a merchant company's trading station. A chaplaincy attached to the Factory at Lisbon was established in the mid 17th century.

Jewish faith to one side and be married in the Church of England's St Mary's at Chatham. The ceremony took place there on 11th December 1821.

Apart from his later sketches of Doctor Slammer and Major Bagstock, there's nothing to indicate how well the nine-year-old Charles Dickens took to his new uncle, nor to five of his six children; but through his life-long friend and biographer John Forster we know that there developed an association between Dickens and the sixth of his new cousins, whom he called James Lamert. However, there's a strange conundrum surrounding this person because, as will be shown as this book develops, there was, in fact, no member of the family called James. The son of Matthew Lamerte described by Dickens and Forster was called George and not James – his other two sons were called Joseph and John. He is consistently called George through an endless number of formal documents. And yet so certain do Dickens and Forster appear when calling him James that we must conclude the young man was formally named George but preferred to be called James by those close to him. It's not uncommon for such a switch of names to be exercised by those who don't take to the names given them by their parents.

It would appear that as a boy George Lamerte was impressed by the wartime exploits of his father and sought to follow in his footsteps, since the records of the Military Academy at Sandhurst show that George was enrolled as a cadet there on 13th August 1815, aged just 13 years and 11 months. He left the Academy on 24th June 1820, without having obtained a commission. It must have been during his periods of leave from Sandhurst and after his return to his family at Chatham that young Charles and he struck a friendship. There was an age gap of ten years between them and it seems odd that Dickens should have taken to the much older George rather than to the younger brothers Joseph and John. But there may be an explanation in George's interest in theatre: Dickens later told Forster that it was Lamerte who first took him to the theatre, besides which Lamerte helped stage amateur theatricals at the spacious and almost uninhabited Ordnance Hospital. If it was, indeed, George Lamerte who first aroused, or nurtured, Dickens' interest in theatre then he was, of course, instrumental in developing one of the major planks of Dickens' life.

Soon after the marriage between Matthew Lamerte and Mary Allen the couple moved to Cork in Ireland, taking with them all the Lamerte children except George, and one of the Dickens' servants, Jane Bonny. Why they should choose this move it's difficult to tell but the earlier birth of Lamerte's son John demonstrates a previous connection with the area. Sadly, it was a catastrophic move for Dickens' aunt. She must have become pregnant very soon after her marriage since just nine months later the following sad announcement appeared in *The Morning Chronicle* for Wednesday September 4th 1822: "Died. On Wednesday last, at Cork, in child bed, of twins, Mary, wife of Mathew Lamert, Esq. Surgeon of the 1st Veterans." Her death must have come as a great shock and a very great loss to all of the Dickens family – for Elizabeth Dickens the loss of a close sister, for John Dickens of someone who had been a mainstay of his family for nearly the whole of his married life, and for the Dickens children the loss of a dear aunt. Matthew Lamerte continued to live in Ireland for the rest of his life and so passes from the remainder of this book. I would like, though, to round off his story. Two years after the death of his second wife he married for a third time, to Susan Travers. Her father had been a prominent figure in the community as Mayor of Cork and she had military brothers: a colonel, a major, a major-general and a rear admiral. Still in his role as army-surgeon it may have been through these brothers that Lamerte met his new wife; and perhaps through their influence that he gained the appointment, in 1830, as Deputy Inspector-General of Hospitals. In 1845 he was listed in a local directory as a doctor and surgeon living at St Luke's Place, Cork. The couple had four more children, two sons and two daughters and he died on 30th November 1848; his third wife lived on to 4th January 1871.[11] From Ireland he maintained contact with Elizabeth Dickens and followed the blossoming career of her famous son: in 1840 Dickens wrote to Forster: "Would you believe, that in a letter from Lamert at Cork, to my mother, which I saw last night, he says 'What do the papers mean by saying that Charles is demented, and further, that he has turned roman-catholic?' - !"[12] It would appear that his daughter Anne continued to live with him since she is reported to have died in Cork, unmarried, in 1886.

When Matthew Lamerte took his new bride and his family to Cork in January 1822 he left behind his eldest son George. Aged 19 George had completed his training at Sandhurst and though he didn't have a commission it was still his purpose to pursue a military career – he and his father probably considered that an opportunity was more likely to arise at Chatham than in Ireland. Though the Dickens family home at The Brook was rather small, room enough was found for George – Aunt Mary, after all, had vacated some space. Room also had to be found for a new baby, born on 11th March 1822 and given the same name as a child who was born and died in Portsmouth, Alfred. He was baptised at St Mary's Chatham on 3rd April and just as the earlier child had been

---

[11] Much of this information is taken from *Burke's Irish Family Records.*
[12] *The letters of Charles Dickens*, Pilgrim edition, vol.2, p128. In the footnotes to this letter the editors of The Pilgrim Letters say that Lamerte left a graphic ms record of his experiences in many military campaigns from 1795-1810.

given Aunt Mary's surname – Alfred Allen Dickens – so was the new baby given her new surname – Alfred Lamert Dickens. With time on his hands and young Charles an adventurous nine-year-old it was probably this time that Dickens later looked back on as the period the two got on so well together. It was to last about six months, after which John Dickens was recalled to London to work at the Navy Pay Office in Somerset House. The whole family decamped, including George, but Charles was left in Chatham with his schoolmaster probably until September, finishing off the last term of his school year.

Chapter Two

George Lamerte's wider family

The similarities between events in *David Copperfield* and those in Dickens' own life have been evident since John Forster's biography in 1872 and I'm bound to draw on both *Copperfield* and Forster as this book progresses. With reference to John Dickens' financial problems I'm struck by the words that Dickens put into the mouth of Micawber, to the effect that he married too early and never recovered from the expense.[13] Dickens may well have heard his father say this and there may be some truth in it – if there is we'll never know – but if there is then it begs the question why wasn't his father able to extricate himself from an early setback? The evidence of his later attitude towards money suggests it was there from the beginning and the fault lay more with his own character than with an inopportune marriage. Micawber's words apart there's no evidence of John Dickens' financial problems until his days at Chatham. Perversely, the problems of which we're aware arose at a time when his salary from the Admiralty was rising to its highest peak. In London in 1816 his pay was £200 a year, which rose in 1817 to £291 and in 1820 to £441.[14] And yet in 1819 he found it necessary to borrow the very large sum of £200. What it was used for we don't know: he didn't own property, or run a horse and carriage. I've sometimes wondered if Dickens' portrayal of Little Nell's grandfather in *The Old Curiosity Shop* was a suggestion that gambling had once been a destructive force in the Dickens family; there's no evidence to suggest this was so but it was not unknown for the Dickenses to draw a veil of silence over unpleasant events in their lives, and to keep skeletons in cupboards through the destruction of revealing letters. Nevertheless, there is no evidence of gambling by John Dickens. Maybe he was seduced into an investment, but if so it must have failed because we see no sign of any additional benefit. Maybe he used it to pay off a number of smaller debts and tradesmen's bills that had built up, maybe even a doctor's bill. For whatever reason he needed money he found, or was introduced to, a man called James Milbourne. Milbourne's roots were firmly set in central London. He ran a well-respected business as a carver, gilder, glass grinder, picture frame and looking glass maker, operating at

---

[13] *David Copperfield*, chapter 12.
[14] *Charles Dickens' Childhood*, op cit.

different times between 1773 and the mid-1850s from three different addresses in the Strand: numbers 221, 347 and finally 195. Number 347 was occupied from the year 1773 and was located at the corner of Wellington Street, where Charles Dickens had his offices of *All the Year Round* half a century later. From 1804 Milbourne took his sons James and Robert into the business, handing the reins over to them when he retired and eventually it passed to his grandson, also James. That his business was successful can be deduced not just from its longevity but also from the savings he accrued. The saved money was put to use by lending out, as he did to John Dickens, a number of the indentures for these transactions having been located by the family through their own research. His lending of money was often operated in partnership with a certain James Scott. Though James Milbourne had a house at Elizabeth Place, Kennington, now Black Prince Road, he lived for a number of years leading up to his death in July 1826, at 81 years of age, with his widowed daughter, Mary Ann Rowley, at 42 Green Street, Mayfair, just behind the Marble Arch end of Oxford Street. His lending partner, James Scott, lived next door at number 41. John Dickens may have known of Milbourne either from his business in the Strand or from Milbourne's residence at Green Street, not far from where John Dickens' mother had worked as housekeeper to the Crewe family. The transaction between them involved Milbourne's payment of £200 to John Dickens and John Dickens' payment to Milbourne of £26 a year for the rest of his life, probably payable in half-year instalments. A deed recording the arrangement was drawn up and signed on 14th August 1819 – John Dickens' brother-in-law and work colleague Thomas Culliford Barrow stood surety for the payments. But John Dickens was not to be relied upon. He appears to have made one half-yearly payment but no more. Milbourne must have unsuccessfully chased for the second payment but when he realised it wasn't going to materialise he finally agreed to full settlement of the debt on 26th May 1821, by a single payment of £213, ie the original loan plus one half-year payment; the debt was settled by John Dickens's guarantor Barrow. The original document was returned to Barrow and kept in his family papers at least through to 1952, with a note written on to state that John Dickens never did refund the outstanding amount[15]. John Dickens' debt to his brother-in-law was hanging over his head when the family moved to London.

The nine-year-old Charles Dickens appears to have had no idea of any financial problems in Chatham, even in retrospect, when as an adult he wrote and passed to Forster a fragment of autobiography. But biographers have drawn attention to another piece of writing, when

---

[15] Some of this was contained in "The deed in *David Copperfield*", by William J. Carlton, *The Dickensian*, June 1952.

Dickens wrote: "I was taken home, and there was Debt at home as well as Death."[16] If the death was that of his Aunt Mary in September 1822 and if this was the time he was brought up from Chatham to the new family home at Bayham Street in Camden Town, then the subject of debt was almost certainly on the lips of his parents. Forster says the earliest impressions received and retained by him in London, were of his father's money involvements and talks of a deed, which in later days he came to understand was a composition with his creditors. A composition, and reference to a deed, strongly implies a formal arrangement probably drawn up by a solicitor; and considering that he had been at Camden Town only a short time I would suggest the debts and the composition were entered into at Chatham rather than London. This view is reinforced by the decision in 1825, after John Dickens' imprisonment and release under the Insolvent Debtors Act, that payment to creditors was made at the office of the solicitor John P. Henslow in Rochester.[17] The main creditor at that time was Richard Newnham, a neighbour of the Dickenses in Ordnance Terrace, who declined to be the assignee, or trustee, for the payments. This composition that John Dickens carried with him to London probably involved regular payments towards settling the debts, payments which, like the Milbourne payments, he was unable to maintain.

He had also borrowed from his mother (if borrowed is the right word, considering there was unlikely to be any intention of repayment) who says in her will, dated 1824, "… my Son John Dickens having had from me ~~large~~ several sums of money some years ago".

The property that John Dickens had rented at 16 Bayham Street was far from extravagant. Located about three miles from the centre of London Camden Town was little more than a village, though it was soon to be caught up in rapid expansion and lost much of the quietness it enjoyed when the Dickenses were there. Brought back from Chatham the young Charles did not like the change, particularly his parents' failure to find the money to send him to school. Suddenly there was a lack of routine and stimulation. Speaking of his father, Dickens later wrote:

"…in the ease of his temper, and the straitness of his means, he appeared to have utterly lost at this time the idea of educating me at all, and to have utterly put from him the notion that I had any claim upon him, in that regard, whatever. So I degenerated into cleaning his boots of a morning, and my own; and making myself useful in the work of the little house; and looking after my younger brothers and

---

16 *All the Year Round*, Christmas 1859: 'The haunted house'; reprinted in *Christmas Stories*. This line has been quoted by Forster, Langton and Kitton.

17 Interestingly Henslow married Frances Stevens, the daughter of Thomas Stevens who owned Gads Hill Place, which Dickens coveted as a child and bought in 1856.

sisters (we were now six in all); and going on such poor errands as arose out of our poor way of living."[18]

There were compensations. He was taken to visit relations: to his grandmother in Oxford Street, who gave him a fat old silver watch; to his uncle Thomas who had rooms above a bookshop in Gerard Street, Soho, the uncle who had paid off John Dickens' debt to James Milbourne; to his godfather Christopher Huffam who lived in a substantial, handsome sort of way as a ship-rigger in Limehouse, close to the Thames; and probably to his recently-acquired relatives in the Lamerte family.

George Lamerte had continued to live with the Dickens family following their move from Chatham to Bayham Street and, being unemployed himself, spent time with young Charles. Dickens later remembered, and told Forster, that Lamerte had made and painted a toy theatre for him. Later, in 1853, Dickens wrote a much-quoted piece called "Gone astray" in which he described himself as a small boy, taken out for the day by "Somebody". It's my judgement that the Somebody was, in fact, Lamerte. If so then Dickens gives us a well-remembered picture of him, a 20-year old man, just up from Chatham and trying to look stylish: "I have an impression that Somebody was got up in a striking manner – in cord breeches of fine texture and milky hue, in long jean gaiters, in a green coat with bright buttons, in a blue neckerchief, and a monstrous shirt-collar. I think he must have come (as I had myself) out of the hop-grounds of Kent. I considered him the glass of fashion and the mould of form."[19]

In the course of the tale, which Dickens claimed at the end was literally and exactly true, the boy and Somebody were parted and an account of the child's inquisitiveness and wandering around London was related. The journey began at St Giles' Church, travelled to Charing Cross, along the Strand and Fleet Street, past St Paul's Cathedral and on to the Guildhall, then into the City and finished at Goodman's Fields. This small part of Whitechapel might seem a strange destination, obscure in comparison with the other landmarks he visited; yet telling, because this was the area where the family of Lamerte's mother lived.

George Lamerte's parents were probably cousins, both families originating in Germany, though I don't know the level of kinship. On George Lamerte's side of the family the surname was spelt sometimes with and sometimes without the final letter 'e', though George Lamerte favoured it with and so I have, throughout this book, followed his example. On his mother's side I've only found the spelling Lamert and

---

[18] Forster, op cit.

[19] *The Dent Uniform edition of Dickens' journalism, volume 3: 'Gone astray' and other papers from Household Words 1851-59*; edited by Michael Slater, Dent, 1998, page157.

have used that spelling for her side of the family, which provides a neat distinction between the two. It's interesting to note that, as an adult, Alfred Lamert Dickens used both spellings.

The Quack Doctors: Lamert Senior and Junior

George Lamerte's mother Sarah was the daughter of Isaac Lamert, a quack medical practitioner; and on his mother's side there were three aunts, Esther, Catherine and Rachel and an Uncle Abraham. Abraham followed his father into quack medicine, as did Abraham's two sons Joseph and Samuel. An early account of Isaac Lamert was published in 1805 in *The London Medical and Physical Journal*[20]. It says he was born in Germany but doesn't explain how he or his family came to Britain. His first work was as a servant in the house of a Mr Goldsmith of Thavies Inn, after which he rented a little shop in Chiswell Street, next to a bookshop run by James Lackington, who went on to achieve great fame and wealth. From his shop Lamert sold chalk balls to whiten buttons and buckles and achieved such perfection at this that he raised enough money to enable him to set up as a maker of quack medicines, probably moving at this stage to 10 Church Street Spitalfields, an address he later claimed to have operated from since 1765. His first concoction was a spirit of wine, sweetened and coloured with treacle, which he called Switzer's Balsam and to lend power to his claims for the "medicine" he assumed the title of Doctor. This self-created Doctor, the article says, insinuated in his hand-bills "that in any disorder incident to the human body, and the afflicted know not the real disorder, or what it proceeds from, by bringing or sending their morning urine, may depend on having their disorder really informed them, as the Doctor's admirable knowledge from the urine has established his fame." His bills inform potential customers that he can accommodate any lady or gentleman with genteel lodgings at his house. The article goes on to say that a vein of piety is assumed in many of his advertisements and the sacred name is introduced to sanction deceit and cover ignorance, with impudent claims of the blessing of God, the intervention of providence and intimations he is the agent of the Almighty. Unabashed by his own outrageous claims Lamert had published in 1787 a self-congratulatory book, consisting mainly of letters from patients, entitled *Pro Bono Publico: an account of the remarkable cures performed by Dr. Lamert and Co.*[21] Also in that year Lamert took on to assist him a "smart active youth, very loquacious, and of sonorous lungs" called Issachar Cohen. Equipping him with a horse and a stock of balsam Cohen was sent off to sell the product all

---

[20] *The London Medical and Physical Journal*, vol 12, June-December 1804, pp425-6.
[21] The sole surviving copy appears to be in the library of The Wellcome Institute in London. It comprises only 16 pages.

over Kent, which he did very successfully. However, Cohen was ambitious and discovering from one of his customers in Hawkhurst that a local apothecary, now dead, had achieved a good reputation, he took over that man's name and became known thereafter as Doctor William Brodum. When he discovered this Lamert ended their connection, announcing it in the *London Gazette*[22] and Doctor Brodum went on to acquire fame as a quack doctor that far exceeded that of his mentor, earning for himself an entry in the *Oxford Dictionary of National Biography*.[23]

After many years Switzer's Balsam may have lost its appeal, or maybe the criticism in the journal article hit sales, because the next advertisement I've found, appearing in 1821, introduces a new product.

"Mr. Hooker, Ipswich, has just received a fresh supply of that invaluable Cordial, The BALM OF LIFE viz. Dr. LAMERT's (sen.) NERVOUS BALSAM, proved by more than 56 years experience of wonderful efficacy and superior to any Medicine ever discovered; many thousands having been cured of lowness of spirits, loss of appetite, trembling and shaking of the hands or limbs, nervous or bilious debility, inward wastings, palsy, palpitation of the heart, indigestion, spasms, flushings of heat and cold, oppression of the breast, dimness of sight, impaired memory, weaknesses, ulcerated throats, consumption, asthmas, shortness of breath, obstinate coughs, and every kind of debility to which the human frame is subject. By taking a tea-spoonful of it twice a day will evince its great efficacy and valuable properties.

Be sure to ask for Dr. LAMERT's NERVOUS BALSAM"[24]

Advertisements such as this appeared in newspapers throughout the country and sales of a cure-all balsam, whatever name it went under, must have proved a steady earner. But he had at least one more string to his bow, extolling his skill in the curing of venereal disease, piles, fistulas and ruptures, all of which, he assures his public, are cured without surgical operation, though he omits to say exactly what his methods involve – who knows, perhaps the application of his Nervous Balsam. Both sexes are provided for. The following leaflet demonstrates not only how he sells his services but also where he lives, how long he has lived there, the very long hours he's available, the accommodation he can provide and, for the shy or ashamed, that access can gained by "a back door round the corner up the gateway, name on the door".

---

[22] *The London Gazette*, 8th July 1788.
[23] Like Lamert William Brodum was put in the spotlight in *The London Medical and Physical Journal*, vol 13, January-June 1805, pp66-75.
[24] This advertisement appeared in *The Ipswich Journal*, December 8th 1821. It included a list of stockists in that area in addition to Mr Hooker of Ipswich, and a list of prices.

"THE VENEREAL DISEASE, effectually cured, Which is well known in the Metropolis, and other parts of the kingdom, many thousands having been saved by DR. LAMERT, SEN., at his old establishment, 10, CHURCH STREET, SPITALFIELDS, Ten Doors from Spitalfields Church, London, Where he has resided more than 55 years, and continues successfully to eradicate every symptom of so dreadful a complaint, whether arising from quacking themselves, or by consulting those ignorant pretenders to medical skill, who by their boasted promises delude the unwary. Those who suspect themselves injured, by an early application, may be relieved in twenty-four hours. In the course of DR. LAMERT'S extensive practice he has witnessed thousands having fallen victims through the pernicious use of mercurials and salivation, which not only debilitate, but eventually destroy the constitution. Slight cases, and even those of long standing, ulcers in the throat, nose, and roof of the mouth, eruptions and blotches in various parts of the body, strictures, dimness of sight, noise in the ears, deafness, nocturnal pains in the limbs, frequently taken and fatally treated as rheumatism, nodes on the shin bones, buboes, shankers and glandular swellings, by a superior mode of treatment, speedily and permanent cured, without confinement or hindrance of business, on terms suitable to the circumstances of each individual.

The Doctor may be consulted daily, by both sexes, in all cases, in different languages, from 8 in the morning, till nine in the evening, as above; and on Sunday from 8 in the morning till 12. Or by letter (post paid) inclosing a fee, for no others are answered, will be duly attended to. The public will please to observe the name and place of abode, as there is another Doctor in the same street.

The piles and fistulas cured without any surgical operation. The Doctor's great skill in the cure of ruptures is too well known to need any comment here, suffice it to say, that where the application of a truss is deemed necessary, the Doctor will apply it without any charge to the Patient. Private apartments for the better accommodation of both sexes, at No. 10, Churchstreet, Spitalfields, a large sign at the front of the house. Advice gratis. A back door round the corner up the gateway, name on the door."[25]

George Lamerte's grandfather Isaac died in 1827, so he was still alive when the Dickens family and their cousin moved to London in 1822 although, if he had been operating since 1765, he must have been aged in his 70s or 80s. In his will, written 27th September 1826 and proved 1st February 1827, he left money to his son Abraham, to his daughters

---

[25] "Leaflets on the treatment of venereal diseases of the early nineteenth century", by A. Fessler, in *The British Journal of Venereal Diseases*, June 1946, pp85-89.

Rachel, Catherine and Esther (but not to his daughter Sarah, George Lamerte's mother, who had, of course, died some years earlier). Money was also left to his grandson, George's younger brother John.[26]

If Isaac Lamert was a remarkable character then so, too, was his son Abraham, who followed his father into quack medicine, similarly taking up the bogus title of Doctor. Since they both operated at the same time and both promoted themselves as Doctor Lamert, Isaac often identified himself as Senior and Abraham as Junior. The son was also credited at times with the strange middle name of Lima. Though always maintaining his link with his father in Spitalfields Joseph spread his appeal further abroad, establishing a base at Queen Street in Bristol and travelling to major towns and cities throughout the country to promote and sell his wares. Self-promotion was part of his stock-in-trade. Wherever he went he would place an advertisement in the local newspapers, announcing his arrival as if it were some great event. In Carlisle, for example, both *The Citizen* journal and *The Carlisle Journal* noted his arrival at the end of September 1829: "This Dr. Lamert is a fearfully dashing gentleman, all powder, with a black servant, and drives a beautiful pair of greys. Vive la Quackery!" Elsewhere he is described with his two-wheeled open chaise, a cape round his shoulders, an eye-glass, a bamboo cane and a "copper face". Such an eye-catching character must have attracted attention wherever he went, as, of course, he intended. His greatest product was The Balm of Zura or Phoenix of Life, which he colourfully promoted as follows, on this occasion at Exeter:

"This great reanimator of nature has been proved, by most extensive private practice, to possess such efficacy as justly entitles it to a universal approbation. It is a perfect restorative in all nervous disorders, headaches, weaknesses, lowness of spirits, dimness of sight, wanderings of the mind, vapours, and melancholy; all kinds of hysteric complaints, asthmas, paralytic affections, and a certain preventive of the gout. It is extremely salubrious in nausea, flatulencies, and obstructions; and is admirably calculated to relieve broken and decayed constitutions, when every other medicine has totally failed!

The medicinal qualities of the BALM OF ZURA, or PHOENIX OF LIFE, are extracted from an Asiatic berry, strongly resembling that of the whitethorn of this country; but its virtues are of the most exhilarating description. It is faithfully prepared from the prescription of the highly-celebrated REMBERTI DODOENS,

---

[26] The National Archives. Records of the Prerogative Court of Canterbury: Will Registers: The will of Isaac Lamert. Ref Prob 11/1721.

Physician to the Turkish Emperor and his harem. In 1588, a present of it was sent by the Sultan to Queen Elizabeth, who prized it exceedingly for its powerful stomachic qualities, as a sweetener of the blood, and as an invigorator of the nervous and debilitated system.

The CORDIAL BALM OF ZURA is prepared only by the sole Proprietor, Dr. LAMERT, and sold, wholesale and retail, at his house, No.54, Queen-square, Bristol; also, by TREWMAN and Co. and R.CULLUM, Exeter; and by most respectable Medicine Venders in Town and Country.

In bottles at 4s.6d. 11s. and £1. – one 11s. bottle contains three at 4s.6d. and that at a pound six times as much, whereby is a saving of seven shillings, duty included.

Beware of impositions, as none are genuine but where the sole Proprietor's name is blown on the bottle, sealed with the initial of the Doctor's name on the cork, and enveloped in the Asiatic arms and directions."[27]

Exotic as he may sound Rembert Dodoens was not a creation of Lamert, but a sixteenth-century physician and botanist whose book *A new herbal or historie of plants* is considered one of the foremost botanical works of the period and was used as a reference book for more than two centuries. Dodoens became the court physician to the emperors of both Austria and Spain and a professor of medicine at the University of Leiden, though the Turkish Emperor and his harem seem to be an elaboration of Lamert's.

Legitimate medical practitioners disliked the Lamerts and the many other quack doctors who widely advertised their wares to a public with poor understanding and knowledge of medicines, and there were frequent attacks in the medical press, sometimes in dubious taste. *The Medical Adviser* related the story of one of Lamert's dissatisfied customers who decided to get his own back. Having wasted his money on the Balm of Zura this customer took his empty bottle to a tavern frequented by Lamert and bided his time. When Lamert had to leave the bar for a short time his customer urinated into the bottle and added brandy and water. On Lamert's return a complaint was made to him that the balm had gone sour. To the merriment of all Lamert first tasted the concoction and with further encouragement drank the whole bottle, just to show it was perfectly safe. Only then was the practical joke explained, to the great wrath of the doctor and the great hilarity of the rest.

Whether it was because of bad press like this, or the ineffectiveness of his product, or even competition, Abraham Lamert's business was a

---

[27] From *Trewman's Exeter Flying Post*, 3rd April 1823.

precarious one and he fell on bad times on more than one occasion, as this notice from *The London Gazette* demonstrates:

"By order of the Court for the Relief of Insolvent Debtors – the petitions of Henry Moore, late of Bath, in the County of Somerset, Merchant; Abraham Lima Lamert, junior (committed by the name of Lima Abraham Lamert), late of High-Street, Borough, Southwark, Surrey, and Queen-Square, Bristol, Somersetshire, Surgeon and Doctor of Medicines; and James Stride, late of Frome, Somersetshire, Auctioneer and Broker, but now prisoners for debt in the King's-Bench prison, in the County of Surrey, will be heard at the Guildhall, in the City of Westminster, on the 26th day of May instant, at the hour of Nine of the Clock in the Morning; and that schedules, containing lists of all the creditors of the said prisoners, annexed to their said petitions, are filed in the Office of the said Court, No. 9, Essex-Street, in the Strand, in the County of Middlesex, to which any creditor may refer; and in case any creditor intends to oppose the discharge of either of the said prisoners, it is further ordered, that such creditors shall give notice in writing of such his intention, to be left at the Office of the said Court, two days at the least before the said 26th day of May, together with the grounds or objections to such discharge, and in default thereof, such Creditor shall be precluded from opposing the said prisoners; and we do hereby declare, that we are ready and willing to submit to be fully examined touching the justice of our conduct towards our creditors. HENRY MOORE. ABRAHAM LIMA LAMERT, jun. JAMES STRIDE."[28]

Further notices relating to his bankruptcy appeared in issues of *The London Gazette* for 21st November 1834 and 23rd January 1835. Soon after this last notice Abraham Lamert travelled to Ireland where he died, in Dublin, on the 4th March 1836; his will was proved in London on 6th April.[29] He left two sons, Joseph and Samuel, both about the same age as Charles Dickens.

Further detailed information about Abraham Lamert, his family and his business can be found in the fascinating transcript of an Old Bailey trial, in which his wife accuses an employee of embezzlement. Heard just two months after Lamert's death, the case begins as follows:

"ELIZABETH LAMERT. I am the widow of Dr. Abraham Lamert, who carried on business at No. 10, Church-street, Spitalfields. He was a patent medicine vender—the prisoner came into his employ about

[28] *The London Gazette* 2nd May 1818, p800.
[29] The National Archives. Records of the Prerogative Court of Canterbury: Will Registers: The will of Abraham Lamert. Ref Prob 11/1860.

four years since—he was clerk and assistant—he was authorized to receive money for medicines that were sold, and to make proper entries of them in the book—there was a day-book kept to enter money received from customers for goods sent out, or medicines sold—this is the book (*looking at one*) in which I have always seen the accounts entered—my husband died on the 4th of March, 1836—on the 19th of May 1835, I left London, and joined him in Dublin, and continued with him until his death—I am his administratrix—the prisoner has not accounted to me, independently of the day book, for 5s., 3d., received from Zaccheus Hunter, on the 9th of July, 1835; nor for 8s. 9d. received from Alfred Willoughby, on the 22nd of August, 1835—he has never accounted for or paid me the sum of 10s., received on the 19th of October, from Mr. James Knight—two days before my husband's death I authorized my son, Joseph Lamert to obtain the prisoner's account from him."[30]

The Doctors Lamert, senior and junior, were, then, the grandfather and uncle of George Lamerte and when the Dickens family and George Lamerte moved to London in 1822 it seems most probable that George, with his father in Ireland, will have spent some time with this other side of his family. That he may have taken young Charley Dickens with him can only be conjecture – Dickens makes no reference to such visits in his fragment of autobiography. In his writings Dickens referred to Spitalfields, as he did to most parts of London, but not in any detail, nor with any connection to quack medicine – in fact, quack doctors were not a target for Dickens' pen.

Doctor Lamert senior had only the one son, but there were four daughters: Sarah, the mother of George Lamerte, and his three aunts Esther, who married a Joseph Nathan, Catherine, who became Catherine Brown, and Rachel. Esther and Catherine have no impact on this book, but Rachel does. It may be that George Lamerte paid calls on all three of his aunts, but we know for sure that there was one he was very well acquainted with, Aunt Rachel. On 23rd May 1799 she had married within the Jewish faith to Aaron Worms at the Great Synagogue in London and they had at least seven children. Aaron Worms, born in Germany in 1775, had an older brother, Henry, seven years his senior and also born in Germany; Henry also had at least seven children. For George

---

[30] Old Bailey Proceedings Online (www.oldbaileyonline.org, 29 June 2011), May 1836, trial of Thomas Gore (t18360509-1335); the full transcript is given as Appendix One to this book

Lamerte here were seven cousins and a further seven cousins by marriage; just as Charley Dickens was his cousin by marriage.

The Worms side of the family

Aunt Rachel and Uncle Aaron had their home and business in Whitechapel, at 63 Greenfield Street in 1802 and later, at least from 1814, at 107 Whitechapel Road[31], Aaron describing himself first under the catch-all trade of merchant and later describing his premises as linen drapers, haberdashers and mercers. Their son Lewis Aaron Worms went into partnership with his father and added to the description "warehousemen and dealers in shoes". There is a short but interesting transcript of a trial at The Old Bailey, dated 19th September 1836, in which John Jackson was indicted for stealing, on the 24th August, 1 shawl, value 5s., the goods of Lewis Worms and another:

"LEWIS WORMS. I live in Whitechapel, and am in partnership with Aaron Worms. About eight o'clock in the morning on the 24th of August, I was walking in front of my shop – I saw the prisoner in the act of taking a shawl from my window – I called to a person in my employ – I collared him – he made resistance, but, with the assistance of half a dozen more, we secured him – he had removed the shawl from inside my window – this is it.

Cross-examined by MR. PHILLIPS. *Q.* How do you mean inside your window? *A.* It hung inside, with many others – I am not aware that any pane of glass had been broken before, but I suppose he must have broken it – my father is in partnership with me – the prisoner appeared not to be drunk, but he pretended to be so.

PETER HAYES. I am foreman to Mr. Worms. I saw the prisoner take the shawl from the window – he threw it down, and we secured him.

Cross-examined. Q. Had he got any distance? *A.* About two yards – he had doubled it up in his hand.

GUILTY. Aged 26. – Confined Eight Days."[32]

For a short time Lewis Worms diversified, setting up at 107 Whitechapel Road with his cousin George Lamerte in the manufacture of boot blacking; but that's a story at the heart of this book, which I'll

---

[31] This information is taken from the records of the Sun Fire Insurance Company, held at the City of London's Guildhall Library.
[32] Old Bailey Proceedings Online (www.oldbaileyonline.org, 29 June 2011), September 1836, trial of John Jackson (t18360919-2200).

return to as we progress. Lewis Aaron Worms was born in 1805, married Hannah Joseph at the Great Synagogue in 1826, had at least nine children, and died in 1890.

Another of the sons of Aunt Rachel and Uncle Aaron was Henry Worms who concentrated on the large-scale manufacture of boots and shoes, expanding from the Whitechapel Road to premises in the Minories, a warehouse in Bishopsgate and a showroom at 275 Oxford Street. He was born about 1808, married Rebecca Nathan in 1836 and died in 1878. His wife may well have been a cousin since his Aunt Esther had married Joseph Nathan. This Henry Worms was named after his uncle, Aaron Worms' brother Henry.

Uncle Henry was at the least a very colourful character and at the most a highly significant icon in the history of Charles Dickens. Born in Frankfurt in 1764, at what age he transferred from Germany to London we don't know, but he is likely to have brought with him his Jewish culture and appearance and a heavy German/Hebrew accent. He married Hannah Levy at the Great Synagogue in London in 1798. We next find him at the age of 40, in 1808, insuring his business premises at 44-45 Nightingale Lane, East Smithfield, where he described himself as a furniture broker and cabinet maker. Two years later he was at 17 Dock Street, Wapping, as a broker of household goods; and the following year in Norton Folgate, still as a broker of household goods.[33] Such a business description might have encompassed a whole range of activities and it may be relevant that many east-end Jews at this time made their living as second-hand dealers. Whatever the nature of his living, in 1811 it failed and he was made bankrupt. The notice of bankruptcy published in *The London Gazette* described his business as "upholsterer, dealer and chapman" and his address as Wapping-Dock-Street.[34] A deposition written on his behalf 14 years later described his position at this time: "… he carried on a Respectable Establishment, as an Auctioneer, Appraiser, Wholesale Carpet and Woolen Warehouse Man for a Long Period in Norton Falgate, till about Twelve Years since, when through unavoidable Misfortunes, he failed in Business and was compelled to open a Shop … and in that Degrading Occupation to preserve a Beloved Wife and Family from Starving, yet by dint of Industry, Attention and Perseverance he maintained them decently till the Death of his Wife, whose irrecoverable Loss he has felt ever since. He has had to

---

[33] This information is taken from the records of the Sun Fire Insurance Company, held at the City of London's Guildhall Library.

[34] The first notice appeared in the issue for 16th March 1811. Further notices recording the progress of the procedure appeared in issues for 23rd March, 30 March, 2nd April, 16th April and 4th June.

encounter the severest Misery and Distress but has met it with Fortitude and Resignation, and had almost surmounted his Difficulties…"[35]

The expansion from "upholsterer, dealer and chapman" to "Auctioneer, Appraiser, Wholesale Carpet and Woolen Warehouse Man" may have been an embellishment to establish respectability but it demonstrates how widely spread his dealings were – a bit of this, a bit of that! After his wife died in 1818 life must have been terribly hard for this 50-year-old German Jew – bankruptcy, an uncertain way of making a living and seven children to provide for, all under the age of 16. We might suppose that temptations came along to help ease the need to earn money and Henry Worms was probably no stranger to the odd questionable transaction. Then, he got caught, together with his brother and three other men – a newspaper report tells the story:

"PUBLIC OFFICE, BOW-STREET. – Yesterday Aaron Worms, Lyon Levy, Henry Worms, Benjamin Israel, and Patrick Neale underwent an examination before Mr. Birnie, charged with having a large quantity of bed furniture found in their possession, which had been stolen from the warehouse of Mr. Miles, in Holborn, to the amount of several hundred pounds. – The discovery was made by a friend of Mr. Miles seeing the furniture to be sold in the Minories, and knowing the pattern to be Mr. Miles's only, gave him information. – The thief is not yet taken. The prisoners Israel and the two Worms were liberated, on they and some friends entering into an undertaking for their appearance at a future day."[36]

We don't know the outcome of this charge but no further report appeared in this newspaper and the Worms brothers appear to have retained their freedom, so a dismissal seems likely. I also have a report that Henry was charged at the Clerkenwell Sessions of 1816 with "uttering bad money", but with a lack of report or repercussions this, too, was probably dismissed.

Things got more serious in 1823, at just the sort of time that 11-year-old Charley Dickens may have been taken visiting by Cousin George. Henry Worms was now operating a "marine store" in Fox Court, a seedy, run-down alleyway leading off Grays Inn Lane, just a few steps from its junction with Holborn. This was the western end of a stretch of streets, lanes and alleyways, bordering the north side of Holborn and reaching across to Field Lane, Saffron Hill and Smithfield, which was

---

[35] This is taken from a petition for clemency, written to the Home Secretary, Sir Robert Peel, in 1825 and quoted in an article "The ancestors of Laurence Worms: the true story of how I am related to Dickens (but not in a good way)", published in the *Antiquarian Booksellers' Association Newsletter*.
[36] *The Morning Chronicle*, Thursday 3rd March 1814. The Lyon Levy referred to could have been his wife's brother.

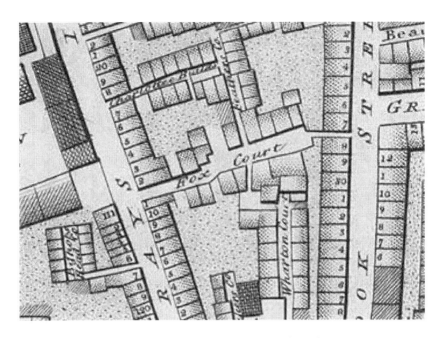

Fox Court from Horwood's map of London

notorious for the poverty and criminality of its inhabitants and the multi-occupancy of its tenements. Fox Court was not an important spot – no more than a small turning, with a sort of crooked elbow halfway down its short length, entered from Grays Inn Lane and exited at the other end through a very narrow built-over alleyway. Shown clearly on the Horwood map of 1792[37] it contained a dozen or so properties some or all of which may have dated back to the 17th century: "In this wretched alley the profligate Countess of Macclesfield was delivered of her illegitimate child, Richard Savage... delivered by a Mrs Wright, a midwife, on Saturday the 16th of January 1697."[38] These old buildings were probably those still standing and described by Henry Mayhew in his classic book *London labour and the London poor*, first published in 1851. In a section headed "The filth, dishonesty and immorality of low lodging-houses" he printed an illustration and the following description:

The illustration presented this week is of a place in Fox-court, Gray's-inn-lane, long notorious as a 'thieves' house', but now far less frequented. On the visit, a few months back, of an informant (who

[37] *Map of London, Westminster & Southwark, shewing every house, 1792-9*, by Richard Horwood. Motco, 2006. ISBN 978-0-9545080-7-4 (CD).
[38] *London recollected: its history, lore and legend*, by Walter Thornbury, Vol 2, The Alderman Press, 1985, p552. Originally published as *Old and New London*.

The thieves' kitchen from Mayhew's London

declined staying there), a number of boys were lying on the floor gambling with marbles and halfpennies, and indulging in savage or unmeaning blasphemy. One of the lads jumped up, and murmuring something that it wouldn't do to be idle any longer, induced a woman to let him have a halfpenny for 'a stall'; that is, as a pretext with which to enter a shop for the purpose of stealing, the display of the coin forming an excuse for his entrance. On the same occasion a man walked into 'the kitchen', and coolly pulled from underneath the back of his smock-frock a large flat piece of bacon, for which he wanted a customer. It would be sold at a fourth of its value."[39]

As a writer Dickens himself often made reference to this same area, in *Oliver Twist*, for example:[40] "...deep in the obscurity of the intricate and dirty ways which, lying between Grays Inn Lane and Smithfield, render that part of the town one of the lowest and worst that improvement has left in the midst of London." And in *On duty with Inspector Field*: "...the courts that are eaten out of Rotten Gray's Inn Lane, where other lodging-houses are, and where (in one blind alley) the Thieves' Kitchen and Seminary for the teaching of the art to children is."[41] He also chose

---

[39] This extract taken from *The illustrated Mayhew's London*, edited by John Canning, Book Club Associates, 1986.

[40] *Oliver Twist*, chapter 41.

[41] "On Duty with Inspector Field", first published in *Household Words*, 14th June 1851; now available in *Dickens' journalism, volume 2: The amusements of the people and other papers*, edited by Michael Slater, Dent, 1996.

to draw attention to Fox Court in his publication *The Household Narrative of Current Events*:

"William Bristol, a young ruffian, was tried on the 21st, at the Middlesex Sessions, for having Attempted to Steal from a person unknown. The prisoner in company with a notorious thief and prostitute, had been detected by a police officer one evening, in Gray's Inn Lane, putting his hand into the pocket of a person passing by, but before he had time to take anything his companion gave the alarm and they ran away, but the man was captured. From the evidence given by the police officer it appeared that the prisoner was a member of a gang of daring thieves, and the "deputy" or, sub-landlord of a notorious den in Fox Court, Gray's Inn Lane, which was known as the "Thieves Kitchen," and which was the rendezvous of burglars, pickpockets, prostitutes, and pot stealers; a regular receptacle of stolen property, and where nightly could be seen thieves, prostitutes, and beggars, of all ages and of both sexes, huddled together indiscriminately, there being in some instances eight or ten men, women and children, all in one bed together. Some short time before, the officer had been on duty near Fox Court, and on contriving to peep into the "Kitchen" through a window, he saw the prisoner in a room with a line tied across it, and from this line was suspended a coat, in the pockets of which were placed pocket-handkerchiefs. A dozen little boys surrounded the prisoner, and each in turn tried his still in removing a handkerchief without moving the coat or shaking the line. If he performed the manoeuvre with skill and dexterity, he received the congratulations of the prisoner; if he did it clumsily or in such a manner as would have led to detection, had the operation been performed in the usual manner in the street, the prisoner beat them with severity, having on the occasion in question knocked down and kicked two of the boys for not having exhibited the requisite amount of tact and ingenuity in extracting the handkerchief. The learned judge said he regretted that the court had not the power of passing such a sentence as would rid the country of the prisoner, but sentenced him to be kept to hard labour for eighteen calendar months."[42]

All of this sounds as though it might have been lifted from the pages of *Oliver Twist*, published 14 years earlier. But, bearing in mind what I shall relate soon, keep in mind the description of the thieves as "pot stealers".

There was, for Dickens, another very personal knowledge of Fox Court, dating from the age of 15, when he worked as a solicitor's clerk in Grays Inn. For just over a year his workplace was at Raymond

---

[42] *The Household Narrative of current events* (for the year 1851,) being a supplement to Household Words, conducted by Charles Dickens. London, 1851. p10.

Buildings, overlooking Grays Inn Lane and almost opposite Fox Court. It was a great delight, apparently, for the office boys to be able to look from the windows on the second floor at life passing along below them, and occasionally to have fun by dropping cherry stones onto the hats of passers-by.[43] Dickens' knowledge of Fox Court did, indeed, date from a very early age, and it was a knowledge he turned back to, I suggest, when he came to write *Bleak House*.

Till now Dickensians have conjectured which place the author had in mind when he wrote of the home of Jo the crossing-sweeper. Fox Court has not been a consideration, but then the link between the Dickens, Lamerte and Worms families has not been known till now. Dickens wrote:

"Jo lives… in a ruinous place, known to the like of him by the name of Tom-all-alone's. It is a black, dilapidated street, avoided by all decent people; where the crazy houses were seized upon, when their decay was far advanced, by some bold vagrants, who, after establishing their own possession, took to letting them out in lodgings. Now, these tumbling tenements contain, by night, a swarm of misery. As, on the ruined human wretch, vermin parasites appear, so, these ruined shelters have bred a crowd of foul existence that crawls in and out of gaps in walls and boards; and coils itself to sleep, in maggot numbers, where the rain drips in; and comes and goes, fetching and carrying fever, and sowing more evil in its every footprint than Lord Coodle, and Sir Thomas Doodle, and the Duke of Foodle, and all the fine gentlemen in office, down to Zoodle, shall set right in five hundred years – though born expressly to do it.

Twice, lately, there has been a crash and a cloud of dust, like the springing of a mine, in Tom-all-alone's; and, each time, a house has fallen. These accidents have made a paragraph in the newspapers, and have filled a bed or two in the nearest hospital. The gaps remain, and there are not unpopular lodgings among the rubbish. As several more houses are nearly ready to go, the next crash in Tom-all-alone's may be expected to be a good one."[44]

It's known that Dickens exercised great control over the subjects and detail of the illustrations that appeared in his novels. There is a moody illustration to accompany the above description and I have little doubt he directed his artist, Hablot K. Brown, to Fox Court to make the drawing. Compared against the map from Horwood both demonstrate a short street, a narrow covered alleyway at the far end and a crooked elbow in its shape. The architecture of the buildings look of an age to

---

[43] "Mr Blackmore engages an office boy" by William J. Carlton, in *The Dickensian*, September 1952, pp162-167.
[44] *Bleak House*, chapter 16.

Tom-all-alone's from *Bleak House*

have been standing when the Countess of Macclesfield gave birth to her illegitimate child in 1697. But Dickens throws in one of those very personal, enigmatic clues that he is known to have used elsewhere: hanging from the front of one of the shops on the left hand side is a gibbeted black doll, the trade sign for marine stores – in fact, marine stores were often known as "dolly-shops". And it was in Fox Court, in

1823, that was located the marine store of Henry Worms.[45] For reasons I shall come to soon it's worth noting that the map shows on the left two exits leading to other buildings, the second, much narrower of the two possibly relating to an archway in the drawing. There are two provisos to make about the illustration from *Bleak House*. Firstly, there is a church tower looming over the street, but there was no such church that close to Fox Court – other commentators have likened it to the tower of St Andrews Holborn, which is about 350 yards from the end of Fox Court; and though the tower was slightly off line and not, I would have thought, visible, I suspect either Brown or Dickens shifted it into the illustration for stylistic or symbolic effect. The second proviso is that Henry Worms occupied his place in the court in 1823 yet *Bleak House* was written in 1852. Nevertheless, contemporary descriptions show that Fox Court changed little in appearance and character throughout the nineteenth century.

Focussing more particularly on the type of shop run by Henry Worms, Dickens showed himself well-acquainted with marine stores and strongly enough absorbed to devote to them one of his *Sketches by Boz*:

"Our readers must often have observed in some by street, in a poor neighbourhood, a small dirty shop, exposing for sale the most extraordinary and confused jumble of old, worn-out, wretched articles, that can well be imagined. Our wonder at the idea of their ever having been bought, is only to be equalled by our astonishment at the idea of their ever being sold again. On a board, at the side of the door, are placed about twenty books – all odd volumes; and as many wine glasses – all different patterns; several locks, an old earthenware pan, full of rusty keys; two or three gaudy chimney ornaments – cracked, of course; the remains of a lustre, without any drops; a round frame like a capital O, which has once held a mirror; a flute, complete with the exception of the middle joint; a pair of curling irons; and a tinder box. In front of the shop window are ranged some half dozen high backed chairs, with spinal complaints and wasted legs; a corner cupboard; two or three very dark mahogany tables with flaps like mathematical problems; some pickle jars, some surgeons' ditto, with gilt labels and without stoppers; an unframed portrait of some lady who flourished about the beginning of the thirteenth century, by an artist who never flourished at all; an incalculable host of miscellanies of every description, including bottles and cabinets, rags and bones, fenders and street door

[45] Michael Slater suggests the black doll in this illustration is a reference to the shop of Krook, but Dickens describes Krook's shop as being adjacent to Lincoln's Inn and not in Tom-all-alone's – *Dickens' Journalism, vol 1: Sketches by Boz and other early papers 1833-39*, edited by Michael Slater, p176.

knockers, fire irons, wearing apparel and bedding, a hall lamp, and a room door. Imagine, in addition to this incongruous mass, a black doll in a white frock, with two faces – one looking up the street, and the other looking down, swinging over the door; a board with the squeezed up inscription 'Dealer in marine stores', in lanky white letters, whose height is strangely out of proportion to their width; and you have before you precisely the kind of shop to which we wish to direct your attention."[46]

I'm not suggesting this sketch by Boz is a specific description of the marine store of Henry Worms but it is a good contemporary view of what such a shop would look like, encompassing the poverty of the neighbourhood, the dirtiness of the shop and the jumble of its contents. The hanging black doll trade sign draws together Dickens' sketch of 1834 and his novel of 1852. One aspect of marine stores that Dickens does not make reference to is that their owners were often known as receivers of stolen goods. Henry Worms was a case in point.

On 29 October 1823 he and his son Solomon appeared in the dock at The Old Bailey, accused of feloniously receiving two iron weights knowing them to have been stolen.[47] The weights were said to have been purloined from a greengrocer in Beauchamp Street, just behind High Holborn, and taken by the thief, George Ballard, about a hundred yards away to the marine store in Fox Court. There, it was claimed, Henry and Solomon Worms paid seven pence for the two. However, a barmaid at the Rose public house in Hatton Wall, a few streets away, gave evidence that Henry Worms was in her bar at the time he was said to be paying for the weights, and a customer at the pub confirmed it. Two of Worms' children, Sarah and Lewis, appeared in court to swear their father was not at home at the time claimed. Henry and Solomon were found not guilty. The transcript of this trial is given at the end of this book as Appendix 2. In this first quarter of the nineteenth century punishment for crime seems, to 21st century eyes, excessively harsh; yet still criminals returned time and again to their bad ways. And so it would seem did the thief in this case, George Ballard, who turned to housebreaking. His youthful career was brought to an end six years later when, at the age of 19, he was sentenced to hang.

Nor, it would seem, could Henry Worms leave behind his bad ways. On the 13th January 1825 he appeared once again in the dock at The Old Bailey, this time accompanied by his son Morris, charged again with receiving stolen goods. The cases seem so petty – the earlier case for

---

[46] "Brokers' and Marine-store Shops", first published *in The Morning Chronicle*, 15th December 1834; now available in *Dickens' Journalism, vol 1*, op cit.
[47] www.oldbaileyonline.org, (14 Mar 2011), October 1823, trial of Henry Worms and Solomon Worms (t18231022-124).

goods with a value of seven pence, this case for a pewter beer mug worth one shilling – pot-stealing. A man of 38, with the Sherlock-Holmesian-name of John Moriarty, who also lived in Fox Court, was accused of stealing the pot from the Fox and Peacock public house in Grays Inn Lane and selling it to the Wormses at their marine store. Henry Worms said he had been out that evening, and produced witnesses to confirm it, and said that he had come home to find a drunken Moriarty at his house. Young Morris Worms, 14 years old, said he had declined Moriarty's offer to sell him the mug but Moriarty had sworn at him, threatened to hit him and thrown the mug into a melting pan under the fire. On this occasion Henry Worms and his witnesses were not believed – Moriarty was found guilty of theft and sent to prison for three months; Morris Worms was found guilty of receiving but wasn't sentenced till later, when he was sent to a House of Correction; whilst poor old Henry, now aged 57, was found guilty and sentenced to be transported to Tasmania for 14 years. It seems a draconian sentence for a petty crime but Henry, as we've seen, had been in trouble before, possibly on more occasions than we know about at this great distance of time; and maybe the authorities saw this as a way rolling up a list of nuisance crimes and getting rid of a pain in the neck.

A transcript of Worms' case is printed as Appendix Three to this book but there are some parts I'd like to draw out here, since they add to our description of his place in Fox Court. A central part of the prosecution's case was that an attempt had been made by Morris Worms to melt the stolen pewter beer mug and to this end witnesses described a very large fire in the shop, with three melting pans and some pewter, very lately melted – such fires and their melting pans were, it seems, a common feature of marine stores. Bearing in mind the map and illustration above it's intriguing to note that a witness described looking down a passage leading to Worms' house: "It is a private house, the shop lies back – there is a board up, with 'Dealer in Marine Stores' on it; there is a back-room, which I call the other shop, where they do their business." We must also note, with interest, that the board and its wording is exactly the same as Dickens described in his sketch. Another witness also described the open passage and a strong fire. Only one witness in either this case or the earlier case in 1823, made reference to Worms being a Jew – this was Thomas Thompson, a Bow Street policeman, who reported Moriarty told him he had sold the stolen pot to a Jew in Fox Court and the policeman did not know of any other Jew than Worms with a shop there.

After his trial and sentence Henry Worms was transferred to a hulk ship, the sort that had made such an impression on the young Charley Dickens a few years earlier. And from the hulk he was eventually sent off to the other side of the world, leaving from Sheerness Downs on 26th April 1825 aboard the ship Medina. The authorities took no account, it would seem, that he left behind eight children, motherless, and most far too young to fend for themselves. Was the responsibility for survival thrown, I wonder, onto the older children? Or perhaps onto their uncles and aunts on the Lamert side of the family? Henry Worms' behaviour during his term of captivity was recorded for posterity in a notebook, together with that of all other prisoners, and is now preserved in the Archives Office of Tasmania; it tells us that on the hulks he was "orderly".[48]

He arrived at Hobart in Van Diemen's Land on 14th September 1825 and though he didn't manage to maintain his earlier orderly conduct for long his record of misbehaviour seems at times to be on a level as petty as the charge which landed him there in the first place. On 20th September 1826 he was recorded to have "missed muster and church last Sunday", which sounds as though he was made to attend church despite being Jewish. Then two years later, on 25th June 1828, he was admonished for "profaning the Sabbath Day by exposing for Sale Cakes & Lollypops at his House in Elizabeth St." In March 1830 he was on the receiving end of crime, when a coat and a pair of trousers were stolen from him, valued at thirteen shillings: James Leach, a man who had already served three 7-year sentences of transportation, was found guilty of receiving the stolen property.[49] Later that same year, on 9th August, things got more serious when he assaulted John Gregory with the intent to commit an unnatural crime, a euphemism for an act of homosexuality. For this he was tried at the Quarter Sessions on 7th September, found guilty and sentenced to forfeit his ticket-of-leave (a form of parole), to be imprisoned in the gaol and kept to hard labour for six months.[50] At the end of these six months he may have celebrated his release a little too enthusiastically since he was charged, on 14th March 1831, with being drunk and was punished with 10 days on the treadmill. Three months later, on 7th June, he repeated the offence and received the same punishment. Within a week or so he was in court again, this time as a witness in a case involving a stolen watch, a long report of which was spelled out in the local newspaper. That section relevant to Worms reads:

---

[48] Archives Office of Tasmania, Item number: CON31/1/45, Location: HOB, Copy Number: Z2556. Transferred from the Sheriff's Office to the Tasmanian State Archives, 6 Dec., 1951, under the terms of the Public Records Act, 1943. Class: - E. Principal Superintendent of Convicts: Alphabetical record book of convicts arriving in Van Dieman's Land. "W" 1816-1830; "Y" 1803-1830. Accession No: 2/176. http://search.archives.tas.gov.au/default.aspx?detail=1&type=I&id=CON31/1/45.
[49] *The Hobart Town Courier*, Saturday 20th March 1830.
[50] *Colonial Times* (Hobart, Tasmania), Friday 10th September 1830.

"Thomas Mills sworn:- ...the number of my watch was 1105; I borrowed some money on it from Worms, who is a Jew, and then lived opposite to the Police-office; he lent me 13s upon it, for 10 days, and I was to give him 2s interest for the advance for 10 days; if not redeemed at the time, it was to become Worms's property; I gave Worms a memorandum, saying I had sold him the watch for 13s; I never saw it again until upon the person of the prisoner.

Henry Worms sworn. – I was not a pawnbroker in March 1830? I know Thomas Mills, and had a silver watch which I bought of him conditionally; I gave him 13s for it: I had a bill and receipt for it; the watch belongs to me; Mills came a day or two after the time, but I had lost the watch."

Worms was one of many who handled the watch over a period of time and the court decided the case was fraught with uncertainty and dismissed the accused.[51]

In 1833, having served eight years of his 14 year sentence Henry Worms was granted a pass to travel a short distance of about 12 miles from Brighton to New Norfolk, close to Hobart – his entries in the record book finish with one word: "Ran". A reward of £2 for his return was offered and a description given: a native of Frankfurt, aged 65, height 5'3", dark brown hair, high temples, grey eyes and crooked teeth. Distinctive as Worms was it would seem that he managed to disappear quite successfully – 5 years later, in December 1838, the Hobart newspaper included his name in a long list of presumably similar absconders invited to come forward and collected their certificates of freedom, the term of their sentence having been completed. A family history researcher has reported that in that same year his son Lewis Henry Worms arrived in Australia, though I haven't seen the documentation for this. No doubt father and son got together and settled in Sydney, where Henry Worms, now aged 74, still managed to get into trouble. On a busy Wednesday at the Sydney Quarter Sessions of 10th August 1842 he was one of 20 people appearing before the court, 8, like him, for larceny, but others for burglary or assault; nine were found not guilty and discharged, the other eleven, including Worms were found guilty and sentenced to terms ranging from one month to three years. Three newspapers listed the outcomes – two said he got six months imprisonment, the other said one month.[52] Thereafter it's difficult to say how Henry Worms ended his days. Other members of the Worms family made their way to Australia in the 1850s and became

---

[51] *Colonial Times* (Hobart, Tasmania) Wednesday 15th June 1831.
[52] *The Sydney Morning Herald*, Monday 15th August 1842; *The Sydney Gazette and New South Wales Advertiser*, Tuesday 16th August 1842; and *Australasian Chronicle*, Tuesday 16th August 1842.

an established family, so it seems likely he remained there. On two occasions, in 1848 and 1852, notices appeared in the newspapers to say the Post Office were holding uncollected letters for Henry Worms.[53] One of these was in Adelaide, which shows he may have travelled. Then, in 1857 his name appeared in a newspaper report on an inquest at Petersham in Sydney – the report said he accompanied a man called William Smith into the bush to load a cart with firewood; the man appeared very ill from drinking and died the next day.[54] So, if this was, indeed, the Henry Worms we have followed and not his son Lewis Henry Worms, nor any other member of the family – and I suspect it was him – then at the age of 89 he was one of the great survivors of a harsh system and a hard life. The sort of person you wouldn't forget.

Three years after this, back in England, Charles Dickens began his 13th novel, *Great Expectations*, in which he created Abel Magwitch, born, it's calculated, in 1768, the same year as Henry Worms;[55] accused of forging and passing stolen banknotes, just as Henry Worms had been accused of passing bad money; and sentenced to transportation for 14 years, the same as Henry Worms. Does it mean anything?

In 1836 Dickens wrote his first novel, *Oliver Twist*, depicting a Jew, about the same age as Henry Worms, a receiver of stolen goods, like Henry Worms, living in "the intricate and dirty ways … lying between Grays Inn Lane and Smithfield", just as Henry Worms did, surrounded by children, just as Henry Worms had been. In *Oliver Twist*, Cruikshank's illustrations of Fagin, whilst not attempting to be a faithful portrait of a real person, complement rather than contradict the description of Henry Worms issued by the Authorities in Van Diemen's Land.

Laurence Worms, a descendent of Henry, has suggested that the marine store general dealer and receiver of stolen goods may have had a great influence on Dickens when creating the character of Fagin, and I think he's right.[56] It has often been suggested that Dickens drew on Isaac Solomons for his Fagin but there's no real evidence for this, the age, build and dress of the two being incompatible. On the other hand the young Dickens may well have been in very much closer proximity to Henry Worms than he ever was to Isaac Solomons, standing next to him

---

[53] *The Sydney Morning Herald*, Monday 1th February 1848 and the *Australian Register* (Adelaide), Monday 23rd February 1852.

[54] *The Sydney Morning Herald*, Tuesday 24th March 1857.

[55] "Dickens, Australia and Magwitch, Part II: The search for *le cas Magwitch*", by Leon Litvack, in *The Dickensian*, Summer 1999, p102.

[56] I'm grateful to Laurence Worms for much of the information on the family backgrounds of the Worms and Lamert families, some of which appears in his article "The Ancestors of Laurence Worms: the true story of how I am related to Dickens (but not in a good way)"; this is available online through the *Newsletter of the Antiquarian Booksellers' Association*.

in his shop in Fox Court, observing his German-Hebrew accent, a man in his late fifties, just 5'3" tall – an old Jew, as Dickens described Fagin. Taken there by his Cousin George Lamerte.

Fagin, by George Cruikshank

Whether it was in Fox Court or in Whitechapel young Charley's visits would have no doubt left on him a strong impression of this Jewish community – the heavy accents, perhaps the way they dressed, the ways they made their living. There is one more link to which it's worth drawing attention. In *Oliver Twist*, when Oliver is snatched from the street while on an errand for Mr Brownlow, he is carried to one of Fagin's safe houses in a 'filthy narrow street, nearly full of old-clothes shops' in the neighbourhood of Whitechapel. The book's illustration of the interior of this Whitechapel house bears looking at twice, because there's Oliver, on his knees, polishing the boots of the Artful Dodger, or, as the Dodger put it 'japanning his trotter-cases'. Whether he does so consciously or otherwise Dickens draws a link in his story between Whitechapel and boot-blacking and then emphasises it with an illustration.

Chapter Three

Blacking

The story of Charles Dickens' childhood

The story of Charles Dickens' childhood is dominated by a single narrative, mostly written down by Dickens himself, then edited, arranged and supplemented by John Forster. The accuracy and truthfulness of his account of his own life was never seriously questioned or tested, reinforced or challenged. Neither of his parents, none of his uncles and aunts, nor any of his brothers and sisters wrote down their own recollections of the childhood of their famous relative. Or if they did, it hasn't survived. Forster claimed a prodigious memory for his friend, but if it frequently failed him we wouldn't know about it. And if Dickens chose to omit particular events or people from his narrative, or to adjust their impact and influence, then we are entirely in his hands – there has been nobody to challenge him. The control he was able to exercise over the history of his own childhood was not so easily exercised over his later history.

Dickens first met John Forster in 1836 and there immediately developed a very strong friendship between the two. Inevitably, Forster also became acquainted with Dickens' family. Yet, according to Forster, for eleven years neither Dickens nor any of his relatives talked to him about the traumatic period of his early years when he was sent out to work in a factory and his father, John Dickens, was imprisoned for debt, not only an inmate of the Marshalsea Prison but also accompanied there by his wife and three of their children. At this time Forster was aware that he had a limited knowledge of his friend's childhood, as might be judged from a letter sent to him by Dickens in November 1846: "Shall I leave you my life in MS. When I die? There are some things in it that would touch you very much, and that might go on the same shelf with the first volume of Holcroft's"[57] What sort of things was Dickens keeping from him, Forster might have wondered, his curiosity aroused again, perhaps, a few months later when he was talking to Charles Wentworth Dilke. Dilke was a friend of both Dickens and Forster, but more importantly an ex-colleague of John Dickens and he related to Forster that while accompanying John Dickens one day he had noticed young Charley engaged in some juvenile employment in a warehouse

---

[57] Pilgrim Letters, vol 4, dated 4th November 1846.

near the Strand. Forster tells us that it was not till the following March or April, 1847, that he was able put to Dickens this anecdote of Dilke's, which struck his friend silent for several minutes. It was not spoken of again for several weeks and then there was another short interlude before Dickens finally told Forster the details of this part of his early life. So, Forster had a verbal account of Dickens' childhood, which he may then have carried in his head or he may have written down; we don't know.

As we've seen from that letter the writing of his own life story had obviously crossed Dickens' mind and maybe he had started to commit it to paper, either as a narrative or as notes. But the Dilke episode, and no doubt Forster's great interest in what his friend had to say, encouraged Dickens to set to with more purpose, and in January 1849 he sent what he had written to Forster. Forster called it Dickens' fragment of autobiography, which he faithfully held in secrecy and trust until after the death of Dickens in 1870. To this Forster added some "after-talk explanatory of points in the narrative, of which a note was made at the time". *The Life of Charles Dickens* by John Forster, the first volume of which was published in 1872, contained these revelations about Dickens' childhood, shocking not only his millions of readers across the world but also his many friends and relatives including, amazingly, his own children.

Following publication some acquaintances from his schooldays came forward with distant and sometimes confused recollections and in the following years Robert Langton, Frederic G. Kitton and William Hughes searched out people who had known the Dickens family, particularly at Chatham. None of these were able to shed further light on the events surrounding John Dickens' imprisonment and his son's employment at the blacking factory. Much closer examination, though, was now paid to Dickens' own writings, which showed the very great extent to which, in his novels, his journalism and his sketches, he had drawn on his early experiences; and particularly so in *David Copperfield*.

Against this background the discovery at The National Archives of documents from the Chancery Court in London, relating to disputes between the people who owned and ran the blacking factory where Dickens was employed and also between them and their rival Robert Warren, has opened up a wealth of information not previously available to us. Where Dickens' young memory and understanding failed him these documents do, in many instances, correct and enhance the account. However, Dickens' account is a powerful personal statement, relating the minutiae of his existence, and his feelings towards his situation and the people around him. In later years, with hindsight, he analysed the effect of this part of his childhood on his development as a man. The court documents cannot change or challenge that account.

The court documents are not about a boy called Dickens, nor do they mention such a boy, but they do describe in great detail the circumstances and the personnel at his place of work and provide a chronology against which his own personal misery took place.

The Chancery Court

There's no more appropriate place to find information relating to Charles Dickens than in Chancery Proceedings. Dickens the author was scathing about the institution. As a youth he had been a reporter, and time spent writing up cases in Chancery established in him a feeling of contempt. Then in 1844 those feelings were reinforced when he obtained an injunction from the court to prevent a pirated edition of *A Christmas Carol* – he won the argument but lost the costs when the pirates declared themselves bankrupt. He found himself out of pocket by the considerable sum of £700. But his most famous attack on Chancery – its expence, its tangled bureaucracy, its slowness – came in *Bleak House* and the case of Jarndyce v Jarndyce. However, frustrating though the proceedings of this ancient court may have been to those who had to go through them, they have left The National Archives with a rich treasure of social and economic history. The millions of Chancery documents held at TNA open a window into the lives and worries of people from the 14th to the 19th centuries.

In July 1826 William Edward Woodd went to the Chancery Court and made a complaint against George Lamerte. In November of the following year Robert Warren made separate complaints against William Edward Woodd and against George Lamerte. Following the complaints it was the usual practice for witnesses to come forward, within a fortnight or so, and provide written statements, or affidavits, sworn under oath, providing evidence to support either the complainant or the defendant. Several months would be allowed for the defendant to make his answer to the complaint. The documents in these three cases were lengthy and detailed but with a wealth of information about the history of Warren's Blacking leading up to and through the period when Dickens worked there.

To start with it must be recognised that boot blacking was a profitable business in the first quarter of the nineteenth century. The state of the roads and footways was such that boots and shoes needed constant protection to maintain a degree of water repellence and flexibility as well as for cleanliness. Many firms manufactured blacking in London and it was despatched for sale throughout the country and throughout the world. There was also a constant demand from the military forces. Charles Day of the blacking firm Day and Martin was reported to have left at least £350,000 when he died in 1836 – with money like that to be made it's little wonder there was great competition in the industry. Two competitors of Day and Martin were the firms of Warren's Blacking.

At the end of the eighteenth century, disputedly in either 1795 or 1798, two brothers, Jonathan Warren and Thomas Warren, each established their own business of making blacking. Jonathan's claim to be first in the field was expressed vehemently, consistently and at length. A plate powder maker named George Garey supported his claim, recording in his affidavit that he knew Jonathan Warren for some years before 1795, when he began manufacturing blacking, and that the two of them exchanged information about their discoveries in their respective creative processes.[58] This evidence not only put Jonathan first in the field but demonstrated that he was working to develop a recipe and that only when he had done so did he begin manufacture. The existence and ownership of this valuable recipe was a matter of contention in the Chancery Court. George Garey also said that for several years after Jonathan Warren began he was not aware of any other person with the name of Warren who was also making blacking. Jonathan's wife Elizabeth, in her affidavit, swore that Thomas Warren was a boot-maker in St Martin's Lane when her husband first started. Jonathan and his brother, she says, then made an agreement to go into partnership and the recipe and method of manufacture was passed on to Thomas. Within a month, Elizabeth Warren claimed, Thomas had reneged on his agreement and proceeded to produce the blacking himself. From that time forward a feud existed between the two sides of the family. Jonathan was always adamant that he was the original inventor and to press his point swore an affidavit stating as much before the Lord Mayor of London. William Glindon, a printer, came forward to swear that he had printed for Jonathan Warren many thousands of copies of this affidavit, which we may conclude were for distribution to customers, in refutation of the claims of the opposition. There is a touch of ordinary family life in Elizabeth Warrren's statement when she recollects that Thomas Warren and his family used to come visiting to their home – a prospect, one imagines, that must have been fraught with potential argument and accusation. Her brother-in-law, she suggests with bitterness, used the occasions to steal the names and addresses of her husband's customers and then seek to supply them with the rival product.

In counter-claim Mary Warren, the wife of Thomas, denied there had ever been an agreement for the brothers to go into partnership, or that

---

[58] Plate powder was used for cleaning silver and silver-plated household objects – it's manufacture, like that of boot-blacking, must have involved some level of chemical manipulation

Jonathan had passed on to his brother the recipe for making blacking. Her case seems weaker than that of the rivals, since neither she nor anybody else demonstrated how Thomas learned the art of manufacturing blacking, if not from his brother. There is no anger or accusation in her statement that Jonathan set up in competition to Thomas, and no suggestion that the recipe was stolen by Jonathan. Whatever was the truth of the beginning of the rivalry, we are told that Thomas Warren operated from his premises at 14 St Martin's Lane and Jonathan from 18 Great Suffolk Street near the Haymarket.

Remarkably, some stone bottles have survived from that time, carrying the names and addresses of the two rivals, sometimes, in each case, just carrying the title of "Warren's Liquid Blacking" and sometimes featuring "J Warren's Liquid Blacking".

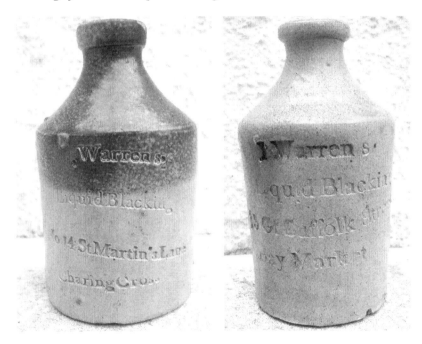

Blacking bottles from Robert Warren (left) and Jonathan Warren (right)

In 1805 Thomas Warren died and his business was taken over by his son Robert, who sought to build and expand through extensive use of advertising. As early as 1808 he was placing advertisements in newspapers up and down the country warning against his uncle's product: [59] Similar advertisements appeared regularly through to the

---

[59] For example, this one from *The Morning Chronicle*, Monday, 18 April, 1808

1820s. Despite the animosity between them both sides of the family managed to continue to trade. Both sides claimed great success for their own business and pointed out the deficiencies in the opposition.

The evidence presented to the court convinces me that it was, indeed, Jonathan Warren who created a recipe for making blacking and who began first to manufacture it. But I'm equally convinced that when Robert Warren took over, following the death of his father, his promotional efforts and organisational skills ensured that his side of the family grew the business and helped it pull ahead of his uncle's. In his own affidavit Robert Warren claimed that in 1816 he needed to move from St Martin's Lane into larger premises due to the "very great increase in his business", and he relocated himself at number 30 in the Strand. Much was made of this address on the packaging of his product. On the other hand Uncle Jonathan was not doing so well and in 1817 he was declared bankrupt.[60] The root of his difficulties might be found in the statement, already mentioned, of the printer William Glindon, who says "in consequence of habits of Intemperance and gaming the said Jonathan Warren afterwards neglected his business and the Trade very

---

WARREN'S Original JAPAN LIQUID BLACKING.—This unrivalled composition, with half the usual labour, produces a jet black, equal to the highest japan varnish; it preserves the leather soft, and prevents its cracking; it is perfectly free from any unpleasant smell, will not soil the linen, and will retain its virtues in any climate.—Sold whole-sale by R. Warren, 14, St. Martins-lane, and retail by the prin-cipal boot makers and oilmen in London, and a shopkeeper in every town in England, in stone bottles 1s. 6d. a pint; 10d. half a pint.—Caution.—The superior quality of this Blacking has induced several persons to sell spurious compositions under the above name, to prevent which; observe " Robert Warren" is signed on each label, and " 14, St. Martin's-lane" is stamped in each bottle of Warren's Blacking.

---

much fell off". Such a view is challenged by William Whalley, who had worked for Jonathan Warren from 1807 and asserted "that during the fifteen years he so Travelled for the said Jonathan Warren as aforesaid the said Jonathan Warren never Abandoned his Business in any manner whatever or left the same". There are contradictions a-plenty here, yet despite the evidence of bankruptcy and the claim of drinking and gambling, still the firm managed to stay afloat. It was, though, all done on a small scale according to another witness, William Arundel, who swore that Jonathan Warren began in a very small way "in fact in a perfect Chandler Shop style compared to the extensive and general

---

[60] Listed in *The London Gazette*, 30 August 1817, p1870

manner" of Robert Warren. Arundel went on to say that in a conversation with Jonathan Warren in 1818 Warren had told him "that from the quantity of Vinegar Treacle and other Articles which Robert Warren was in the habit of purchasing for his business of a Blacking manufacturer he was carrying on a most extensive business and would certainly make a rapid fortune – while on the other hand the business which he the said Jonathan Warren was doing was scarcely sufficient to pay his rent and expences". Arundel is relentless in his attack on Jonathan Warren: "And this Deponent lastly saith that during all the years that this Deponent was acquainted with the said Jonathan Warren he was as Deponent verily believes a Man always in very needy and distressed circumstances and was as Deponent hath been informed and also believes a considerable time a Prisoner in White Cross Street Prison and also a Prisoner in the Fleet Prison for Debt." This evidence may have had substance to it or not (no reference to his imprisonment appears in The London Gazette), but the fact that Arundel's affidavit was made jointly with Thomas Warren's widow, Mary, demonstrates which side of the argument he supported.

But Jonathan Warren came up with a new strategy for his business. In 1821, when his property in Great Suffolk Street was pulled down, he took the opportunity to find new premises in Hungerford Market, located nearby to his nephew's in the Strand. The sketch opposite illustrates excellently the very close proximity of Robert Warren's place in the Strand and the turning to Hungerford Market.[61]

Two affidavits were given to the court by Samuel Mann, who proudly announced that he was acting beadle to the parish of St Martin in the Fields. Of greater relevance to this book was his role as rent collector for the Hungerford Estate, owned by Henry Wise of Offchurch in Warwickshire, a position he had filled for the previous eight years. His affidavit says Jonathan Warren rented a property not at Hungerford Stairs but in Little Hungerford Street, taking it from February 1821 at a rent of £60 a year. Mann declares that Little Hungerford Street had no more than 12 houses, none of which was numbered 30, but that soon after moving in Jonathan Warren painted the number 30 on the door, in imitation of the 30 used on the front of Robert Warren's property in the Strand; and also had painted on the wall facing the River Thames a large white area over which was painted in very large legible black characters "Warrens 30 Blacking Warehouse".

Another witness was James Phillipps of Little Hungerford Street, a Custom House Agent and Lighterman, who "remembers that about Five

---

61 This sketch is taken from *John Tallis's London Street Views*, 1838-1840, published by The London Topographical Society, 2002. At this later date Robert Warren had gone into partnership with Russell and Wright.

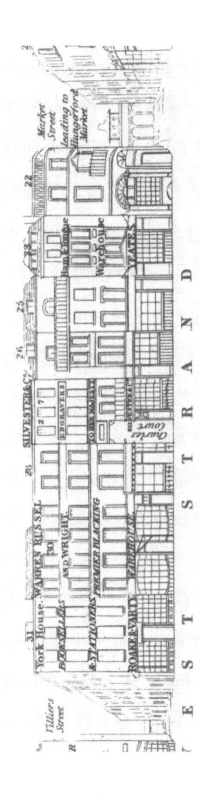

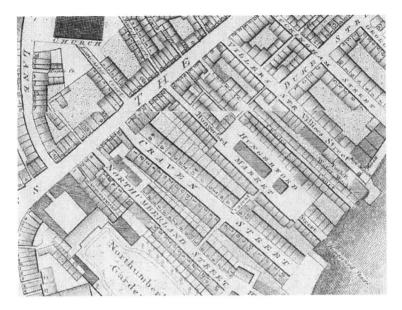

Horwood's map[62] showing the Strand, Hungerford Market and Hungerford
Stairs. Robert Warren's Blacking was on the west
corner of the Strand and Villiers Street, and Jonathan Warren's
Blacking faced the river on the east corner of Hungerford Stairs

Hungerford Market by Thomas Shepherd, looking towards the Thames.
It was down here that young Charles Dickens trudged each day to
Jonathan Warren's blacking factory, the last house on the left

[62] *Map of London, Westminster & Southwark, shewing every house, 1792-9*, by Richard
Horwood. Motco, 2006. ISBN 978-0-9545080-7-4 (CD)

Years after the said Robert Warren had been established as a Blacking Manufacturer at Number Thirty Strand Jonathan Warren came to reside in Little Hungerford Street aforesaid and shortly afterwards put up His name and a large number thirty precisely in imitation of the Plaintiffs Robert Warrens number Thirty and in other respects as regards their name similarly done and gave little Hungerford Street the appellation of Hungerford Stairs which name the Place never had before or since And this Deponent also saith that the true number of the House in which the said Jonathan Warren resided was number six and not number Thirty".

Whatever justification Jonathan Warren may have had for resentment against his brother and his nephew his own re-positioning of his business and the re-numbering of the property is clear intention of a move to blur the distinction between the two operations, and to gain advantage from the more successful of the two. It smacks of sharp practice. But having moved in February 1821 Jonathan Warren would appear to have resigned himself, within six months or so, to losing the battle between the two rivals, and to have decided to sell up. The following small ad appeared in *The Times*[63]:

> **PARTNERSHIP.—WARREN's Original BLACKING MANUFACTORY**, established upwards of 20 years.—Any respectable Person who can command from 300l. to 500l., may immediately engage in the above concern, an additional capital being requisite to execute the orders of an increasing connexion. The advertiser will conduct the manufacturing department, for which he expects to draw a very moderate weekly stipend, while the receipts and disbursements pass through the partner's hands, which will be ample security for any sum he may advance. Letters addressed, post paid, to Jonathan Warren, 4, Dean-street, Fetter-lane, will meet immediate attention.

The suggestion that he continue to make the product while the new purchaser owns and runs the business is, perhaps, an indication that his interest and ability lay in the technical and mechanical aspects of the work, rather than on the promotional and financial side. Clearly he wasn't overwhelmed with offers. More than twelve months passed before Jonathan Warren entered into an agreement with William Edward Woodd, signed on 8th November 1822.

William Edward Woodd

Search as you might through the numerous indexes of biographies of Dickens, or through the twelve volumes of the Pilgrim edition of Dickens' letters, or through the indexes to more than 100 years of *The*

---

63 *The Times*, Monday, 10 September 1821

Dickensian and you'll not find a reference to William Edward Woodd, oddly spelt with a double-d. Yet it was Woodd who employed the young Dickens in the blacking warehouse, it was Woodd who paid the child his 5 or 6 shillings a week, and it was the labels produced for Woodd that Dickens pasted onto pots of blacking.

The family of Woodd was extensive and ancient, first recorded in Shropshire in the 15th century, moving to Oxfordshire in the 17th century and to Richmond-upon-Thames in the 18th century.[64] The name of Basil, often accompanied by a second name, confusingly appears at many generations of the family through several centuries. The grandfather of William Edward Woodd, named George Basil Woodd, was twice married, producing nine children by his first wife and a further seven by his second wife, the first child born in 1750 and the last 33 years late in 1783. The first of all these children, George Woodd, baptised at Richmond-upon-Thames, was the father of William Edward Woodd; the last son to be born was Basil George Woodd who, in the first half of the 19th century, made a fortune as a wine merchant and purchased valuable land and property in Hampstead. Little enough is known about William Edward Woodd's father, George, but we do know he was a soldier, a Major in the 43rd Regiment of Foot, which fought extensively in the American War of Independence; that he married Sarah Foreman at Bexley in Kent on 2nd May 1775, and that he died in Ipswich on 8th December 1798. William Edward Woodd was the youngest son of George Woodd, though I don't know of any other siblings, and he was born in Cork, Ireland on 24th March 1797.[65] The substance of the Irish connection is not obvious but was maintained through the first half of the nineteenth century. With the death of his father depriving the boy before he reached the age of two, he must have been brought up by his mother; but even this support was lost when he was thirteen years old, his mother dying on 3rd May 1810. She was buried at the Grosvenor Chapel in London's South Audley Street, Mayfair, where a memorial to her was erected on one of the walls. If she was interred in the vault of the Chapel then she lays there now, with many others more famous than her, isolated and undisturbed since the vault was sealed in 1859, a mysterious place that nobody any longer knows how to access. With such a large family behind him no doubt the orphaned Woodd was taken in, cared for and educated, and if he had money left to him then that,

64 *Pedigrees and memorials of the family of Woodd, formerly of Shinewood , Salop, and Brize Norton, Oxfordshire; now of Conyngham Hall, co. York, and Hampstead, Middlesex, and of the family of Jupp of London and Wandsworth.* Privately Printed, London: Mitchell and Hughes, 24 Wardour Street, Soho, W. 1875.

65 Confusingly there was another William Edward Woodd, born 4th November 1790 to the Rev. Basil Woodd (1760-1832) and his wife Ann, but that child died an infant.

too, would have been taken care of, though as the youngest son of a soldier it's unlikely to have amounted to a fortune.

William Edward Woodd next comes to our attention ten years later, when he married Sophia Lamerte, the daughter of Matthew Lamerte, as shown in the previous chapter. The wedding took place in Central London at St Martin in the Fields on 18th March 1820. Then, two years later he became the purchaser of Jonathan Warren's blacking manufactory. At the time of the purchase Woodd had a counting house at 26 Tokenhouse Yard, just behind the Bank of England, though what business he was engaged in I haven't been able to determine. Tokenhouse Yard at that time was populated by a range of businesses typical of the City, mostly under the catch-all headings of stockbrokers and merchants, but with a sprinkling of auctioneers and appraisers, silkmen, brush makers and engravers. Woodd was the first occupant of the street to take up the manufacture of blacking. His agreement gave him complete ownership of Jonathan Warren's blacking manufactory, including continued use of the name, in exchange for an annual payment of £250 to be paid to Jonathan Warren for seven years or, should he die, to his wife, Elizabeth. As suggested in the advertisement Jonathan Warren continued to run the manufacturing side of the business, and was paid a wage for doing so, and Woodd, who had no previous experience in this field, engaged a clerk to manage the office, which was operated, to begin with, from his existing counting house. The office clerk was his brother-in-law, George Lamerte. Prior to his appointment Lamerte had no obvious means of financial support, so up to this point he was probably still living with the Dickens family in Bayham Street, Camden Town, as John Forster later recorded.

The coming together of Warren, Woodd and Lamerte was a strange mix. Jonathan Warren was the old hand and though I don't have his date of birth he was described, when he died two years later, as elderly. Woodd on the other hand was aged just 25 when he bought into the business and Lamerte was even younger, aged 20. At some point Lamerte moved out of Bayham Street, probably when a regular income gave him the confidence to do so, though he maintained contact with the Dickenses.

In the court documents Lamerte gives a personal insight to his employment by his brother-in-law:

"this Defendant George Lamerte was educated at the Royal Military College at Sandhurst and intended for the Army and ... in October One thousand eight hundred and twenty two the Complainant William Edward Woodd prevailed on this Defendant George Lamerte to give up his then views in life and engage with the

Complainant William Edward Woodd in the Manufacture of Blacking"[66]

In January 1823 George Lamerte and the office side of the operation was moved from Tokenhouse Yard to join the manufacturing side at Hungerford Stairs.

"the said William Edward Woodd having little or no knowledge of the Art of Manufacturing Blacking he desired this Deponent to pay the most particular attention to that part of the business and to obtain all possible information regarding it from the said Jonathan Warren … this Deponent undertook the whole management of the concern for his Employer and he constantly assisted the said Jonathan Warren in Manufacturing Blacking and was taught and fully instructed in the said art by him"[67]

Though now owned by Woodd, competition between Jonathan Warren's blacking and Robert Warren's blacking continued as it had done for twenty years. Indeed, new blood, new capital and a new competitive zeal appears to have improved sales. It may be an indication of his success that within twelve months Woodd was looking round for new premises, preferably in one of the busy streets, such as Oxford Street, Strand or Piccadilly, with stabling for three or four of the horses used to cart his blacking to customers or to the docks, and with entrance to a yard through a gateway.[68]

WANTED, the LEASE of a HOUSE, with front shop and entrance through a gateway : if stables for three or four horses it would be preferred : the situation would be more desirable if in or leading to any of the principal streets, viz. Oxford-street, Strand, or Piccadilly. Direct, with particulars, to W.E.W., Jonathan Warren's blacking manufactory, 30, Hungerford-stairs, Strand.

Promoting the product

Much of the rancour between the two firms of Warren's Blacking arose from the way they presented and promoted their products. In her affidavit the wife of Jonathan Warren declared that from an early date her husband printed large placards to advertise his blacking, to which were attached the names and addresses of customers and dealers. She then complained that her brother-in-law and his family copied down the details and sought to steal away their customers. He also produced labels to identify his product and is said to have advertised in the

---

[66] From the pleadings in the case of Woodd v Lamerte, The National Archives, ref C 13 865 12. See p107-150

[67] From the affidavit of George Lamerte in the case of Warren v Lamerte, The National Archives ref C 31/448. See p172

[68] This small ad appeared in *The Times* on 3rd September 1823

newspapers, though I haven't found examples of either. On the other side of the divided family the same promotional material was produced by Robert Warren. But if the ability of ephemera to survive the ravages of time is any guide to its ubiquity then we must applaud the efforts of Robert Warren rather than Jonathan. From the time he took over, following the death of his father, we find a much greater use of his advertising in the newspapers, such as the example on page 43. Clearly he saw wide-spread promotion as the route to greater success, not just with increased use of newspaper advertising, but also with innovative ideas. One idea that caught on with the public was the introduction into his placards and handbills of verse – pretty bad verse, it has to be said, and maybe noticed and remembered just because it was so bad. But it caught the attention and was recollected in a number of writings through the nineteenth century, including the works of Dickens. Dickens wrote of the shabby-genteel lodger in *Seven Dials*, about whom "rumours are current in the Dials, that he writes poems for Mr Warren";[69] and then in *The Pickwick Papers* Tony Weller announces "Poetry's unnat'ral; no man ever talked poetry 'cept a beadle on boxin-day, or Warren's blackin', or Rowland's oil, or some of them low fellows". Robert Warren appears to have revelled in the fame – or infamy – of this aspect of his advertising, celebrating it with the publication of a book of "Warreniana" in, or soon after, 1820. The book, said to have been compiled by William Gifford,[70] comprises a series of pastiches in the styles of well-known writers, such as Washington Irving, William Wordsworth and Leigh Hunt, all of whom sing the praises of Warren's Blacking. It's all very tongue-in-cheek, yet the Introduction, if it's not as creative as the body of the book, does at least provide us with a small piece of biographical information, telling us that Gifford and Warren attended school together at Ashburton in Devon, since when "five and forty springs have now passed", ie sometime between 1775 and 1780.

Robert Warren had other ideas to help impress his product on the minds of the public: street advertising, including the novel idea of men walking around London encased in model blacking-bottles; and the making and giving out of tokens representing farthing coins. These tokens may well have been used to pay customers who returned empty bottles for re-use, a practice that I remember was still in common use, for glass bottles, when I was a child in the 1950s, and is alluded to by Dickens in *Hard Times*:

---

[69] *Sketches by Boz: Seven Dials*
[70] William Gifford, 1756-1826, English critic, editor and poet, famous as a satirist and controversialist; first editor of the *Quarterly Review*, from 1809-1824.

Boots and Shoes 1 (28a)

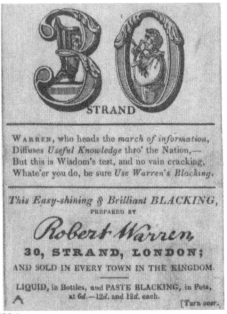

Boots and Shoes 1 (28c)

Bodleian Library, University of Oxford: John Johnson Collection

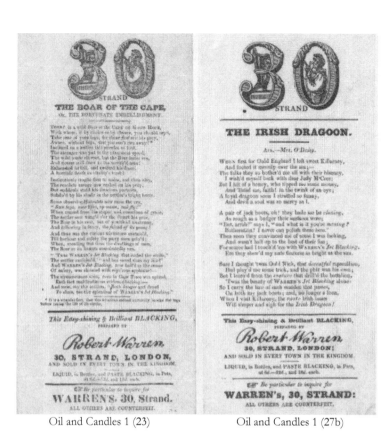

Oil and Candles 1 (23)

Oil and Candles 1 (27b)

Oil and Candles 1 (24a)

Oil and Candles 1 (24b)

Bodleian Library, University of Oxford: John Johnson Collection

Oil and Candles 1 (27a)   Oil and Candles 1 (26a)

Oil and Candles 1 (24c)

Bodleian Library, University of Oxford: John Johnson Collection

Both sides of a Robert Warren token,
resembling a farthing

Street advertising:
a sketch by George Scharf

"I am Josiah Bounderby of Coketown. For years upon years, the only pictures in my possession, or that I could have into my possession, by any means, unless I stole 'em, were the engravings of a man shaving himself in a boot, on the blacking bottles that I was overjoyed to use in cleaning boots with, and that I sold when they were empty for a farthing a-piece, and glad of it!'"

A common motif in his advertising was a boot that shone so brilliantly because of the application of Warren's Blacking that a man could shave in the mirror-like sheen, as recollected by Josiah Bounderby, or that a cat might be alarmed by seeing its own reflection, or that a cock might rise up to fight a supposed rival. But more important than all of these, Robert Warren had, from 1816, one marketing ploy that was to run throughout all his promotional material: to impress upon the public the image of "30 Strand", his business address. It appeared prominently on placards, newspaper adverts, billboards and tokens; but of particular relevance to the cases before the Chancery Court, and of the work before the young Charles Dickens, it appeared prominently on the labels attached to his products. Much space in the documents of the Chancery Court is devoted to the description of labels, placards and bills, and much of the complaint of Robert Warren is aimed at the deliberate imitation of his designs by his rivals. The use of the contrived address of 30 Hungerford Stairs was a particular cause of annoyance:

"...the house and premises in which Deponents carry on their said trade or business is situated in the Strand aforesaid and numbered 30 and is in fact not far distant from Hungerford Stairs Strand aforesaid and that the said No 30 the No of their said house and premises is printed in the Centre of the said placards and bills or labels in very large and conspicuous characters and that the word Strand is printed towards the bottom of Deponents said placards and bills or labels also in large and conspicuous Characters   That said Defendants have caused the said No 30 to be printed in the centre of their said placards and bills or labels in Characters of the same size and as conspicuous as those in which such No is printed in said Deponents said placards and bills or labels and that they have also caused the address of Hungerford Stairs Strand to be printed towards the bottom of their said placards and bills or labels in large and conspicuous characters..."[71]

Close imitation, claimed Robert Warren, misled customers who frequently purchased his rival's product, not perceiving any difference in

---

[71] The National Archives, Court of Chancery: Records of Equity Side: the Six Clerks: Affidavits, Michaelmas Term 1827, box I-Z: Affidavits in the case of Warren v Woodd. Ref C 31/448

the packaging and not realising they had made a mistake until it was too late. As proof of which he persuaded several shopkeepers to come forward and swear they had been duped. In their defence Woodd and Lamerte carefully pointed out the many differences in their packaging, Lamerte forensically so:

"...the ground pattern in the Plaintiffs Label is of different form and better executed than the Defendants that the words "real Japan Blacking" in Plaintiffs Label are red with Black at the tops and Bottoms of the Letters the same words in the Defendants Label are in reddish Characters that in the Plaintiffs Label next follows "made by" and in the Defendants Label "made by the late Manufacturer to" In the Plaintiffs Label the names "Robert Warren" are printed in White Characters upon a Black Ground with a broad red Bar Through the Centre and the same names in small red Letters upon the large Letters the Defendants Label has "Jonathan Warren" printed in the most conspicuous manner so that no person could mistake the same unless intentionally the Words "Jonathan Warren" being printed in distinct white Letters upon a black Ground, that the Plaintiffs Label contains two lines of poetry either in white characters upon a Black Ground or in Black Letters upon a White Ground, that the defendants Label has no poetry but the following words "Proprietors Geo Lamerte & Co. White Chapel Road" and since the dissolution of the Partnership and this Deponents Removal as aforesaid the words "proprietor Geo Lamerte" 56 Mansell Street" And this Deponent saith that the labels of the Plaintiffs as well as the Defendant each contain two tablets and that the borders or patterns of those of the Defendant are obviously different from those of the Plaintiff And this Deponent has been informed and believes that it has been the practice of all or nearly all Blacking makers to use similar tablets with printed sentences for many years last past And this Deponent saith that in the plaintiffs first Tablet on his Label is printed as follows "This composition with half the usual labour, produces a most brilliant jet Black, fully equal to the highest Japan Varnish affords peculiar nourishment to the leather; will not soil the finest linen, and will retain its virtue in any Climate" The Defendants first Tablet contains as follows "In consequence of the many inferior composition offered to the Public for this superior Article none is genuine unless signed Geo Lamerte & Co." and since the dissolution of the partnership the words "& Co." have been omitted. The Plaintiffs second tablet on his label is thus "Use – stir it till it is well mixed, then lay on your brush as thin as possible; black the Boot or Shoe all over; apply your shining Brush immediately and in one minute it will produce the most Brilliant lustre and jet black

John Johnson Collection, Labels 1 (16)

BLACKING LABELS

John Johnson Collection, Labels 1 (11b)

John Johnson Collection, Labels 1 (9a)

BLACKING LABELS

John Johnson Collection, Labels 1 (14)

Bodleian Library, University of Oxford: John Johnson Collection

ever beheld" The Defendants second tablet is as follows "Use – Stir your blacking well from the bottom applying it to the boot or shoe as usual, and it will immediately produce a brilliant polish" And this Deponent saith that the figures "30" in this Deponents label vary in many respects from the same figures in the Plaintiffs label but especially in as much as the Plaintiffs figures contain the representation of a Boot and a Man shaving and the Defendants figures contain the representation of a looking Glass and a monkey Shaving and the Plaintiffs number has "30" printed in small figures upon the larger ones which the Defendants has not And this Deponent saith that in the Plaintiffs Label is printed the word "Strand" in White Characters upon a Black Ground with a Broad Red Bar and in this respect also the Defendants label is totally at variance with the other for the Defendants label contains the words "Hungerford Stairs Strand" in conspicuous White Characters upon a Black Ground, each Label bears the price at one Corner and the Plaintiffs Label contains in the other corner his name printed in Black Characters upon a White Ground or white Characters on a black Ground…"

All of this demonstrates the importance attached to the labels which played such a large part in Dickens' work at the blacking factory. But if advertising and labelling were important to the success of each enterprise so, too, were the efforts of the salesmen.

The Salesmen

The salesmen, sent to all parts of the UK to take orders, played a prominent part in the Chancery Court documents, primarily to support or dispute the claims that shopkeepers were misled to believe they were buying one make of Warren's Blacking believing it to be the alternative on offer. They are referred to as "travellers" or "agents".

In their advertising and in their statements to the Court the owners of each blacking firm emphasised the pervasiveness of their products by claiming it could be bought in every town and city in the country, and the evidence from the travellers certainly shows how widespread was their network. The most interesting of the salesmen was John Thomas Lamerte, the brother of George Lamerte. In July 1824, aged just 18, he was employed by Woodd, on commission, to sell blacking in London and Kent. This would have necessitated regular visits to "headquarters", to hand in orders and to collect handbills and placards; and although he would have been well known to the Dickens family and Charles, from when they were all living at Chatham, there is no reference to him in Dickens' fragment of autobiography. Intriguingly John Thomas Lamerte, referring to Woodd's employment of his brother George in

1823, says he was unacquainted with the circumstances at that time because of "a coolness subsisting between this Deponent and certain branches of his Family". This would seem to indicate a falling out either with his brother or with Woodd, or perhaps with both. Nevertheless, the difficulty was overcome and Woodd employed him, and when Woodd and George Lamerte parted company in October of that year the younger brother was employed by the elder on a more permanent basis, and with a vastly wider scope: "this Deponent saith", was written in his affidavit, "that he is accustomed to frequent various parts of England Ireland Scotland Wales, Guernsey and Jersey soliciting orders for Blacking". That sounds like an awful lot of travelling. But he wasn't the only one – Robert Warren, though he was the head of the firm, also travelled widely. By great coincidence both Robert Warren and John Thomas Lamerte arrived in Exeter in Devon at the same time, in May 1826, staying at the same hotel, and an altercation occurred between them which found its way into the affidavits:

> "And this Deponent saith in the month of May One thousand eight hundred and twenty six ... he well remembers he met the Plaintiff Robert Warren at Exeter ... soliciting and taking orders at that place in a fair and Tradesman like way and being at the Globe Inn and seeing the said Plaintiff but mistaking him for another person upon the said Plaintiffs leaving the Room this Deponent asked the Waiter whether his name was Harris the Waiter said no and went out of the Room the Plaintiff again returned and approaching this Deponent said my name is not Harris but to the best of this Deponents recollection he added it is Warren and he continued I am not ashamed of my name if you are of yours the said Plaintiff then reproached this Deponent with selling his Employers Blacking under a fictitious name falsely representing that the person whose name was so used was dead And this Deponent then recommended the said Plaintiff if he had any complaints to make to address them to the principals and not to Deponent who was merely a Traveller but this Deponent nevertheless flatly denied the truth of the Accusation"[72]

The same incident, viewed from the opposing side, appears in the affidavit of Robert Warren. And as some further proof that Robert Warren got about the country just as much as his travellers I found the following reference to a visit he made to Dunbar in Scotland:

> "To The Banking Company, Dunbar,   From B. W. for Robert Warren, 14 St. Martin's Lane, London. Dated 7th December 1813.
> Gents, I have this day had a two £ Bank of England Note ret'd. the No. 27540 Dated 19th May 1813 taken into the Bank 6th Day of Dec'

---

[72] For the full transcript see p 181

1813, which my Brother received of you when he was at Dunbar. You can have the Note sent you through the medium of your Banker in London.

I remain, Your most Obed. Serv' B[enjamin] W[arren], for Rob't Warren."[73]

If my estimation of Robert Warren fell when he appeared to be the older, experienced factory-owner bullying and harangueing the young John Thomas Lamerte, then I couldn't help but find some admiration for his determination to travel the length and breadth of the country in pursuit of more business, work he could easily have delegated to his travellers. Four further salesmen were brought forward to swear their statements, two for George Lamerte and two for Robert Warren. William Whalley, of 4 Kings Row, Pentonville, was a loyal employee, starting with Jonathan Warren as early as 1807, staying with him until he sold the business to Woodd in 1822 and continuing to work for his new employer through to the time of the court case in 1827; his affidavit swore that Jonathan Warren's blacking was only sold under that name and never in pretence of being the blacking of Robert Warren. Thomas Quarmby of 8 Langdale Street in Whitechapel swore to the same effect and, like William Whalley, had known Jonathan Warren for a considerable time and was on intimate terms with him. His testimony, though, is additionally interesting since he relates a first-hand account of the employment arrangements of George Lamerte:

"... about the same time the above named Defendant George Lamerte was also taken into the service and employ of the said William Edward Woodd and had the principal management of the Business as well in the Manufactory as in the Counting house And this Deponent saith that he has repeatedly seen and been present when the said Defendant and the said Jonathan Warren were engaged together in Manufacturing large quantities of Blacking and the said Defendant was learning from the said Jonathan Warren his method and art of making that article and he this Deponent saith that he continued so engaged for the space of between one and two years and that during that time the said Defendant became well known to all the Customers of the said William Edward Woodd..."[74]

He also had the common-sense to point out the similarities in the styles of labels across several blacking manufacturers:

"... And this Deponent Saith that about two or three years ago Messieurs Day and Martin Blacking makers altered the Ground of their Labels to a reddish Colour that soon after the said Plaintiff

---

[73] From the website Bankingletters.co.uk. This website also shows a Robert Warren halfpenny token, similar to the farthing token shown above.

[74] For the full transcript see pp162-164

Robert Warren altered his to a somewhat similar colour and that about twelve months since the said Defendant and Lewis Worms altered the Ground of their labels also to a similar colour or nearly so..."[75]

These two witnesses appear to be solid and reliable, with a history behind them and an attention to detail. On the other hand the traveller delivered to the court by Robert Warren, Robert Ashdown of 32 Crooked Lane in the City of London, swore that Woodd sought fraudulently to steal orders from Robert Warren, but had his evidence shredded by two witnesses who claimed that, on behalf of Warren, he gained employment with Woodd solely to gather or manufacture false evidence. This stinks of dirty practice.

---

[75] For the full transcript see pp162-164

Chapter Four

1824

The documents from the Court of Chancery demonstrate very well the history of the two firms of Warren's Blacking, bringing into focus the principal characters and the frictions that existed between them. And though there were claims and counter-claims over how successful or not were the two firms, the evidence would seem to show that, up to 1822, Robert Warren was flourishing and Jonathan Warren was struggling. However, the injection of new energy, outlook and finance from October 1822, when Woodd bought Jonathan Warren's business, appears to have turned around their prospects – sufficiently, at least, to cause concern to Robert Warren, who claimed in his affidavit against Woodd that Woodd had sold "a very great quantity of Blacking and to a large amount in value … and that these Deponents have thereby sustained great loss and injury".[76]

No 2 Chandos Street stands on the corner, nos 3 and 4 are combined as one; the entrance to the yard at the back is via the very narrow Castle Court

[76] For the full transcript see pp216-220

Woodd's decision to look for new premises, as we've seen from the small ad placed in *The Times*, may have been driven by the need to find more space and as a result of his success. The property chosen was at number 3 Chandos Street, Covent Garden, not one of the principal streets first envisaged but busy nevertheless and not far distant from Hungerford Market and the Strand. Knowing the date of this move would go some way towards understanding when Dickens started his unwelcome job and for how long he suffered it. We've seen the search for new premises was under way on 3rd September 1823, and George Lamerte says the move was made at the beginning of 1824. If so, then it may well have been during the first week of January, since property moves were usually associated with Quarter Days. Woodd makes no reference to Chandos Street, saying that the business was carried on at Hungerford Stairs until Christmas 1824, which is a clear error of fact. Of course, it is possible that for a time both locations were in use – however, Lamerte says quite clearly that the business was moved, even though the old address was still afterwards used on their packaging.

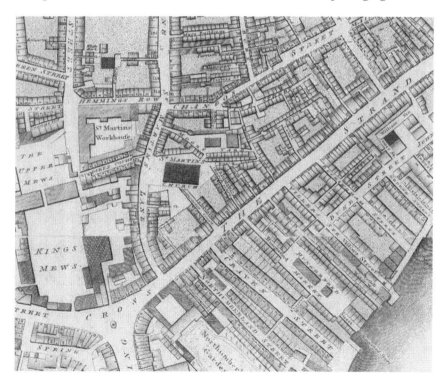

Hungerford Market is towards the bottom right corner, Chandos Street runs north of, and parallel with, the Strand; Robert Warren's Blacking was close to the corner of Strand and Villiers Street

3 Chandos Street, with the attached no. 4

The new premises were, in fact, two properties knocked into one, numbers 3 and 4, providing a substantial area for his operations. The Horwood map, shown below, describes its position, on the south side of Chandos Street, one house from the corner into Bedford Street. The only illustration I've seen of these premises, shown on the previous page, depicts a ground floor and three upper floors and it's likely there was a basement. The upper rooms of one of the two properties were of higher proportions than the other, and it can be clearly seen that at ground level the complete width of both properties was comprised of shop windows. Dickens' fragment of autobiography provides some precise details about his new workplace:

"Next to the shop at the corner of Bedford Street in Chandos Street are two rather old-fashioned houses and shops adjoining one another. They were one then, or thrown into one, for the blacking-business;[77] and had been a butter-shop.[78] Opposite to them was, and is, a public-house, where I got my ale, under these new circumstances. The stones in the street may be smoothed by my small feet going across to it at dinner- time, and back again. The establishment was larger now, and we had one or two new boys. Bob Fagin and I had attained to great dexterity in tying up the pots. I forget how many we could do in five minutes. We worked, for the light's sake, near the second window as you come from Bedford Street; and we were so brisk at it that the people used to stop and look in. Sometimes there would be quite a little crowd there. I saw my father coming in at the door one day when we were very busy, and I wondered how he could bear it."

The second window refers to the one to the right of the door. Dickens writes of being busy and of one or two new boys being taken on but his description fails to express the size of the blacking factory, the range of tasks involved in the business, the volume of output and the numbers of workers engaged. For a better comprehension of the running of a blacking factory we must turn to an article published in *The Penny Magazine* in 1842, which gives a detailed description of operations at Day and Martin's.[79] Located in High Holborn Day and Martin's was a purpose built factory and operated on a larger scale than the business in Chandos Street, yet the processes would have been much the same.

Though each manufacturer developed his own special recipe, with minor refinements, the main ingredients of blacking were vinegar, supplied in casks of 60 gallons, oil, supplied in larger casks, and ivory-

---

[77] Horwood's map shows them joined together as early as 1799

[78] After the blacking factory left it changed yet again, this time to become a curriers, a leather-worker's where techniques of dressing, finishing and colouring to tanned hide makes it strong, flexible and waterproof

[79] The full transcript, with illustrations, is given as Appendix 4, page 266

black[80] or something similar, in casks of nearly a ton each. The odour of vinegar pervaded the whole factory. These ingredients were mixed in large tubs, each containing 100 gallons, and Day and Martin operated as many as 100 tubs, which must have taken up an enormous amount of space. Bottles for liquid blacking and pots for paste blacking were both made of brown glazed earthenware, principally supplied from the Derbyshire potteries and transported to London in large crates, packed in straw, each crate containing about 1200 bottles and weighing half-a-ton. Thousands of these bottles and pots would be emptied from their crates and arranged on shelves, ready for use. The manufacturers would also re-use old bottles, so space had to be found for coppers and tubs of steaming water in which to wash them. Blacking sold to the armed forces was packed in round tins about 3 inches in diameter, earthenware bottles and pots being far too heavy to form part of a soldier's kit. The consistency of the blacking was varied to suit bottles, pots and tins. The containers were filled direct from the mixing tubs, the expertise of the men doing the filling being a mix of speed with the ability to avoid spilling blacking onto the bottle or pot. The full bottles were lined up along benches for the next stage of the process, corking. Corks were delivered to the factory in sacks containing up to fifteen thousand corks which, when sorted into appropriate sizes, were passed to two-man teams. The first in the team placed a cork in each bottle while the second followed on and rammed it tight with a wooden mallet till the top was level with the rim of the bottle. A cork was not sufficiently fixed to prevent leakage of liquid blacking so the preparation and application of a sealing wax was called for. Supplies of resin, turpentine and colourant had to be brought in, which were mixed and melted in a special furnace, special care being taken to avoid accidents with this dangerous hot wax. It was poured into containers to cool and later lumps of it were re-melted when needed to seal the bottles. The observer at Day and Martin's was obviously impressed with the technique of sealing:

"When melted, it has a cream like consistence, and presents the well known red colour. This apparatus being ready, and placed close beside the ranges of filled bottles, a workman proceeds to seal the corks. He has no brush, no ladle, no contrivance for pouring the wax on the cork, but, holding the bottle upside down, he just immerses the corked surface in the liquid wax. Practice has enabled the men to effect the dipping so exactly, that the wax rarely comes over the sides of the bottle. The apparently simple matter of reversing the bottle again, without scattering the wax, or causing it to flow over the sides

---

[80] a black powder, originally made from ivory, but later from bone

of the bottle, is effected by a peculiar movement of the wrist and hand, impossible to describe and difficult to imitate."[81]

As with all the procedures, speed was important and when we're told a man could seal 1200 bottles in an hour it helps build a picture of the scale of proceedings. The next description relates directly to the work carried out by 12-years-old Charles Dickens, the pasting of labels:

"One man or boy can paste as many labels as two others can attach to the bottles, so that they work together in groups of three. On the bench is placed on the one side a large tub of paste, and on the other a ranged series of filled and sealed bottles. A heap of labels is laid down face downwards, and the paster pastes them one by one with a brush. The dexterity in this simple act is not in the pasting, but in a peculiar final touch with the brush, by which the pasted label is jerked off the heap, and caught in the left hand. So rapidly is this effected, that one man will paste a label, jerk it off the heap, catch it in his left hand, and lay it on one side, nearly two thousand times in an hour; for one man can thus paste a hundred and sixty dozen labels in this time. As fast as the labels are pasted, the other two workmen attach them to the bottles. Each one takes a bottle in his left hand, and a pasted label in his right, and attaches the one to the other by two or three touches which the eye can scarcely follow. To a spectator it seems that almost before the bottle is taken fairly into the hand, it is laid down again, properly labelled. Let any uninitiated person endeavour thus to secure sixteen labels per minute to as many bottles, and see what progress he will make."[82]

When the bottles were filled, sealed and labelled they then had to be packed into casks, ready for despatch. At Day and Martin they made their own casks, so employed a team of coopers, and though they may not have done the same at Warren's they would still have needed to buy them in and allow space for storage. Bottles and pots were arranged in layers and rings in the casks, liberally secured and protected with straw padding. Porters would then transport them to the yard for loading on to waggons, ready for carrying across London or to close destinations, or to the docks for shipping further afield. In my investigations into Henry Worms, for example, I noticed newspaper advertisements for auctions of casks of Warren's Blacking in Australia. One of the criteria that William Edward Wooodd was looking for in his new premises, as shown in the advertisement he placed, was sufficient stabling for three or four horses. Presumably space to house the waggons was also needed. None of this would happen, of course, without a command centre – the office, or counting house, from which supplies would be calculated, ordered and

---

[81] See p278
[82] See p281

paid for; to which travellers and agents passed the orders they had taken; from which invoices were issued, payments collected in, and wages calculated and paid.

Such, then, was the range of activity in a blacking factory, demonstrating the extent of space needed for the men to operate and the large areas necessary for the storage of materials. The image of a young Charles Dickens shown as the frontispiece to this book, depicts a solitary lad, pitiful in his private misery, designed to arouse our sympathy. Till now it never occurred to me that there was a busy workforce behind him, hauling crates, mixing smelly ingredients, rapidly filling, sealing and labelling, packing and transporting the finished product.

The affidavits of George Lamerte and a number of other witnesses make it clear that, from the time he was engaged in 1822 through to 1824, Lamerte learned the working of the business from top to bottom, albeit with the experience of the elderly Jonathan Warren to guide him. William Edward Woodd may have decided strategic direction – how to finance and promote growth, where to find new premises that would put his business in the public eye, when to take on additional staff – but Lamerte was very much a hands-on manager. There is evidence, both in the court documents and elsewhere, that Woodd often spent time in Ireland. The detailed descriptions of the blacking business laid out before us in the court documents and in the article on Day and Martin allow us a good understanding of the responsibility taken on by Lamerte. The weight already on his shoulders became considerably heavier in August 1824 when Jonathan Warren dropped down dead. On 21st August the following small item appeared in the newspapers:[83]

> SUDDEN DEATH.—This morning, about nine o'clock, Mr. Jonathan Warren, an elderly gentleman, the original inventor of Warren's japan blacking, and uncle to the present proprietors belonging to that firm, having gone into the shop of Mr. Homewood, an oilman, in the Strand, to purchase some articles, he suddenly fell forwards on some bottles in the shop, and expired.

The journalist appears ignorant of the schism in the Warren family, bringing uncle and nephews together under the same banner, which they certainly were not. At the time of the death Woodd was in Ireland and Lamerte found himself running everything by himself. Still a young man,

[83] *Jackson's Oxford Journal*, Saturday 21 August 1824.

just passing his 22nd birthday at this time, the strain of running all aspects of the business appears to have tested his patience and judgement. First of all, goaded and insulted by a letter from John Dickens, he exploded and told young Charley he would no longer be able to keep him at the factory. Dickens' mother pacified Lamerte, who agreed to take Charley back but John Dickens, either out of stubbornness or from a feeling of compassion for his son, or a feeling of guilt about the trials he had been put through, refused to send him back and with a largesse he probably couldn't afford started to make arrangements for him to resume his schooling. Lamerte then argued violently with Woodd. The nature of their argument is recorded in the Chancery Court Pleadings but to appreciate the likely heat of their altercation a little imagination is needed to see beyond stilted court language:

"And this Defendant George Lamerte says ... that in or about the month of October One thousand eight hundred and twenty four this Defendant George Lamerte required the Complainant William Edward Woodd to come to a settlement and to define on what terms this Defendant George Lamerte was to continue in such manufactory when this Defendant George Lamerte and the Complainant William Edward Woodd disagreed and the Complainant William Edward Woodd remarked to this Defendant George Lamerte that there was plenty of room in the Blacking Trade and that Lamerte was an excellent name for it to which remark this Defendant George Lamerte made answer No Mr. Woodd from the treatment you have shewn towards me let me observe that I have had the manufactory of Jonathan Warrens blacking and the many improvements I have made in it to your advantage shall now be placed to my account you know I have no other trade or profession and I therefore most certainly shall take that which is the only course I have left and take your advice and set up as a Blacking maker but not in the name of Lamerte but that of late Manufacturer to Jonathan Warren"[84]

This was no ordinary row. Here were two young men, brothers-in-law, one probably feeling his considerable efforts were not being appreciated, complaining about the treatment he had received, the other thinking, perhaps, that his younger relative was getting above himself. Woodd, having taken on an inexperienced youth, only, perhaps, because he thought he was helping his wife's brother, seems to have felt confident enough of the strength of his position to tell Lamerte if he didn't like his job at Chandos Street then he could go and find a job with some other blacking manufacturer. Calling his bluff, and with all the confidence of youth, Lamerte felt he knew enough about the business not to work for

---

[84] The full transcript is given at pp133-4

somebody else but to set up on his own account – not to join a competitor, but to become a competitor.

And so the two split up. History repeated itself: just as the brothers Jonathan and Thomas Warren argued and created two rival businesses, so too did these brothers-in-law argue and create two rival businesses. Woodd carried on at Chandos Street for about two months, after which he took a new partner, Stephen Pilcher, and moved to less prominent premises at 9 Noble Street, near the City of London's Guildhall. George Lamerte turned to his relatives in the East End, persuading his cousin Lewis Worms to go into partnership with him and to operate their new enterprise from the Worms property at 107 Whitechapel Road. Rivalry in the production of Warren's Blacking took on a bizarre twist. Robert Warren continued to advertise his 'genuine' blacking, Woodd advertised the strapline he had bought of 'Jonathan Warren's original Japan Blacking' and Lamerte set up with the logo 'manufacturer to the late Jonathan Warren'. There may, even, have been a fourth complication, since at some point Jonathan Warren's eldest son, also called Jonathan, stepped into the business, setting up with a partner called William Grigg and promoting himself on his labels as "Jonathan Warren, eldest son of of the late celebrated inventor of that name". The Warren/Grigg partnership was dissolved in 1829, so must have been established sometime between 1824 and 1829 and was operating at the same time as the other three "Warren's". There was a strange coincidence attached to the business of Jonathan Warren junior, which had its premises at 53 Hatton Garden – 12 years later, when writing *Oliver Twist,* Dickens wanted a first-hand observation of the performance of the notorious magistrate Allan Stewart Laing, whom he transformed into Mr Fang, and he asked a fellow-journalist, Thomas Haines, if he could smuggle Dickens into Laing's police court some morning.[85] The coincidence is that the police court was at 54 Hatton Garden, right next door to Warren's Blacking.

Going to Court

A label for the blacking of Jonathan Warren junior can be seen on page 59. Despite being the one person most entitled, in many ways, to call his product Warren's Blacking the occupant of 53 Hatton Garden appears to have failed in his enterprise and fades from view. Woodd may have expected the same outcome for Lamerte, but if he did then he was disappointed and it seems likely that Lamerte took trade from his brother-in-law. And to such an extent that about 18 months later, on 26th July 1826, William Edward Woodd and Stephen Pilcher made a

---

[85] Letter to Haines 3 June 1837 – *Pilgrim Letters*, vol 1, p267

complaint before the Right Honorable John, Earl of Eldon, Lord High Chancellor of Great Britain, at the Court of Chancery. The written Pleading laid out their Complaint and concluded:

"May it please your Lordship the Premises considered to grant unto your Orators not only his Majestys most gracious writ of Injunction issuing out of and under the seal of this honorable Court to be directed to the said Defendants George Lamerte and Lewis Worms and each of them and their and each of their Agents Servants and Workmen severally to restrain them from pasting or affixing upon the said Bottles and pots containing the composition or Blacking and paste manufactured by them the said Defendants or either of them as aforesaid any labels hitherto used by them as aforesaid or other labels being the same or colourable imitations of the labels hereinbefore mentioned to be used by your Orators as such partners as aforesaid in the sale of their said liquid Blacking or Paste Blacking as aforesaid or any other label or description by which such Composition or liquid Blacking and paste so manufactured shall be described or represented as being the composition or Blacking actually made or manufactured by your Orators or shall have the appearance of being so described or represented and more particularly any label or labels having the name or firm of Jonathan Warren subscribed or annexed either actually or apparently and ostensibly as a signature thereto and from selling Bottles and pots containing respectively the composition or liquid Blacking and paste Blacking manufactured by them the said Defendants or either of them or by any person or persons by their or either of their order or direction or with their or either of their knowledge or privity with such labels pasted or affixed thereon as aforesaid, but also his Majestys most gracious Writ or Writs of Subpena to be directed to the said George Lamerte and Lewis Worms and their Confederates thereby commanding them at a certain day and under a certain pain therein to be limited personally to be and appear before your Lordship in this honourable Court and then and there full true direct and perfect answer make to all and singular the Premises and further to stand to perform and abide such further Order direction and Decree therein as to your Lordship shall seem meet   And your Orators shall ever pray" .

It can only be imagined what sort of rifts this caused in the families. Perhaps Woodd took the action in anger, perhaps in fear that his business would fail from the competition. Maybe he considered that Lamerte would be frightened by the prospect of a court case, and would stop promoting his link with Jonathan Warren; or perhaps give up blacking altogether. If so, then he mistook Lamerte's determination. The wheels of justice grinding slow, it was four months, on 22nd

November 1826, before George Lamerte and Lewis Worms called his brother-in-law's bluff and placed before the Court their Answer to the Complaint. Now it was the turn of Woodd to consider his next step. For whatever reason he let the case lapse and on the 27th July 1827 Lamerte's counsel went back to court:

"Upon notification this day made unto this Court by Mr Wakefield of Counsel for the defendants It was alleged that the plaintiffs have exhibited their Bill in this Court against the defendants It appears by the six clerks certificates now produced and received that the defendants put in their answer thereto on the 22nd day of November last and that no other proceedings have since been had in this cause. It was therefore prayed that the plaintiffs Bill may stand dismissed out of this Court with costs for want of presentation which is agreed accordingly and it is thereby referred to the Master in Rotation to tax the said costs."[86]

Two weeks later the costs were calculated and granted to George Lamerte:

"9th. August 1827   In Pursuance of an order made in this Cause bearing date the 13th. Day of July last whereby it was ordered that the plaintiffs Bill should stand dismissed out of this Honorable Court with Costs for want of prosecution and it was referred to me to tax the said Costs I have been attended by the Clerk in court and Solicitors for the plaintiffs and for the Defendants and in their presence have proceeded to tax the said Defendant his Costs of this Suit the Bill of which has been brought in before me accordingly and the said Defendants Bill of such Costs amounting to the Sum of £32..7..2   I have taxed at the Sum of £30..18..4   including therein fourteen shillings and two pence for a Subpoena and personal service thereof and which must be deducted in case the said taxed Costs are paid before such Subpoena is sued out Which I humbly certify to this Honorable Court   Jns Stephen" [87]

And so that particular dispute, as far as the Court of Chancery was concerned, came to an end. Whether or not it continued in the 19th century parlours of the Woodd and Lamerte families we can only surmise; whether Sophia Woodd took the side of her husband or her brother is anybody's guess. It's the stuff, isn't it, of a 19th century novel?

---

[86] The National Archives, Court of Chancery: Decrees and Orders in the course of a suit, C 33/759/1416, Woodd v Lamerte
[87] The National Archives, Chancery Records, Masters reports and certificates C 38/1385 covering "W" names for 1827.

Robert Warren
as he appeared on his own halfpenny tokens

Robert Warren goes to Court

Standing on the sidelines, awaiting the outcome of the case, was the third blacking manufacturer, Robert Warren. Warren made his move on 13th November 1827, his barrister Mr Horne appearing before the Lord Chancellor[88] in the Court of Chancery to seek an injunction against George Lamerte. The complaint in full appears in Chapter Six, but the accounts next day in *The Times* and *The Morning Chronicle* give a much better flavour to an otherwise stale process. First from *The Times*:

"COURT OF CHANCERY, Tuesday, Nov. 13. Warren's Blacking. Mr Horne moved for an injunction that George Lamert should be restrained by the injunction of the Court from vending a spurious imitation of the celebrated blacking called "Warren's." The notoriety of the plaintiff, Robert Warren, was so well established, - his

---

[88] The Lord Chancellor was John Scott, first Earl of Eldon, 1751-1838; he was replaced in May 1827 by Lord Lyndhurst.

reputation had acquired such a lustre, - that it was unnecessary for the counsel to do more than mention his name, in order to put the Court in possession of his character and merits. All the walls in the town spoke eloquently in his praise, and he was universally acknowledged to be the only reall blacking-maker that Europe had produced.

The Lord Chancellor thought that the names of "Day and Martin" had shone in the same career.

Mr Horne said, that was once. Day's glories were eclipsed by the brighter beams of this new luminary, Mr Warren: his blacking was unrivalled, and not to be mentioned in the same day with any body else's. His bill stated, in terms of urgent and just complaint, that the defendant, Mr Lamert, - who was as it were a stranger – a foreigner to the part of town where Mr Warren resided, - had, with the unfair design of vending his own spurious composition in the place of Mr Warren's, counterfeited the bill which was pasted on the outside of the vessels which contained the genuine blacking, and placed them on his own. This was the injury for which Mr Warren sought redress. Mr Lamert lived somewhere in Goodman's-fields, and yet he pretended to sell blacking made at No. 30, in the Strand. The bills were in court for his Lordship's inspection. They were evidently piracies of the plaintiff's, but the blacking, he assured his Lordship, was by no means a *colourable* imitation of the genuine article prepared by Mr Warren.

The bills were put in, and very scrupulously and closely examined by the Lord Chancellor, who asked if there was any body of the name of Warren connected with the defendant.

Mr Horne said "No, there was not."

His Lordship said he saw the bill stated the blacking to be made in one instance by Jonathan and in the other by Robert Warren.

Mr Horne said that was a mere artifice to evade the law, and he trusted it would not succeed.

The injunction was granted."[89]

Then from *The Morning Chronicle*:

"COURT OF CHANCERY. – Tuesday. Special Injunction – Warren's Blacking.

Mr Horne stated that he had been instructed to move for a special injunction upon an *ex parte* application, in a case which called for the immediate interposition of the Court. The Plaintiff was Mr Robert Warren, of blacking notoriety; and the defendant Mr George Lamert, who had thought fit, most fraudulently, to use the name of the plaintiff in the sale of his spurious blacking. The case, as it appeared

---

[89] *The Times*, Wednesday 14th November 1827, p3

upon the bill, supported by affidavit, was this: the defendant well knowing that the very best blacking was sold by none but Mr Warren [a laugh] –

The Lord Chancellor thought "Day and Martin" were entitled to some share of notoriety in that line.

Mr Horne begged to differ from his Lordship: for Day and Martin were completely out of court, at least on this occasion. The facts were these: - The article in question was accustomed to be sold in bottles, as well as boxes, labelled in large characters, with the name and address of the plaintiff at full length. His Lordship, in way of his perambulations round the outskirts of the town, might have been amused with these characters written on the walls, and might not perhaps require to be told that "Warren's Blacking, 30, Strand," was the plaintiff's in the present suit. This address was invariably fixed on the bottles (here some of the blacking bottles were handed up to the Court, and the curious examination of them by his Lordship excited considerable merriment). The defendant lived in quite a different part of the town – viz. in Mansell-street, in the Minories, but had thought proper to sell to the public blacking in bottles labelled so nearly similar to those of the plaintiff, as to deceive the purchasers of his spurious article. The defendant, therefore, being a person of no celebrity either with respect to his person, or the article which he sold, had fraudulently resorted to this artifice to gain a profit, and injure the plaintiff. It was in proof that the defendant's customers had themselves upbraided him with the cheat, and on many occasions had compelled him to refund the money and take back his blacking. The jars were expressly sold by the defendant as Warren's blacking, and the Learned Counsel conceived, under these circumstances, there could be no difficulty in granting the injunction.

The Lord Chancellor asked if any person connected with the defendant was named Warren?

Mr Horne replied in the negative. There was no "Warren," no number "30," and no "Hungerford;" all of which were fraudulently put upon the label in imitation of the plaintiff's label.

The Lord Chancellor asked if Mr Horne thought an action would lie in such a case? He perceived that on one label was the name of Jonathan Warren, and on the other Robert Warren.

Mr Horne said that this was only an artifice to evade the law, but it fortunately had not succeeded. – Injunction granted."[90]

Buoyed-up by his success Robert Warren moved quickly to re-inforce his position, placing a notice in the newspapers designed to scare Lamerte's

---

[90] *The Morning Chronicle*, Wednesday 14th November 1827

customers from placing further orders:

"COURT OF CHANCERY. – An injunction has this day been granted by the Lord Chancellor to restrain G. Lamerte from making or selling any blacking with labels in imitation of the genuine Warren's Blacking, which he has been in the habit of doing by using the fictitious name of Jonathan Warren, and otherwise imitating the genuine labels of Robert Warren, 30, Strand. It is therefore strongly recommended, that those shopkeepers, or others, who have any of the counterfeit blacking, as above described, do return it to the parties from whom they received it, which they are justified in doing. By neglecting this notice they will be liable to the heavy expenses and penalties of a suit in Chancery, which will be immediately commenced against them. The genuine blacking is signed "Robert Warren, 30, Strand," on each label, all others are counterfeit, and of very inferior quality. – London, No. 13, 1827."[91]

Not taking any chances that this notice might be missed by those for whom it was intended, Warren had copies of it made and sent out to customers of Lamerte, together with the following letter, a copy of which was re-routed to Lamerte by a sympathiser:

"Blacking Manufactory 30 Strand Novr. 16th. 1827

Sir Being informed you have a quantity of the Counterfeit Blking in imitation of the genuine Warrens Blking made by me, I beg to recommend the annex'd Notice to your serious attention presuming you have been deceived by the close imitation, and having no wish to proceed to extremities without giving an opportunity for your immediately discontinuing a practice so injurious to my trade and reputation as a Blking Manufacturer I have to request you will take the earliest means in your power to stop such proceedings. The most effectual will be to return the spurious Blking to the parties from whom you receive it I shall be further obliged by your favouring me with an order for a supply of the genuine Blking A line by post will meet immediate attention from

Sir your obdt. Servant Robert Warren."[92]

In this very busy week for the bullish Robert Warren there was, straightaway, another major irritation to be dealt with, as recorded in his affidavit by the new occupant of the premises at Hungerford Stairs:

"John Wood of Hungerford Market in the City of Westminster Clicker maketh oath and saith that prior to Michaelmas last this Deponent hired the House he now resides in at Hungerford Market his Tenancy to commence from Michaelmas last that on the Front

---

91 *The Times*, Monday 19th November, p1
92 The National Archives, reference C 31/448, Affidavits in the case of Warren v Lamerte in the Chancery Court. See Chapter 7 of this book, p178

next the River was written or painted in very large and legible Characters in Black upon a White Ground "Warrens 30 Blacking Warehouse" And this Deponent saith that the said Figures and words so being on the River Front of this Deponents House Mr. Harnett of Northumberland Street Solicitor called upon this Deponent twice and asked this Deponent if he would give his consent to have the said words and figures obliterated because if he refused it would occasion him a great deal of Trouble That this Deponent assented provided he was put to no expence about it and in a few days afterwards that is in the last week the Plaintiffs men came and effaced the said Words and Figures so as that they are now scarcely legible unless the person desirous of reading them knew what had been scratched out And this Deponent saith that the front of the said House next the Street had borne a Number and that very lately some person without his knowledge or consent obliterated such number and has painted the No 6 upon his said Door in lieu thereof And this Deponent saith that on the morning the words and figures were obliterated as before described the said Plaintiff Robert Warren came down before his Men and inspected the said words and figures John Wood [signature]

Sworn at the Public Office Southampton Buildings Chancery Lane in the County of Middlesex this nineteenth day of November 1827 Before me

H Cross [signature]"

Robert Warren seemed to sweep all before him. Less than a week after his first appearance in the Chancery Court he was back again, this time appearing before the Vice Chancellor, seeking an injunction against William Edward Woodd. The newspapers carried a short report:

"VICE CHANCELLOR'S COURT. Monday, November 19. Warren v Wood, Pitcher, and others. This was an application made by Mr Warren, the blacking-maker, for an injunction to restrain the defendants from vending blacking labelled "Jonathan Warren, 30 Strand." The Vice-Chancellor, finding that the circumstances of this case were precisely similar to those upon which the Lord Chancellor had lately granted an application of the same sort, granted the injunction now prayed for."[93]

For a week or so Robert Warren must have been cock-a-hoop, getting the law on his side, seriously impeding the operations of these two rivals and frightening their customers. But then he suffered a reversal, and a rebuke from the Court. Once again, the newspapers, including this one from *The Times*, give the best accounts:

---

[93] *The Examiner*, Sunday 25th November 1827

"COURT OF CHANCERY, Tuesday, Nov. 27. Warren v. Lamert. Mr Sugden moved that the injunction obtained some days ago by Mr Warren, the blacking-maker, in the Strand, against the defendant, should be dissolved. The plaintiff had stated in his affidavits, that there was no person of his name in the defendant's firm, that the use of such a name was obviously for the purpose of injuring him in the sale of his blacking, by passing off a spurious article on the public as of his composition. The affidavits stated also, that the labels on the jars, and the jars themselves, were so nearly imitated by the defendant, as to be mistaken without a close scrutiny.

Mr Horne interrupted Mr Sugden, by reminding him that this was the appeal day, and requesting him to postpone his motion.

Mr Sugden regretted the urgency of the case was so great that he could not attend to his friend's suggestion.

Mr Horne complained that the notice had been too short.

Mr Sugden replied, that it was as long as his client was compelled by the practice of the Court to give, and the plaintiff could not expect more from him after the manner in which the injunction had been obtained. He then went on to state the substance of the defendant's affidavits, which was, that so long ago as the year 1798, one Jonathan Warren, an uncle of the plaintiff, had discovered a valuable method of making liquid blacking, which he manufactured and sold for many

Lincoln's Inn old hall, showing the Court of Chancery in session, 1808

years at Hungerford-stairs, near the Strand, and that the house in which he lived was numbered, or known, as Number 30. He had painted upon this house, in very large characters, "Warren's Blacking, No. 30," and this inscription remained there until within a short period of the present time, when the plaintiff's solicitor had prevailed upon the owner of the house to have it obliterated. In the year 1821 Jonathan Warren died, but had continued to carry on the trade of a blacking-maker up to the time of his death, in partnership with a Mr Wood. After the death of Jonathan Warren, Mr Wood made proposals to the defendant Lamert to join him as a partner, which he did, and they continued to carry on business together. The elder Warren and his partner, as well as the defendant who succeeded, had always used labels and jars in some degree resembling those of the plaintiff, because almost all blacking resembled one another. They had called their blacking "Warren's Blacking," as they submitted they had a right to do, after the ingenious person who had discovered it, and he hoped his Lordship's decision this day would give them the right of continuing to do so. He complained of the attempts which the plaintiff had made to ruin the defendant by means of letters and advertisements in the public papers, threatening their customers with bills in Chancery, and all the other frightful penalties of the law, for doing that which they had a right to do – viz., to deal with the defendants for blacking. This had succeeded to so great an extent as to cause very serious loss to the defendant; for although nothing could be more ridiculous than the plaintiff's threats, people who wanted to buy blacking would like to buy it at places where they would not be molested. The defendant complained that he was reduced to the verge of ruin by the means which the plaintiff had resorted to for the purpose of preventing the sale of his manufacture. He therefore hoped that the Lord Chancellor would forthwith dissolve this injunction, and that in such a manner, as would show the plaintiff he had no right to attack a competitor in the manner he had selected.

Mr Wakefield was heard on the same side.

Mr Horne, for the plaintiff, contended that the defendant's conduct was such as did not entitle him to the protection of a court of justice. He had endeavoured, and it could not be denied, to make an article manufactured by himself pass off with the public for one which was manufactured by the plaintiff. He had copied the plaintiff's bills and labels so nearly, that to an unpractised eye no difference appeared; and although he had inserted his own place of residence, he had done so in characters that could hardly be seen. As to the statement about the uncle and Hungerford stairs, it was clearly unfounded. The place to which he alluded did not contain 30 houses, so there could be no "N. 30" there. The way in which "Warren's Blacking, No. 30, Strand," was introduced into the label, could be for no other purpose than to imitate that sold and made by the plaintiff.

The Lord Chancellor said he had particularly asked, whether any person of the name of Warren was connected with the defendant when he had granted the injunction, and he was assured there was not, and that all reference to him was a fiction. This turned out to be untrue.

Mr Horne said he had been dead several years, so that it was true no connexion existed between him and the defendant.

The Lord Chancellor asked if such a man chose to make and sell blacking, and to write over his door "Warren's Blacking," had he not a right to do so?

Mr Horne said that case was different from this, which was one of palpable imitation.

The Lord Chancellor said it appeared he did live at Hungerford stairs.

Mr Horne. – But not at "No. 30. Strand."

The Lord Chancellor said, that whatever right Jonathan Warren had, the defendant derived from him, and he might, in order to keep up the sale of his goods, make allusion to the former place of its manufacture, notwithstanding he had removed to another part of the town.

Mr Horne believed, if it had been expected that this motion would be made to-day, an answer would have been given to the defendant's case. Wood, the alleged partner of the defendant, was at this moment engaged in a suit with him, in which he denied his right to make this blacking. There could be no doubt of the unfairness of the defendant's intention, for no sooner had the plaintiff changed the colour of his placards, than the defendant imitated the alteration.

The Lord Chancellor said that the plaintiff had rested for six or seven years without attempting to establish the right which he now contended for. His Lordship also reprehended in strong terms the manner in which the affidavit alluded to events which had passed many years ago, by such expressions as "lately," and "some time since." At the same time there could be no doubt that the defendant had attempted an imitation of the plaintiff's placards, for so much were they alike, that without a close examination the difference could not be detected. For this, however, the plaintiff, if he had any remedy at all, would find it at law, and his tardiness in bringing forward his claim was a proof, satisfactory to his Lordship's mind, that there was no necessity for the interference of the Court. He should therefore dissolve the injunction, but, considering the defendant's conduct, he would do so without costs. His Lordship said also, that the means adopted by the plaintiff in inserting letters and advertisements in newspapers were extremely unjustifiable."[94]

Accounts from two other newspapers are transcribed in Appendix Five, covering much the same ground, though with small differences depending on what the Court reporters decided to omit from the proceedings and what to leave in. If either the journalist or the barristers were not exactly right in all their facts, they were very nearly so; and I was impressed that the Lord Chancellor grasped the essential points of the case and saw the weaknesses in the case put by Robert Warren's barrister. Warren must have been greatly disappointed by the cold water poured on his case by the Lord Chancellor. There was to be a repeat performance of all this the following day, when Counsel for William Edward Woodd appeared in the court of the Vice-Chancellor seeking, and getting, dismissal of Warren's injunction in the parallel case – the newspaper report on Woodd's case is also transcribed in Appendix Five.

And so, as far as this book is concerned, the battles in the blacking business fizzled out. I've not found further documents in The National Archives although, such is the complexity of the archive of the Chancery Court, there may well be something hidden somewhere.

Sworn signature of George Lamerte

---

[94] *The Times*, Wednesday 28th November 1827, p3

Chapter Five

Charles Dickens' account

Charles Dickens' emotional and personal account of his time at Warren's Blacking sits in sharp contrast to the formality of pleadings, affidavits and injunctions from the Court of Chancery. I've repeated his account here, using those elements relating to the blacking factory but leaving out his otherwise day-to-day existence, his wandering of the streets and his descriptions relating to the Marshalsea. Forster's relevant linking paragraphs are added in italics. From this excerpt we can assess how accurate, or not, Dickens and Forster were in their accounts of this crucial period in Dickens' life.

"The person indirectly responsible for the scenes to be described was the young relative James Lamert, the cousin by his aunt'smarriage of whom I have made frequent mention, who got up the plays at Chatham, and after passing at Sandhurst had been living with the family in Bayham-street in the hope of obtaining a commission in the army. This did not come until long afterwards, when, in consideration of his father's services, he received it, and relinquished it then in favour of a younger brother; but he had meanwhile, before the family removed from Camden-town, ceased to live with them. The husband of a sister of his (of the same name as himself, being indeed his cousin, George Lamert), a man of some property, had recently embarked in an odd sort of commercial speculation; and had taken him into his office, and his house, to assist in it. I give now the fragment of autobiography of Dickens.

This speculation was a rivalry of 'Warren's Blacking, 30, Strand,'--at that time very famous. One Jonathan Warren (the famous one was Robert), living at 30, Hungerford Stairs, or Market, Strand (for I forget which it was called then), claimed to have been the original inventor or proprietor of the blacking-recipe, and to have been deposed and ill used by his renowned relation. At last he put himself in the way of selling his recipe, and his name, and his 30, Hungerford Stairs, Strand (30, Strand, very large, and the intermediate direction very small), for an annuity; and he set forth by his agents that a little capital would make a great business of it. The man of some property was found in George Lamert, the cousin and brother-in-law of James. He bought this right and title, and went into the blacking-business and the blacking-premises.

--In an evil hour for me, as I often bitterly thought, its chief manager, James Lamert, the relative who had lived with us in Bayham Street, seeing how I was employed from day to day, and knowing what our domestic circumstances then were, proposed that I should go into the blacking-warehouse, to be as useful as I could, at a salary, I think, of six shillings a week. I am not clear whether it was six or seven. I am inclined to believe, from my uncertainty on this head, that it was six at first, and seven afterwards. At any rate, the offer was accepted very willingly by my father and mother, and on a Monday morning I went down to the blacking-warehouse to begin my business life.

The blacking-warehouse was the last house on the left-hand side of the way, at old Hungerford Stairs. It was a crazy, tumble-down old house, abutting of course on the river, and literally overrun with rats. Its wainscoted rooms, and its rotten floors and staircase, and the old gray rats swarming down in the cellars, and the sound of their squeaking and scuffling coming up the stairs at all times, and the dirt and decay of the place, rise up visibly before me, as if I were there again. The counting-house was on the first floor, looking over the

Hungerford Stairs
showing Warren's Blacking to the right of the gates[95]

---

[95] Note the window on the first floor where Dickens sat to work; and the area of wall where Warren's name was painted and later erased.

coal-barges and the river. There was a recess in it, in which I was to sit and work. My work was to cover the pots of paste-blacking; first with a piece of oil-paper, and then with a piece of blue paper; to tie them round with a string; and then to clip the paper close and neat, all round, until it looked as smart as a pot of ointment from an apothecary's shop. When a certain number of grosses of pots had attained this pitch of perfection, I was to paste on each a printed label, and then go on again with more pots. Two or three other boys were kept at similar duty down-stairs on similar wages. One of them came up, in a ragged apron and a paper cap, on the first Monday morning, to show me the trick of using the string and tying the knot. His name was Bob Fagin; and I took the liberty of using his name, long afterwards, in *Oliver Twist*.

Our relative had kindly arranged to teach me something in the dinner-hour; from twelve to one, I think it was; every day. But an arrangement so incompatible with counting-house business soon died away, from no fault of his or mine; and, for the same reason, my small work-table, and my grosses of pots, my papers, string, scissors, paste-pot, and labels, by little and little, vanished out of the recess in the counting-house, and kept company with the other small work-tables, grosses of pots, papers, string, scissors, and paste-pots, down-stairs. It was not long before Bob Fagin and I, and another boy whose name was Paul Green, but who was currently believed to have been christened Poll (a belief which I transferred, long afterwards again, to Mr. Sweedlepipe, in *Martin Chuzzlewit*), worked generally, side by side. Bob Fagin was an orphan, and lived with his brother-in-law, a waterman. Poll Green's father had the additional distinction of being a fireman, and was employed at Drury Lane theatre; where another relation of Poll's, I think his little sister, did imps in the pantomimes.

A certain man (a soldier once) named Thomas, who was the foreman, and another named Harry, who was the carman and wore a red jacket, used to call me 'Charles' sometimes, in speaking to me; My rescue from this kind of existence I considered quite hopeless, and abandoned as such, altogether.

When the family left the Marshalsea they all went to lodge with the lady in Little College Street, a Mrs. Roylance, who has obtained unexpected immortality as Mrs. Pipchin; and they afterwards occupied a small house in Somers-town. But, before this time, Charles was present with some of them in Tenterden Street to see his sister. Fanny received one of the prizes given to the pupils of the Royal Academy of Music.

I could not bear to think of myself--beyond the reach of all such honorable emulation and success. The tears ran down my face. I felt as if my heart were rent. I prayed, when I went to bed that night, to be lifted out of the humiliation and neglect in which I was. I never had suffered so much before. There was no envy in this.

I am not sure that it was before this time, or after it, [June 29th 1824] that the blacking-warehouse was removed to Chandos Street, Covent Garden. It is no matter. Next to the shop at the corner of Bedford Street in Chandos Street are two rather old-fashioned houses and shops adjoining one another. They were one then, or thrown into one, for the blacking-business; and had been a butter-shop. Opposite to them was, and is, a public-house, where I got my ale, under these new circumstances. The stones in the street may be smoothed by my small feet going across to it at dinner-time, and back again. The establishment was larger now, and we had one or two new boys. Bob Fagin and I had attained to great dexterity in tying up the pots. I forget how many we could do in five minutes. We worked, for the light's sake, near the second window as you come from Bedford Street; and we were so brisk at it that the people used to stop and look in. Sometimes there would be quite a little crowd there. I saw my father coming in at the door one day when we were very busy, and I wondered how he could bear it.

Now, I generally had my dinner in the warehouse. Sometimes I brought it from home, so I was better off. I see myself coming across Russell Square from Somers-town, one morning, with some cold hotch-potch in a small basin tied up in a handkerchief. I had the same wanderings about the streets as I used to have, and was just as solitary and self-dependent as before; but I had not the same difficulty in merely living. I never, however, heard a word of being taken away, or of being otherwise than quite provided for.

At last, one day, my father, and the relative so often mentioned, quarreled; quarreled by letter, for I took the letter from my father to him which caused the explosion, but quarreled very fiercely. It was about me. It may have had some backward reference, in part, for anything I know, to my employment at the window. All I am certain of is, that, soon after I had given him the letter, my cousin (he was a sort of cousin, by marriage) told me he was very much insulted about me, and that it was impossible to keep me after that. I cried very much, partly because it was so sudden, and partly because in his anger he was violent about my father, though gentle to me. Thomas, the old soldier, comforted me, and said he was sure it was for the best. With a relief so strange that it was like oppression, I went home.

My mother set herself to accommodate the quarrel, and did so next day. She brought home a request for me to return next morning, and a high character of me, which I am very sure I deserved. My father said I should go back no more, and should go to school. I do not write resentfully or angrily; for I know how all these things have worked together to make me what I am; but I never afterwards forgot, I never shall forget, I never can forget, that my mother was warm for my being sent back.

From that hour until this at which I write, no word of that part of my childhood which I have now gladly brought to a close has passed my lips to any human being. I have no idea how long it lasted; whether for a year, or much more, or less. From that hour until this my father and my mother have been stricken dumb upon it. I have never heard the least allusion to it, however far off and remote, from either of them. I have never, until I now impart it to this paper, in any burst of confidence with any one, my own wife not excepted, raised the curtain I then dropped, thank God.

Until old Hungerford market was pulled down, until old Hungerford Stairs were destroyed, and the very nature of the ground changed, I never had the courage to go back to the place where my servitude began. I never saw it. I could not endure to go near it. For many years, when I came near to Robert Warren's in the Strand, I crossed over to the opposite side of the way, to avoid a certain smell of the cement they put upon the blacking-corks, which reminded me of what I was once. It was a very long time before I liked to go up Chandos Street. My old way home by the borough made me cry, after my eldest child could speak.

In my walks at night I have walked there often, since then, and by degrees I have come to write this. It does not seem a tithe of what I might have written, or of what I meant to write.

The substance of some after-talk explanatory of points in the narrative, of which a note was made at the time, may be briefly added. He could hardly have been more than twelve years old when he left the place, and was still unusually small for his age; much smaller, though two years older, than his own eldest son was at the time of these confidences. His mother had been in the blacking-warehouse many times; his father not more than once or twice. The rivalry of Robert Warren by Jonathan's representatives, the cousins George and James, was carried to wonderful extremes in the way of advertisement; and they were all very proud, he told me, of the cat scratching the boot, which was their house's device. The poets in the house's regular employ he remembered, too, and made his first study from one of them for the poet of Mrs. Jarley's wax-work. The whole enterprise, however, had the usual end of such things. The younger cousin tired of the concern; and a Mr. Wood, the proprietor who took James's share and became George's partner, sold it ultimately to Robert Warren. It continued to be his at the time Dickens and myself last spoke of it together, and he had made an excellent bargain of it."

Much of Dickens' understanding of the rivalry in the Warren family is accurate but there is one fundamental error in his account - made by Dickens and repeated by Forster – that has misled Dickens scholars and biographers for the past 140 years, which was to call George Lamerte by the name of James. Now, it is just possible that Dickens, when it came to writing his fragment of autobiography, simply forgot his cousin's name. In an age when many children might call their elders "sir" or "mister" it may be that the young boy didn't often use his cousin's first name, and so it didn't become as embedded in his memory as it could have been. On the other hand, this may have been one of those situations – I've come across many – where somebody prefers to use a name different from the one they've been given. So, did George Lamerte prefer to be called James, and everybody in the family talked of James and not of George? Whatever is the explanation for the mis-placed name, it is clear from the extensive Chancery Court documents that there was no person connected with operations at Warren's Blacking with the name of James Lamert; nor is that first name to be found in any of the many other documents I've researched. When Dickens says that James attended Sandhurst, it was in fact George who did so, as the court statement avers, and as the Royal Military Academy confirmed to William J. Carlton in 1964.[96] When Dickens says James was employed to manage Warren's Blacking, it was in fact George. Only once does Dickens mention George Lamerte, when he names him as the purchaser of Warren's, describing him as the cousin and brother-in-law of James. There never was a James <u>and</u> a George. Maybe Dickens got the wrong end of the stick – we know now it was Woodd who bought Jonathan Warren's business, and it was Woodd who was the brother-in-law of Lamerte; so somehow the boy Dickens mistook Woodd for George Lamerte, adding to the confusion over the name of James. It would clarify future Dickens biography if the correct names of these two main players in this important part of his life replaced the two incorrect names. Forster's introduction of "a Mr. Wood", mis-spelt, has him quite erroneously buying a share from a non-existent James Lamert and going into partnership with George Lamert, when the only partner Woodd had was Stephen Pilcher, who he teamed up with from the end of 1824.

If the names of George Lamerte and William Edward Woodd are diminished by inaccurate use, then so, too, are the people themselves

---

[96] *The Dickensian*, Winter 1964: In the blacking warehouse, by William J. Carlton.

diminished in this real-life drama, through a lack of interest shown in them by Dickens. We can read some kindness into the few comments made about George Lamerte – his initial offer of employment seemed to be a helpful response to the family's desperate situation; he kindly arranged to teach Dickens during the lunch hour; and having been offended by Dickens' father he was magnaminous enough to change his mind when appealed to by Dickens' mother. But even from the maturity of adulthood Dickens, when writing his fragment of autobiography, failed to recognise any affection in Lamerte, or capacity for hard work. He offers no substance to the character of Lamerte. And from the moment he left his work in Chandos Street never again did Dickens leave any acknowledgment of George Lamerte, in his letters, his speeches, his reported conversations or his writings. With one exception: the "Gone Astray" paper referred to on page 15, when Lamerte is metamorphosed into "Somebody".

Nor is any mention made of John Thomas Lamerte, the younger brother who must have been part of the family at Chatham, and who, as a traveller for the business, must have called in regularly to the office to drop off his orders and to receive further instructions. His was a familiar face, later forgotten or ignored by Dickens. Another familiar face from Chatham who might have called at the factory, but is not referred to, was Sophia Lamerte, brother of George and wife of Woodd. Forster tells us that Dickens's mother visited the warehouse many times, evidence, I believe, that she worried for him. But the adult Dickens gave her a hard time when he thought back to his father's decision to take him out of Warren's – 'I never afterwards forgot, I never shall forget, I never can forget my mother was warm for my being sent back'[97] Any concern she may have had for the welfare of her son does not appear to have been shared by her husband, who visited, according to Forster, only once or twice, albeit for some of the time the Marshalsea prevented this. Another strange omission from Dickens' account is any mention of the founder of the business, Jonathan Warren, undoubtedly an important figure in the story. Having read in the affidavits that Jonathan Warren was a gambler, it did occur to me that Dickens remembered him very well indeed and later transformed the old man who had to sell his blacking business into Little Nell's grandfather in *The Old Curiosity Shop*, who similarly lost his business through gambling. However, Warren's history, his presence in the factory, his training of Lamerte and, finally, his death, all failed to make sufficient impact on Dickens for a reference in the fragment of autobiography.

---

[97] John Forster, *The life of Charles Dickens*, chapter 2

Dickens reflects little sense of urgency in the running of the factory, no great degree of busy-ness, nor the involvement of a great many workmen, all of which might suggest a less than successful business. On the other hand he does talk of his instructions to cover a certain number of grosses of pots before going on to paste labels on them – this suggests at least three gross, or nearly 450, before moving on to another batch. We don't know how many gross were dealt with each day but with Bob Fagin and Paul Green working alongside him at the same rate, this adds up to a very substantial number of pots, an indication, I'd suggest, of good sales figures. Dickens' account specifies his task of covering and labelling pots of paste blacking and makes no reference to involvement with the labelling of bottles of liquid blacking, or of filling tins; but his alter ego, David Copperfield, when describing the similar work at Murdstone and Grinby's warehouse says:

> "I know that a great many empty bottles were one of the consequences of this traffic, and that certain men and boys were employed to examine them against the light, and reject those that were flawed, and to rinse and wash them. When the empty bottles ran short, there were labels to be pasted on full ones, or corks to be fitted to them, or seals to be put upon the corks, or finished bottles to be packed in casks. All this work was my work, and of the boys employed upon it I was one."[98]

There may, then, have been a wider range of work for Dickens than the single, repetitive task described in the fragment of autobiography. His observation that he was taken into the factory to be as useful as he could be suggests being directed to different tasks as and when needed. The description from *David Copperfield* represents a workplace closer to that described in the Day and Martin article, though still short of it.

Although Jonathan Warren is left out by Dickens, there are two other characters who are included: Thomas the foreman and Harry the carman; in *David Copperfield* these become Gregory the foreman and Tipp the carman. The Court documents include affidavits from a number of the warehouse workers, but none relate to the names put forward by Dickens. John Harrison was a foreman to Lamerte and Joseph Lampit the foreman to Woodd; Woodd's carman was called John Wright.

Dickens' descriptions of the rat-infested warehouse and the shop-front at Chandos Street, with its throng of onlookers, bring a touching, human appeal that contrast with the the somewhat dry and mechanical descriptions I've had to lift from court documents, newspaper adverts and magazine articles. His account tugs at the heartstrings, all the time inviting sympathy for the vulnerable child and admiration for his rise

---

[98] David Copperfield, chapter XI

from so low a point to great fame and fortune. If he laid it on a bit thick at times, well, that carried through all his writings: great veins of the grotesque, caricature and melodrama. As an example, I like his exaggerated avoidance of the Hungerford Stairs area: "Until old Hungerford market was pulled down, until old Hungerford Stairs were destroyed, and the very nature of the ground changed, I never had the courage to go back to the place where my servitude began. I never saw it. I could not endure to go near it." – Not very long, in fact, since the market and the stairs were demolished in 1831 to make way for a completely new structure, leading into the first Hungerford Bridge across the Thames. So, he avoided it all the way up to the age of 19! And then headed straight back there, taking lodgings in Buckingham Street, just round the corner, in 1831 and in Cecil Street, close by, in 1833.

How long did it last?

In my book *Charles Dickens' Childhood* I proposed that Dickens' employment at Warren's lasted from February 1824 to March 1825. In the light of the details provided in the case of Woodd v Lamerte I suggest that both the start date and the finish date need re-examination. In the court papers Lamerte points to the move from Hungerford Stairs to Chandos Street taking place 'about the beginning of the year 1824'. Such timing makes it almost impossible that Dickens started at Warren's in February of that year; it must have been earlier. Until now Forster's biography has been the sole source of information about Dickens's time at the factory and in seeking to fix dates subsequent biographers, including myself, have been led by the sequencing of Forster's account. Forster dealt first with the Dickens family's move from Bayham Street to Gower Street North, then with John Dickens's arrest and imprisonment in the Marshalsea and then with Charley's employment at Warren's. He doesn't assert this sequence but readers might, and have, assumed it. But if George Lamerte, writing in November 1826, says that 30 Hungerford Stairs was vacated at the beginning of 1824 then that must carry very much more credibility than anything John Forster might hint at in the 1870s. Throughout his life, both as an author and as an editor, Dickens was sharply aware that a story had to be well told, that it had to capture the attention and imagination of the reader – it was a point he urged many times on contributors to his periodicals *Household Words* and *All the Year Round*. I don't doubt he was telling such a story when he wrote his fragment of autobiography, shaping it, perhaps, with similar emphases as those used by Thomas Holcroft[99]. So, much is made of the horrors of

---

[99] Dickens wrote to Forster, 4 November 1846: 'Shall I leave you my life in MS. When I die? There are some things in it that would touch you very much, and that might go on the same shelf with the first volume of Holcroft's' (Pilgrim Letters, vol 4). Similarities

the warehouse at Hungerford Stairs and not so much of his time at Chandos Street. If Warren's Blacking was moved from Hungerford Stairs to Chandos Street at the beginning of 1824 and Charley started work round about his birthday on 7th February, then his time in the rat-infested building would have been short, perhaps non-existent, and his account, and reaction to it, inflated. However, can the case be made that he started earlier than has so far been suggested, and that his account and reaction are justified? I think it can.

Forster's cut-and-paste job on Dickens's fragment separates what might have been closer together in the original. Of the time when George Lamerte (aka James) was living with the family in Bayham Street, Dickens wrote: 'So I degenerated into cleaning his boots of a morning [ie his father's], and my own; and making myself useful in the work of the little house; and looking after my younger brothers and sisters (we were now six in all); and going on such poor errands as arose out of our poor way of living.' Forster then ends the first chapter with the family's financial decline and John Dickens's arrest. For suitable impact Forster deals with Dickens and Warren's Blacking in a new chapter and soon moves on to Dickens's own words: '...James Lamert, the relative who had lived with us in Bayham Street, seeing how I was employed from day to day, and knowing what our domestic circumstances then were, proposed that I should go into the blacking warehouse...'. These two sentences may well have been closer together in Dickens's account than in Forster's and Lamerte's offer of employment for Charley might have taken place at Bayham Street rather than at Gower Street North and therefore sometime in 1823. It's not easy for writers on Dickens to give up the hugely appealing idea that he began his hated drudgery within days of his 12th birthday, but it's a notion that appears nowhere in Forster. Had it been the case would either Dickens or Forster have let it go without comment? Probably not. Of course, it could be considered even more poignant that he was just eleven years old when he began – and even that is one year older than he had David Copperfield begin at Murdstone and Grinby.

If he began his work sometime in 1823, can we now say with any greater certainty when he ended it? Lamerte and Woodd parted company in October 1824 and we must assume Woodd continued with Chandos Street before his move to Noble Street at Christmas 1824. Since Dickens says he left his employment after his father argued with Lamerte, it follows that he left at or before October 1824, or that he followed Lamerte to Whitechapel Road. The latter seems unlikely since

---

between Holcroft's and Dickens's autobiographies were drawn out by John Harrison Stonehouse in his book *Green leaves: new chapters in the life of Charles Dickens*, Piccadilly Fountain Press, rev ed, 1931 – see Appendix 6.

there was a break, for Lamerte, of 2-3 months between leaving Chandos Street and starting in Whitechapel. Such a break would surely have been noted by Dickens. So, it's most likely he left in or before October 1824. In *Charles Dickens's Childhood* I calculated a much later date, relying on that part of the fragment of autobiography where Dickens says he travelled into Warren's from Somers Town and I provided evidence from the rate books that his parents did not move into their new home at Johnson Street in Somers Town until after 29th September 1824 and probably not until Christmas 1824. It's difficult to reconcile the information we now have, but one answer may be connected to the family's stay, after John Dickens's release from prison, with Mrs Roylance.[100] Though her address was, strictly speaking, in Camden Town it was little more than a quarter-mile further out from Johnson Street, and a journey into Warren's from Mrs Roylance's would inevitably have passed through Somers Town. What we can say with certainty is that Dickens was removed from Warren's some time after his father's release from prison on 28 May 1824 and with a high degree of probability before George Lamerte argued with Woodd in October 1824. I still give weight to Dickens's own view of his time at Warren's: 'I have no idea how long it lasted; whether for a year, or much more, or less'.

I suggest now that young Charley started at Hungerford Stairs in September 1823, that he was moved to Chandos Street in January 1824, when the business was relocated, and that his father removed him from Warren's Blacking in either September or October 1824.

This book has concentrated on the business of blacking production and on those people connected with Warren's Blacking, in an attempt to fill out the background against which Dickens was employed, and to test his own account, bearing in mind the new information that has become available. If the circumstances of his employment came as a great shock to the 11-12 year old boy, so, too, were there monumental events unfolding in his family life. Between September 1823 and October 1824 he and his family were moved out of Bayham Street and into Gower Street North, from which address his father was arrested and imprisoned in the Marshalsea; gradually the family's furniture and possessions were sold and Gower Street North given up; Charley was moved in first with Mrs Roylance and then into a back-attic in Lant Street, while the rest of the family moved into the Marshalsea with his father; when his father was released from prison the family moved in temporarily with Mrs Roylance, then spent a short time at an unknown address in Hampstead, before finally finding some stability at their new home in Johnson Street,

---

[100] See Allen, *Charles Dickens' Childhood.*

Somers Town. And at last Charley was released from Warren's Blacking and given the opportunity of a return to school.

This was, indeed, a time of great turmoil in the life of an 11-12 year old boy: life at the blacking factory was bad enough but life outside was even worse. If I haven't dwelt on that life outside in this book, it should, nevertheless, not be forgotten or laid aside. There is no better account than Dickens' own, as presented to us in Forster's biography; and readers might also find of interest the additional material provided in my book *Charles Dickens' Childhood.*

Chapter Six

What happened afterwards

Robert Warren

We know what subsequently happened to Dickens but what of the other players in this episode of his life? Robert Warren stayed in the blacking business, at some time taking partners to become Warren, Russell and Wright, still operating from 30 the Strand. He died in 1849 but the business continued, becoming in 1913 the Chiswick Polish Company Ltd., makers of Cherry Blossom polish[101], and now subsumed into Reckitt Benckiser plc. The contents of his will give some indication of the success of his business.[102] With twelve children and his wife pregnant with the thirteenth he had a lot of provision to make, but then he also appears to have had plenty of wealth to distribute. Much of his investment went into property, with a main residence at 87 Gloucester Place, Portman Square, a wealthy area of Marylebone. Though he owned the freehold on his business premises at 30 Strand he also had the acumen to buy up numbers 26, 37 and 38. Just around the corner he held the freehold on 1 Buckingham Street; then further afield he owned 35 Devonshire Street, Queen's Square, now re-named Boswell Street, close to Great Ormond Street. Even further away he had six freehold properties at New Dorset Street in Brighton, on the south coast. Back in London he held the leases to 19 houses at Shadwell and the freehold to four properties being built at White Hart Court, Leicester Square. Perhaps most interesting of all his properties was The Saracen's Head on Snow Hill, an inn that Dickens knew well and featured prominently in *Nicholas Nickleby*, the London headquarters of Wackford Squeers. Warren also owned a property in nearby Skinner Street. Besides property Robert Warren's other big investments were in shares. He held 306 shares in the recently formed London and Westminster Bank, a forerunner of todays Natwest; 100 shares in the Peninsula and Orient Steam Navigation Company (P. & O.), and unstated numbers of shares in the London and Brighton Railway, Eastern Counties Railway, South Western Railway and Northern and Eastern Railway. There was also

---

101 Information taken from the *Oxford Dictionary of National Biography*.
102 The National Archives. Records of the Prerogative Court of Canterbury: Will Registers: The will of Robert Warren. Ref Prob 11/2089.

£200 in Spanish Bonds and £5800 in Bank of England 3% Annuities. The will does not mention how much he owned of Warren, Russell and Wright or to whom he left his share, but it's possible he had already passed this over to his eldest son, also called Robert: certainly Robert received the freehold of 30 Strand. This list of his assets shows that Robert Warren made a great success of his business but though we don't know the monetary value of his properties or his shares it would probably be fair to say that it didn't add up to the £350,000 left by his other blacking rival Charles Day.

George Lamerte

George Lamerte also continued, for some years, to manufacture blacking, first dissolving his partnership with Lewis Worms in 1827 and moving from 107 Whitechapel Road to another Whitechapel address at 56 Mansell Street, Goodman's Fields and then to 100 London Wall. In the affidavit of John Thomas Lamerte (page 181) he gives his address as 56 Mansell Street, Goodman's Fields, so John was living and working with his brother; and this reminded me of Dickens' story "To be read at dusk" in which a tale is related of Mr James and Mr John who were in business together at Goodman's Fields. Since Dickens referred to George Lamerte as James throughout his autobiographical fragment I wondered if this story could be a nod in the direction of the Lamerte brothers. If this were the case it demonstrates that the Dickenses maintained some contact with, or awareness of, George Lamerte after the argument in Chandos Street. The details of Mr James and Mr John, in the story, do not, though, bear any resemblance to the Lamertes.

George Lamerte's ties with Whitechapel were reinforced in January 1827, when he married Harriet Oppenheim. She was the daughter of Henry Oppenheim who, like Lamerte, had businesses in Mansell Street, at numbers 17 and 27. Henry Oppenheim, undoubtedly Jewish, was described variously as a warehouseman, toy merchant, looking-glass manufacturer and cabinet maker. He and his family later moved out to Tottenham. George Lamerte's first child George Fead Lamerte was born in 1828 and baptised at St Mary's Whitechapel, followed by Ricardo George in 1830 and Jane Sarah in 1831, also baptised at Whitechapel. After that they must have moved out to Finchley where Harriet was born in 1833, Matilda in 1835 and Amy Charlotte in 1837. From 1839 they were at Salters Buildings, Walthamstow, where they are listed in the 1841 census. Sophia was baptised at Walthamstow in 1839, Matthew in 1841 and John Joseph in 1845. George Lamerte was declared insolvent in 1842, described in the London Gazette as a blacking manufacturer of

Providence Row, Finsbury[103]. He died in 1868 and his wife Harriet lived on till 1888 – she, at least, may have read Forster's account of Warren's Blacking and queried the detail.

George Lamerte and the theatre

If there was one thing for which Dickens was grateful to George Lamerte it was the fascination with theatre that Lamerte aroused or fostered in his young friend. We hear of their pursuit of this interest in Chatham and then of Lamerte building a toy theatre at Bayham Street. But there is another feature of their enthusiasm that has not previously come to light.

The Adelphi Theatre in the Strand, 1830

In 1806 a theatre was established in the Strand called the Sans Pareil, which changed its name in 1819 to The Adelphi Theatre. Just around the corner from 3 Chandos Street it was also close to Hungerford Stairs and almost opposite Robert Warren's. Knowing George Lamerte's interest we should not be surprised if he became involved in one of the many available London theatrical establishments, but where could be

---

103 *The London Gazette*, 8 July 1842

more convenient than The Adelphi? On the 13th January 1824 *The Times* published an announcement:

ADELPHI THEATRE, Strand. – By Authority of the Lord Chamberlain. – This evening, Jan.13, and to-morrow, will be presented, The heart of Mid Lothian; or, The Lily of St Leonard's – After which (16th time), an entirely New Grand and Magnificent Christmas Pantomime, with New Scenery, Machinery, Tricks, Properties, Dresses, and Decorations, that has been the whole Summer in preparation, and on which no labour of expense has been spared in the production, entitled DOCTOR FAUSTUS AND THE BLACK DEMON; or, Harlequin and the Seven Fairies of the Grotto."

Interior of the Adelphi Theatre, 1808
(at that time called the Sans Pareil)

The announcement then goes on to describe some of the characters and actors and a list of the settings for the production, one of which settings is surprisingly listed as "Interior of Jonathan Warren's Blacking Warehouse, Hungerford Stairs". We have to see here the hand of George Lamerte; and perhaps the voice of Dickens whispering in our ear "Pantomime" and "Harlequin".

Moving on 20 months, to the 7th October 1826, the name of Mr Lamerte starts to appear in the cast lists at the Adelphi – not in any prominent roles but rather as background characters, part of a crowd, one of the officers, one of the sailors. He may, even, have had to pay for his appearances, a practice not uncommon in some London theatres at that time. For him, I would guess, it was a form of entertainment and not a source of income or a route to a new livelihood. And, if the newspapers are anything to go by, a jolly good form of entertainment it was! The following account of his first night, in which he appeared in the second of three pieces, *La Fete des Nations*, lays out the atmosphere which probably attracted him to The Adelphi:

"ADELPHI THEATRE. The Adelphi Theatre opened on Saturday evening. It continues under the management of Messrs. Terry and Yates, whose ability and experience in theatrical matters eminently qualify them for the superintendence of such an establishment. Last season the Adelphi, for the first time, raised itself in public estimation above the rank and humble level of our minor theatres, and gave ample promise of an earnest competition with houses of higher and more established repute. If that promise has not been as yet quite realized, there is no reason to presume, from the performance at this Theatre on Saturday, that it has been lost sight of or abandoned. Considerable improvements have been made since last season. The boxes are lined with red silk of a rich and costly texture; the panels of the boxes have been slightly re-touched and gilded afresh; much of careful attention has been bestowed on scenic decoration, and altogether the interior of the house presents quite a new, neat, and elegant appearance. The melodramatic burletta of *The Pilot* led the entertainments of the evening. As this piece was performed one hundred and eight nights last season, we may be well excused from making many observations on this, its one hundred and ninth representation. Suffice it to say, that the popularity it has enjoyed is not undeserved. The melodramatic acting in it by Mr. T.P. Cooke, in the part of *Tom Coffin*; the *Captain Boroughcliff* (a genuine Yankee riglar), by Mr. J. Reeve, who has been gathering fresh laurels for his comic fame by a successful season at the Haymarket; and the Pilot, by Terry, are three as felicitous speciments of genuine and sterling comedy as are to be met with in the whole range of modern dramatic literature. The only alterations in the cast of characters were the first appearance of Mrs. Hughes, late of Drury-lane, in the part of *Miss Katherine Plowden*, and of "a young Lady," in the character of *Cecilia*. Mrs. Hughes is a smart, lively and agreeable actress. To gaiety of spirits, and a cheerful expression of countenance, she unites a clear enunciation in the dialogue of the play, and possesses a voice, though of limited power, yet of considerable flexibility and sweetness. These are qualities that go a great way in conciliating public favour, and Mrs. Hughes may, therefore, reasonably expect no small share of that very fickle, yet very useful commodity. As to the "Young Lady," whose name we could not, and cared not to learn; it is as likely that she will always continue as "unknown to fame," as she at present is to us. Allowance is no doubt to be made for the incompleteness of self-possession in a first appearance – but where there is the absence of promise of any kind, either in singing, speaking, or acting, it may be pardoned us to delicately hint that the candidate for fame in these attributes has mistaken the profession and walk in life in which eminence is attainable to her or him. In a new Burletta, *La Fete des Nations*, which followed the play, there were some dances gracefully executed by Miss Pitt, Hawthorne, Engelina, and Melanie Duval. The *Corps de Ballet* altogether is very creditable to the Establishment. *La Fete des Nations* was followed by a new Comic Opera, called *Old Love and Young Love*. The title of it serves as a clue to the plot, which consists of two elderly guardians (Terry and Elliot) becoming enamoured of their Ward (Miss Boden). The young lady, however, naturally bestows her affections on the son of one of the old gentlemen. The match, as usual, from interested motives, is opposed by the Guardians, which obliges the young lover to assume various disguises, to run "hair-breadth 'scapes," and encounter all the obstacles which the opposition of the Guardians offers to his alliance with *Amelia*. The winding up of the piece, which is neither very pleasant nor yet very dull, Young Love, as may be supposed, is victorious; and, by a well-contrived stratagem, marriage takes place between *Amelia* and *Frederick*. Wrench and Yates, on whom the principal interest of the piece depended, went through their disguises, and sustained their parts throughout with much animation. It was favourably received. The house was crowded to excess."[104]

Lamerte, in his part of Coriphes, fares even worse with his anonymity than the un-named Young Lady, receiving no mention whatsoever from the reviewer. Nevertheless, he appeared in this piece for 18 performances between 7th October 1826 and 7th April 1827. Concurrently he appeared for 18 performances as one of Cadi's Officers in *The Barber and his Brothers*, between 2nd and 22nd November 1826; for 25 performances as Terence O'Hod in *The Harlequin and the Eagle*, between 26th December 1826 and 27th January 1827; for 4 performances as one of the sailors in *The Pirate's Doom*, between 12th February and 31st March 1827; and for 3 performances as one of the cavalieri in *Don Giovanni* between 20th and 26th March 1827.[105]

Sixty-eight appearances over a period of seven months represents a considerable commitment, especially when he was, at the same time,

---

[104] *The Morning Chronicle*, Monday 9th October 1826.
[105] All of this information is taken from the work carried out on The Adelphi Theatre Project at the University of Eastern Michigan.

running a business and dealing with the Chancery Court. And then there was the small matter of a short walk to the church of St Martin in the Fields, at the top of the Strand, for his marriage, on 8th January 1827, to Harriet Oppenheim. All of this aside, I would be surprised if there were not more performances, both before and after this seven month period, and probably at other theatres as well. Lists of other London theatre programmes are not as available or accessible as those for The Adelphi but diligent research might well reveal a wider career treading the boards for George Lamerte.

There is no evidence that George Lamerte and the Dickens family maintained contact after Charley left Chandos Street, which may be an indication that the argument which caused the departure resulted in a permanent rupture in the relationship. On the other hand, we are very well aware (because he told us) that Dickens maintained an interest in theatre while he attended school at the Wellington House Academy, and expanded that interest into a passion as a young man. Part of his passion embraced The Adelphi Theatre. In *Pickwick* Dickens thought back to his time at the solicitors' office of Ellis and Blackmore in 1827-28, just after those recorded appearances by George Lamerte, and amusingly described the typical activities of a range of office clerks: "There is the salaried clerk – out of door, or in door, as the case may be – who devotes the major part of his thirty shillings a week to his personal pleasure and adornment, repairs half-price to the Adelphi at least three times a week, dissipates majestically at the cider cellars afterwards, and is a dirty caricature of the fashion, which expired six months ago."[106] Dickens was not a salaried clerk on thirty shillings a week, but his knowledge of the half-price tickets and the availability of cider cellars suggests The Adelphi may well have been one of his own destinations for entertainment, and possibly encouraged by, or to see, his cousin and friend George Lamerte. One person he certainly did see at The Adelphi from about this time was the actor Charles Matthews, who staged his unique performances as "Charles Matthews at Home" between 1828 and his death in1835. Matthews made a big impact on Dickens and when he considered going into the acting profession himself he prepared for an audition at Covent Garden Theatre in 1832 by working up one of Matthews' routines. He was too unwell to attend the audition and soon after was diverted into journalism, but he always maintained affectionate memories of Charles Matthews at The Adelphi. Not that he restricted himself to The Adelphi – when he gave up the work as a solicitor's clerk and set out to establish himself as a reporter he spent his time, as he later

---

[106] *The Pickwick Papers*, chapter XXX.

told Forster, visiting a theatre every night, with very few exceptions, for at least three years.[107]

The Adelphi also holds the distinction of being the first theatre to stage a plagiarised version of one of Dickens' stories. His Sketch "The Bloomsbury Christening" appeared in *The Monthly Magazine* in August 1834 and within two months had been adapted for the stage by John Baldwin Buckstone, under the heading of "The Christening". Its first performance at The Adelphi was on 13th October 1834.[108] Dickens was good-humourdly irritated but nevertheless wrote a review of the piece for *The Morning Chronicle*. Through to 1836 he was sent regularly by the editor of *The Morning Chronicle* to write reviews of Adelphi productions until, eventually, the popularity of *The Pickwick Papers* and the novels that followed ensured he could give up his work on the *Chronicle*. His link to The Adelphi didn't end there, however, as they mounted adaptations of *Pickwick* in 1837, *Nicholas Nickleby* in 1838, *Oliver Twist* in 1839 and *The Old Curiosity Shop* in 1840. Dickens maintained good relations with Frederick Yates, the actor-manager of The Adelphi, until Yates' death in 1842.

Dickens' link to The Adelphi, then, was a strong one; and so, too, was George Lamerte's, dating from 1824, and treading the boards there on at least 68 occasions. It wouldn't be at all surprising, would it, if Lamerte took the boy along to the theatre, encouraging his interest, just as he had in Chatham and at Bayham Street? Since Dickens, the author of his own history, didn't tell us about this particular piece of encouragement from his cousin there has been no reason for biographers to imagine it. But perhaps this was one part of the tithe of what he might have written. Undoubtedly, discovery of Lamerte's on-going fascination with theatre and his substantial involvement with The Adelphi, extends our understanding of his possible influence on Dickens.

Before leaving the subject of The Adelphi Theatre it's worth remarking that it still operates from the same site today, having been re-built four times. I'd like to be able to report that *Oliver: the Musical* was first staged there in the 1960s, but the christening of Lionel Bart's progeny took place a short walk away in St Martin's Lane.

Joseph Richard Lamerte

There is reference in Forster to a younger brother of George Lamerte (aka James) who took up the army commission belatedly offered to George. This was Joseph Richard Lamerte, who became a Captain in the 37th Regiment of Foot. In December 1846 the regiment embarked from

[107] *Pilgrim Letters*, Vol 4, p245
[108] *Pilgrim Letters*, vol 2, p42

Chatham and after four months arrived at Colombo in Ceylon, on 10th March 1847. Great sickness followed their arrival and 60 men died. Four companies were sent on attachment, three to Trincomali and another to Galle. Just before November 1848 disturbances in the Kandy brought part of the regiment into the field, 100 men with a hand full of the Ceylon Rifle Regiment, were sent to re-establish order by forcibly dispersing an armed mob. The anticipated danger of this operation may have persuaded Captain Lamerte to ensure he left his affairs in order. For this, or some other reason, he wrote out his will as follows:

"Off Cochin[109] on Bd. Ship Pottinger Novr. 5 1848
In the event of my death I will and bequeath my personal property as follows all deposits and credits in the hands of my Agents at home (viz Cox & Co/ or with Messrs. Fforbes & Co of Bombay) to my sister Hannah or in the event of her death previously to my niece Sophia Woodd. The Canteen of plate presented to me by the 76th Regt. to my brother John during his lifetime & at his death to my brother George's son Ricardo to be handed down from him to the eldest male representative of the family excepting Ensign George Fead Lamert now of the 37th Regt. The proceeds of any saleable property about my person and any ready money in my possession to my niece Sophia Woodd. I declare the foregoing to be my last made will & Testament up to this date   Off Cochin lying in the Roads November 5th 1848 – J.R. Lamert"

His death must have followed soon after, though I don't have a date. The granting of administration of the estate, about seven months later, is recorded at the end of the will:

"On the 1st June 1849 Admon (with the will annexed) of the Goods Chattels and credits of Joseph Richard Lamert late a Captain in Her Majestys 78th Regiment of foot Esquire Bachelor at Sea deceased was granted to George Lamert the natural and lawful Brother and one of the next of kin having been first sworn duly to administer. No Executor of Residuary Legatee." [110]

This, then, was the younger brother for whom, according to Forster, George/James relinquished his commission in the army. It refers to his brothers George and John and also to his sister Hannah and his niece Sophia Woodd.

For a family tree of the Lamerte family see page 294.

---

109 Cochin lies on the south west coast of India, below Bombay
110 The National Archives. Records of the Prerogative Court of Canterbury: Will Registers: The will of Joseph Richard Lamert. Ref Prob 11/2095.

William Edward Woodd

William Edward Woodd, having moved from Chandos Street to Noble Street in 1825, was still in business when Robert Warren went to court against him in November 1827. But while there is evidence of Lamerte continuing to produce blacking for many years it's not clear if Woodd did the same. The name of William Edward Woodd and the business he owned under the name of Jonathan Warren simply fade from the scene. Forster reported that Woodd eventually sold up to Robert Warren but I haven't been able to verify this. I did, though find several references to Woodd and his family on the website 'Families in British India Society': firstly, to the will of George Leslie Woodd of Bombay, Lieutenant in Her Majesty's 86th Regiment of Foot, who died 22 December 1847, the son of William Edward Woodd of Brickfields Road, Cork, half-pay Lieutenant of the Derby Militia; secondly to Sophia Woodd, travelling between Portsmouth and Bombay in 1853; and thirdly to the burial of Miss Eliza Sarah Woodd, at Kotree, Bombay on 20 June 1853, the eldest daughter of the late W.E. Woodd, Esq, formerly of Richmond Surrey, latterly of Cork Ireland. All of this points to a reinforcement of his earlier connection with Ireland. His death on 21 February 1851 in Westminster, with his burial in South Audley Street, Mayfair, is confirmed by a newspaper report: 'DEATH. – In London, in the 54th year of his age, Lieutenant William Edward Wood, of the Derbyshire Militia'[111].

For a family tree of William Edward Woodd's family see page 296.

The Worms Family

The Worms line is difficult to follow, since it comprised large families and the same names were often used by each branch of the family. It starts off simply enough, with two brothers, Henry Worms, who we've seen was transported to Australia, and Aaron Worms who married George Lamerte's aunt Rachel. There was reportedly a third brother, Lewis, who did not live in London and does not feature in this story.

On Henry's side there were eight children, one of whom, Lewis Henry, emigrated to Australia to join his father, as noted earlier in the book. My knowledge of Lewis Henry's family is sketchy, but he appears to have left a daughter, Sophia, back in London who went on to become a furrier. He must have taken other members of his family with him: a Matthew Aaron Worms was running a shop selling boots and shoes in George Street, Sydney in 1866, and there are records of a marriage between another Lewis Henry, probably a son, marrying Amelia Harris in Sydney in 1868, where he also set up as a boot and shoe dealer; the

---

[111] *Jackson's Oxford Journal*, 1 March 1851.

birth of Lewis and Amelia's children followed soon after, Charles Frederick in 1869 and Henry William in 1870, and probably their grandchildren Ethel Lane in 1895 and Lewis Henry in 1906, all in New South Wales. Worms family descendants still live in Australia. All of Henry's other children remained in London, three of the daughters, Catherine, Matilda and Frances, also going into the fur trade. The eldest daughter of Henry, Sarah, had a school on Clerkenwell Green. Two of Henry's sons, Morris and Solomon, lived in the area of Saffron Hill, which Dickens knew well and used for backdrops in *Oliver Twist* and *Little Dorrit*. Morris had a second-hand furniture shop in Seven Dials, another area that loomed large in the childhood imagination of Dickens, and Solomon dealt in recycled building materials. Another son, Philip ran an auction house in Chelsea.

On the side of the other brother, Aaron Worms, there were seven children, one of whom, Henry Worms, diversified into the large-scale manufacture and wholesaling of boots and shoes with premises in the Minories as well as a warehouse in Bishopsgate and a showroom in Oxford Street. A second son, Lewis Aaron, we've already been introduced to as the blacking partner of George Lamerte. One of Lewis Aaron's sons, Samuel Lewis Worms, emigrated to New Zealand and established a branch of the family there, with one of Samuel's sons, Alfred Joseph living through to 1943. Lewis Aaron had nine other children, one of whom, Rosetta, is listed in London directories for 1879 and 1885 as a Woollen Bootmaker at 31 Euston Road – connections with the boot and shoe trade seem to echo through the years and across the globe! Other children of George Lamerte's partner, Lewis Aaron were Joseph, Sarah, Rebecca, Matilda and Matthew.

For a family tree of the Worms family see page 295.

Chapter Seven

Pleadings in the case of Woodd v Lamerte

This document is held at The National Archives at Kew in London, catalogued at reference C 13/865/12, with the heading Woodd v Lamerte. It contains firstly the joint Complaint of William Edward Woodd and Stephen Pilcher against George Lamerte and Lewis Worms, and secondly the joint Answer of George Lamerte and Lewis Worms. The Complaint comprises six large sheets of parchment and the Answer three sheets. All sheets are clearly written and legible but, as was the style at that time, are written in a continuous flow of language, with virtually no punctuation, no separation of sentences and no paragraphs. Throughout there is a constant repetition of words and phrases, random capitalisation of words and regular spelling-out of dates. Although the content of what's being said is fascinating, the manner in which it's presented can make for tedious reading. I have, therefore, broken down the never-ending flow into understandable chunks. This is my own transcription and as far as I'm aware nobody else has attempted the same task. It is accurate to the best of my ability, so any mis-spellings and inaccuracies of fact are copied from the original and not of my own making.

<u>The Complaint of William Edward Woodd and Stephen Pilcher</u>

26 July 1826   To the Right Honorable John Earl of Eldon Lord High Chancellor of Great Britain. –

Humbly Complaining shew unto your Lordship your Orators William Edward Woodd and Stephen Pilcher both of Number 9 Noble Street in the City of London Blacking Manufacturers That Jonathan Warren the elder late of Hungerford Stairs in the Strand in the County of Middlesex but now deceased from the Year One Thousand seven hundred and ninety eight up to the Month of November One thousand eight hundred and Twenty two carried on the Business of manufacturing Blacking of a superior quality for the cleaning of Boots Shoes and other Articles of black Leather according to an original Recipe in his possession and that the said Blacking so manufactured by him as aforesaid was prepared in paste and also in a liquid state and that such of the said Blacking as was sold and disposed of by them in a liquid state was so sold and disposed of by the Name of "Jonathan Warrens Original Japan Blacking" – and that such as was sold by him in a paste state was so sold by the name and description of "Jonathan Warrens Japan Water proof paste Blacking"

and such Blacking so manufactured and sold by the said Jonathan Warren as aforesaid was highly approved of by the Public and the Name of the said Jonathan Warren became by means of the great Reputation of such Blacking extensively known and established for the Sale of the said Blacking both in a liquid and paste state

And your Orators further shew unto your Lordship that the said Jonathan Warren made and devised to himself considerable profits from the Sale of the said Blacking so manufactured by him from such Recipe as aforesaid and that your Orator William Edward Woodd having some time in or about the Month of November One thousand eight hundred and twenty two became desirous of purchasing the aforesaid Recipe so belonging to the said Jonathan Warren as aforesaid as also the permission of the said Jonathan Warren to authorize your last named Orator to Manufacture such Blacking for his own sole use and benefit and the good will of the said Jonathan Warrens said Business and all his Interest therein your last named Orator at or about the time last mentioned contracted and agreed with the said Jonathan Warren the Elder to purchase of him for the Consideration and for the term hereinafter mentioned the said Recipe and the use of the Name of him the said Jonathan Warren in making and selling of the said Blacking and all his right Title and Interest in the same and in his the said Jonathan Warrens said Business

and in pursuance of such last mentioned arrangement an Agreement in writing bearing date on or about the eight day of November One thousand eight hundred and Twenty two was duly made and entered into and executed by and between the said Jonathan Warren the Elder of the One part and your last named Orator of the other part whereby after Reciting the several matters hereinbefore stated and that it had been agreed by your last named Orator that he would pay and allow to the said Jonathan Warren the several Sums of Money therein more particularly mentioned for his own Use and benefit for Seven Years in Case the said Jonathan Warren should so long live and for such further

Term or successive Terms as your last named Orator should elect on giving such Notice as therein mentioned

and that your last named Orator would also conduct and carry on the said Manufactory of Blacking and find and provide the materials and necessary things at his own expence Cost and Charges and the said Jonathan Warren for the Considerations therein mentioned thereby agreed with your last named Orator during the Term aforesaid and until such further term as your last named Orator should elect as therein also mentioned to permit your last named Orator to make use of the Name of the said Jonathan Warren in his labels and Advertizements to that Public and that he the said Jonathan Warren should not carry on the said Manufactory on his own Account or otherwise than for the benefit of your last named Orator and under his direction and that he should forthwith furnish your last named Orator with the original Recipe for making the said Blacking and afford him every means and facility in his power for the carrying on of the said concern for the sole use and benefit of him your last named Orator

And in such last mentioned Agreement there was contained a Proviso that if the said Jonathan Warren should die leaving his then Wife Elizabeth Warren him surviving then your last named Orator would so long as the said Manufactory of Blacking should be carried on for his benefit pay and allow without deduction to the said Elizabeth Warren the Yearly Sum of Two hundred and fifty pounds as by such Agreement now in the custody or possession of your Orator reference being thereunto had when produced will appear

and your Orators further shew unto your Lordship that immediately upon the execution of the said Agreement the said Jonathan Warren delivered up to your Orator William Edward Woodd possession of the said Recipe and your last named Orator thereupon commenced the manufacturing of Blacking and manufactured and sold large quantities thereof both in a paste and liquid state using the Name of the said Jonathan Warren both in his labels and advertisements for the sale thereof as the Manufacturer of such Blacking both in a paste and liquid state

And your Orators further shew unto your Lordship that some time in or about the Month of December One thousand eight hundred and Twenty four your Orators agreed that in Consideration of an adequate premium paid to your Orator William Edward Woodd by your Other Orator That your Orator Stephen Pilcher should participate with your Orator William

Edward Woodd in the benefit of the Said Recipe and the manufacturing of the said Blacking and that they should enter into Copartnership together for the manufacturing and selling the aforesaid Blacking and divide the profits derived therefrom in equal halves and that they should become equally liable to the payments reseived by the said Agreement of the said eighth day of November One thousand eight hundred and Twenty two to the said Jonathan Warren and his said Widow and your Orators have accordingly ever since the said Month of December One thousand eight hundred and twenty four held and enjoyed the said Recipe in partnership together and have as such Copartners as aforesaid ever since made and manufactured the said Jonathan Warrens said Blacking and sold and disposed of large quantities thereof both in a paste and in a liquid State

And your Orators further shew that up to Christmas One thousand eight hundred and twenty four they carried on the Business of Manufacturing the said Blacking at Hungerford Stairs in the Strand where the said Jonathan Warren had originally carried on such Business but that at Christmas One thousand eight hundred and Twenty five your Orators removed their said Manufactory to Number 9 Noble Street aforesaid where they have ever since carried on the same

And your Orators further shew unto your Lordship that the said Recipe by which such Blacking was originally manufactured by the said Jonathan Warren has ever since been manufactured by them as aforesaid is exceedingly valuable and that the Blacking so produced therefrom and known or designated by the aforesaid name of Jonathan Warrens Japan Water proof Blacking is of very excellent quality and superior to other compositions of the same nature and that your Orators by their own personal exertions and assiduity and also at great expence have succeeded in forming an extensive connection for the sale of such Blacking as well in the Liquid as in the paste State to Merchants Shopkeepers Dealers and others who purchase the same for exportation or for the purpose of reselling the same by retail and that from the intrinsic excellence of the said Blacking it has acquired great Credit in the public estimation and a preference has been therefore invariably given to the said Blacking prepared by your Orators over other compositions of the like nature and in consequence thereof the Business in which your Orators are engaged as aforesaid had been extremely profitable

And your Orators further shew unto your Lordship that the said Blacking has been always and is now sold by your Orators when in a liquid state in Stone bottles containing Pints three quarters of a pint and

110

a quarter of a pint each and that on each of such Bottles there now is and hath been for many years past pasted a label and that such Label is in the words or to the effect following that is to say – "Warren's Original Japan liquid Blacking made only by Jonathan Warren established 1798 – 30 Hungerford Stairs Strand – Nothing has yet been offered to the public equal to this Blacking or giving an elegant black lustre to Leather which it also preserves soft and pliable and prevents from cracking It being of an Oily preparation." -

And your Orators further shew that the said label contains on the right side thereof certain directions for using the same which are in the words or to the effect following that is to say – "Use; stir it well from the bottom with a stiff stick, Rub the stick on a soft brush, then black your Boot and shine it while wet, Don't put the Boot to the fire to dry." -

And your Orators further shew unto your Lordship that the said Blacking hath been always and now is sold by your Orators when in a paste state in stone pots and that on each of such pots there hath been for many years and is now pasted a label in which such composition is described in the words or to the effect following that is to say - "This composition is only one fourth the price of Warrens liquid Blacking and possesses all its good qualities which are so well known. it would be superfluous for the proprietors to say any thing in its praise Directions for use; -   Mix a little of the Paste with water to the consistency of liquid Blacking, after the dirt is brushed off the Boot black it and shine it before it gets dry" -

And your Orators further shew that each of such labels purports to be signed or subscribed in the Name of the said Jonathan Warren and that in order to prevent the imitation of their said labels and the fraud upon your Orators and upon the public consequential thereon your Orators have Caused their said Labels to be printed after a particular design and that those which are affixed to the said Bottles containing the said liquid Blacking have the large figures of 30 printed in the middle thereof and that those which are affixed to the said Pots containing the paste as aforesaid have an Irish Harp with the figures 30 under the same in the centre thereof and the description of the said composition being engraved in a circle at the left side of all such labels and the directions for using the same on the right side thereof as by such labels reference being thereunto had when produced will appear

And your Orators further shew unto your Lordship that your Orators have for some time past caused to be printed and circulated certain hand

Bills for the purpose of recommending their said Blacking which are printed on Red paper with the Royal Arms at the Top thereof and such hand bills are in the words or to the effect following that is to say

Warren's Military Blacking Song - Tune British Grenadiers
Some talk of Day and Martin who thinks their Blacking fine
And some say Statham Turner and Landers make Boots shine
But the Grenadiers Old Englands pride who fought at Waterloo
Must "ask for Warrens Blacking" which others far outdo

To keep you all from doubting and fearing a mistake. –
You must ask for the Original of Jonathan Warren's make. –
For perchance if you get Roberts' whose Surname is the same.
Your Boots will loose their lustre and you your shining fame"

as by such Songs and Verses reference being thereunto had when produced will appear

And your Orators further shew unto your Lordship that the said Jonathan Warren departed this life on or about the Twenty first day of August One thousand eight hundred and twenty five leaving the said Elizabeth Warren his widow him surviving and that the said Elizabeth Warren became thereupon entitled to receive the said Annuity of Two hundred and fifty Pounds

And your Orators further shew unto your Lordship that previously to your Orator William Edward Woodd entering into such Copartnership with your other Orator as aforesaid and some time in the year One thousand eight hundred and twenty three he took into his employ as a Clerk in his said Business George Lamerte of Whitechapel Road in the County of Middlesex one of the Defendants hereafter named and that the said George Lamerte continued to act as such Clerk as aforesaid in your Orator William Edward Woodd's service up to the month of October in the said year One thousand eight hundred and Twenty four when he left the same

And your Orators further shew unto your Lordship that some time in or about the Month of November in the said year One thousand eight hundred and twenty four the said George Lamerte and Lewis Worms (who is the other defendant hereinafter named) entered into Copartnership together as Blacking Manufacturers at Number 107 Whitechapel Road aforesaid under the Stile or Form of "Lamerte & Co." and they have ever since continued to carry on such Business under such

Stile or form accordingly and that the said George Lamerte and Lewis Worms have as your Orators have lately discovered formed a design to make vend and sell a certain composition not made by your Orators but made by them the said George Lamerte and Lewis Worms or by some persons or person by their Order or directions or with their knowledge or privity as and for the said Composition called Jonathan Warrens Japan Water proof Blacking and so sold by your Orators as such purchases under the said late Jonathan Warren as aforesaid and with some such view or design they the said George Lamerte and Lewis Worms or some persons or person on their behalf or with their direction have or has made large quantities of liquid Blacking and put the same into stone Bottles of the same size and make as those used by your Orators and they the said George Lamerte and Lewis Worms or some persons or person on their behalf or with their direction have or has also made large quantities of paste Blacking and put the same into Pots of the same size and make as the said Pots so used by your Orators in sales of the said Jonathan Warren's said Paste Blacking as aforesaid and they have pasted or affixed to such Bottles and Pots labels in the same or nearly the same Words and figures and to a similar purport or effect as the labels affixed to the said Bottles and Pots so sold by your Orators as aforesaid and in Order the more closely to imitate your Orators said labels and so affixed to the said Bottles and Pots so sold by them as aforesaid and the better to deceive the public thereby the said George Lamerte and Lewis Worms have employed the same person to print their said Labels as hath for some time past been employed by your Orators to print theirs and the said Bottles and Pots so labelled as aforesaid have been from time to time sold and delivered by them the said George Lamerte and Lewis Worms to various persons in Order that the same might be sold by such Persons as Bottles and Pots containing the same Paste or Liquid Blacking so made by your Orators as such purchasers under the said Jonathan Warren as aforesaid and they have actually represented to various persons and particularly to some persons who have been in the habit of purchasing of your Orators the said Blacking so manufactured by them as aforesaid that such Blacking so made and sold by them the said George Lamerte and Lewis Worms as aforesaid is the Original Jonathan Warren's real Japan Water proof Blacking and that the same actually comes from or has been made by your Orators or they otherwise have made some such Representations to some such or the like effect

And your Orators further shew unto your Lordship that many Persons have been deceived by such Representations and have been thereby induced to purchase of the said George Lamerte and Lewis Worms the said Composition or Blacking manufactured by them or by their Order or direction as and for the composition or Blacking manufactured by your Orators as the Original Blacking of the said Jonathan Warren as aforesaid and divers other Persons have been induced by means of such fraudulent deception to purchase of the said George Lamerte and Lewis Worms Bottles and Pots of the said Composition or Blacking and other Persons have bought Bottles and Pots of the said Composition or Blacking knowing the same to be manufactured by the said George Lamerte and Lewis Worms or by some other person or persons than your Orators to the intent to sell the same again by means of the labels affixed thereto as and for the composition or Blacking manufactured by your Orators and the said George Lamerte and Lewis Worms have therefore been enabled by the means aforesaid to dispose of large quantities of the said composition or blacking manufactured by them or by some other person or persons other than your Orators

And your Orators having sustained great injury from the deception practised by the said George Lamerte and Lewis Worms in manner of aftersaid they have frequently by themselves and their Agents applied to the said George Lamerte and Lewis Worms and requested them to desist from pasting or affixing on the said Bottles and Pots containing the said Blacking and Paste or Composition so manufactured by them the said George Lamerte and Lewis Worms or by any person or persons by their Order or direction or with their knowledge or privity or in any other manner using such labels as are before mentioned or any other labels being Copies or fac similies or colourable imitations of the labels used by your Orators as such Partners as aforesaid

And your Orators have also requested the said George Lamerte and Lewis Worms to desist from selling the Bottles and Pots containing the said liquid Blacking and Paste or Composition manufactured by them or by their Order or direction or with their knowledge or privity with such labels pasted or affixed thereon and to account with your Orators for the profits made by them the said George Lamerte and Lewis Worms from the sale of the said Composition or blacking so manufactured as aforesaid but which has nevertheless been represented by the labels pasted or affixed thereto as the Composition or Blacking made by your Orators and your Orators were in hopes that such their just and reasonable requests would have been complied with as in Justice and equity ought to have been the case,

But now so it is may it please your Lordship that the said George Lamerte and Lewis Worms combining and confederating to and with divers persons at present unknown to your Orators (but whose names when discovered your Orators pray they may be at liberty to insert herein with apt and proper words to charge them as parties Defendants hereto and contriveing how to wrong and injure your Orators in the Premises they the said Defendants at some times pretend that they never have in any manner represented or endeavoured to represent the said Composition or Blacking so made and sold by them as aforesaid as the same composition or Blacking as was made and sold by the said late Jonathan Warren and as now made and sold by your Orators as such purchasers under him as aforesaid

and that the said labels so affixed to their said Bottles and Pots as well as the said hand Bills so circulated by them as aforesaid are not in any respect of a similar purport or effect to the said labels so affixed by your Orators to the said Bottles of the said Blacking and to the said Pots of Paste so sold by them as aforesaid or to the said hand Bills so circulated by your Orators as aforesaid but that the same materially differ therefrom -

Whereas your Orators charge the contrary of such pretences to be true and that the said labels so used and affixed by the said Defendants to the said Bottles and Pots of the composition so sold by them as aforesaid as well as the said Hand Bills so circulated by them as aforesaid do materially and closely resemble in every respect the said labels and hand Bills so used and circulated by your Orators as aforesaid
and that if there be any differences between them the same is merely trifling and only colourable and as evidence thereof your Orators Charge that the said labels are printed of the same type and in the same or nearly in the same manner as the labels so used by your Orators as aforesaid and that on the said Labels which the said Defendants so fix or cause to be affixed to the said Pots of Paste so made and sold by them as aforesaid there is a Harp described in the centre thereof with the figure of 30 under the same and that such Harp very nearly resembles the aforesaid Harp so described on your Orators aforesaid labels which are so affixed to the pots of paste so sold by your Orators as aforesaid

and that the description of the said Blacking and the direction for using the same as stated on the said Labels so affixed to the said Pots of Paste Blacking so sold by the said Defendants as aforesaid are similar in every respect to the aforesaid description and directions for use contained in your Orators said labels so affixed to the said Pots of Paste so sold by your Orators as aforesaid and that the said labels of the said Defendants so affixed to their said Pots differ only from those so affixed by your

Orators to the said Pots of Paste so sold by your Orators in the following particulars

that is to say that instead of the words "Jonathan Warrens No. 9 Noble Street established 1798" printed in the said Labels so affixed to the said Pots and Bottles so sold by your Orators as aforesaid the Said Defendants have introduced into the labels so affixed by them to the said Pots and Bottles as aforesaid the words late Manufacturer to Jonathan Warren 107 Whitechapel Road London but that the words late "Manufacturer to" and "107 Whitechapel Road" are with a view to deceive the public and with a view to prevent the same being immediately observed printed only in small characters although with a view also of imposing on the Public the words "Jonathan Warren" are printed in large Letters in the said Defendants labels and in the same manner as the same words are printed in your Orators said labels

And your Orators further charge that the only other difference between your Orators said labels so affixed to the said Pots of Paste so sold by them as aforesaid and the said labels affixed to the said Pots of Paste so made and sold by the said Defendants as aforesaid is that at the bottom of your Orators said Labels the words Jonathan Warren are printed Whereas at the bottom of each label of the said Defendants there are printed the initials "G.L. & Co." -

And your Orators further charge that the hand Bills so circulated by the said Defendants as aforesaid differ only from those so circulated by your Orators in the second and third from last lines thereof and that such four last lines are in the words or to the effect following that is to say
    "To keep you all from doubting and fearing a mistake
    "You must Ask for the superior of George Lamerte's make
    "For perchance you get other and think it be the same
    "Your Boots will loose their lustre and you your shining fame"
all which the said Defendants will at other times admit

But then they pretend that they have not in fact sold or disposed of the Blacking so made by them as aforesaid as or for the Blacking so made by your Orators as aforesaid or ever represented it to be such Whereas Your Orators charge the contrary of such pretences to be true and especially they charge that the said Defendants have sold to divers persons the Blacking so manufactured by your Orators from such Recipe as the purchasers thereof from the said Jonathan Warren as aforesaid as the Blacking of the said Jonathan Warren deceased and as an Article which they the said Defendants were rightfully and lawfully entitled to sell and dispose of and that they have so sold the same under a fraudulent representation that the said Blacking was the same Blacking as was originally manufactured by the said Jonathan Warren the elder notwithstanding that they the said Defendants well knew such Representation to be untrue

and as the same evidence of such last mentioned matters your Orators further charge that the said Defendant George Lamerte or some person in his employ and on his behalf some time in or about the Month of August ~ " ~ " ~ One thousand eight hundred and Twenty Five ~ " ~ " ~ applied to a Mr. Lombard of Mary le bone Street in the County of Middlesex (who had been some time previously thereto a regular Customer of your Orators) and asked him whether he wanted any of Jonathan Warren's Blacking or to such or the like effect and that the said Mr. Lombard believing that the said Defendant George Lamerte had proper authority to sell the same observed that the said Blacking was not brought by the same Carman as usually brought the goods sold by your Orators said house and asked why your Orators had changed the same to which the said Carman replied that the Carman who usually brought the Blacking was ill and unable to attend his Business or otherwise some conversation took place between the said Mr. Lombard and the said Carman to some such or to the like effect and your Orators further charge that your Orators Carman who usually brought the said Blacking was not ill at the time so alledged as last mentioned and that he was only represented so to be in Order to further the fraudulent plan of the said Defendants in selling the aforesaid Blacking of Jonathan Warren

And your Orators further charge and humbly insist that for the reasons and under the circumstances aforesaid the said Defendants and their Agents Servants and Workmen ought to be severally restrained by the Injunction of this honourable Court from pasting or affixing upon the Bottles and Pots containing the composition or liquid Blacking and paste Blacking manufactured by them as aforesaid any labels hitherto used by them as aforesaid or other labels being the same or colorable imitations of the labels before mentioned to be used by your Orators as such Partners as aforesaid or any other labels or descriptions by which such composition or Blacking so manufactured shall be described or represented as being the Composition or Blacking actually made and manufactured by Jonathan Warren or shall have the appearance of being so described or represented and more particularly any label or labels having the name of Jonathan Warren subscribed or annexed either actually or apparently and ostensibly as a signature thereto and from selling the Bottles containing the said Composition manufactured by them the said Defendants or by any person or persons by their Order or direction or with their knowledge or privity with such labels pasted or affixed thereon

And your Orators charge that the said Defendants ought to set forth a full true and particular Account of the quantity and number of Bottles of Composition or liquid Blacking and paste Blacking which have been manufactured by the said Defendants or by any person or persons by their Order or direction or with their knowledge or privity and which have been sold by them with such labels or descriptions passed or affixed thereupon as aforesaid or any other Labels in imitation or resemblance of your Orators said labels and when and to whom and for what Terms & money the same have been sold and what has been the amount of the profit resulting from the sales thereof and how the said Defendants compute and make out the same

All which actings doings and pretences of the said Confederates are contrary to equity and good conscience and tend to the manifest wrong and injury of your Orators   In consideration whereof and for as much as your Orators are Remediless in the Premises by the strict Rules of the Common Law and cannot have adequate relief therein save only in a Court of equity where matters of this nature are properly cognizable and relievable

To the end therefore that the said George Lamerte and Lewis Worms and their confederates when sworne may upon their several and respective Corporeal Oaths according to the best of their several and respective knowledge remembrance information and belief full true [????] Answer make to all and singular the several matters aforesaid and that as fully and particularly as if the same were here repeated and that they thereunto distinctly interrogated

and more especially that they may in manner aforesaid Answer and set forth Whether the said Jonathan Warren did not from and up to the time hereinbefore mentioned in that behalf or from and up to some and what other time carry on the Business of Manufacturing Blacking of a superior quality for the cleaning of Boots Shoes and other Articles of Black Leather according to an Original Recipe

And whether he did not carry on such Business by manufacturing such Blacking according to an Original Recipe in his possession or how otherwise and whether the Blacking so manufactured so by him as aforesaid was not prepared in paste and whether or not also in a liquid State or how otherwise

And whether such of the Blacking as was sold and disposed of by him in a liquid state was not so sold and disposed of by the Name of Jonathan Warren's Original Japan Blacking or how otherwise

And whether such as was sold by him in a paste state was not so sold by the name and description of Jonathan Warren's Japan Water proof paste Blacking or by some and what other name or how otherwise

And whether such Blacking so manufactured and sold by the said Jonathan Warren as aforesaid was not highly approved of by the public or how otherwise

And whether the name of the said Jonathan Warren did not become, And whether or not by means of the great reputation of such Blacking, extensively known and established for the sale of the said Blacking both in a liquid and Paste state or how otherwise

And whether the said Jonathan Warren did not make and devise to himself considerable income and what profits from the sale of the said Paste Blacking so manufactured by him from such Recipe as aforesaid or how otherwise

and whether your Orator William Edward Woodd did not at or about the time hereinbefore mentioned in that behalf or at some and what other time became desirous of purchasing the said aforesaid Recipe so belonging to the said Jonathan Warren as aforesaid and also the permission of the said Jonathan Warren to authorize your last named Orator to manufacture such Blacking for his own Sole use and benefit And whether or not also the good Will of the said Jonathan Warrens said Business and all his interest therein or how otherwise

And Whether your last named Orator did not at or about the time hereinbefore mentioned in that behalf or at some and what other time Contract and Agree with the said Jonathan Warren the elder to purchase of him and whether or not for the consideration and and for the term hereinbefore stated in that behalf or for some other and what other Consideration or for some and what other term the said Recipe and the use of the name of him the said Jonathan Warren in making and selling of the said Blacking and all his Right Title and Interest in the same   And whether or not in the said Jonathan Warrens said Business

And whether in pursuance of such last mentioned arrangement such Agreement bearing such date is hereinbefore stated in that behalf or some and what other Agreement of some and what other date was not duly made and entered into by and between the said Jonathan Warren and your Orator William Edward Woodd or how otherwise and whether such last mentioned Agreement was not of such purport or effect as hereinbefore stated in that behalf as far as the same is hereinbefore setforth or of some and what other purport or effect And whether immediately upon the execution of the said Agreement the said Jonathan Warren did not deliver up to your last named Orator possession of the said Recipe And whether your last named Orator did not thereupon commence the manufacturing of Blacking at Number 9 Noble Street aforesaid or how otherwise

And whether he did not manufacture and sell large or some and what quantities thereof both in a paste and liquid state And whether he did not use the name of the said Jonathan Warren both in his labels and advertisements for the sale thereof as the Manufacturer of such Blacking both in a paste and liquid state or how otherwise

And whether at or about the time hereinbefore mentioned in that behalf or at some and what other time your Orators did not agree that in consequence of an adequate premium paid to your Orator William Edward Woodd by your other Orator he your Orator Stephen Pilcher should participate with your Orator William Edward Woodd in the benefit of the said Recipe and in the profits arising from the manufacturing of the said Blacking and that they should enter into Copartnership together for the manufacturing and selling the aforesaid Blacking and that they should divide the profits derived therefrom in equal halves And whether it was not agreed that they should become equally liable to the payments reserved by the said Agreement of the said eighth day of November One thousand eight hundred and twenty two to the said Jonathan Warren and his said widow or how otherwise

and whether your Orators have not accordingly ever since the time hereinbefore mentioned in that behalf or some and what other time held and enjoyed the said Recipe in Partnership together or how otherwise

And whether they have not as such Copartners as aforesaid ever since made and manufactured the said Jonathan Warrens said Blacking And whether they have not sold and disposed of large or some and what quantities thereof in paste and in liquid state or how otherwise

And whether up to Christmas One thousand eight hundred and Twenty four or up to some and what other time your Orators did not carry on the business of manufacturing the said Blacking at Hungerford stairs aforesaid where the said Jonathan Warren had originally carried on such business or how otherwise

And whether at or about the time hereinbefore mentioned in that behalf or at some and what other time your Orators did not remove their said manufactory to Number 9 Noble Street aforesaid or otherwise and whether they have ever since therein carried on the said Business or how otherwise

And whether the said Recipe by which such blacking was Originally Manufactured by the said Jonathan Warren and by which the same has been since manufactured by your Orators is not exceedingly valuable or how otherwise

And whether the Blacking so produced therefrom or known and designated by the aforesaid Name of Jonathan Warrens Japan Waterproof paste Blacking is not of very excellent quality And whether or not superior to other compositions of the same Nature or how otherwise

And whether your Orators by their own personal exertions and assiduity and Whether or not at a great or some and what expence have not succeeded in forming an extensive connection for the sale of such Blacking And whether or not also as well in the liquid as in the paste state to Merchants Shopkeepers Dealers and others who purchased the same for exportation or for the purpose of reselling the same again by retail or how otherwise

And whether from the intrinsic excellence of the said Blacking it has not acquired great credit in the public estimation or how otherwise And whether a preference has not been therefore invariably given to the said Blacking prepared by your Orators over other Compositions of the like Nature or how otherwise

And whether in consequence thereof the Business in which your Orators are engaged as aforesaid has not become extremely profitable or how otherwise

And whether the said Blacking has not been always and is not now sold by your Orators when in a liquid state in stone Bottles or how otherwise And whether such Bottles do not contain Pints, three quarters of a pint and a quarter of a Pint each or how otherwise

And whether on each of such Bottles there is not now and hath not been for many years past pasted a label   And whether such label is not in such words or to such effect as hereinbefore stated in that behalf or in some and what other words or to some and what other effect

And whether the said label does not contain on the right side thereof certain direction for using the same   And whether such directions are not in such words or to such effect as hereinbefore stated in that behalf or in some and what other words or to some and what other effect

And whether the said Blacking hath not been always and is not now sold by your Orators when in a paste state in stone pots or how otherwise And whether on each of such pots there hath not been for many years and is not now pasted a label   And whether in such label the said Composition is not described in such words or to such purport or effect as hereinbefore setforth in that behalf or in some and what other words or to some and what other purport or effect   And whether each of such labels do not purport to be signed or subscribed in the Name of the said Jonathan Warren or how otherwise and whether in Order to prevent the imitation of their said labels and the fraud upon your Orators and upon the Public consequential thereon or for some and what other purpose your orators have not caused their said labels to be printed after a particular design or how otherwise

And whether such labels as are affixed to the said Bottles containing the said liquid Blacking have not the large figures of 30 printed in the middle thereof or how otherwise   And whether such labels as are affixed to the pots containing the Paste have not an Irish harp with the figures 30 under the same in the center thereof and the description of the said composition engraved in a circle on the left side of all such labels and the directions for using the same on the right side thereof or how otherwise

And whether your Orators have not for some and how long time past caused to be printed and circulated certain hand Bills   And whether or not for the purpose of recommending their said Blacking and whether the same hand Bills are not printed on Red Paper   And whether or not with the Royal Arms at the top thereof   And whether such hand Bills are not in such words or to such effect hereinbefore set forth in that behalf or in some and what other words or to some and what other purport or effect

And whether the said Jonathan Warren did not depart this life at or about the time hereinbefore mentioned in that behalf or at some and what other time   And whether he did not leave the said Elizabeth Warren his Widow him surviving   And whether the said Elizabeth Warren did not become thereupon entitled to receive the said Annuity of Two hundred and fifty Pounds or how otherwise

And whether previously to your Orator William Edward Woodd entering into such Copartnership with your other Orator as aforesaid and whether or not at or about the time hereinbefore mentioned in that behalf or at some and what other time he did not take into his employ as a Clerk in the said Business the said Defendant George Lamerte or how otherwise

And whether the said Defendant George Lamerte did not continue to act as such Clerk as aforesaid in your Orator William Edward Woodd's service up to the time hereinbefore mentioned in that behalf or up to some and what other time   And whether he did not leave your last named Orators service at or about the time last mentioned or at some and what other time

And whether at or about the time hereinbefore mentioned in that behalf or at some and what other time the said Defendant George Lamerte and the said Defendant Lewis Worms did not enter into Copartnership as Blacking Manufacturers at Whitechapel Road aforesaid   And whether or not under the stile or form of Lamerte And Company   And whether they have not ever since continued to carry on such Business under such stile or form accordingly or how otherwise

And whether the said Defendants have not formed a design to make and sell a certain composition not made by your Orator but made by them the said Defendants or by some and what person or persons

And whether or not by their Order or directions or with their knowledge or privity as and for the said Composition called Jonathan Warrens Japan Water Proof Paste Blacking and so sold by your Orators as such purchasers under the said late Jonathan Warren as aforesaid or how otherwise

And whether with such view or design or with some and what other view or design they the said Defendants or some and what persons of person And whether or not on their behalf or with their direction have or has not made large or some and what quantities of liquid Blacking or how otherwise And whether they have not put the same into Stone Bottles And whether such Stone Bottles or some and which of them were not of the same size and make as those made by your Orators or how otherwise and in what respects or respects did they differ therefrom And whether they the said Defendants or some and what other persons or person on their behalf or with their direction have or has not also made large or some and what quantities of paste Blacking and whether they have not put the same into pots of the same size and make as the said Pots so used by your Orators in the sale of the said Jonathan Warren's said Paste Blacking as aforesaid or how otherwise and whether they have not also pasted or affixed to such Bottles labels in the same or nearly the same words and figures and to a similar or same and what other purport or effect as the labels affixed to the said Bottles and Pots so sold by your Orators as aforesaid or how otherwise And whether or not in Order the more closely to imitate your Orators said labels so affixed to the said Bottles and Pots so sold by them as aforesaid

And whether or not the better to deceive the public thereby the said Defendants have not employed the same person to print their said labels and hath for some time past been employed by your Orators to print theirs or how otherwise

And whether the said Bottles and Pots so labelled as aforesaid have not been from time to time sold and delivered by them the said Defendants to various or some and what persons And whether or not in Order that the same might be sold by such Persons in Bottles and Pots containing the same Paste or liquid Blacking so made by your Orators as such purchasers under the said Jonathan Warren as aforesaid or how otherwise

And whether the said Defendants have not actually represented to various or some and what persons And particularly whether or not to some and what persons who have been in the habit of purchasing of your Orators the Blacking so manufactured by them as aforesaid that such Blacking or composition so made and sold by them the said Defendants as aforesaid is the Original Jonathan Warrens real Japan Water proof Blacking and that the same actually comes from or has been made by your Orators or otherwise and whether they have not made some such or some other representations to some such or the like or some other and what effect

And Whether many or some and what persons have not been deceived by some representations or how otherwise   And whether such persons or some and which of them have not been thereby induced to purchase of the said Defendants the said composition or blacking manufactured by them or by their Order a direction as and for the Composition or Blacking manufactured by your Orator as the Original Jonathan Warrens as aforesaid or how otherwise

And whether divers or some and what other persons and whom by name have not been induced and whether or not by means of such fraudulent deception to purchase of the said Defendants Bottles and Pots of their said Composition or Blacking or how otherwise

And whether other and what persons have not bought Bottles and Pots of the said Composition or Blacking knowing the same to be manufactured by the said Defendants or by some and what other Persons or Person then your Orators to the intent to sell the same again by means of the labels affixed thereto as and for the composition or Blacking manufactured by your Orators or how otherwise and how do the said Defendants make out the contrary

And whether the said Defendants have not therefore been enabled by the means aforesaid to dispose of large or some and what quantities of the said Composition or Blacking manufactured by them or by some and what other person or persons than your Orators or how otherwise   And whether your Orators have not sustained great or some and what injury from the deception practised by the said Defendants in manner aforesaid or how otherwise

And whether your Orators or some and what other persons or person have or hath not and how often and when made or caused to be made some applications or requests to the said Defendants or One and which of them for some such or the like purposes as hereinbefore stated in that behalf or for some and what other purposes   And whether the said Defendants have not and for what reasons refused or declined to comply therewith

And that the said Defendants may in manner aforesaid Answer and set forth Whether the said labels so used and affixed by the said Defendants to the Bottles of the composition so used by them as aforesaid   And whether or not as well as the said hand Bills so circulated by your Orators as aforesaid do not materially and closely resemble in every or some and what respect the said labels and hand Bills so used and circulated by your Orators as aforesaid or how otherwise

And that the said Defendants may setforth in what particulars instances or instance there is any variation or difference between them and in what such variation or difference consists   And whether if there be any difference between them the same is not merely trifling and whether or not only colourable or how otherwise and whether the said labels or some and which of them are not printed of the same Type and whether or not in the same or nearly in the same manner as the labels so used by your Orators as aforesaid or have otherwise and in what respect do they differ therefrom

And whether on the said Labels which the said Defendants so fix or cause to be affixed to the said pots of Paste so made and sold by them as aforesaid there is not a harp described in the centre thereof with the figures of 30 under the same or how otherwise   And whether such Harp does not very nearly or in some and what respect resemble the aforesaid Harp so described on your Orators aforesaid labels which are so affixed to the pots of Paste so sold by your Orators as aforesaid or how otherwise and in what respect do the same differ therefrom

And whether the description of the said Blacking and the directions for using the same as stated on the said labels so affixed to the said Pots of Paste Blacking so sold by the said Defendants as aforesaid are not similar in every or in some and what respect to the aforesaid description and directions for use contained in your Orators said labels so affixed to the said Pots of Paste so sold by your Orators as aforesaid or how otherwise

And whether the said labels of the said Defendants so affixed to the said Pots do not differ only from them so affixed by your Orators to the said Pots of Paste so sold by your Orators in such Particulars as hereinbefore particularly mentioned and set forth in that behalf or in some and what other particulars

And whether the said words and figures "late Manufacturers to" and "107 Whitechapel Road" are not and whether or not with a view to deceive the Public   And whether or not also with a view to present the same being immediately observed printed only in small characters or how otherwise and with what other view in particular are they so printed And whether with a view also of imposing on the public or with some and what other view or for some and what reason in particular the words "Jonathan Warren" are not printed in large Letters in the said Defendants Labels and whether the same are not printed in the same manner as the same words are printed in your Orators said labels or how otherwise

And whether the only other difference between your Orators said labels so affixed to the said Pots of paste so sold by them as aforesaid the said labels affixed to the said Pots of Paste so made and sold by the said Defendants aforesaid is not that at the bottom of your Orators said labels the words "Jonathan Warren" are not printed or how otherwise And whether at the bottom of each label of the said Defendants there are not printed the initials "G. L & Co." or how or otherwise and in what manner or in what other respects do the same differ

And whether the Songs and Hand Bills so circulated by the said Defendants as aforesaid do not differ only from those so circulated by your Orators in the second and third from last lines thereof or how otherwise And whether such four last lines are not in such words or to such purport or effect as hereinbefore setforth in that behalf or in some and what other words or to some and what other purport or effect

And that the said Defendants may in manner aforesaid Answer and set forth whether the said Defendants have not sold to various or some and what persons the Blacking so manufactured by your Orators of such Recipe as the purchasers thereof from the said Jonathan Warren as aforesaid as the Blacking of the said Jonathan Warren And whether or not as an Article which they the said Defendants were rightfully and lawfully entitled to sell and dispose of or how otherwise

And whether they have not so sold the same under a fraudulent representation that the said Blacking was the same Blacking as was originally manufactured by the said Jonathan Warren or how otherwise And whether they the said Defendants did not well know such representation to be untrue or how otherwise

And whether the said George Lamerte or some and what person in his employ And whether or not on his behalf at or about the time hereinbefore mentioned in that behalf or at some and what other time apply to the said Mr. Lombard And whether he did not ask the said Mr. Lombard whether he wanted any of Jonathan Warren's Blacking or to such or the like or some and what other purport or effect or how otherwise And whether the said Mr. Lombard had not been some and

127

how long time previously thereto a regular Customer of your Orators or how otherwise And whether the said Mr. Lombard did not believe that the said Defendant George Lamerte had proper authority to sell the same And whether the said Mr. Lombard did not observe that the Blacking was not brought by the same Carman as brought the Goods sold by your Orators said house And whether he did not ask why your Orators had changed the same And whether the said Carman did not reply that the Carman who usually brought the Blacking was ill and unable to attend his Business or how otherwise and whether some conversation did not take place between the said Mr. Lombard and the said Carman to some such or the like or some and what other effect And whether Your Orators Carman who usually brought the said Blacking was ill at the time so alledged as last mentioned or how otherwise And whether he was not only represented so to be in Order to further the fraudulent plan of the said Defendants in selling the aforesaid Blacking of Jonathan Warren or how otherwise

And whether for the Reasons and under the Circumstances aforesaid the said Defendants and their Agents Servants and Workmen ought not to be severally restrained by the Injunction of this honourable Court from pasting or affixing upon the Bottles and Pots containing the composition or liquid Blacking and Paste Blacking manufactured by them as aforesaid any labels hitherto used by them as aforesaid or other labels being the same or Colourable imitations of the labels before mentioned to be used by your Orators as such partners as aforesaid or any other label or description by which such Composition or Blacking so manufactured shall be described or represented as being the Composition or Blacking actually made and manufactured by Jonathan Warren or shall have the Appearance of being so described or represented and more particularly any label or labels having the name of Jonathan Warren subscribed or annexed either actually or apparently and ostensibly as a signature thereto and from selling the Bottles containing the said Composition manufactured by them the said Defendants or by any person or persons by their Order or direction or with their knowledge or privity with such labels pasted or affixed thereon and if not why not

And that the said Defendants may set forth a full true and particular Account of the quantity and Number of Bottles of Composition or liquid Blacking and Paste Blacking which have been manufactured by the said Defendants or by any person or persons by their Order or direction or with their knowledge or privity and which have been sold by them with such labels or descriptions pasted or affixed thereupon as aforesaid or any other Labels in imitation or resemblance of your Orators said labels and when and to whom and for what Sums of money the same have been sold and what has been the Amount of the profit resulting from the sale thereof and how the said Defendants make out and compute the same

And that the said Defendants and each of them their and each of their Agents Servants and Workmen may he severally restrained by the Injunction of this honourable Court from pasting or affixing upon the Bottles and pots containing the Composition of Blacking and Paste manufactured by them the said Defendants or either of them as aforesaid any labels hitherto used by them as aforesaid or other labels being the same or colourable imitations of the labels hereinbefore mentioned to be used by your Orators as such partners as aforesaid in the sale of their said liquid Blacking or paste Blacking as aforesaid or any other label or description by which such Composition of liquid Blacking and paste so manufactured shall be described or represented as being the Composition or Blacking actually made and manufactured by your Orators or shall have the appearance of being so described or represented and more particularly any label or labels having the name or firm of Jonathan Warren subscribed or annexed either actually or apparently and ostensibly as a signature thereto and from selling Bottles and Pots containing respectively the composition or liquid Blacking and paste Blacking manufactured by them the said Defendants or either of them or by any person or persons by their or either of their Order or direction or with their or either of their knowledge or privity with such labels pasted or affixed thereon as aforesaid

And that an Account may be taken under the direction of the honourable Court of the Numbers of Bottles of liquid Blacking and Paste Blacking which have been manufactured by the said Defendants or by any person or persons by their Order or direction or with the knowledge of either of them upon any such labels as hereinbefore mentioned have been pasted or affixed and which have been sold by them the said Defendants and of the profits which have arisen from the sale thereof   And that the said Defendants may be decreed to pay to your Orators the Amount of such profits as ascertained by such Accounts

And that your Orators may have such further and other Relief and that all such necessary directions may be given for the further and better effectuating the matters aforesaid as to your Lordship shall seem meet and the circumstances of the Case may Require

May it please your Lordship the Premises considered to grant unto your Orators not only his Majestys most gracious writ of Injunction issuing out of and under the seal of this honorable Court to be directed to the said Defendants George Lamerte and Lewis Worms and each of them and their and each of their Agents Servants and Workmen severally to restrain them from pasting or affixing upon the said Bottles and pots containing the composition or Blacking and paste manufactured by them the said Defendants or either of them as aforesaid any labels hitherto used by them as aforesaid or other labels being the same or colourable imitations of the labels hereinbefore mentioned to be used by your Orators as such partners as aforesaid in the sale of their said liquid Blacking or Paste Blacking as aforesaid or any other label or description by which such Composition or liquid Blacking and paste so manufactured shall be described or represented as being the composition or Blacking actually made or manufactured by your Orators or shall have the appearance of being so described or represented and more particularly any label or labels having the name or firm of Jonathan Warren subscribed or annexed either actually or apparently and ostensibly as a signature thereto and from selling Bottles and pots containing respectively the composition or liquid Blacking and paste Blacking manufactured by them the said Defendants or either of them or by any person or persons by their or either of their order or direction or with their or either of their knowledge or privity with such labels pasted or affixed thereon as aforesaid, but also his Majestys most gracious Writ or Writs of Subpena to be directed to the said George Lamerte and Lewis Worms and their Confederates thereby commanding them at a certain day and under a certain pain therein to be limited personally to be and appear before your Lordship in this honourable Court and then and there full true direct and perfect answer make to all and singular the Premises and further to stand to perform and abide such further Order direction and Decree therein as to your Lordship shall seem meet And your Orators shall ever pray

Wm Phillimore

The Answer of George Lamerte and Lewis Worms

Sworn at the Public Office Southampton Buildings in the County of Middlesex on the 7th day of November 1826 by both the Defendants before me H Cross

22nd November 1826   The joint and several Answers of George Lamerte and Lewis Worms the two Defendants to the Bill of Complaint of William Edward Woodd and Stephen Pilcher Complainants

These Defendants now and at all times hereafter saving and reserving to themselves all and all manner of benefit and advantage which may be had or taken to the said Complainants said Bill of Complaint by way of exception for answer hereto or unto so much thereof as these Defendants are advised it is in any wise necessary or material to make answer unto answering say

they have heard and believe that Jonathan Warren in the said Bill of Complaint mentioned for several years previously to the year one thousand eight hundred and twenty two carried on the business of a Blacking Manufacturer in great obscurity and on a very confined scale

And these Defendants say that they have heard and believe that Robert Warren in and for several years previously to the year One thousand eight hundred and twenty two and since that time carried and now does carry on the business of a Blacking manufacturer at No 30 in the Strand and that the said Business of the said Robert Warren was lucrative and extensive

And this Defendant George Lamerte says and the other Defendant believes that this Defendant George Lamerte was educated at the Royal Military College at Sandhurst and intended for the Army and that in October One thousand eight hundred and twenty two the Complainant William Edward Woodd prevailed on this Defendant George Lamerte to give up his then views in life and engage with the Complainant William Edward Woodd in the Manufacture of Blacking in the manner and circumstances herein after mentioned

And this Defendant George Lamerte says and this other Defendant believes that in October One thousand eight hundred and twenty two the Complainant William Edward Woodd carried on the business of a Blacking Manufacturer having his Counting house in Tokenhouse Yard and his manufactory or warehouse at a House in Hungerford Stairs Strand and employing the said Jonathan Warren as his manufacturer and selling such blacking under the name of the said Jonathan Warren

And this Defendant George Lamerte says and this other Defendant believes that the Complainant William Edward Woodd was anxious to take advantage of the reputation of the said Robert Warren and to vend the Blacking so manufactured by the said Jonathan Warren as and for the Blacking of the said Robert Warren and for such purposes the Complainant William Edward Woodd was desirous of having hand bills and labels printed which should be colorable imitations of those used by the said Robert Warren

And this Defendant George Lamerte says and this other Defendant believes that the original number of the House at Hungerford Stairs occupied by the Complainant William Edward Woodd for his said Manufactory was 25 and that No 30 Hungerford Stairs was occupied by a Shoemaker and that the Complainant William Edward Woodd for the purposes of the said Hand Bills and labels exchanged numbers with the said Shoemaker and thereupon advertised his Blacking "30 Hungerford Stairs Strand" the figures 30 and the word Strand being printed in a conspicuous Character and the words Hungerford Stairs in a small character

And these Defendants say they are now in possession of a label of the said Robert Warren which is in the words and figures following that is to say "Warrens original Japan Liquid Blacking sold wholesale by the proprietor Robert Warren. The Boot by Warrens Blacking cleaned does shew, Each feature fairer than then the mirrors glow. Nothing has yet been offered to the public equal to this Blacking for giving an elegant black lustre to leather which it also preserves soft and pliable and prevents from cracking it being of an oily preparation [image of large number 30 with sketch of two people contained] use. Stir it well from the bottom with a stiff stick rub the Stick on a soft brush then black your boot and shine it while wet. Don't put the boot to the fire to dry Strand   caution observe each label is signed thus Robert Warren price 1.s No 13 Ask for Warrens Blacking"   but for their greater certainty these Defendants crave to refer to the said label

And these Defendants say they are in possession of labels used by the Complainant William Edward Woodd which are in the exact words and figures of the said label of the said Robert Warren with the exception that for the word "Robert" the word "Jonathan" is subscribed and that the words "Hungerford Stairs" and the words "Counting house No 26 Tokenhouse Yard City" are added

And these Defendants say that the said figure 30 are printed on the portrait of a Man shaving by the reflection of a Boot and that the same device was adopted by the Complainant William Edward Woodd   And these Defendants say that to render the number 30 more conspicuous the said Robert Warren has caused the same number 30 to be printed in a large black character with the number 30 in white character thereon and that the same device was adopted by the Complainant William Edward Woodd

And this Defendant George Lamerte says and this other Defendant believes that in the month of October One thousand eight hundred and twenty two the Complainant induced this Defendant George Lamerte to engage with him as aforesaid but no Agreement or understanding was entered into or come in respect of such engagement and that in January One thousand eight hundred and twenty three the Complainant removed his Counting house to the said Manufactory at Hungerford Stairs where this Defendant George Lamerte at the express request of the Complainant William Edward Woodd undertook the whole management and superintendence of the said manufactory and counting house

And this Defendant George Lamerte says and this other Defendant believes that the blacking manufactured by the said Jonathan Warren was of inferior quality and Much complained of and in consequence this Defendant altered the mode of manufacturing the Blacking which greatly improved the quality and extended the sale thereof and the article so manufactured by this Defendant George Lamerte obtained great reputation under the name of Jonathan Warrens Blacking

And this Defendant George Lamerte says and this other Defendant believes that about the beginning of the year One thousand eight hundred and twenty four the Complainant William Edward Woodd moved his said Business from Hungerford Stairs to No 3 Chandos Street When the Complainant William Edward Woodd made a small alteration in his own hand bills and labels but continued the figures 30 and the words Hungerford Stairs Strand in conspicuous characters

And this Defendant George Lamerte says and this other Defendant believes that the said Jonathan Warren died in the month of August One thousand eight hundred and twenty four and this Defendant George Lamerte thereupon exclusively manufactured the said Blacking the Complainant William Edward Woodd being then in Ireland

And this Defendant George Lamerte says that during the period from the month of October One thousand eight hundred and twenty two until the death of the said Jonathan Warren this Defendant George Lamerte never saw or heard of any receipt by or from which the said Jonathan Warren manufactured Blacking nor did he manufacture the same upon scientific principles or according to any settled rule and that this Defendant George Lamerte introduced into the said manufactory the principles and settled rules by which this Defendant George Lamerte manufactured such blacking

And this Defendant George Lamerte says and this other Defendant believes that in or about the month of October One thousand eight hundred and twenty four this Defendant George Lamerte required the Complainant William Edward Woodd to come to a settlement and to define on what terms this Defendant George Lamerte was to continue in such manufactory when this Defendant George Lamerte and the Complainant William Edward Woodd disagreed and the Complainant William Edward Woodd remarked to this Defendant George Lamerte that there was plenty of room in the Blacking Trade and that Lamerte was an excellent name for it to which remark this Defendant George Lamerte made answer "No Mr. Woodd from the treatment you have shewn towards me let me observe that I have had the manufactory of Jonathan Warrens blacking and the many improvements I have made in it to your advantage shall now be placed to my account you know I have no other trade or profession and I therefore most certainly shall take that which is the only course I have left and take your advice and set up as a Blacking maker but not in the name of Lamerte but that of late Manufacturer to Jonathan Warren or this Defendant George Lamerte used words to that effect some days after which the Complainant William Edward Woodd required this Defendant George Lamerte to write out the receipt by which the Blacking had been made which this Defendant George Lamerte refused to do alleging as the fact is that he had never been furnished with any receipt by the said Jonathan Warren but had improved upon the practice of the said Jonathan Warren and should now turn such improvement to his this Defendants George Lamerte's own advantage

And this Defendant George Lamerte saith that the said Jonathan Warren frequently informed him that he had no particular receipt for the manufacture of the said Blacking

And these Defendants say that this Defendant George Lamerte being so disengaged as aforesaid these Defendants agreed to carry on the trade of Blacking makers in copartnership together and they commenced such Business in Whitechapel Road in the month of January One thousand eight hundred and twenty five and then began and have ever since used bottles hand bills and labels of a similar description to those complained of by the said Complainants said Bill of Complaint and that with the full knowledge of the Complainant William Edward Woodd

however these Defendants say that in all the said hand bills and labels it is expressly stated that the Blacking therein mentioned was made by the late manufacturer to Jonathan Warren and that these Defendants have put in the said hand bills and labels or any of them alleged or pretended that the said Blacking was made by or after any receipt of the said Jonathan Warren and that when these Defendants so commenced business as aforesaid they caused a circular Letter to be extensively distributed and which is in the words and figures following that is to say "Geo Lamerte & Co respectfully beg leave to acquaint Merchants Captains and others they have opened a manufactory in the Whitechapel Road for the sale of the Real Japan Blacking made by the late manufacturer to Jonathan Warren and in consequence of their establishment being contigious to the East and West India Docks they are enabled to forward shipping orders to any amount with the greatest expedition on the shortest notice a large stock being in constant readiness for that purpose on the following very low terms Liquid Blacking pints @ 12/- per doz. ¾ pints @ 8/- Do. ½ pints @ 4/- Do. Paste Blacking in pots and tin boxes @ 4/- 8/- and 12/- per dozen subject to the following discounts £10 and upwards 15 per cent 15 Do. 20 Do. 25 Do. 35 Do. 30 Do. 50 Do. 35 Do.   G. L. having been in the manufactory of the late Jonathan Warren 2 years previous to his death and until the last 3 months sole manufacturer of all blacking bearing his name since his decease can confidently assure those who may kindly favour him with their commands that they will meet with every satisfaction   It being the study of the firm to make their article with the very best materials and the greatest care being taken in getting it up consequently they feel no hesitation in saying their Blacking is equal to any that is made in the Kingdom and far superior to some they can warrant it to remain as good and perfect after it has been conveyed to any distance as when it first leaves the manufactory   orders directed as under will meet with due attention
107 Whitechapel Road January 20th 1825"

but for their greater certainty these Defendants crave to refer to such circular or letter

And these Defendants to the best of their knowledge information and belief deny that the said Jonathan Warren did from and up to the time in the said Bill mentioned or from and up to any other time carry on the business of manufacturing Blacking of a superior quality for the cleaning Boots Shoes and other Articles of Black Leather as according to an original Recipe or that he did carry on such business by manufacturing such Blacking according to an original Recipe in his possession or any otherwise than as aforesaid or that the Blacking so alleged to have been manufactured by him as in the said Bill is stated was prepared in paste and also in a liquid state but these Defendants admit that the Blacking so manufactured as hereinbefore is mentioned was prepared in paste and also in liquid state and that such of the blacking as was sold and disposed of in a liquid state was sold and disposed of by the name of Jonathan Warrens original Japan Blacking and that such as was sold in a paste state was so sold by the name of Jonathan Warrens Japan Water proof paste Blacking but these Defendants say they never knew the said Jonathan Warren sell or dispose of such Blacking whether Liquid or paste in his own account but always as the servant of the Complainant William Edward Woodd

however these Defendants to the best of their knowledge information and belief deny that such Blacking manufactured and sold by the said Jonathan Warren as aforesaid was highly approved by the public or any otherwise than as aforesaid or that the name of the said Jonathan Warren did become by means of the great reputation of such Blacking extensively known and established for the sale of the said Blacking both in the Liquid and paste state or any otherwise than that by the improvements introduced by this Defendant George Lamerte the name of Jonathan Warren became extensively known and the reputation of the said Blacking established

but these Defendants to the best of their knowledge information and belief deny that the said Jonathan Warren did make and derive to himself considerable or any profits from the sale of the said Blacking so alleged to have been manufactured by him from such recipe as in the said Bill mentioned or any otherwise than as aforesaid and that the said Jonathan Warren always appeared to this Defendant George Lamerte to be in very narrow and mean circumstances

and save as hereinbefore is mentioned these Defendants say they do not have and are unable to set forth as to their belief or otherwise whether the Complainant William Edward Woodd did at or about the time in the said Bill mentioned or at any or what other time become desirous of purchasing the aforesaid alleged recipe so alleged to be belonging to the said Jonathan Warren as in the said Bill is stated and also the permission of the said Jonathan Warren to authorize the last named Complainant to manufacture such Blacking for his own sole use and benefit or whether also the good will of the said Jonathan Warrens said Business and all his interest therein or how otherwise or whether the last named complainant did at or about the time in the said Bill mentioned or at any other time contract and agree with the said Jonathan Warren the elder to purchase of him for the consideration and term in the said Bill mentioned or for any other term the said alleged recipe and the use of the name of him the said Jonathan Warren in making and selling of the said Blacking and all his right title and interest in the same and in the said Jonathan Warrens business excepting only that these Defendants to the best of their knowledge information and belief deny that the said Jonathan Warren had any recipe to sell and that as these Defendants believe the Complainant William Edward Woodd originally engaged the said Jonathan Warren to manufacture Blacking for him the Complainant William Edward Woodd in order to take a fraudulent advantage of the reputation of the said Robert Warren as is hereinbefore more particularly mentioned whereupon some time in the latter end of the year One thousand eight hundred and twenty two some memorandum was agreed or made between the parties but these Defendants are ignorant of the contents thereof and have heard and believe that the Complainant William Edward Woodd after the death of the said Jonathan Warren disclaimed or objected to the validity thereof and save as aforesaid these Defendants do not know and are unable to set further as to their information belief or otherwise whether in pursuance of such alleged arrangement such Agreement bearing such date as in the said Bill mentioned or any other Agreement of any other date was duly made and entered into by and between the said Jonathan Warren and the said Complainant William Edward Woodd any otherwise than as aforesaid or whether such last alleged Agreement was of such purpose and effect as in the said Bill stated in their behalf as far as the same is therein mentioned and set forth or of any other purport and effect but these Defendants say that to the best of their knowledge information and belief they deny that immediately or upon the execution of the said alleged Agreement the said Jonathan Warren did deliver up to the said last mentioned Complainant possession of the said alleged recipe or that thereupon the said last named Complainant did commence the manufacturing of Blacking at Noble Street in the said Bill mentioned or any otherwise than that after the Complainant William Edward Woodd had for the fraudulent purpose aforesaid engaged the said Jonathan Warren as aforesaid he commenced Business at No 25 Hungerford Stairs Strand and afterwards changed that number to 30 as herein before is mentioned and thence removed to Chandos Street and afterwards to Noble Street aforesaid but the Complainant did not remove to Noble Street aforesaid until several months after the death of the said Jonathan Warren however these Defendants admit that the Complainant William Edward Woodd did by means of the said Jonathan Warren and this Defendant George Lamerte and in manner aforesaid but not otherwise manufacture and sell large quantities of Blacking both in paste and Liquid state and that he did use the name of the said Jonathan Warren both in his Labels and Advertizements for the sale thereof as the Manufacturer of such Blacking both in a paste and in a liquid state

And these Defendants say they do not know and are unable to setforth as to their belief or otherwise whether at or about the time in the said Bill mentioned or at any other time the Complainants did agree that in consequence of an adequate premium paid to the Complainant William Edward Woodd by the Complainant Stephen Pilcher that the Complainant Stephen Pilcher should participate with the Complainant William Edward Woodd in the benefit of the said alleged recipe and in the profits arising from the manufacturing of the said Blacking and that they should enter into Copartnership together for the manufacturing and selling the aforesaid Blacking and that they should divide the profits derived therefrom in equal halves and that they should become equally liable to the payments reserved by the said alledged Agreement of the eighth of November One thousand eight hundred and twenty two to the said Jonathan Warren and his said Widow or otherwise than that on or about the month of December One thousand eight hundred and twenty five the Complainants began to carry on the said business in partnership together under the style or form of Woodd and Pilcher but these defendants to the best of their knowledge information and belief deny that the Complainants have accordingly ever since the time in the said Bill mentioned or any other time held and enjoyed the said alledged recipe in partnership together or any otherwise than that there is no such recipe or that the Complainants have as such Copartners as aforesaid ever since made and manufactured the said Jonathan Warrens Blacking

but these Defendants say they have heard and believe that the Complainants have ever since the month of December One thousand eight hundred and twenty four made and manufactured a blacking which they call Jonathan Warrens Blacking but which is an article very inferior to the one manufactured by this Defendant George Lamerte and sold by the Complainant William Edward Woodd as Jonathan Warrens blacking but these defendants say they do not know and are unable to setforth as to their belief or otherwise whether the Complainants have sold and disposed of large or what quantities of the blacking so made by them in Paste and in a Liquid state or how otherwise except that these Complainants believe the Complainants have sold and disposed of some of such Blacking in paste and in a liquid state and the defendant George Lamerte says and this defendant believes that the Complainant William Edward Woodd carried on the said business in Hungerford Stairs aforesaid until the beginning of the year One thousand eight hundred and twenty three when he removed as aforesaid to Chandos Street Covent Garden and thence as these defendants have heard and believe the Complainant did in or about Christmas One thousand eight hundred and twenty five remove to Noble Street aforesaid but Save as aforesaid these defendants do not know and are unable to setforth as to their belief or otherwise whether up to Christmas One thousand eight hundred and twenty four or up to any or what other time the Complainant William Edward Woodd did carry on the business of manufacturing the said Blacking at Hungerford Stairs aforesaid where the said Jonathan Warren had originally carried on such Business as aforesaid or how otherwise or save as aforesaid whether at or about the time in the said Bill mentioned or at any or what other time the Complainants did remove their said Manufactory to No. 9 Noble Street aforesaid or how otherwise but these defendants say they have heard and believe that the Complainants have ever since Christmas One thousand eight hundred and twenty four carried on the said business in Noble Street aforesaid

however these defendants say they do not know or believe that the pretended recipe by which it is alleged the said Blacking was originally prepared by the said Jonathan Warren and by which it is alledged the same has been since manufactured by the Complainant is exceedingly valuable or how otherwise than that the same is of no value whatever and these defendants say that to the best of their knowledge information and belief they deny that the blacking so produced from such pretended recipe or known or designated by the aforesaid name of Jonathan Warrens Japan and Water Proof paste Blacking is of very excellent quality superior to other Compositions of the same nature or any otherwise than that the same is of a very inferior quality however these defendants say that the Blacking manufactured by this defendant George Lamerte and sold by the Complainant William Edward Woodd by the name of Jonathan Warrens Japan Water proof paste blacking was of very excellent quality and superior to most other Compositions of the same nature

And these defendants say they do not know and are unable to setforth as to their belief or otherwise whether the Complainants by their own personal assiduity or at a great or any or what expence have succeeded in forming an extensive connexion for the Sale of such Blacking or whether also as well in the liquid as the paste state to Merchants Shop keepers dealers and others who purchased the same for exportation for the purpose of reselling the same again by retail or how otherwise but these defendants to the best of their knowledge information and belief say that from the intrinsic excellence of the said Blacking it has acquired great credit in the public estimation or any otherwise than that it is not as these Defendants believe held in estimation by the public And the Defendants to the best of their knowledge information and belief deny that a preference has therefore been invarriably or ever given to the said Blacking prepared by the Complainants over other compositions of the like nature or any otherwise than as aforesaid or that in consequence thereof the business in which the Complainants were engaged as aforesaid has become extremely profitable or any otherwise than as aforesaid however these Defendants say they admit that the said Blacking has been always and is now sold by the Complainants when in a liquid state in Stone Bottles and that such Bottles do contain pints three fourths of a pint and a quarter of a pint each and that on each of such bottles there is now and has been for many years past pasted a label however these defendants say that the said labels have varied from time to time and were at first such colorable imitations of the said Robert Warrens labels as hereinbefore is mentioned and that in consequence of Complainants having been made the picture of the man shaving by the reflection of a boot was omitted and afterwards the Complainants used labels stating that the blacking was made by the proprietors of the Original recipe of the late Jonathan Warren and added their address No 9 Noble Street but still omitting their own names and that these defendants are in possession of several of such labels differing in some respects from each other but that they all describe the said liquid Blacking in the same words as those used by the said Robert Warren in his labels and give directions for its use in the same words as the directions given by the said Robert Warren And these defendants admit that some of the said labels are in such words or to such effect as in the said Bill stated so far as the same are therein setforth and that the said labels contain on the right side thereof directions for using the same and that such directions are in such words and to the purport and effect as in the said Bill stated but for their greater certainty these defendants crave to refer to such labels however they say that in the labels of the said Robert Warren as well as in the labels of the Complainants the description of the Blacking is on the left and the directions for the use on the right side of the said labels and these defendants believe that the said Blacking hath been always and is now sold by the Complainants when in a paste state in Stone pots or in tin boxes and that on each of such pots or boxes there has been for many years and is now pasted a label and that on such labels the composition is described in such words as in the said Bill mentioned but for their greater certainty these defendants crave to refer thereto however these defendants admit that each of such labels do purport to be subscribed or signed in the name of Jonathan Warren in imitation of the said Robert Warrens labels which purport to be subscribed or signed by him and these defendants to the best of their knowledge information and belief deny that in order to prevent the imitation of their said labels and the fraud upon the Complainants and upon the public consequential thereon the Complainants have caused their said labels to be printed after a particular design but these defendants say that the design of the said labels is similar to those of other blacking manufacturers with additions made thereto for the purpose of imposing the blacking of the Complainants upon the public as the Blacking of the said Robert Warren and save as aforesaid these defendants to the best of their knowledge information and belief deny that the said labels printed after the particular design or any otherwise than as aforesaid

however these defendants admit that such labels as are affixed to the said Bottles containing the said liquid Blacking have the large figures of thirty printed in the middle thereof but these Defendants say that many of such labels have as aforesaid small figures of thirty printed on the said large figures of thirty however these defendants admit that such labels as are affixed to the pots containing the paste have an Irish Harp with the figures thirty under the same in the centre thereof and the description of the said Composition engraved in a circle on the left side of all such labels and the directions for using the same on the right side thereof but for their greater certainty these defendants crave to refer thereto

and these defendants say they have heard and believe that the Complainants have for some time past caused to be printed and circulated certain hand bills but for how long or time these Defendants say they do not know and are unable to setforth as to their belief or otherwise however these defendants believe the Complainants have caused the said hand bills to be published and circulated for the purpose of recommending their said blacking   And that some hand bills are printed on red paper and with the loyal Arms at the top thereof and that such hand bills are in the words or to such effect as in the said bill setforth in that behalf   And this defendant George Lamerte says and this other defendant believes that such words were the original composition of this defendant George Lamerte

and these Defendants admit that the said Jonathan Warren did depart this life at or about the twenty first of August One thousand eight hundred and twenty four the time in the said Bill mentioned and that he did leave Elizabeth Warren in the said bill mentioned his widow him surviving but whether the said Elizabeth Warren did thereupon become entitled to the said annuity of Two hundred and fifty pounds or how otherwise these defendants do not know and are unable to setforth as to their belief or otherwise save and except as aforesaid and that these Defendants have heard and believe the Complainant William Edward Woodd has refused to pay the same

and save as aforesaid these Defendants deny that previously to the Complainant William Edward Woodd entering into Copartnership with the Complainant Stephen Pilcher as aforesaid or at or about the time in the said Bill mentioned or save as aforesaid at any other time the Complainant William Edward Woodd did take into his employ as a Clerk in the said business the said Defendant George Lamerte or how otherwise than as aforesaid or save as aforesaid that this Defendant George Lamerte did continue to act as such Clerk as aforesaid in the Complainant William Edward Woodd's service up to the time in the said Bill mentioned or up to any other time or any other than as aforesaid however these defendants admit that this Defendant George Lamerte did as aforesaid leave the Complainant William Edward Woodd's service at or about the time in the said Bill and hereinbefore in that behalf mentioned

And these defendants admit that in January One thousand eight hundred and twenty five and not in November One thousand eight hundred and twenty four these Defendants did enter into Copartnership as Blacking Manufacturers at Whitechapel Road aforesaid under the style or form of Lamerte and Company and that they have ever since continued to carry on such business under the said style or form accordingly but these Defendants deny that they these defendants have formed a design to make vend and sell a certain composition not made by the Complainants but by them the said Defendants or by any person or persons by their order or directions or with their knowledge or privity as and for the said composition called Jonathan Warrens Japan Water proof blacking and so sold by the Complainant as such alleged purchases under the said late Jonathan Warren as in the said Bill mentioned or any otherwise than as aforesaid and that these defendants do not believe the Complainants are

such purchasers under the said Jonathan Warren as aforesaid and that in fact these defendants have formed no such design but have as they submit they were and are entitled to do made vended and sold a certain composition not made by the Complainants but made by or by the direction of these defendants as and for a blacking Manufactured by the late Manufacturer to the said Jonathan Warren though these defendants admit it would have been more correct and nearer the truth had these Defendants described such blacking as manufactured by the person who had made the composition called Jonathan Warren's Japan Water proof paste blacking in as much as the said Jonathan Warren was merely the Servant of the Complainant William Edward Woodd

and these Defendants deny that with such view or design in the said bill in that behalf mentioned or with any other view and design they these Defendants or any person or persons on their behalf or with their directions have or has made large or any quantities of liquid Blacking excepting only these Defendants have in the regular course of their trade made large quantities of liquid blacking and has put the same to Stone Bottles and that such Stone bottles were the same size and make as those used by the Complainants but these defendants say that such Stone bottles are as these defendants believe commonly and invariably used by all blacking Manufacturers however these defendants admit that they have made some quantities of paste Blacking and that they have put the same into Stone pots of the same size and make as the said pots so used by the Complainants in the Sale of the said Jonathan Warrens said paste Blacking as aforesaid but these defendants say such pots are as these defendants believe commonly and invariably used by all blacking Manufacturers

but these defendants deny that they have also affixed or pasted to such Bottles lables in the same or nearly the same words and figures and to a similar purport and effect as the labels affixed to the bottles and pots so sold by the Complainants as aforesaid or any otherwise than that the description and the directions for the use of the said liquid Blacking is in different words to the description and directions for the use of the liquid blacking of the Complainants and that in none of the said labels whether used for the said liquid or the said paste blacking is the same described otherwise than as made by the late manufacturer to Jonathan Warren with the address of these defendants added thereto

And these defendants deny that in order the more closely to imitate the complainants said labels to affixed so the said Bottles and pots so sold by them as aforesaid or the better to deceive the public thereby these defendants commenced their said respective partnership concerns nearly at the same time and that this defendant George Lamerte being know to Mr. J------------ Smith an engraver in Saint Martins Lane who had formerly been employed by the Complainant William Edward Woodd these defendants employed the said Mr. J-------------- Smith to design and engrave the lables of these Defendants but these defendants say that to the best of their knowledge and belief the said Mr. J------------- Smith was not then employed by the Complainants to print and engrave their labels and these defendants also employed a Mr. Foster of Worship Street to print some hand bills as consequence of the said Mr. Foster having been known to the brother of this defendant George Lamerte for several years which Mr. Foster has as these defendants believe printed some hand bills for the Complainants

however these defendants deny that the said bottles and pots so labelled as in the said Bill in that behalf mentioned have been from time to time or at any time delivered by the said defendants to various or any persons or person in order that the same might be sold by the said persons or person in Bottles or pots containing the said paste or liquid blacking so made by the Complainant as such alledged purchasers under the said Jonathan Warren as in the said Bill mentioned or any otherwise than as aforesaid

and these defendants deny that they have actually represented to various or any persons or particularly to any persons who have been in the habit of purchasing of the Complainants Blacking so Manufactured by them as aforesaid that such blacking or composition so made and sold by these defendants as the original Warrens real Japan Water proof blacking and that the same actually comes from or has been made by the Complainant or any otherwise than that no such representations have been made but these defendants say they may have represented as the fact is that this Defendant George Lamerte had manufactured much of the Blacking which the Complainant William Edward Woodd has sold as the Original Japan Water proof Blacking and that the blacking of these Defendants was greatly superior to that of the Complainants but save as aforesaid these Defendants to the best of their recollection and belief deny they have made any representations to some such or the like effect as in the said Bill mentioned or to any other effect or that many or any persons have been deceived by such alledged representations or any otherwise than as aforesaid or that any persons have been thereby induced to purchase of these Defendants the said Composition or Blacking manufactured by them or by their order or direction as and for the Composition of Blacking manufactured by the Complainant as the original Jonathan Warrens as in the said Bill mentioned or any other otherwise than as aforesaid or that divers or any other persons have been induced by means of such alleged fraudulent deception to purchase of these Defendants Bottles and Pots of the said Composition or Blacking

144

or any otherwise than as aforesaid or that other persons have bought Bottles and Pots of the said Composition or Blacking knowing the same to be manufactured by these Defendants or by some other person or persons than the Complainants to the intent to sell the same again by means of the labels affixed thereto as and for the Composition or Blacking manufactured by the Complainants or any otherwise than as aforesaid as these Defendants make out by the facts and circumstances aforesaid

And these Defendants to the best of their knowledge information and belief deny that they have been enabled by the means in the said Bill in that behalf most untruly alledged to dispose of large or any quantity of the said Composition or Blacking manufactured by them or by other persons or person than the Complainants or any otherwise than as aforesaid or that the Complainants have sustained great or any injury from the deception in the said Bill untruly alledged to have been practiced by these Defendants in manner in the said Bill untruly alledged or any otherwise than as aforesaid

And these Defendants say they received a Letter dated the sixth October one thousand eight hundred and twenty five nearly a year after these Defendants had commenced Business as aforesaid signed Ja----- Boxer in the words following that is to say

"Sir – I am informed that you assume to sell Blacking under the name of Jonathan Warrens greatly to the injury of the ffirm who you are well aware have the exclusive right to sell the same, I must request of you to give me on behalf of that ffirm an account of the Blacking sold or to make compensation for the injury done to my clients by their loss of Sale and to desist from the future use of the name or any artful imitation of it for the sale of your Blacking otherwise legal proceedings will be instituted against you"

but for their greater certainty these Defendants crave to refer to such letter to which an Answer was returned by the Solicitors of these Defendants denying the charge in the said letter

And save as aforesaid these Defendants to the best of their knowledge recollection and belief deny that the Complainant or either of them or any other persons have or hath often or ever made or caused to be made any application and requests to these Defendants or either of them for any such or the like purposes in the said Bill stated or for any other purposes relating to the matters in and by the said Bill complained of or any of them or that the said labels used and affixed by these Defendants to the Bottles of the composition so used by them as aforesaid as well as the said handbills so circulated by them as aforesaid materially or closely resemble in every or any respect the said labels and handbills so used and circulated by the Complainants as aforesaid or any otherwise than as aforesaid and that one material difference or variance between the labels and handbills of the Complainants and those of the Defendants is that some of the labels and handbills of the Complainants untruly and fraudulently describe their Blacking as made by the Proprietors of the Receipt of Jonathan Warren and others of such labels untruly describe the said Blacking as Jonathan Warrens Japan Water proof paste Blacking, whereas the said labels and handbills of these Defendants expressly describe the Blacking of these Defendants as made by the late Manufacturer to Jonathan Warren

but save as aforesaid these Defendants are unable to setforth in what particular instances or instance there is any variation or difference between them or in what such difference consists except as aforesaid and by referring to the said labels and handbills as these Defendants crave to do for their greater certainty but these Defendants submit and insist that the difference between the said labels and handbills of these Defendants and those of the Complainants are not merely trifling but one substantial and real   And these Defendants say that none of the said labels are printed of the same type the same being engraved and not printed from any Type and that the said labels are not printed in the same or nearly the same manner as the labels so used by the Complainants as aforesaid but in what respect they differ these Defendants save as aforesaid and by reference to the said labels are unable to setforth as to their knowledge belief or otherwise

however these Defendants admit that on the said labels which these Defendants so fix or cause to be fixed to the said Pots of Paste so made and sold by them as aforesaid there is a harp described in the centre thereof with the figures of 30 under the same but these Defendants say they affix similar labels on their Bottles of liquid Blacking which as these Defendants believe are not done by the Complainants

And these Defendants were induced to have such last mentioned labels engraved at the suggestion of some irish Customers and such labels are x x x x by these Defendants generally confined to the Blacking intended for Irish Sale but except as all harps have a resemblance to each other these Defendants deny that the said harp does in any respect resemble the harp so described on the complainants aforesaid labels so affixed to the Pots of Paste so sold by the said Complainants as aforesaid but in what respect they differ therefrom these Defendants are unable to setforth except that the harp on the labels of these Defendants are differently shaped and are in the shape of Irish harps with the figure of an Angel in front have fewer strings and are more ornamented than those of the Complainants which are in the shape of Welsh harps but for their greater certainty these Defendants crave leave to refer to such labels

however these Defendants admit that the description and the directions for using the same as stated in the said labels so affixed to the said Pots of Paste Blacking so sold by these Defendants as aforesaid are similar in substance but not in every respect to the aforesaid description and direction for use contained in the Complainants said labels so affixed to the said Pots of Paste so sold by the Complainants as aforesaid as must necessarily be the case as the qualities of Blacking and the mode of using the same are necessarily described and in similar terms for all Blacking ought to produce a black and shining lustre and all Blacking is used in a similar way but these Defendants deny that their said labels were copied or taken from those of the Complainant

And these Defendants deny that the said labels of these Defendants so affixed to their said Pots to differ only from those so affixed by the Complainants to the said Pots of Paste so sold by the Complainants in such particulars as in the said Bill particularly mentioned and setforth but on the contrary the said labels of these Defendants are signed   G L & Co. and those of the Complainants are signed Jonathan Warren and the harps differ from each other as hereinbefore setforth but these Defendants deny that the words and figures "late Manufacturer to" and "107 Whitechapel Road" are with a view to deceive or impose upon the public or with a view to prevent the same being immediately observed printed only in small characters but these Defendants deny that such labels are engraved in different characters as is customary in most if not all labels used by Blacking makers

And that the greater part of such labels are in the smaller character than the words and figures ("late Manufacturer to" and "10")   Whitechapel Road but with what view in particular the said words and figures were so engraved these Defendants are unable to setforth as to their belief or otherwise but these Defendants deny that with a view of imposing on the public or with any other view or for any reason in particular the words "Jn Warrren" are printed in large letters in these Defendants labels or that the same are printed in the same manner as the same words are printed in the Complainants said labels excepting that in some of the

Complainants said labels the same ornamental letters are used as in the labels of these Defendants

however these Defendants deny that the only other difference between the Complainants said labels so affixed to the said Pots of Paste so sold by them as aforesaid and the said labels so affixed to the said Pots of Paste so made and sold by these Defendants as aforesaid is that at the bottom of the Complainants said labels the words "Jonathan Warren" are printed And at the bottom of each label of these Defendants there are printed the initials "G L & Co" but in what other respect do the same differ these Defendants have hereinbefore setforth

however these Defendants admit that the songs and handbills so circulated by these Defendants do differ only from those so circulated by the Complainants in the second third and fourth last lines thereof And these Defendants say that the said Song was the original composition of this Defendant George Lamert however these Defendants admit that the four last lines are in the words and to the purport and effect in the said Bill mentioned

however these Defendants deny that they have sold to various or any persons the Blacking so manufactured by the Complainants from such pretended Recipe as the Purchasers thereof from the said Jonathan Warren as aforesaid as the Blacking of the said Jonathan Warren or as an Article which they the said Defendants were rightfully and lawfully entitled to sell or dispose of any otherwise than that they have not sold any such Blacking And these Defendants deny that they have so sold the same under a fraudulent representation that this Blacking was the same Blacking as was originally manufactured by the said Jonathan Warren or any otherwise than as aforesaid or that these Defendants did well know the said representations to be untrue or any otherwise than that no such representations were ever made

And this Defendant George Lamert denies and this other Defendant believes such denial to be true that this Defendant George Lamerte did in August One thousand eight hundred and twenty five or at any other time make such application to Mr. Lombard in the said Bill mentioned or any other application but these Defendants say that one of the persons employed by these Defendants to obtain orders did as these Defendants have been informed and believe on behalf of these Defendants at or about the time in the said Bill mentioned apply to the said Mr. Lombard but these Defendants say they do not know and are unable to setforth as to their belief or otherwise whether the said Mr.

148

Lombard had been some time previous thereto a regular Customer to the Complainants but these Defendants say that to the best of their knowledge information and belief they deny that such person asked the said Mr. Lombard whether he wanted any of Jonathan Warren's Blacking or to such or the like or any other purport and effect as aforesaid that such person did as these Defendants have heard and believe represent to the said Mr. Lombard as the fact is that the Blacking of these Defendants was prepared by the late Manufacturer to Jonathan Warren and thereupon shewed to the said Mr. Lombard one of these Defendants Cards and which Cards are except to the prices at the bottom thereof at the bottom in the words following that is to say "The Real Japan Blacking made by the late Manufacturer to Jonathan Warren and sold wholesale at G   Lamerte & Cos. Manufactory Whitechapel Road" but for greater certainty these Defendants crave to refer to one of the said Cards however these Defendants say that the said Mr. Lombard having given an Order for some Blacking the same was sent to him accompanied by an Invoice in the words and figures following that is to say – "London Augt. 3rd 1826 Mr. Lombard Bot. of G Lamerte & Co. Japan Blacking Manufacturers Whitechapel Road 1 doz liquid Blg. @ 12/- 1 .. .. @ 8/- .. 8 - 1 .. @ 4/5 per Cent discount .. 1 .. 0.. 19.. 0 - 14 to the dozen"   but for their greater certainty these Defendants crave to refer to the said Invoice   And these Defendants submit and insist that the said Card as well as the said Invoice on the face of it disclosed to the said Mr. Lombard that he was not buying the Blacking of the Complainants and that if the said Mr. Lombard had been such regular Customer of the Complainants as represented by the said Bill he must have known that their Warehouse was in Noble Street and not in Whitechapel Road   And that he was dealing with a totally different ffirm And these Defendants to the best of their knowledge information and belief deny that the said William Lombard was in any respect deceived or that he believed the said Defendant George Lamert had proper authority to sell the Blacking in the said Bill in that behalf mentioned or that the said Mr. Lombard did observe that the Blacking was not brought by the same Carman that brought the Goods sold by the Complainants said House or that he did ask why the Complainants had changed or that the said Carman did reply that the Carman who usually brought the Blacking was ill and unable to attend his Business or any otherwise than that no such inquiry was made and no such answer given or that any Conversation did take place between the said Mr. Lombard and the said Carman to such or the like or any other effect but these Defendants say they do not know and are unable to setforth as to their belief or otherwise whether the complainants said Carman who usually brought the said Blacking was ill at the time so alledged as last mentioned or how

otherwise but these Defendants to the best of their knowledge information and belief deny that he was only represented so to be in order to further the fraudulent plan of these Defendants in selling the aforesaid Blacking of Jonathan Warren any otherwise than that no such representation was made and that no such fraudulent plan existed
and these Defendants submit and insist that they ought not to be restrained as sought and prayed by the said Bill of Complaint And these Defendants submit and insist that the Complainants have no right to appropriate the name of the said Jonathan Warren to the Blacking manufactured by them even if they could prove (which these Defendants do not believe) that such Blacking was manufactured according to a receipt of the said Jonathan Warren

And that these Defendants are well justified in the use of the labels handbills and songs used and circulated by them And that the same are not colorable imitation of the labels handbills and songs of the Complainants but are in substance and effect different And that if the contrary were the case (which these Defendants deny) then these Defendants submit and insist that the labels and handbills of the Complainants having been originally colorable imitations of the labels and handbills of the said Robert Warren and intended to defraud the said Robert Warren and impose upon the Public the Complainants are not entitled to the aid or assistance of this Honorable Court,

Without this that there is any other matter cause or thing in the said Complainants said Bill of Complaint contained material or effectual in the law for these Defendants to make answer unto and not herein and hereby well and sufficiently answered avoided traversed or denied is true to the knowledge and belief of these Defendants All which matters and things these Defendants are ready and willing to aver maintain and prove as this Honorable Court shall direct and humbly pray to be hence dismissed with their reasonable costs and charges in the Law in this behalf most wrongfully sustained./ Geo Lamerte   Lewis Worms

Sworn by both the Defendants at the Public Office Southampton Buildings in the County of Middlesex this 22nd day of November 1826 Before me W Wingfield

Chapter Eight

Affidavits in the case of Warren v Lamerte

These documents are held at The National Archives at Kew in London, catalogued at reference C 31/448. They are contained in a box with affidavits from a great many other cases, all relating to the Michaelmas Term 1827, and dealing with Complainants whose names begin with the letters I-Z. Within the box they are maintained in first-letter order, but not all documents relating to the case of Warren v Lamerte are kept together. The Affidavits were written by officers of the Court and signed by the witnesses. Paper about the size of A5 was used. I have arranged the transcripts that follow here in chronological order of the date they were originally written.

1 Robert Warren and Benjamin Warren, blacking manufacturers
2 James Harnett, solicitor for Robert and Benjamin Warren
3 Thomas Harrison, labourer
4 John Harrison, foreman, George Lamert's blacking warehouse
5 John Henderson, traveller for Robert Warren's Blacking
6 Richard Latham, William Neall, Daniel Jiggens, and Edward
    Selth, employees of George Lamerte
7 Thomas Quarmby, commission agent for George Lamerte
8 Sarah Scott, servant to George Lamerte
9 James Smith, printer to Jonathan Warren
10 John Wood, clicker, Hungerford Market
11 Henry Walker, gentleman, friend to George Lamerte
12 William Glindon, printer to William Edward Woodd
13 Samuel Mann, rent collector for Hungerford estate
14 George Lamerte, blacking manufacturer
15 George Lamerte, blacking manufacturer
16 John Thomas Lamerte, brother to George and traveller for his
    business
17 James Phillipps, custom house agent and lighterman, Little
    Hungerford Street
18 Samuel Mann, rent collector for Hungerford estate
19 William Dixon, clerk to solicitor for George Lamerte
20 George Whitehead and his wife Ann, grocer and cheesemonger

[1. The affidavit of Robert Warren and Benjamin Warren]
In Chancery Between Robert Warren and Benjamin Warren,
plaintiffs and George Lamerte, Defendant

Robert Warren and Benjamin Warren both of No. 30 the Strand in the County of Middlesex Blacking Manufacturers the Plaintiffs in this Cause severally and respectively make oath and say And First this Deponent the said Robert Warren for himself saith that in or about the year One thousand eight hundred and five he commenced the trade or business of a Blacking Manufacturer and that for the purpose of raising and establishing such business he was in the habit of advertising in the Public Newspapers and circulating placards and hand bills. And of travelling and sending other persons to travel for him to most parts of England for the purpose of procuring Customers for the Article so manufactured by him. And that by means of the industry of this Deponent he succeeded in establishing a very large and extensive business having Customers in most towns in England and that he carried on his Business in Saint Martins Lane in the said County of Middlesex from the said year One thousand eight hundred and five until about the year One thousand eight hundred and sixteen when he removed to No. 30 in the Strand aforesaid where he carried on his said Business alone until the year One thousand eight hundred and twenty two And Deponent also saith that in the said year One thousand eight hundred and twenty two he took into Partnership his Brother Benjamin Warren and that Deponent and his said Brother have ever since carried on and do still carry on the said trade or business in Copartnership together at No.30 in the Strand aforesaid And both these Deponents say that as the said Business had been established in the name of Robert Warren alone the Deponents did not like to change the name or style under which the same was established and that such Business has therefore notwithstanding such Copartnership been carried on and is still carried on in the name of Robert Warren alone and that for the purpose of keeping up and carrying on such extensive Business as aforesaid they have continued and still are in the habit of circulating such Placards and hand bills or labels as aforesaid and also of sending Travellers to receive Orders from their Customers residing in the different parts of England – that the Article so manufactured by them as aforesaid is sold by them in bottles and also in boxes or jars and that Deponents with the view of distinguishing the Article so sold by them from that sold by others in the same trade or business with Deponents Deponents have been in the habit of pasting or affixing one of such hand bills or labels as aforesaid on each of such bottles and boxes or jars And these Deponents say that the above named Defendant George Lamerte now of 56 Mansell Street Goodmans fields near the Minories in the County of Middlesex has for some time past also carried on the trade or business of a Blacking Manufacturer and that about two years ago Deponents believe he began to travel abut the Country with the view of procuring orders for his Blacking but that not having acquired a name or reputation as a Manufacturer of Blacking he met with little or no encouragement that the said George Lamerte (as deponents have been lately informed and believe) for the purpose of procuring a sale of his Blacking began both by himself and also by means of travellers or Agents employed by him for that purpose falsely and to the great loss and injury of Deponents to represent to the Customers of Deponents and to the public in general that his the said Defendant's house or business was a branch or part of the house or business of Deponent Robert Warren No. 30 Strand (meaning Deponents house or business) and that their style or firm was George Lamerte Jonathan Warren & Co. and that their warehouse for the shipping and sending of Goods was No. 30 Hungerford Stairs Strand and that the said Defendant and his Travellers or Agents accordingly solicited and obtained orders for Blacking as and for the house of the Deponent Robert Warren of the Strand Deponents said house or firm being thereby meant and intended or understood for Deponents say that the article so manufactured by them was at that time well known by the description of "the Blacking of Warren of the Strand" and that Deponents Said house or firm was in fact at that time and is now the only house of that name carrying on such trade or business as aforesaid in the Strand And these Deponents also say that to aid and assist such fraudulent representations as aforesaid the said Defendant also caused to be printed and circulated placard and hand bills or labels in imitation of and similar to those of Deponents and that he also pasted or caused as Deponents believe one of such hand Bills or labels to be pasted on each of the Bottles and Boxes of Jars containing the Blacking so as aforesaid manufactured by him in order the more easily to pass off and sell the same to the Customers of Deponents and the public in general as and for the article so manufactured by Deponents and that by such false and fraudulent representations and contrivances of the said Defendant George Lamerte as aforesaid many persons both customers of these deponents and others who intended and were as Deponents believe desirous of purchasing Deponents Blacking have been led to purchase and have actually purchased the article so manufactured by the said Defendants conceiving as Deponents verily believe that they were purchasing the Blacking manufactured by Deponents and that by means thereof the said Defendant hath been enabled to sell and hath actually sold and does still sell a very great quantity of his Blacking and to a very large amount in value as and for the article so as aforesaid manufactured by these Deponents and that Deponents have thereby sustained great loss and injury in their said trade or business and this Deponent the said Robert Warren for himself further saith that some time since he met a person who he believes was the Brother of the said Defendant being then travelling through Exeter in Devonshire soliciting and taking Orders as aforesaid and this Deponent the said Robert Warren then remonstrated with him upon the impropriety of his conduct in representing to Deponents Customers and others that he was selling and taking Orders for the house of this Deponent when in fact he was not authorised so to do but the said person accused himself by saying that he was only a Traveller and that if Deponent had any complaint to make he must apply to his employers thereby meaning the said Defendant   And both these Deponents also say that they have been informed and verily believe that there is no such person as Jonathan warren or any other person in partnership with the said Defendant and that the name of Jonathan Warren is fictitious and merely assumed for the purpose of imposing upon the Customers of these Deponents and upon the public in general and to lead them to believe that the said Defendant's house of Business is a branch of or connected with the house of Business of those Deponents and thereby enable the said Defendant to sell and dispose of his Blacking as and for the Article so manufactured as aforesaid by these Deponents   And these Deponents also say that their house and premises in which they carry on their said trade or business is situate and being No 30 in the Strand and is in fact not far distant from Hungerford Stairs Strand aforesaid and that the said No. 30 being the number of their said house and premises is printed on their said placards and bills or labels in very large and conspicuous Characters and that the said Defendant has also caused the said No 30 to be printed on his said placards and Bills or labels in characters of the same size and appearance as those in which such Number is printed in Deponents said placards and Bills or labels and that the said Defendant has selected that Number in consequence of such being the number of Deponents said house and premises and that he has selected the address of Hungerford Stairs Strand on account of its vicinity to Deponents said house and premises in the Strand with the view of aiding and assisting his said false and fraudulent representations and contrivances and inducing the public the more easily to believe that the article so sold by the said Defendant is in fact the article so as aforesaid manufactured and sold by the Deponents for these Deponents say that their said house or firm has been for years known by the name and description of Robert Warren of No. 30 Strand and that the said Defendant has in fact no House or place for Business belonging to - - - - - - - or occupied by him at No. 30 Hungerford Stairs Strand nor ever had   And these Deponents also say that the placards and Bills or labels so printed and circulated by the said Defendant if not precisely similar to those printed and circulated by Deponents they are nevertheless a very close imitation of them and that the said Defendant contrived and caused the same to be printed solely for the purpose of enabling him by reason of their very great similarity to those of Deponents to sell and dispose of his Blacking as and for Deponents Blacking and that many persons who were desirous of purchasing Deponents Blacking have been deceived or misled by them and have actually purchased the Blacking of the said Defendant intending to purchase and conceiving they were purchasing Deponents Blacking   And these Deponents also say that on the sixth day of November instant they received a letter from Thomas Brough one of Deponents travellers dated the fourth day of November instant then being at Merthyr in Wales travelling to take orders for these Deponents in the way of Deponents said Business and in which Letter is contained a passage and which passage these Deponents believe to be true to the effect that the Brother of the above named Defendant had arrived there and was selling Blacking under the name of Jonathan Warren and representing that he was one of the Family (meaning as Deponents believe the family of Deponents) and was doing Deponents a very great deal of injury on that Journey which embraces the west of England and South Wales   And these Deponents also further say that they have been informed and verily believe the same to be true that several persons have been imposed upon and prevailed upon to give Orders for Blacking to the Agents or Travellers of the said Defendant conceiving that they were giving orders for Blacking to the Agents or Travellers of these Deponents and that when the said Defendant had furnished his said Blacking the imposition was detected and some persons had returned the same back to the said Defendant although many persons had been induced to keep the said the said Goods of the Defendant as they were taken in – many persons having an apathy or objection to the trouble of sending the Defendants Goods back which must in such cases have been done at their own expence and which in many instances would actually amount to more than the value of the Blacking.   And these Deponents lastly say that by Reason of the daily frauds practised by the said Defendant and his Travellers and Servants upon these Deponents as hereinbefore more fully detailed these Deponents have sustained and are daily sustaining very Considerable loss and are injured in their good name and credit as Blacking Manufacturers by such doings

Robert Warren [signature]   Benjamin Warren [signature]

Sworn respectively by the Deponents Robert Warren and Benjamin Warren at the public office Southampton Buildings Chancery Lane London this 12th day of November 1827 before me

R H Eden [signature]

[2. The affidavit of James Harnett]
In Chancery   Between Robert Warren and Benjamin Warren, Plaintiffs and George Lamerte, Defendant

James Harnett of Northumberland Street Strand in the County of Middlesex Gentleman the Solicitor for the above named Plaintiffs in this Cause Maketh Oath and saith that he this Deponant did on the tenth day of November instant personally serve the above named Defendant George Lamerte with a Subpoena issued out of and under the Seal of this Honorable Court by delivering the said Subpoena to and leaving the body of the said Subpoena so under Seal as aforesaid with them at his House or residence No 56 Mansell Street Goodmans Fields in the said County of Middlesex by which said Subpoena the said Defendant was directed to appear in this Honorable Court on the twelfth day of November instant at the suit of the said Plaintiffs in this Cause as appeared to this Deponent by the said Subpoena

James Harnett [signature]

Sworn at the Public Office Southampton Buildings Chancery Lane this 12th day of November 1827 before me

R H Eden [signature]

[3. The affidavit of Thomas Harrison]
In Chancery   Between Robert Warren and Benjamin Warren, Plaintiffs and George Lamerte, Defendant

Thomas Harrison of No 42 Castle Street Leicester Square in the County of Middlesex Labourer – maketh oath and saith that on Saturday the tenth day of November instant this Deponent went to the house or shop of the above named Defendant George Lamerte situate at No 56 Mansell Street Goodmans fields in the County of Middlesex where he saw the said Defendant and asked him for six bottles of Warrens Blacking – that the said Defendant gave this Deponent six Bottles of Blacking with the labels pasted thereon respectively marked A.B.C.D.E. F. now produced and shewn to this Deponent and that this deponent paid him four shillings for them and at the same time again asked the said Defendant if this (meaning the said six bottles of Blacking then in his hands) was Warrens Blacking in answer to which the said Defendant replied yes it is Warrens Blacking and again added it is the Original Warrens Blacking   And this Deponent also saith that there appeared many hundred bottles of Blacking similarly labelled in the said Defendants shop exposed for sale   And this Deponent also saith that on the comparing the labels or placards on the said Bottles of Blacking so sold by the said Defendant to this Deponent with the labels or placards used upon the Bottles of Blacking usually sold by the above named plaintiffs this Deponent conceives and believes that the labels of the said

Defendants were made expressly to imitate the labels or placards of the said plaintiffs for the purpose of deceit   And this Deponent also saith that the six bottles of blacking with the labels or placards thereon pasted and respectively marked No1   No2   No3   No4   No5   No6 are bottles containing blacking manufactured by the plaintiffs and that the labels pasted upon the said bottles respectively are the plaintiffs labels and the same as those usually sold by them in the way of their aforesaid trade or business

Thomas Harrison [signature]

Sworn at the public office southampton Buildings Chancery Lane London this 12th. day of November 1827 before me

R H Eden [signature]

[4. The affidavit of John Harrison]
In Chancery   Between Robert Warren and Benjamin Warren, Plaintiffs and George Lamerte, Defendant

John Harrison of No 42 Castle Street Leicester Square in the County of Middlesex late fforeman in the employment of the above named Defendant George Lamerte at No 56 Mansell Street Goodmans fields near the Minories in the said County Blacking Manufacturer Maketh oath and saith that he hath seen several of the placards and hand bills or labels printed and circulated upon the Bottles of Blacking sold by the said Defendant that such placards labels or hand bills were made by the said Defendant similar and to represent the placards and hand bills or labels printed and circulated by the above named plaintiffs upon their bottles of blacking with a view of inducing many of the Customers of the above named plaintiffs and the public in general to believe that the blacking sold by the said Defendant was a branch of the Blacking and formed part of the Blacking manufactured by or under the name of the plaintiff Robert Warren of No 30 Strand and that this Deponent of his own knowledge knows that the No 30 and the general appearance of the labels upon the said Defendants' Bottles of Blacking were expressly put on to deceive the customers of the said plaintiffs and to induce them and the public in general to believe that the Blacking manufactured and sold by the said Defendant was in fact manufactured by Jonathan Warren and that Jonathan Warren's was a branch or part of the house or business of Robert Warren   And this Deponent also saith that the said George Lamerte has no partner and that the name of Jonathan Warren is fictitious and put on solely to deceive   And this deponent also saith that during the time he was in the employment of the said defendant as such foreman as aforesaid the travellers sent out by the said defendant to take orders for "Warrens Blacking" as the said defendant then and as deponent believes still calls it had frequently received orders for goods to

157

be delivered that is to say "Warrens Blacking" and that such goods so ordered as "Warrens Blacking" had been sent out and delivered and that many persons had afterwards returned it to the said defendant on finding that they were deceived in the Blacking so sent out and delivered not being Warrens Blacking of No 30 Strand although deponent in most instances knows that persons similarly imposed upon had kept the Blacking and paid for it rather than have the trouble of sending it back to the said defendant   And this deponent further saith that in the presence and hearing of this deponent several persons had made complaints to the said Defendant of the imposition so practised by him and his travellers upon them and gave him orders not to send them any more of his Blacking   And this Deponent saith that when some of such Blacking had been so returned to the said defendant for not being "Warrens Blacking" meaning the Blacking manufactured by the said plaintiffs this deponent heard the said defendant ask why the parties had returned and being answered because it was not Robert Warrens blacking of the Strand he shook his head and appeared disappointed And this deponent also has known the Defendants carter bring back several quantities of blacking ordered in the same way and returned for the same reasons

John Harrison [signature]

Sworn at the public office Southampton Buildings Chancery Lane in the County of Middlesex this 12th day of November 1827 before me

R H Eden [signature]

[5. The affidavit of John Henderson]

In Chancery   Between Robbert Warren and Benjamin Warren, Plaintiffs and George Lamerte, Defendant

John Henderson of Camden Town in the County of Middlesex one of the Travellers employed by the above named Plaintiffs in the way of their Trade of Blacking Manufacturers and Alice Hall of No 5 Junction Place Kentish Town in the said County of Middlesex Spinster severally and respectively make oath and say – and first this Deponent Alice Hall for herself saith that this Deponent hath been in the habit of dealing with the above named Plaintiffs for Blacking between one and two years now last past under the name of Robert Warren and that on or about the Ninth day of June now last past a person called upon this Deponent and pretended that he was one of Mr Warrens Travellers meaning as Deponent then believed the above named Plaintiff Robert Warren and asked this Deponent whether she wanted any Blacking and this Deponent being in want of a Dozen Bottles of Blacking and believing that the person so calling upon Deponent and soliciting orders for Warrens Blacking had applied from the House of the above named

Plaintiffs No. 30 Strand with whom this Deponent was then in the habit of dealing for Blacking this Deponent gave the person so calling upon her an order for one dozen of small Bottles of Blacking and that shortly after a person called and left with this Deponent Thirteen small bottles of Blacking as and for a Dozen and for which this Deponent paid him Four shillings the person who brought the said Blacking to this Deponent pulled out a number of receipts and asked Deponent where several Persons whom he named and who resided in Deponents neighbourhood lived apparently with a view of delivering them Blacking that this Deponent was surprised at the question because being in the Habit of coming so often from the said Plaintiffs House with Blacking (as Deponent thought) he ought to have known better than Deponent where the parties for whom he enquired resided this Deponent became suspicious and asked him whether he had not brought Warrens Blacking meaning the Plaintiffs Blacking to which the Deponents Carter replied Yes I have brought it from Warrens and was told to bring it here and I know no more about it that Deponents Nephew George Hall was standing by Deponent in her shop at the time and hearing the conversation between Deponent and the said Defendants Carter the said George Hall remarked to Deponent the Blacking is not right Aunt it is Jonathan Warren on the Bottles that Deponent then said to the Carter it is a mistake altogether I have never ordered any Blacking from you where did you bring it from in reply to which he said from Warrens I said it is wrong I never ordered any in this name and wished the man to take it back and return Deponents money but he went away directly got into his Cart and drove off which astonished and annoyed this deponent very much at the time and this deponent lastly saith that when the man put down the blacking in the first instance on Deponents Counter the resemblance of the Placards upon the bottles and the No 30 was so close an imitation that Deponent felt no hesitation in paying the money for it conceiving that she was buying the Plaintiffs Blacking and not the Defendants   And this Deponent the said John Henderson for himself saith that a few days afterwards he called upon the said Deponent Alice Hall who informed Deponent of the fraud so practised upon her by said Defendant George Lamert or his Agents that he looked at the bottles containing the blacking so sold to her and that the same was the Defendants Blacking   And that this Deponent in the Course of his travelling to take orders for the above named Plaintiffs in the way of their trade or business of Blacking Manufacturers has discovered many frauds practised by the said Defendant or his Travellers of a similar description to that Practised upon the other Deponent Alice Hall and that the labels pasted upon the bottles of Blacking which the Defendant is in the daily habit of selling are in imitation of the Plaintiffs labels upon their bottles of Blacking and done solely with a view of imposing upon the Plaintiffs Customers and the Public in General and to enable the said Defendant to sell his Blacking as and for Warrens Blacking to the great injury and loss of the said Plaintiffs

Alice Hall [signature]

John Henderson [signature]

Sworn respectively by the Deponents John Henderson and Alice Hall at the public Office Southampton Buildings Chancery Lane London this 12th day of November 1827. before me –

R H Eden [signature]

[6. The affidavit of Richard Latham, William Neall, Daniel Jiggens and Edward Seth]

In Chancery   Between Robert Warren and Benjamin Warren, Plaintiffs and George Lamerte, defendant

Richard Latham of 28 Weston Street Somers Town in the County of Middlesex Labourer William Neall of No 28 Bakers Row Whitechapel Road in the said County labourer Daniel Jiggens of No 3 Peacock Court Minories in the County of Middlesex And Edward Selth of 44 Cannon Street Road in the said County of Middlesex labourer severally make oath and say and first this deponent Richard Latham for himself saith that this deponent was in the employ of the said defendant And Lewis Worms as Blacking makers for the Space of about three months and down to the dissolution of their partnership on the thirty first day of August last and that from such last mentioned day to the present time this deponent has been foreman to the said defendant   And the said deponent William Neall for himself saith that he entered the Service of the said defendant and Lewis Worms on the third day of June last and has continued in the Employ of the said defendant to the present time And the said deponent Daniel Jiggens for himself saith that he entered the service of the said defendant in September last and has continued in his Employ to the present time   And the said deponent Edward Selth saith that he entered the Service of the said defendant and Lewis Worms on the seventh day of May last And has continued in the employ of the Said defendant to the present time and all these deponents Severally say that each of these deponents has Sold and delivered the Blacking made by the said defendant and Lewis Worms and by the said defendant since the dissolution of the said Copartnership to various Customers applying for the same   And they have also respectively taken out and delivered large quantities thereof and each of these deponents Speaking for himself saith that he has in no instance nor did the said defendant and Lewis Worms during their partnership or the said defendant since the termination thereof to each of these deponents knowledge and belief represent or Cause it to be represented to any person or persons whomsoever that the said Defendant, or that the said Defendant and his late partner were in any manner whatsoever either directly or indirectly connected in Trade or otherwise with any person or persons carrying on the Trade or business of Blacking Manufacturers at No. 30 Strand or that the said Defendant or the said Defendant and his late Partner sold the Blacking manufactured by the said Plaintiff Robert Warren Individually or by the said Robert Warren and Benjamin Warren as Copartners, and each of these Deponents further saith that during the said partnership all goods to the best of their knowledge and belief were sold publicly avowedly and ostensibly as the manufacture of the said Defendant only or of the said Defendant and Lewis Worms as Partners And this Deponent Edward Selth for himself saith that on Thursday the eleventh day of October last about one o'Clock in the Afternoon being the time when the men were going to Dinner this Deponent saw John Harrison of N. 42 Castle Street Leicester Square in in the County of Middlesex then in the employment of the said Defendant take a pot of blacking from the Defendants shop secrete it in his hat and carry the same away with him that as soon as this Deponent had what he considered a favourable opportunity viz on the Friday following he communicated the circumstance to the said Defendant – who thereupon discharged him the said John Harrison from his Service, that the said John Harrison afterwards summoned the said Defendant for wages and attended such Summons and the said Defendant this Deponent and William Neall attended but upon these parties making their appearance the said John Harrison left the place and abandoned his Summons And this Deponent verily believes that he was actuated in doing so by the fear of Public exposure and this Deponent the said William Neal for himself saith that he attended the last mentioned Summons that he saw the said John Harrison in the Office and that he verily believes that the said John Harrison left the Office and abandoned the Summons from the apprehension of being publicly exposed as above mentioned

Rd Latham [signature]
Wm Neall [signature]
E Selth [signature]
D Jiggins [signature]
Sworn by the Deponents Richard Latham William Neall Daniel Jiggens and Edward Selth at the Public Office Southampton Buildings in the County of Middlesex this fifteenth day of November 1827 before me
Jam: C: Cox [signature]

[7. The affidavit of Thomas Quarmby]
In Chancery   Between Robert Warren and Benjamin Warren,
Plaintiffs and George Lamerte, Defendant

Thomas Quarmby of No 8 Langdale Street Cannon Street Road in the County of Middlesex Commission Agent maketh oath and saith that in and prior to the year One thousand eight hundred and twenty two this Deponent was upon terms of intimacy with Jonathan Warren whom this Deponent believes was the original Inventor of the Blacking which has ever since been sold under his name and who at the time before alluded to carried on his business of a Blacking maker and had his Manufactory at No 30 Hungerford Stairs Strand   That in or about the month of September One thousand eight hundred and twenty two the said Jonathan Warren sold and disposed of his trade and business with the permission to use the name of the said Jonathan Warren in conducting the same as this Deponent has been informed and verily believes to William Edward Woodd who for some time conducted the said trade or business at No. 30 Hungerford Stairs aforesaid in the name of the said Jonathan Warren and was aided and assisted in the Manufacture of his Blacking by the said Jonathan Warren personally   And this Deponent further saith that by the recommendation of the said Jonathan Warren this Deponent was taken into the Service and employ of the said William Edward Woodd as a Town Traveller in vending the said Article in the name of the said Jonathan Warren as aforesaid   That about the same time the above named Defendant George Lamerte was also taken into the service and employ of the said William Edward Woodd and had the principal management of the Business as well in the Manufactory as in the Counting house   And this Deponent saith that he has repeatedly seen and been present when the said Defendant and the said Jonathan Warren were engaged together in Manufacturing large quantities of Blacking and the said Defendant was learning from the said Jonathan Warren his method and art of making that article and he this Deponent saith that he continued so engaged for the space of between one and two years and that during that time the said Defendant became well known to all the Customers of the said William Edward Woodd whilst so trading under the name of the said Jonathan Warren as aforesaid   And this Deponent further saith that the above named Defendant commenced his Business as a Blacking maker in Copartnership with one Lewis Worms about January One thousand eight hundred and twenty five having their Manufactory in Whitechapel Road and that the said Copartnership was dissolved on the thirty first day of August last since which time the said Business has been conducted and carried on by the said Defendant individually on his own account at No. 56 Mansell Street Goodmans fields   That in the year One thousand eight hundred and

162

twenty five this Deponent was employed by the said Defendant and Lewis Worms to sell for them on Commission in London and its vicinity the Blacking Manufactured by them and that since the dissolution of the Partnership he has carried on the business for the said Defendant in like manner   And this Deponent further saith that the said Jonathan Warren for a considerable time prior and up to the time of his leaving off business and the said William Edward Woodd after he purchased the business of the said Jonathan Warren and down to the present time each of them used labels containing the No. 30 printed in large characters in the centre of their Labels which were pasted on their bottles of Blacking And this Deponent saith that the said Defendant and Lewis Worms used on their first commencement of business the Label No 1 the Card No 2 and the Invoice No 3 now produced and shewn to this Deponent   And this Deponent saith that early in the month of January of the present year the said Defendant and Lewis Worms altered their Labels and adopted two others No 4 and 5 now produced and shewn to this Deponent and since the Dissolution of the said partnership the said Defendant has used the Labels No. 6 and 7   The Invoice No. 8 and 9 the Card No. 10 the direction Card No. 11 and the Shop placard No 12 now respectively produced and shewn to this Deponent   And this Deponent saith that he has sold for the said Defendant and Lewis Worms during their partnership and for the said Defendant since the dissolution of their partnership a very considerable quantity of blacking manufactured by them and that he has in the course of their business distributed several hundreds of the Cards before mentioned as Numbered respectively 2 and 10   And this Deponent further saith that in all instances as this Deponent verily believes in which Bills of parcels have been delivered for Goods sold by him on the account aforesaid such Bills of parcels have been written upon one or other of the Invoices before mentioned as numbered 3. 8 and 9   And this Deponent further saith that in soliciting custom for his Employers he never in any manner either directly or indirectly induced or attempted to induce the persons with whom he was dealing to believe that the persons for whom he was employed were in any manner connected with the said Plaintiff or either of them but on the contrary this Deponent invariably stated to such persons that the Blacking which he was vending was precisely similar to that which had been made and sold by Jonathan Warren the original Inventor at No. 30 Hungerford Stairs Strand and that if this Deponent had used any such deception it would have been immediately detected by a perusal of any of the Labels Cards placards and Invoices hereinbefore referred to   And this Deponent Saith that about two or three years ago Messieurs Day and Martin Blacking makers altered the Ground of their Labels to a reddish Colour that soon after the said Plaintiff Robert

163

Warren altered his to a somewhat similar colour and that about twelve months since the said Defendant and Lewis Worms altered the Ground of their labels also to a similar colour or nearly so   And this Deponent further saith that the Labels now in use by the said Deft differ in almost every particular from those in use by the said Plaintiffs or the said Plaintiff Robert Warren   And this Deponent further saith that at the time when he first entered the service of the said William Edward Woodd in manner as hereinbefore mentioned the said Jonathan Warren made an affidavit before the then Lord Mayor that he was the sole inventor of Warrens Blacking and the said Jonathan Warren delivered the said Affidavit to this Deponent for the purpose of being shewn to the various customers but such Affidavit has been lost

Thomas Quarmby [signature]

Sworn at the Public Office Southampton Buildings Chancery Lane in the County of Middlesex this fifteenth day of November 1827 before me Jam: C: Cox [signature]

[8. The affidavit of Sarah Scott]
In Chancery   Between Robert Warren and Benjamin Warren, Plaintiffs and George Lamerte, Defendant

Sarah Scott of No. 56 Mansell Street Goodmans Fields in the County of Middlesex Widow Servant to the above named Defendant maketh Oath and Saith that on Saturday the tenth day of November instant a Man whom this Deponent believes to be Thomas Harrison of No. 42 Castle Street Leicester Square in the County of Middlesex Labourer came to her Masters Shop in Mansell Street aforesaid and asked this Deponent for six one Shilling Bottles of Blacking   at this Time this Deponent was alone in the Shop and the said Defendant was up stairs and the Shilling Bottles being upon a high stack in her Masters the Defendants Shop which she could not conveniently reach she called the Defendant down Stairs   he reached the Bottles and handed them to the Customer who paid the wholesale price for them four shillings   this Deponent remained in the Shop and the Man asked the Defendant if those Bottles were Warrens Blacking to which the Defendant replied they were made by the late Manufacturer to Jonathan Warren who was then Dead   the Man then asked the Defendant whether it was the same as Warrens in the Strand to which the Defendant replied no it was made by him the Defendant and and that he the Defendant had been Manufacturer to the late Jonathan Warren he then said he wanted to sent it to the Country and asked the Defendant for a Shop placard and the Defendant gave him one similar to the placard marked A now produced and shewn to this Deponent and the said Man thereupon went away   And this Deponent saith she took no other order for six one shilling Bottles of Blacking on

164

that day   And this Deponent further Saith that she has occasionally
lodged with the Mother of Edward Selth the Defendants Shop Boy
which induced the said Edward Selth to place Confidence in this
Deponent and the said Edward Selth informed this Deponent that John
Harrison one of the Defendants then was in the habit of Robbing his
Employer and that he had seen him put a pot of Blacking in his Hat and
carry it away with him privately whereupon this Deponent strongly urged
the said Edward Seth to inform his Master the Defendant thereof as it
was his bounden Duty to do and the said Edward Selth followed her
Advice and Recommendation and imparted the Circumstance to the
Defendant who thereupon discharged the said John Harrison from his
Service
Sarah Scott [signature]
Sworn at the Public Office Southampton Buildings in the County of
Middlesex this sixteenth day of November 1827before me
Jns Stephen [signature]

[9. The affidavit of James Smith]
**In Chancery   Between Robert Warren and Benjamin Warren,
Plaintiffs and George Lamerte, Defendant**
James Smith of number sixteen Saint Martins Lane in the City of
Westminster printer maketh Oath and Saith that in the year one
thousand eight hundred and twenty two he first became acquainted with
Jonathan Warren late of number thirty Hungerford Stairs Strand
Blacking maker deceased that the said Jonathan Warren has many times
stated to this deponent and in his hearing that he was the sole inventor
of Warrens Japan Blacking and he has also told this deponent that he
had deposed to that Fact before the Lord Mayor and all which
information this deponent believes to be true.   And this deponent saith
he has seen many placards of Warrens Blacking with the copy of a
Deposition thereon purporting to have been sworn by the said Jonathan
Warren and which this deponent believes was a copy of the affidavit
before referred to.   And this deponent saith that in the said year one
thousand eight hundred and twenty two he was privy to and well knew
that the said Jonathan Warren sold the Goodwill of his Trade as a
Blacking maker to William Edward Woodd and this deponent did
business in the way of his trade for the said Jonathan Warren before he
relinquished the trade and for the said William Edward Woodd after he
purchased the said trade   And this deponent saith that after the said sale
and purchase the said William Edward Woodd carried on and conducted
the said business of a blacking Maker in the name of Jonathan Warren at
number thirty Hungerford Stairs Strand in the same manner as the said
Jonathan Warren had previously done and this deponent has seen the

said Jonathan Warren manufacturing Blacking for the said William Edward Woodd and that after the death of the said Jonathan Warren the said defendant manufactured Blacking for the said William Edward Woodd in like manner   And this deponent further saith that as well before as subsequently to the decease of the said Jonathan Warren his deponent has seen the placard now produced and shewn to this deponent marked G and that similar placards were to this deponents knowledge exhibited in various Shops in London   And this Deponent further saith that John Harrison a Person lately in the employ of the said defendant on Saturday the seventeenth day of November instant called upon this deponent and enquired when this deponent had seen the defendant – he then alluded to the Chancery suit instituted by the plaintiffs against the defendant and he communicated to this Deponent that a charge had been fabricated against him by the defendant to his injury of stealing Blacking and that he had given the defendant a helping hand adding that he was a damned mean Fellow that he the Communicant knew a few things about the defendant of which he should have the full Benefit as he the Informant was determined to use every means to obtain Revenge or to that or the like effect.

James Smith [signature]
Sworn at the public office Southampton Buildings in the County of Middlesex This nineteenth day of November 1827 before me
H Cross [signature]

[10. The affidavit of John Wood]
In Chancery   Between Robert Warren and Benjamin Warren, Plaintiffs and George Lamerte, Defendant
John Wood of Hungerford Market in the City of Westminster Clicker maketh oath and saith that prior to Michaelmas last this Deponent hired the House he now resides in at Hungerford Market his Tenancy to commence from Michaelmas last that on the Front next the River was written or painted in very large and legible Characters in Black upon a White Ground "Warrens 30 Blacking Warehouse"   And this Deponent saith that the said Figures and words so being on the River Front of this Deponents House Mr. Harnett of Northumberland Street Solicitor called upon this Deponent twice and asked this Deponent if he would give his consent to have the said words and figures obliterated because if he refused it would occasion him a great deal of Trouble   That this Deponent assented provided he was put to no expence about it and in a few days afterwards that is in the last week the Plaintiffs men came and effaced the said Words and Figures so as that they are now scarcely legible unless the person desirous of reading them knew what had been scratched out   And this Deponent saith that the front of the said House

166

next the Street had borne a Number and that very lately some person without his knowledge or consent obliterated such number and has painted the No 6 upon his said Door in lieu thereof And this Deponent saith that on the morning the words and figures were obliterated as before described the said Plaintiff Robert Warren came down before his Men and inspected the said words and figures

John Wood [signature]

Sworn at the Public Office Southampton Buildings Chancery Lane in the County of Middlesex this nineteenth day of November 1827 Before me

H Cross [signature]

[11. The affidavit of Henry Walker]

In Chancery   Between Robert Warren and Benjamin Warren, Plaintiffs and George Lamerte, Defendant

Henry Walker of Ranelagh Grove Pimlico in the County of Middlesex Gentleman maketh Oath and Saith That he has been intimately acquainted with the above named Defendant for the space of ten years and upwards last past that the he well remembers the said Defendant being engaged as a Clerk to his Brother in Law William Edward Woodd and that he was informed at that Time by the Said Defendant and believes that the said William Edward Woodd had purchased the Business of a Blacking Manufacturer from Jonathan Warren and was carrying on the same in the Name of the said Jonathan Warren at No. 30 Hungerford Stairs Strand and Deponent Saith he very frequently called upon the said Defendant at that place and there became acquainted with the Jonathan Warren named in the Defendants Blacking Labels and he frequently held Conversations with the said Jonathan Warren and that upon one of those occasions he well Remembers having seen the said Defendant and Jonathan Warren engaged together in the actual Manufacture of Blacking and he understood and believed and still believes that the said Jonathan Warren taught and instructed the said Defendant in his art of making Blacking And this Deponent further Saith that after the Decease of the said Jonathan Warren and during his further continuance in the employ of the said William Edward Woodd the said Defendant was the sole manufacturer of the Blacking vended by the said William Edward Woodd as Jonathan Warrens Original Blacking And this Deponent further Saith that he has frequently heard the said Jonathan Warren say and this Deponent believed it to be true that he the said Jonathan Warren was the sole Inventor of the Blacking which for many years past has been known by the appellation of Jonathan Warren's Blacking And this Deponent Saith that at the Time he went to No. 30 Hungerford Stairs in manner as aforesaid he has seen very considerable numbers of the Placard marked A now produced and shewn to this

Deponent and that the said Placards as well before the Death of the said Jonathan Warren as afterwards were distributed to a very considerable extent and made as public as possible and that every pains was taken by the said Jonathan Warren and the said William Edward Woodd and those who were in his Employ to give to the said Placard every possible publicity

Henry Walker [signature]

Sworn at the Public Office Southampton Buildings in the County of Middlesex this 20th day of November 1827 Before me

Jas. Howse [signature]

[12. The affidavit of William Glindon]

In Chancery   Between Robert Warren and Benjamin Warren, Plaintiffs and George Lamerte, Defendant

William Glindon of No. 57 Rupert Street Haymarket in the City of Westminster Printer maketh oath and saith that he became acquainted with Jonathan Warren Blacking maker deceased about the year One thousand eight hundred ------- and such intimacy subsisted during the remainder of his life   And this Deponent saith that the said Jonathan Warren was the Inventor of Warrens original Japan Blacking and sold Blacking under the Designation of Warrens Blacking from the year One thousand eight hundred --------- until he disposed of his business to William Edward Woodd as hereinafter mentioned and in the year One thousand eight hundred and twenty two the said Jonathan Warren gave to this Deponent an Affidavit of that fact sworn by the said Jonathan Warren before the then Lord Mayor of London That he afterwards printed many thousand Copies thereof at the instance of the said Jonathan Warren   And this Deponent saith that about March One thousand eight hundred and twenty one the said Jonathan Warren removed to Hungerford Stairs Strand in the City of Westminster having engaged premises there for the purpose of his Trade and he or William Edward Woodd his Successor Numbered the said House with the Number 30 which with the words "Warrens Blacking Warehouse" he or one of them painted in large black Characters on a white ground on the River front of the premises   And this Deponent saith the said Jonathan Warren carried on an extensive business as a Blacking Manufacturer at the place last aforesaid and was at considerable expence by placards and otherwise in bringing Warrens Blacking of which he was the original Inventor as aforesaid into public use and repute but in consequence of habits of Intemperance and gaming the said Jonathan Warren afterwards neglected his business and the Trade very much fell off   And this Deponent saith that the said Jonathan Warren some time about October One thousand eight hundred and twenty two sold and disposed of his

said Business to William Edward Woodd upon the terms that the said William Edward Woodd should have permission to use the name of the said Jonathan Warren that the said Jonathan should continue to Manufacture the Blacking and as a Termination should be paid by a per centage and upon this Deponents recommendation provision was made for the Wife of the said Jonathan Warren in the event of her surviving her said Husband   And this Deponent witnessed the Agreement between the said parties to that effect, That upon the Agreement being entered into the said William Edward Woodd took possession of the said Manufactory at Hungerford Stairs aforesaid and continued there until a few months before the death of the said Jonathan Warren   And this Deponent saith that the said William Edward Woodd about the month of October One thousand eight hundred and twenty two took the said Defendant into his employ   And this Deponent has frequently seen the said Jonathan Warren and the said Defendant engaged together in making Warrens Blacking   And this Deponent has been informed and believes that the said Jonathan Warren imparted the Art to the said Defendant and instructed the said Defendant in the process of making the Japan Blacking called Warrens Blacking   And this Deponent saith the Defendant was engaged in managing and conducting the whole concern for the said William Edward Woodd and became acquainted with all the Customers,   That this Deponent in One thousand eight hundred and twenty one and One thousand eight hundred and twenty two printed Shop Placards and others for the said Jonathan Warren for the purpose of promoting the Sale of Blacking therein called Warrens Blacking and in years One thousand eight hundred and twenty two and One thousand eight hundred and twenty three he printed similar placards for the said William Edward Woodd for the like purpose and for the Sale of Blacking bearing the same designation   And this Deponent saith that the Placard shown and now produced to this Deponent marked G is one of such placards so printed for the said William Edward Woodd as aforesaid and contain a Copy of the Affidavit before mentioned   That this Deponent almost always received his orders from and was paid by the said Defendant
William Glindon [signature]
Sworn at the Public Office Southampton Buildings in the County of Middlesex this twentieth day of November 1827 Before me
Jas: Howse [signature]

[13. The affidavit of Samuel Mann]
In Chancery   Between Robert Warren and Benjamin Warren, Plaintiffs and George Lamerte, Defendant

Samuel Mann of Number 9 Hungerford Street Strand in the City of Westminster Chinaman maketh oath and saith that he has resided in his present Residence for ten years last past and during the eight years preceding One thousand eight hundred and twenty seven this Deponent has received the Rent of the House and premises now occupied by John Wood of Hungerford Market in the City of Westminster Clicker And this Deponent saith that Jonathan Warren late Blacking maker deceased hired the said House now occupied by the said John Wood on the twenty fifth day of March One thousand eight hundred and twenty one and commenced his business of Blacking Maker upon the said premises at that time the house bore no Number but the said Jonathan Warren or William Edward Woodd his Successor had the No 30 painted on the Door next the Street and one of them whitened part of the Wall on the River front and wrote or painted thereon in very large legible black characters "Warrens 30 Blacking Warehouse" And this Deponent saith that the said Jonathan Warren often told this Deponent and this Deponent believes it to be true that the said Jonathan Warren was the original Inventor of Warrens Blacking and issued placards to that effect and this Deponent although living in the Neighbourhood does not believe that that fact was ever doubted or denied And this Deponent saith that towards the latter part of the year One thousand eight hundred and twenty two whilst the said Jonathan Warren was carrying on his Trade in Blacking he introduced the said William Edward Woodd into the concern and this Deponent was at that time informed and believes it to be true that the said William Edward Woodd was to be permitted to carry on the said Business in the name of the said Jonathan Warren that the said Jonathan Warren was to Manufacture the Article and receive a per centage or some other allowance upon the quantity sold, that after this transaction William Edward Woodd paid the rent but this Deponent gave Receipts to him in the name of Jonathan Warren for the same And this Deponent verily believes that the before mentioned writing on the River front of the said House formerly occupied by the said Jonathan Warren has remained thereon from the year One thousand eight hundred and twenty two until very lately And this Deponent remembers that the said Defendant was engaged in the said Manufactory about the time that the said William Edward Woodd took possession thereof and continued there until the said William Edward Woodd quitted

Saml. Mann [signature]

Sworn at the Public Office Southampton Buildings in the County of Middlesex this 21st day of November 1827 – Before me

E Wingfield [signature]

170

In chancery   Between Robert Warren and Benjamin Warren, plaintiffs and George Lamerte, Defendant

George Lamerte late of White Chapel Road in the County of Middlesex but now of No 56 Mansell Street Goodmans Fields Blacking Manufacturer the above named Defendant maketh oath and saith that he has lately been informed and believes it to be true that in the latter part of the year One thousand eight hundred and twenty two William Edward Woodd the Brother in Law of this Deponent purchased the goodwill of the trade or Business of a Japan Blacking Manufacturer of Jonathan Warren the Original and Sole Inventor of the Real Japan Blacking and which article was made and sold as this Deponent has lately been informed and believes by the said Jonathan Warren from the year One thousand seven hundred and ninety eight down to the time when the said William Edward Woodd purchased the said goodwill as aforesaid And this Deponent saith that in pursuance of an Agreement or understanding the true contents and particulars whereof have within a few days been communicated to this Deponent and made between the said Jonathan Warren and the said William Edward Woodd the said Jonathan Warren manufactured and assisted in manufacturing the said Japan Blacking for the said William Edward Woodd from about the said month of October One thousand eight hundred and twenty two until the death of the said Jonathan Warren which took place about the twenty first day of August One thousand eight hundred and twenty four and the said William Edward Woodd in pursuance of the said Agreement or understanding hereinbefore mentioned with the permission of the said Jonathan Warren carried on his Blacking Trade under the name of form of "Jonathan Warren"   And this Deponent saith that in or about the said month of October One thousand eight hundred and twenty two the said William Edward Woodd prevailed on this Deponent to abandon his then views in life and engage with the said William Edward Woodd in the Manufactory of Blacking   That the place where the said Jonathan Warren had previously carried on his trade and the premises which he relinquished to the said William Edward Woodd upon his making such purchase were situated at Hungerford Stairs Strand and had been to the best of this deponents recollection the No. 25 but the said William Edward Woodd as this Deponent has been informed and believes or the said Jonathan Warren or one of them in or before the said month of October One thousand eight hundred and twenty two altered the Number of the said premises by substituting No 30 for the previous number   And the said premises have borne the No 30 ever since until within a few days when the Plaintiffs or one of them as this Deponent has been informed and believes caused the said No 30 to be effaced from the River front of the said premises And this Deponent saith that in October One thousand eight hundred and twenty two the said William Edward Woodd having little or no knowledge of the Art of Manufacturing Blacking he desired this Deponent to pay the most particular attention to that part of the business and to obtain all possible information regarding it from the said Jonathan Warren   That this Deponent undertook the whole management of the concern for his Employer and he constantly assisted the said Jonathan Warren in Manufacturing Blacking and was taught and fully instructed in the said art by him and that after the death of the said Jonathan Warren this Deponent was the sole Manufacturer of Blacking for the said William Edward Woodd for about the space of three months following   That in managing the correspondence and the other Branches of the Business this Deponent gained a very general acquaintance in the trade and was known either personally or by name to most of the Customers of the said William Edward Woodd   That about the beginning of the year One thousand eight hundred and twenty four the said William Edward Woodd removed his said Business from Hungerford Stairs Strand to No 3 Chandos Street and afterwards again removed to Noble Street Cheapside yet the said William Edward Woodd has continued upon his labels the words "Warrens Blacking" and the name of "Jonathan Warren" the Number "30" in large figures in the Centre and "Hungerford Stairs Strand" underneath with the knowledge of the said Plaintiffs and without any objection being made thereto to this Deponents knowledge and belief except within the present month of November   And this Deponent saith that having manufactured Blacking with the aid and assistance and under the Instruction of the said Jonathan Warren the Inventor and having afterwards for some time been the sole Manufacturer of Blacking for the said William Edward Woodd trading under the firm of and known to the Public as Jonathan Warren this Deponent conceived and does believe that he was guilty of no Infraction of Law by describing himself in his placards and Labels as late Manufacturer of Japan Blacking to Jonathan Warren 30 Hungerford Stairs Strand   And this Deponent saith that until the said month of October One thousand eight hundred and twenty two this Deponent was unacquainted with the person name and Trade or Business of the said Jonathan Warren but he has lately been informed and believes it to be true that the said Jonathan Warren first established himself publicly as a Blacking Manufacturer in the year One thousand seven hundred and ninety eight as aforesaid   And this Deponent saith that in the beginning of January One thousand eight hundred and twenty five he commenced business as a Blacking Manufacturer in White chapel [flead] aforesaid in Copartnership with one Lewes Worms   That the said Copartnership was dissolved on the thirty first day of August last whereupon this Deponent removed his Manufactory from White Chapel Road aforesaid to No. 56 Mansell Street his present residence where he carried on his Trade upon his own individual account   And this Deponent denies that he ever carried on trade under the form of "George Lamerte Jonathan Warren & Co." or that he ever stated or represented that he had any connexion or partnership or otherwise with any person of the name of Robert Warren or of Jonathan Warren save as herein before is mentioned   And this Deponent saith that the only use he has ever made of the name of Jonathan Warren and which name this Deponent denies to have been a fictitious name was to represent himself as late Manufacturer to Jonathan Warren the Inventor of the real Japan Blacking meaning thereby as late Manufacturer to William Edward Woodd trading under the style or form of Jonathan Warren with the permission of the said Jonathan Warren the Sole Inventor of the said Blacking as aforesaid   And this Deponent saith that from the commencement of his business in January One thousand eight hundred and twenty five to the present time this Deponent has used labels which he pasted on his pots and Jars of Liquid Blacking and paste containing the Number 30 in large figures in the Centre and with as this Deponent believes the privity and knowledge of the said Plaintiffs but without any objection having been made thereto by them to this Deponent   And this Deponent denies that his Labels are a close imitation of those used by the said plaintiffs and that he contrived and caused the same to be printed solely for the purpose of enabling him this Deponent by reason of their very great similarity to those of the plaintiffs to sell and dispose of his blacking as and for the Blacking of the Plaintiffs   And this Deponent saith that no persons to this Deponents knowledge and belief have been deceived or misled by them or have actually purchased the Blacking of this Deponent intending to purchase and conceiving that they were purchasing the plaintiffs said Article or commodity and fraudulent representations or otherwise deceived or misled the customers of the plaintiffs or others by stating to them or any of them or inducing them or any of them to believe that his this Deponents House or Business was a branch or part of the said plaintiffs said House or Business   And this Deponent denies that such Customers and others have in consequence dealt with this Deponent and purchased Blacking of him to a large amount in value conceiving and believing that they were dealing with the said plaintiffs said House or firm and were purchasing the said plaintiffs said Blacking or that this Deponent his said late partner Travellers or Agents have ever directly or indirectly sold this Deponents Blacking as and for the Article manufactured by the said Plaintiffs or passed off his commodity as or for the said Plaintiffs   And this Deponent saith that by reason of the connection he formed whilst with the said William Edward Woodd this Deponent upon embarking in trade at once obtained extensive Custom And this Deponent says that he selected and used in his labels the number 30 in consequence of the premises wherein the said Blacking Manufactory was first conducted by the said William Edward Woodd in the name of Jonathan Warren bearing that particular number at and during the time whilst this Deponent was in his employ   And this Deponent says that in his labels and placards he has printed Hungerford Stairs Strand not on account of its vicinity to the said Plaintiffs said House and premises in the Strand but solely for the reasons last mentioned and for no fraudulent purposes or contrivances whatsoever and that this Deponent has inserted in all his Labels from January One thousand eight hundred and twenty five to the present time to the knowledge of the Plaintiffs as this Deponent verily believes and without any complaint thereof Jonathan Warren 30 Hungerford Stairs Strand and two Tablets as herein after mentioned That this Deponent never had nor has he ever stated or represented that he had or has a house or premises or place for business or for Shipping goods belonging to or occupied or held by him at Hungerford Stairs Strand   And this Deponent saith that the several placards Labels Invoices Cards and direction Cards now produced and shewn to this Deponent and numbered respectively 1, 2, 3, 4, 5, 6, 7, 8, 9, 10, 11 12. are those which have been in use by this Deponent and his late partner and by this Deponent since their separation for twelve months and upwards now last past,   And this Deponent saith that the Label No. 4 bears if any the nearest resemblance to the Labels in use by the said Plaintiffs but this Deponent denies any deceptions similarity for the reasons hereinafter mentioned that is to say the ground pattern in the Plaintiffs Label is of different form and better executed than the Defendants that the words "real Japan Blacking" in Plaintiffs Label are red with Black at the tops and Bottoms of the Letters the same words in the Defendants Label are in reddish Characters that in the Plaintiffs Label next follows "made by" and in the Defendants Label "made by the late Manufacturer to"   In the Plaintiffs Label the names "Robert Warren" are printed in White Characters upon a Black Ground with a broad red Bar Through the Centre and the same names in small red Letters upon the large Letters the Defendants Label has "Jonathan Warren" printed in the most conspicuous manner so that no person could mistake the same unless intentionally the Words "Jonathan Warren" being printed in distinct white Letters upon a black Ground, that the Plaintiffs Label contains two lines of poetry either in white characters upon a Black Ground or in Black Letters upon a White Ground, that the defendants Label has no poetry but the following words "Proprietors Geo Lamerte & Co. White Chapel Road" and since the dissolution of the Partnership and this Deponents Removal as aforesaid the words "proprietor Geo Lamerte" 56 Mansell Street" And this Deponent saith that the labels of the Plaintiffs as well as the Defendant each contain two tablets and that the borders or patterns of those of the Defendant are obviously different from those of the Plaintiff And this Deponent has been informed and believes that it has been the practice of all or nearly all Blacking makers to use similar tablets with printed sentences for many years last past And this Deponent saith that in the plaintiffs first Tablet on his Label is printed as follows "This composition with half the usual labour, produces a most brilliant jet Black, fully equal to the highest Japan Varnish affords peculiar nourishment to the leather; will not soil the finest linen, and will retain its virtue in any Climate" The Defendants first Tablet contains as follows "In consequence of the many inferior composition offered to the Public for this superior Article none is genuine unless signed Geo Lamerte & Co." and since the dissolution of the partnership the words "& Co." have been omitted. The Plaintiffs second tablet on his label is thus "Use – stir it till it is well mixed, then lay on your brush as thin as possible; black the Boot or Shoe all over; apply your shining Brush immediately and in one minute it will produce the most Brilliant lustre and jet black ever beheld" The Defendants second tablet is as follows "Use – Stir your blacking well from the bottom applying it to the boot or shoe as usual, and it will immediately produce a brilliant polish" And this Deponent saith that the figures "30" in this Deponents label vary in many respects from the same figures in the Plaintiffs label but especially in as much as the Plaintiffs figures contain the representation of a Boot and a Man shaving and the Defendants figures contain the representation of a looking Glass and a monkey Shaving and the Plaintiffs number has "30" printed in small figures upon the larger ones which the Defendants has not And this Deponent saith that in the Plaintiffs Label is printed the word "Strand" in White Characters upon a Black Ground with a Broad Red Bar and in this respect also the Defendants label is totally at variance with the other for the Defendants lable contains the words "Hungerford Stairs Strand" in conspicuous White Characters upon a Black Ground, each Label bears the price at one Corner and the Plaintiffs Label contains in the other corner his name printed in Black Characters upon a White Ground or white Characters on a black Ground And the Defendants Label in like manner contains his name And this Deponent saith that in his present labels now in use and lastly hereinbefore referred unto, his this Deponents name is printed in three different places And this Deponent saith that almost all the variances hereinbefore described between the two labels exist in the smaller labels used for paste Blacking And this

Deponent saith that he believes that all his Customers except as aforesaid Knew that they were dealing with this Deponent and Lewis Worms or with this Deponent individually and not with or on account of any person whomsoever bearing the Surname of Warren   That this Deponent sells by far the larger quantity of his Blacking in the Country and upon Credit and all Bills of parcels delivered have invariably as this Deponent believes been written upon one or other of the Invoices hereinbefore referred to under the No. 3 or 8 in like manner all packages Cases or Casks of Goods forwarded to order have been directed upon one of the direction Cards hereinbefore referred to under No. 9   That this Deponent has distributed in great numbers the Cards hereinbefore referred to under No. 2. 9. 12. That very few goods if any have ever been forwarded by this Deponent either alone or in partnership without inclosing as this Deponent verily believes the Shop placard No 11 and that each respective Bottle Pot or Case of Liquid Blacking or paste bore one or other of this Deponents before mentioned Labels with the exception of cases supplied to the Army   And this Deponent verily believes it to be true that no person who has read either of the last mentioned Placards Labels or Invoices could be deceived thereby or induced to believe that the said Deponent or his late partner had any connection with the House Concern or Business of the said plaintiffs but on the contrary any person reading the same must thereby be convinced that the Defendant and his late partner or the said Defendant alone were trading upon their or his own individual separate account unconnected with any other person whatsoever   And this Deponent saith that since he has been engaged in making Blacking he has made it his constant study to improve the Article as much as possible that this Deponent has a knowledge of Chemistry and has in consequence been enabled to make very considerable Improvements in the Manufacture of his Blacking and this Deponent verily believes that the Blacking made by him is equal to that made by any other Manufacturer in London   And this Deponent also believes that his Blacking is in every respect very far superior to that Manufactured by the Plaintiffs   And this Deponent denies that any Blacking was ever sold by this Deponent or by his Travellers or Agents to this Deponents knowledge and belief to Alice Hall of No 5 Junction place Kentish Town in the said County of Middlesex in the manner and under the circumstances described in the Affidavit of the said Alice Hall Sworn in this cause on the twelfth day of November instant   And this Deponent saith that John Harrison the person who has made an affidavit in this cause having been in this Deponents Service as his Foreman was discharged by him on the fourteenth July last that this Deponent subsequently employed one Richard Latham as his foreman that having been applied to in the month of October last to receive back the said

John Harrison into his Service this Deponent engaged him as a Labourer on the ninth day of October last but in a few days Edward Selth one of this Deponents Servants having communicated to this Deponent that he had seen the said John Harrison secrete a pot of Bottle of Blacking in his Hat and carry it away – this Deponent taxed him with the Robbery and dismissed him from his Service   And this Deponent saith that the said John Harrison afterwards Summoned him for wages and attended such Summons but upon this Deponent and his witnesses one of whom was the said Edward Selth making their appearance the said John Harrison went away and abandoned his said Summons   And this Deponent has been informed and believes it to be true that the said John Harrison is at present in the Employ of the said plaintiff   And this Deponent saith that on Saturday the tenth day of November instant a person whose name this Deponent has been informed was Thomas Harrison the Brother of the said John Harrison as the Deponent believes called at this Deponents House in Mansel Street Goodman's Fields and Sarah Scott this Deponents Servant called this Deponent down stairs to give the said Thomas Harrison some Blacking she could not conveniently reach this Deponent accordingly delivered the Blacking to the Customer who paid the wholesale price   The said Thomas Harrison then asked this Deponent if the Bottles were Warrens Blacking to which this Deponent replied they were made by the late Manufacturer to Jonathan Warren who was then dead the person then asked Deponent whether the Blacking was the same as Warrens in the Strand to which this Deponent replied no, it was made by the Deponent himself and that he this Deponent had been Manufacturer to the late Jonathan Warren   The said Thomas Harrison then said he wanted to send it to the Country and asked this Deponent for a Shop placard   And this Deponent thereupon referred unto No 11   And this Deponent further saith that an Advertizement appeared in the Newspaper called the John Bull of Sunday the eighteenth day of November and in the following words that is to say "Court of Chancery   An Injunction has this day been granted by the Lord Chancellor to restrain G Lamerte from making or selling any Blacking with Labels in imitation of the genuine Warrens Blacking which he has been in the habit of doing by using the Fictitious name of Jonathan Warren and otherwise imitating the genuine Labels of Robert Warren 30 Strand.   It is therefore strongly recommended that those Shop keepers or others who have any of the Counterfeit Blacking as above described, do return it to the parties from whom they received it, which they are justified in doing.   By neglecting this Notice they will be liable to the heavy expence and penalties of a Suit in Chancery which will be immediately commenced against them.   The genuine Blacking is signed "Robert Warren "30 Strand" on each Label – all others are

Counterfeit and of very inferior quality. London 13th November 1827"
And this Deponent saith that the said Advertizement has appeared in
several of the London and as this Deponent has been informed and
believes Country Newspapers And this Deponent verily believes that
the said Advertizement was thus publicly advertised by the said plaintiffs
or one of them or by his or their order or under his or their sanction and
at his or their expence And this Deponent submits that the said
Advertizement is a gross abuse of the Writ of Injunction granted by and
issuing out of this Honorable Court and solely for the purpose of
counteracting the mischievous effects thereof this Deponent has been
under the necessity of and has published a counter Advertizement as
follows that is to say "In Chancery Warren and another v Lamerte An
Injunction has been granted by the Court on an exparte statement, as is
usual, restraining the Defendant from selling Warrens Blacking with
particular Labels and as the Defendants Case will in a few days be before
the Public he trusts to their liberality to suspend their Judgement in the
mean time 56 Mansell Street November 17th 1827 George Lamerte."
And this Deponent saith that he has received a Letter from Iltid Evans
of Bridge End in the County of Glamorgan Wales of which the
following is a Copy
"Messrs. Geo: Lamerte & Co.
Gentn. Having received a printed Letter from the genuine Blacking
Manufacturer Mr. Robert Warren of 30 Strand which he informs me of
an injunction been granted by the Lord Chancellor in consequence of
using fictitious name of Jonathan Warren which I will relate as follows it
troubles me but very little I shall feel obliged to you to send me answer
by return of post with the particulars with respects to Mr. J.T. Lamerte
I am Gentlemen Yours respectfully Iltid Evans"
And this Deponent saith that the said Letter as setting out the letter
received by the said Iltid Evans from the said Robert Warren contains a
Verbatim Copy of the Advertizement first hereinbefore set forth with a
Letter in the following words
"Blacking Manufactory 30 Strand Novr. 16th. 1827
"Sir Being informed you have a quantity of the Counterfeit Blking in
imitation of the genuine Warrens Blking made by me, I beg to
recommend the annex'd Notice to your serious attention presuming you
have been deceived by the close imitation, and having no wish to
proceed to extremities without giving an opportunity for your
immediately discontinuing a practice so injurious to my trade and
reputation as a Blking Manufacturer I have to request you will take the
earliest means in your power to stop such proceedings. The most
effectual will be to return the spurious Blking to the parties from whom
you receive it I shall be further obliged by your favouring me with an

order for a supply of the genuine Blking A line by post will meet immediate attention from

Sir your obdt. Servant "Robert Warren" Bridge End Novr. 18th 1827"

And this Deponent saith that the said Letter of the said Iltid Evans is directed to Messrs. George Lamerte & Co. Blacking Manufacturers White Chapel Road London   And this Deponent saith that at the time of such direction being written the said Iltid Evans did not bear in recollection as this Deponent believes that this Deponent had terminated his partnership with the said Lewis Worms   And this Deponent saith he has received other Letters from various Customers in Ireland England and elsewhere informing him that they had received printed Copies of the said Avertizement of the said plaintiffs similar to that hereinbefore set forth accompanied by a Letter from the said plaintiffs soliciting the Custom of those to whom the said printed advertisements had been forwarded   And this Deponent verily believes that the said Plaintiffs have availed themselves of the said Writ of Injunction to send similar advertisements with similar solicitations for Custom to the Dealers in Blacking generally throughout England Ireland Scotland and Wales

Geo Lamerte [signature]

Sworn at the Public Office Southampton Buildings in the County of Middlesex This 23rd. day of November 1827 Before me

G Wilson [signature]

[15. The second affidavit of George Lamerte]

In chancery   Between Robert Warren and Benjamin Warren, plaintiffs and George Lamerte, Defendant

George Lamerte of No 56 Mansell Street Goodmans Fields in the County of Middlesex the above named Defendant and William Dixon the younger of Jewry Street in the City of London Gentleman severally make oath and say And first this Deponent George Lamerte for himself saith that having been informed that William Grayline of Whitechapel Road in the County of Middlesex Oilman had received a Letter from the above named plaintiffs he this Deponent George Lamerte applied to the said William Grayling for the same and received from him the advertizement and Letter in print of which the following is a copy

"Blacking Manufactory 30 Strand London

Sir   Being informed you have been selling and now have a quantity of the counterfeit article in imitation of the genuine Warrens Blacking made by me I beg to recommend the annexed Notice to your very serious attention presuming you have been deceived by the close imitation and having no wish to proceed to extremities without giving an opportunity for your immediately discontinuing a practice so injurious to my trade and reputation as a Blacking Manufacturer I have to request you will take the earliest means in your power to stop such proceedings The most effectual will be to return the Spurious Blacking to the parties from whom you received it I shall feel further obliged by your favouring me with an order for a supply of the Genuine Blacking A line by post will meet with immediate attention from,

Sir, Your obedient servant, Robert Warren"

"Court of Chancery An injunction has this day been granted by the Lord Chancellor to restrain G. Lamerte from making or selling any Blacking with Labels in imitation of the genuine Warren's Blacking which he has been in the habit of doing by using the fictitious name of Jonathan Warren and otherwise imitating the genuine Labels of Robert Warren 30 Strand – It is therefore strongly recommended that those shopkeepers or others who have any of the Counterfeit Blacking as above described do return it to the parties from whom they received it which they are justified in doing By neglecting this Notice they will be liable to the heavy expences and penalties of a suit in Chancery, which will be immediately commenced against them – The genuine Blacking is signed "Robert Warren 30 Strand," on each Label all others are counterfeit and of very inferior quality

London 13th. November, 1827"

And the said Deponent George Lamerte further saith that the said Letter and notice is directed to Mr Grayling oilman 99 Whitechapel Road And saith that the said William Grayling is a regular customer of this Deponent And this Deponent further saith that he verily believes that advertisements and letters similar to these hereinbefore set forth have been generally circulated by the above named Plaintiffs and saith he has been informed and believes it to be true that great numbers of the said Notices or advertizements and Letters have been distributed by the Travellers and other persons in the employ of the said Plaintiffs and that such persons have at the time of delivering the same informed those to whom they were delivered (many of whom are customers of this Deponents) that such advertizements were circulated by the order or under the sanction of the High Court of Chancery And this Deponent William Dixon for himself saith that he had perused the Newspaper of the Eighteenth day of November instant known by the name of "The John Bull" and saith that such Newspaper contains an advertisement or notice corresponding with that hereinbefore lastly set forth and that he this Deponent enquired at the Office where the said John Bull newspaper is printed and published and was informed by Edward Shackell the publisher thereof that he could not state who had delivered such Notice or Advertizement at his office but that it had been sent there and the insertion thereof paid for by the said plaintiff Robert

Warren accompanied by a printed Letter of Instruction which is in the words and figures following that is to say
"30 Strand London 15th. Novr. 1827
Sir Have the goodness to insert the above in a conspicuous part of your paper Twelve times weekly at ten shillings and ^ ^ ^ ^ pence each All former orders void on receipt of this (should you have any) I shall feel particularly obliged by your inserting the first three or four as paragraphs I am Sir Your obedient Servant Robert Warren
To the John Bull 40 Fleet St."
And this Deponent William Dixon further saith that the said Notice of advertizement or one similar thereto has been inserted in several other town and country newspapers   And also on the cover of a weekly publication called "the Lancer" at the instance by the order and at the expence of the said Plaintiffs or their agents or servants as this Deponent has been informed and verily believes.
Geo Lamerte [signature]
W. Dixon [signature]
Sworn by both Deponents at the Public Office Southampton Buildings in the County of Middlesex this 24th day of November 1827. Before me R H Eden [signature]

[16. The affidavit of John Thomas Lamerte]
In Chancery Between Robert Warren and Benjamin Warren, Plaintiffs and George Lamerte Defendant
John Thomas Lamerte of 56 Mansell Street Goodmans Fields in the County of Middlesex the Brother of, and Traveller to, the above named George Lamerte, the Defendant, maketh oath and saith he knows that in the year One thousand eight hundred and twenty three the said Defendant was engaged in the Service of his Brother in Law William Edward Woodd at No. 30 Hungerford Stairs Strand in the Trade of a Blacking Maker but a coolness subsisting between this Deponent and certain branches of his Family this Deponent was unacquainted with any further circumstances regarding that connection at that time, but about July in the year One thousand eight hundred and twenty four this Deponent was employed by the Defendant on the part of the said William Edward Woodd to sell his blacking called Jonathan Warrens Blacking on Commission and for this purpose the Deponent solicited custom in London and Kent, This Commission Agency continued until the latter part of the year One thousand eight hundred and twenty four when the Defendant quitted the employ of the said William Edward Woodd and upon the Defendants entering into the Business of a Blacking Maker in January One thousand Eight hundred and twenty five in Copartnership with Lewis Worms this Deponent commenced a

similar Commission Agency for them which lasted until about the twelfth June One thousand eight hundred and twenty five when this Deponent engaged himself as a regular Traveller to the said Defendant and Lewis Worms and continued that employ with the Defendant and Lewis Worms during the remainder of their Copartnership and with the Defendant subsequent to the dissolution of the joint concern and down to the present time And this Deponent saith that he is accustomed to frequent various parts of England Ireland Scotland Wales Guernsey and Jersey soliciting orders for Blacking made by the late Manufacturer to Jonathan Warren And this Deponent saith that the several Labels Placards Headings for Invoices Cards and Direction Cards respectively Numbered 1.2.3.4.5.6.7.8.9.10.11.12 and now produced and shewn to this Deponent are those used by the said Defendant and Lewis Worms during the partnership and by the said Defendant subsequently And this Deponent further saith that in a great Number of the Instances when this Deponent has taken a Country order the Customer has entered that Order in his own Books and this Deponent has at the request of such person signed the order "George Lamerte & Co." or "G. Lamerte" as the Case might be so that all such Customers well know that George Lamerte and his partner or George Lamerte alone were the persons or person with whom the Customer was trading That the Defendant sells by far the larger quantity of his Blacking in the Country and upon Credit and all Bills of Parcells delivered have invariably as this Deponent believes been written upon one or other of the Invoices hereinbefore referred to under the No. 3 or 8 in like manner all Packages Cases or Casks of Goods forwarded to order have been directed upon one of the Direction Cards hereinbefore referred to under No. 9 That this Deponent has distributed many thousands of the Cards hereinbefore referred to under No. 2. 9. 12 that very few goods if any have ever been forwarded by the Defendant either alone or in partnership without enclosing as this Deponent verily believes the Shop Placard No 11 and that each respective Bottle Pot or Case of Liquid Blacking or paste bore one or other of the Defendants before mentioned Labels And this Deponent verily believes it to be true that no person who has read either of the last mentioned placards Cards Labels or Invoices could be deceived thereby or induced to believe that the said Defendant or the said Defendant and his late Partner had any connection with the House, concern or Business of the Plaintiffs but on the contrary any person reading the same must thereby be convinced that the Defendant and his late Partner or the said Defendant alone were trading upon their or his own individual separate Account unconnected with any other person or persons whomsoever And this Deponent saith that, save as appears in and by the Affidavit Sworn by the said Plaintiffs in this Cause on the twelfth day of November instant, since he has been employed by the said Defendant and his late partner or by the said Defendant he has never in soliciting custom in any instance whatever either directly or indirectly endeavoured to obtain an order or to sell Goods as Travelling in connection or on account of the said Plaintiffs or either of them or as a Branch or part of the House or Business of the said Plaintiff Robert Warren No. 30 Strand nor has this Deponent ever represented in any Instance or upon any occasion stated or described that the firm of his Employers or Employer was George Lamerte Jonathan Warren & Co. nor has this Deponent ever heard nor does this Deponent believe that either the Defendant or Lewis Worms during their said partnership or the said Defendant since the termination thereof have or has stated that they or he were or was a Branch or part of the House or Business of the Defendant Robert Warren 30 Strand or that their or his Firm was "George Lamerte Jonathan Warren & Co. And this Deponent further saith that he this Deponent never did nor does he believe that the said Defendant and Lewis Worms or either of them ever did Represent to any one that the Warehouse and Shipping place of the said Defendant and Lewis Worms or either of them was at Hungerford Stairs Strand And this Deponent says he never described nor does this Deponent believe nor has he ever heard that the said Defendant and Lewis Worms or either of them did ever describe the Blacking sold by this Deponent or his said last mentioned Employers was the Blacking manufactured by the Plaintiffs or either of them nor has this Deponent done nor does he believe his said last mentioned Employers or either of them have ever done any other Act whatsoever to deceive the Plaintiffs customers or any of them or the Public at large into a belief that he travelled for or on Account of any other person than his real Employers or Employer for the time being and that the Blacking which this Deponent has sold as last aforesaid he has never described in any other manner than as Blacking made by the late Manufacturer to Jonathan Warren And this Deponent saith that on some occasions when he has described the said Blacking in manner last aforesaid he has been asked whether the late Jonathan Warren deceased was related to the Plaintiff Robert Warren to which this Deponent has replied that the said Jonathan Warren was as this Deponent believed Uncle to the Plaintiff Robert Warren And this Deponent says that he ever sold any Blacking as being manufactured by any house or firm carrying on business in the Strand but this Deponent saith that he said William Edward Woodd and Stephen Pilcher his Partner make and vend Blacking under the denomination of Warrens Blacking but not in the Strand aforesaid And this Deponent saith that in the course of his Journies he frequently solicits an order as is usual throughout the Trade of the Customers of the Plaintiffs and very often has succeeded but this Deponent denies that he has ever obtained such orders or any of them by means of fraud or deception or otherwise than in the way of fair and honorable competition   And this Deponent saith in the month of May One thousand eight hundred and twenty six as appears by this Deponents Letter written to the Defendant on the first day of January One thousand eight hundred and twenty six and as he well remembers he met the Plaintiff Robert Warren at Exeter being the same meeting as is referred to in the said Affidavit sworn in this cause by the said Plaintiff on the twelfth day of November instants soliciting and taking orders at that place in a fair and Tradesman like way and being at the Globe Inn and seeing the said Plaintiff but mistaking him for another person upon the said Plaintiffs leaving the Room this Deponent asked the Waiter whether his name was Harris the Waiter said no and went out of the Room   the Plaintiff again returned and approaching this Deponent said my name is not Harris but to the best of this Deponents recollection he added it is Warren and he continued I am not ashamed of my name if you are of yours the said Plaintiff then reproached this Deponent with selling his Employers Blacking under a fictitious name falsely representing that the person whose name was so used was dead And this Deponent then recommended the said Plaintiff if he had any complaints to make to address them to the principals and not to Deponent who was merely a Traveller but this Deponent nevertheless flatly denied the truth of the Accusation   And this Deponent saith that he never represented that there was such a person as Jonathan Warren living or in partnership with the Defendant and Lewis Worms or with the Defendant individually but that such a person had existed and was the original Inventor of Warrens Blacking and that the Article sold by this Deponent was made by the late Manufacturer to the said Jonathan Warren as aforesaid   And this Deponent believes the said Plaintiff never made any representation to the Defendant as he was urged by this Deponent to do   And this Deponent further saith that in the month of November One thousand eight hundred and twenty six this Deponent met Mr -------- Groombridge (whom this Deponent believes was a Traveller in the Employ of the said Plaintiffs) at Launceston in Cornwall and the said ------- Groombridge as representing his Employers complained that this Deponent had been selling his principals Blacking to John George Tallow Chandler and Shopkeeper of that place as and for the Blacking of the Plaintiffs or one of them whereupon this Deponent denied the fact and proposed that the said Mr ------- Groombridge should accompany this Deponent to the House of the said John George in order to come to the truth of the matter which was assented to and this Deponent and the said Mr ---------- Groombridge forthwith went to John Georges House and asked him as to the truth of the accusation when the said John George told the said Mr - - - - - - Groombridge that he had given this Deponent the order for the Defendant as the late Manufacturer to Jonathan Warren and that there was no mistake about it   And this Deponent saith that he arrived at Merthyr in Wales on Sunday the fourth day of November instant for the first time in his life and that this Deponent neither solicited nor took any orders before the following day namely the fifth day of November instant   And this Deponent denies that the orders he took and the Goods he sold at Merthyr aforesaid on the occasion aforesaid or on any part of his last Journey to the West of England were taken or sold under the name of Jonathan Warren and under the representation that he the said Jonathan Warren was one of the Family meaning the Defendants Family save and except if asked the question this Deponent stated that the said Jonathan Warren was the Uncle of the said plaintiff Robert Warren and the original Inventor of Warrens Blacking as aforesaid and that he this Deponent travelled for the late Manufacturer to the said Jonathan Warren but this Deponent denies that he ever stated he travelled for or on account of any person bearing the Surname of Warren

John Thomas Lamerte [signature]

Sworn at the Public Office Southampton Buildings in the County of Middlesex this 21st. day of November 1827 Before me

W Winfield [signature]

This is the affidavit referred to by the annexed affidavit of John Thomas Lamerte sworn this 23rd day of November 1827 Before me

G Wilson [signature]

[16a The qualifying affidavit of John Thomas Lamerte]
In Chancery   Between Robert Warren and Benjamin Warren, Plaintiffs and George Lamerte, Defendant

John Thomas Lamerte of number fifty six Mansell Street Goodmans Fields in the County of Middlesex the Brother of and Traveller to the above named defendant maketh Oath and saith that the name "Groombridge" in the annexed affidavit was written by mistake and error and ought to have been instead thereof "Goombridge".   And this deponent saith that at the time he swore the said annexed affidavit he verily believed that "Goombridge" was the name written therein instead of "Groombridge"

John Thomas Lamerte [signature]

Sworn at the public Office Southampton Buildings in the County of Middlesex the 23rd. of November 1827 before me

G Wilson [signature]

[17. The affidavit of James Phillipps]

In Chancery   Between Robert Warren and Benjamin Warren, Plaintiffs and George Lamerte, Defendant

James Phillipps of Little Hungerford Street Strand in the County of Middlesex Custom House Agent and Lighterman Maketh Oath and saith that he this Deponent and this Deponents Father in his life time have resided nearly thirty years in Little Hungerford Street Strand and that he this Deponent has been in the constant habit of shipping and transmitting Goods consisting of Blacking manufactured by the above named Plaintiffs to various parts of England Ireland and Scotland   And this Deponent further saith that Little Hungerford Street is but a short Street and only contains twelve Houses and that there is not now nor ever was to the knowledge or belief of this Deponent any House in the said Street having the number 30 upon it -   And this Deponent also saith that he well remembers the above named Plaintiff Robert Warren when he resided in Saint Martins Lane and carried on business there that his business became and was extremely extensive and that his premises in Saint Martins Lane were too small to enable him to carry on his business there – that in or about the year one thousand eight hundred and sixteen the said Robert Warren removed to No 30 in the Strand and that shortly after his so doing the name of Robert Warren and No 30 Strand were placed in very large Letters and figures in front of his House and that he was also in the constant habit of advertising his Blacking as Robert Warrens Blacking No 30 Strand   And this Deponent also saith he Remembers that about five years after the said Robert Warren had been established as a Blacking Manufacturer at No 30 Strand the said Jonathan Warren came to reside in Little Hungerford Street aforesaid and shortly afterwards put up his name and a large number 30 precisely in imitation of the Plaintiff Robert Warrens No. 30 and in other respects as regarded the name similarly done and gave Little Hungerford Street the appellation of Hungerford Stairs which name the place never had before or since -   And this Deponent also saith that the true number of the House in which the said Jonathan Warren resided was No. 6 and not No 30

James Phillipps [signature]

Sworn at the Public Office Southampton Buildings Chancery Lane in the County of Middlesex this 26th day of Novr. 1827 before me

T: P: Stratford [signature]

[18. The affidavit of Samuel Mann]

In Chancery   Between Robert Warren and Benjamin Warren, Plaintiffs and George Lamerte, Defendant

Samuel Mann of Hungerford Street Strand in the Parish of Saint Martin in the fields in the County of Middlesex the acting Beadle of the said Parish Maketh oath and saith that he this Deponent hath been for many years Collector of the Rents of the Estate of the Reverend Henry Wise of Offchurch in the County of Warwick Clerk which Estate is situate in Hungerford Market Hungerford Street Little Hungerford Street and various other places adjoining thereto, and that on the ninth day of February one thousand eight hundred and twenty one Jonathan Warren named in the pleadings in this Cause applied to this Deponent to take a Lease of a House situate and being in Little Hungerford Street Hungerford Market that this Deponent required a reference as to character of the said Jonathan Warren who referred Deponent to a Baker in Whitcomb Street that this Deponent made enquiries and at last let to the said Jonathan Warren a House situate and being in Little Hungerford Street for one year at the yearly rent of Sixty Pounds that soon after the said Jonathan Warren took the said House he put up a large number 30 precisely in imitation of the No. 30 then used by the above named Plaintiffs   And this Deponent also further saith that he has been from the year One thousand eight hundred and eighteen to the year one thousand eight hundred and twenty six in the habit of collecting the Rents of the said Hungerford Estate and that during the whole of that period and for many years before and up to the present time there were not nor are there in fact more than twelve houses in Little Hungerford Street where the said Jonathan Warren resided   And this Deponent further saith that neither of them had any such number as that of 30 until the said Jonathan Warren came to reside there   And this Deponent also saith that he remembers that Robert Warren came to reside at No. 30 in the Strand some time in or about the year one thousand eight hundred and sixteen and that shortly afterwards he put in front of his house in large projecting letters the name of Warrens Blacking Warehouse – 30 – and also – the name of Robert Warren and that the said name - designation and No. 30 have Continued there from that to the present time

Saml Mann [signature]

Sworn at the public office Southampton Buildings Chancery Lane London this 26 day of November 1827 before me

T P Stratford [signature]

[19. The affidavit of William Dixon]

In chancery   Between Robert Warren and Benjamin Warren, Plaintiffs and George Lamerte, Defendant

William Dixon the younger of number twenty Jewry Street Aldgate in the city of London Clerk to William Dixon the Elder of the same place

Gentleman Solicitor for the above named defendant maketh oath and saith that he did on Saturday the twenty fourth day of november instant serve Mr. Richard Mills who acts as Clerk in Court for the abovenamed plaintiffs with a notice in writing purporting that this honorable court would be moved before the Lord High Chancellor of Great Britain on Tuesday next the twenty seventh day of november instant or so soon after as Counsel Could be heard that the Injunction granted in this cause dated the seventeenth day of this month of November might be disolved by delivering to and leaving with the copying Clerk of the said mr. Richard Mills at his seat in the six Clerks Office a true copy of such notice

W. Dixon Junr. [signature]
Sworn at the public office Southampton Buildings in the County of Middlesex this 26ᵗʰ day of November 1827 before me
T. P Stratford [signature]

[20. The affidavit of George Whitehead and Ann Whitehead]
In Chancery   Between Robert Warren and Benjamin Warren, plaintiffs and George Lamerte, Defendant
George Whitehead of No. 37 Wardour Street in the Parish of Saint Ann Soho in the County of Middlesex Grocer and Cheesemonger and Ann the Wife of the same George Whitehead severally make Oath and say And first this Deponent George Whitehead for himself saith that about three years ago -------------- this Deponent was applied to by a Traveller of the above named Defendants who called at the House of this Deponent and asked this Deponent if he was in want of any of Warrens Blacking   that this Deponent had been for many years in the habit of dealing with the House of Robert Warren of No 30 in the Strand for Blacking and that when the said Traveller called upon the Deponent for orders for Blacking this Deponent was in want of a few dozens of bottles of Blacking and that believing that the said person had applied from the House of Robert Warren of the Strand aforesaid this Deponent gave him an order for Blacking and a day or two afterwards a quantity of Blacking more than this Deponent had ordered was left at this Deponents House in his absence   And this Deponent Ann Whitehead for herself saith that she knew of the said George Whitehead having ordered a quantity of Blacking as she believed of Robert Warren of No. 30 in the Strand and that soon after the said order was given a quantity of Blacking being more than the number of bottles of Blacking ordered was delivered to her this Deponent during the absence of the Deponent George Whitehead and that she believed it was the Said Robert Warrens Blacking and acting under such belief she this Deponent paid for the said Blacking so left as aforesaid and was not aware of the fraud that had

188

been committed by the Defendant in affixing labels on his said bottles of blacking similar to those on the bottles of the said Robert Warren until the Deponent George Whitehead on a closer inspection of them found that the said bottles of Blacking were not the bottles of Blacking sold by the said Robert Warren and that had she been apprised of it before she certainly would not have taken them in And this Deponent George Whitehead for himself further saith that the general appearance of the Bottles and the labels upon them were so similar to those used by Robert Warren of the Strand that this Deponent at first did not discern that the said bottles of Blacking were not the bottles of Blacking of the said Robert Warren but on closer looking into them found that they were the Blacking of the above named Defendant who was at that time and still is a perfect stranger to this Deponent this Deponent never having bought any Blacking either before or since of him the said Defendant but on the contrary gave particular directions that no more of the said Blacking of the said Defendants should be taken in

George Whitehead [signature]

Ann Whitehead [signature]

Sworn at the Public office Southampton Buildings Chancery Lane in the County of Middlesex by both the Deponents George Whitehead and Ann Whitehead this 26th day of November 1827 before me

T P Stratford [signature]

Chapter Nine

Pleadings in the case of Warren v Lamerte

This document is held at The National Archives at Kew in London, catalogued at reference C 13/909/36, with the heading Warren v Lamerte. It contains firstly the joint Complaint of Robert Warren and Benjamin Warren against George Lamerte, and secondly the Answer of George Lamerte. The Complaint comprises two large sheets of parchment and the Answer a further two sheets. Like the Pleadings in Chapter Seven this transcript is my own and is not available elsewhere; as before, I have broken it down into more easily digestible chunks.

The Complaint of Robert Warren and Benjamin Warren

In Chancery, 12 November 1827, Inter by Allen
To the Right Honorable John Singleton Baron Lyndhurst of Lyndhurst[112] in the County of Southampton Lord High Chancellor of Great Britain. –

Humbly complaining shew unto your Lordship your Orators Robert Warren and Benjamin Warren both of No. 30 in the Strand in the County of Middlesex Blacking Manufacturers That your Orator Robert Warren many years prior to the year One thousand eight hundred and twenty two commenced the trade or business of a Blacking Manufacturer

And your Orators further shew your Lordship that for the purpose of raising and establishing such business he was in the habit of Advertising in the public Newspapers and of circulating placards and hand bills and that he was also in the habit of travelling or sending other persons to travel for him to most parts of England for the purpose of procuring Customers for the Article so Manufactured by him

---

112 From May 1827 the Lord Chancellor was John Singleton Copley, Baron Lyndhurst, 1772-1863.

And your Orators further shew unto your Lordship that by the ways and means aforesaid your Orator Robert Warren succeeded in raising and establishing long prior to the said year One thousand eight hundred and twenty two a very large and extensive business having Customers in most Towns in England and that such business was carried on in the name of your Orator Robert Warren alone

And your Orators further shew unto your Lordship that in or about the said year One thousand eight hundred and twenty two your Orator Robert Warren took his Brother your Orator Benjamin Warren into Partnership with him and that your Orators have ever since carried on and do still carry on the said trade or business in Copartnership together but your Orators shew that such business having been carried on and established as aforesaid under the name of your Orator Robert Warren alone your Orators did not like to change the name or style under which the same was conducted and that such business has therefore notwithstanding such Copartnership continued to be carried on and is still carried on in the name of your Orator Robert Warren alone

And your Orators further shew unto your Lordship that for the purpose of keeping up and carrying on such extensive business as aforesaid they have continued and still are in the habit of circulating such Placards and Hand bills or labels as aforesaid and also of sending Travellers to receive Orders from their Customers residing in the different parts of England

And your Orators further shew unto your Lordship that the article so Manufactured by them as aforesaid and by other persons in the same trade or business with your Orators is sold by them in Bottles and also in boxes or jars and that your Orators with the view of distinguishing the Article so sold by them from that sold by others in the same trade or business with your Orators have been in the habit of pasting or affixing one of such handbills or labels as aforesaid on each of such Bottles and boxes or jars

And your Orators further shew unto your Lordship that George Lamerte of Mansell Street Minories in the County of Middlesex the Defendant hereto has for some time past carried on the trade or business of a Blacking Manufacturer   And your Orators further shew unto your Lordship that the said Defendant about two years ago also began to travel about the Country with the view of procuring Orders for his Blacking but that not having acquired a name and reputation as a Manufacturer of Blacking he did not meet with much encouragement And your Orators further shew that the said Defendant thereupon as your Orators have lately discovered for the purpose of procuring a sale for his Blacking began both by himself and also by means of Travellers or Agents employed by him for that purpose falsely and to the great loss and injury of your Orators to represent to the Customers of your Orators and to the public in general that his the said Defendants house or business was a branch or part of the house or business of Robert Warren No. 30 Strand thereby meaning and intending your Orator's said house or business and that their style or firm was George Lamerte Jonathan Warren and Co. and that their Warehouse for the Shipping and sending of Goods was No. 30 Hungerford Stairs Strand and the said Defendant and his said Travellers or Agents accordingly solicited and obtained Orders for Blacking as and for the house of Robert Warren of the Strand your Orators said house or firm being thereby meant and intended or understood for your Orators shew that the Article so as aforesaid Manufactured by them was at that time well known by the description of the Blacking of Warren of the Strand and that your Orator's said house or firm was in fact that time and is now the only house of that name carrying on such trade or business as aforesaid in the Strand

And your Orators further shew unto your Lordship that to aid and assist such false and fraudulent representations as aforesaid the said Defendant also caused to be printed and circulated placards and handbills or labels in imitation of and similar to those of your Orators and that he also pasted one of such hand bills or labels on each of the bottles and boxes containing the Blacking so as aforesaid Manufactured by him the said Defendant in order the more easily to pass off and sell the same to the Customers of your Orators and the public in general as and for the article so as aforesaid manufactured by your Orators

And your Orators further shew unto your Lordship that by such several false and fraudulent representations and contrivances of the said Defendant as aforesaid many persons both Customers of your Orators and others who intended and were desirous to purchase your Orators Blacking have been led to purchase and have actually purchased the Article so as aforesaid Manufactured by the said Defendant conceiving that they were purchasing the Blacking of your Orators

And your Orators further shew unto your Lordship that by the means and in the manner aforesaid the said Defendant hath been enabled to sell and hath actually sold and does still sell a very great quantity of his Blacking and to a large amount in value as and for the Article so as aforesaid manufactured by your Orators and that your Orators have thereby sustained great loss and injury in their said trade and business and your Orators have by themselves and their Agents frequently and in a friendly manner applied to the said Defendant and requested him to desist from making such false and fraudulent representations as aforesaid and from using the name of your Orators and from soliciting or taking orders as and for the house or business of your Orators and also to desist from imitating or copying your Orators said Placards and hand bills or labels

And your Orators well hoped that such their just and reasonable requests would have been complied with as in justice and equity they ought to have been But now so it is May it please your Lordship the said George Lamerte combining and confederating with divers persons at present unknown to your Orators whose names when discovered your Orators pray they may be at liberty to insert in this their Bill with apt words to charge them as parties Defendants hereto and contriving how to injure and oppress your Orators in the premises the said Defendant George Lamerte absolutely refuses to comply with your Orator's aforesaid reasonable requests and he threatens and intends to continue such false and fraudulent representations and practices as aforesaid unless he shall be restrained therefrom by the Injunction of this Honorable Court

and to countenance such his unjust conduct and refusal he sometimes pretends that he is really carrying on the trade or business of a Blacking Manufacturer in Partnership with one Jonathan Warren and other persons at No. 30 Hungerford Stairs Strand aforesaid Whereas your Orators Charge the contrary thereof to be true and that the said Defendant carries on such trade or business by himself alone and not in Partnership with any other persons or person And your Orators in particular charge that the said Defendant is not in Partnership with or in any way connected with any person of the name of Jonathan Warren in his said trade or business for they charge that such name is a fictitious name and only made use of by the said Defendant in order the more easily to sell and dispose of his Blacking as and for the Article so as aforesaid Manufactured by your Orators And your Orators therefore charge that he ought to be restrained from using such name

And your Orators further Charge that the house and premises in which they carry on their said trade or business is situated in the Strand aforesaid and Numbered 30 and is in fact not far distant from Hungerford Stairs Strand aforesaid And that the said No. 30 the number of their said house and premises is printed on their said placards and bills or labels in very large and conspicuous Characters And your

Orators further charge that the said Defendant has also caused the said No. 30 to be printed on his said placards and bills or labels in characters of the same size and appearance asthose in which such Number is printed in your Orators said placards and bills or labels And your Orators charge that the said Defendant has selected that Number in consequence of such being the Number of your Orator's said house and premises and that he has selected the address of Hungerford Stairs Strand on account of its Vicinity to your Orators said house and premises in the Strand with the view of aiding and assisting his said false and fraudulent representations and contrivances and of inducing the public the more readily to believe that the Article so sold by the said Defendant is in fact the Article so as aforesaid Manufactured and sold by your Orators for your Orators charge that their said house or firm has been for some years known by the name and description of Robert Warren of No. 30 Strand and that the said Defendant has in fact no house or premises or place for business belonging to or occupied or held by him at No. 30 Hungerford Stairs Strand

but then the said Defendant pretends that his said placards and bills or labels are in other respects very unlike those of your Orators whereas your Orators charge the contrary thereof to be true for your Orators charge that if such placards and bills or labels are not precisely and in all respects similar to those used by your Orators as aforesaid they are nevertheless a very close imitation thereof and that the said Defendant contrived and caused the same to be printed solely for the purpose of enabling him by reason of their very great similarity to those of your Orators to sell and dispose of his Blacking as and for the Blacking of your Orators And your Orators charge that such Bills or Labels of the said Defendant are in fact so close an imitation or Copy of those of your Orators that many persons who were desirous of purchasing your Orators Blacking have been deceived or misled by them and have actually purchased the Blacking of the said Defendant intending to purchase and conceiving that they were purchasing your Orators said Article or commodity to the very great loss and injury of your Orators

And your Orators further Charge that many persons both customers of your Orators and others have been also deceived or misled by such false and fraudulent representations of the said Defendant and his said Travellers or Agents that his house or business was a branch or part of your Orators said house or business and that such persons have in consequence dealt with the said Defendant and purchased Blacking of him to a large amount in value conceiving and believing that they were dealing with your Orators said house or firm and were purchasing your Orators said Blacking   And your Orators charge that they have thereby sustained great pecuniary loss and damage and they therefore Charge that the said Defendant ought to account with your Orators for the profits made by him by such unfair and fraudulent means as aforesaid and to pay over such profits unto your Orators

All which actings pretences and refusals of the said Defendant George Lamerte are contrary to Equity and good conscience and lend to the manifest wrong and injury of your Orators in the premises   In tender consideration whereof and for as much as your Orators are without remedy in the premises at Common Law and can only have adequate relief in a Court of Equity where matters of this sort are properly cognizable and relievable

To the End therefore that the said Defendant George Lamerte and his Confederates when discovered may upon their several and respective corporal Oaths according to the best and utmost of their several and respective knowledge remembrance information and belief full true perfect and distinct Answer make to all and singular the matters aforesaid and that as fully and particularly as if the same were here repeated and they thereunto severally and distinctly respectively interrogated and more especially that the said Defendant George Lamerte may in manner aforesaid answer and set forth

Whether your Orator Robert Warren did not many and how many years prior to the year One thousand eight hundred and twenty two commence the trade or business of a Blacking Manufacturer or how otherwise   And whether for the purpose of raising and establishing such business your Orator was not in the habit of Advertising in the public Newspapers and of circulating placards and hand bills or how otherwise And whether he was not also in the habit of travelling or sending other persons to travel for him to most or some and what parts of England for the purpose of procuring Customers for the Article so Manufactured by him or how otherwise   And whether by the ways and means aforesaid or some and which of them or some other and what ways and means   And whether in fact your Orator Robert Warren did not succeed in raising and establishing long and how long prior to the said year One thousand eight hundred and twenty two a very large and extensive business or how otherwise And whether or not having Customers in most or some and what Towns or other Places in England   And whether such business was not carried on in the name of your Orator Robert Warren alone or in whose name was the same carried on   And whether in or about the said year One thousand eight hundred and twenty two or at some other and what time your Orator Robert Warren did not take his Brother your Orator Benjamin Warren into Partnership with him or how otherwise And whether your Orators have not ever since carried on and do not still carry on the said trade or business in Copartnership together or how otherwise And whether for the reasons aforesaid or some other and what reasons   And whether in fact such business has not notwithstanding such Copartnership continued to be carried on and is not still carried on in the name of your Orator Robert Warren alone or in whose name is the same carried on

And whether for the purpose of keeping up and carrying on such extensive business as aforesaid your Orators have not continued and are not still in the habit of circulating such placards and handbills or labels as aforesaid or how otherwise   And whether they have not continued and are not still in the habit of sending travellers to receive orders for their customers residing in the different and what parts of England or how otherwise   And whether the article so manufactured by your Orators as aforesaid and by other persons in the same trade or business with your Orators is not sold by them in bottles and also in boxes or jars or how otherwise And whether your Orators with the view of distinguishing the article so sold by them from that sold by others in the same trade or business with your Orators or with some other and what view have not been in the habit of pasting or affixing one of such handbills or labels as aforesaid on each of such bottles and boxes or jars or how otherwise

And whether the said Defendant has not for some and what period of time also carried on the trade or business of a Blacking manufacturer And whether the said Defendant about two years ago or how long since did not also begin to travel about the Country with the view of procuring orders for his blacking or how otherwise   And whether the said Defendant had at that time acquired a name and reputation as a manufacturer of blacking   And if he shall pretend that he had then that he may setforth and discover in what manner in particular and in what place or places in particular he had acquired such name and reputation And whether your Orators have not lately discovered or how otherwise

And whether the said Defendant in fact did not for the purpose of procuring a sale for his blacking begin both by himself and also by the means of travellers or agents employed by him for that purpose or how otherwise falsely and to the great loss and injury of your Orators to represent to some or one and which of the customers of your Orators and to the public in general that his the said Defendants house or business was a branch or part of the house or business of Robert Warren Number 30 Strand   And whether the said Defendant did not thereby mean and intend your Orators said house or business or how does the said Defendant make out the contrary thereof and whether the said Defendant and his said Travellers or Agents or some or one and which of them did not also represent that their Style or firm was George Lamerte Jonathan Warren & Co. or how otherwise   And that their warehouse for the shipping and sending of goods was number 30 Hungerford Stairs Strand or how otherwise   And whether the said Defendant and his said Travellers or Agents or some or one and which of them did not accordingly solicit and obtain orders for blacking as and for the house of Robert Warren of the Strand or how otherwise   And whether your Orators said house or firm was not thereby meant and intended or understood or how otherwise

And whether the Article so as aforesaid manufactured by your Orators was not at that time well known by the description of the blacking of Warren of the Strand or how otherwise And whether your Orators said house or firm was not in fact at that time and is not now the only house of that name carrying on such trade or business as aforesaid in the Strand or how doth the said Defendant make out the contrary thereof and whether to aid and assist such false and fraudulent representations as aforesaid the said Defendant did not also print or cause to be printed and circulated placards and handbills or labels in imitation of and similar to those of your Orators or how otherwise   And whether he did not also paste or cause to be pasted one of such handbills or labels on each of the bottles and boxes or jars containing the blacking so as aforesaid manufactured by him the said Defendant   And whether or not in order the more easily to pass off and sell the same to the Customers of your Orators and the public in general as and for the article so as aforesaid manufactured by your Orators or how otherwise   And whether by such several false and fraudulent representations and contrivances of the said Defendant as aforesaid many persons both customers of your Orators and others or some and what persons who intended and were desirous to purchase your Orators blacking have not been led to purchase and have not actually purchased the article so as aforesaid manufactured by the said Defendant or how otherwise   And whether such persons did not at the time conceive that they were purchasing the blacking of your Orators or how otherwise   And whether by the means and in the manner aforesaid or by some such or the like or some other and what means the said Defendant hath not been enabled to sell   And whether he hath not actually sold   And whether he does not still sell a very great quantity of his blacking and to a large amount in value as and for the article so as aforesaid manufactured by your Orators or how otherwise

And whether your Orators have not thereby sustained great or some and what loss and injury in their said trade or business or how otherwise And whether your Orators have not by themselves and their agents or how otherwise made such applications and requests to the said Defendant George Lamerte hath not refused to comply with such requests and why And whether the said Defendant does not threaten and intend to continue such false and fraudulent representations and practices as aforesaid unless he shall be restrained therefrom by the Injunction of this Honorable Court or how otherwise

And whether the said Defendant does not carry on such trade or business as aforesaid by himself alone or how otherwise And whether he carries on such trade or business in partnership with any other and what persons or person And whether the said Defendant is in partnership with or in any way connected with any person of the name of Jonathan Warren in his said trade or business and if he shall allege that he is then that the said Defendant may setforth and discover who the said Jonathan Warren is and where he resides now and where he did reside two years ago and in what way he is connected with the said Defendant in his said trade or business And whether such name is not a fictitious name or how otherwise And whether such name is not merely made use of by the said Defendant in order the more easily to sell and dispose of his blacking as and for the article so as aforesaid manufactured by your Orators or how otherwise or for what other purpose is such name made use of by the said Defendant And whether the said Defendant ought not to be restrained from using such name and if not why not And whether the house and premises in which your Orators carry on their said trade or business is not situated in the Strand aforesaid and numbered 30 or how otherwise And whether it is not in fact not far distant from Hungerford Stairs Strand aforesaid or how otherwise And whether the said number 30 the number of your Orators said house and premises is not printed on their said placards and bills or labels in very large and conspicuous characters or how otherwise And whether the said Defendant has not also caused the said number 30 to be printed on his said placards and bills or labels in characters of the same size and in appearance as those in which such number is printed in your Orators said placards and bills or labels or how do such characters differ in size or appearance from those of your Orators said placards and bills or labels And whether the said Defendant has not selected that number in consequence of such being the number of your Orators said house and premises or for what other reason did he select it   And whether he has not selected the address of Hungerford Stairs Strand on account of its vicinity to your Orators said house and premises in the Strand or on what account did the said Defendant select such address And whether the said Defendant did not select such number of such address or one and which of them with the view of aiding and assisting his said false and fraudulent representations and contrivances or how otherwise

And whether or not with the view of inducing the public the more readily to believe that the article so sold by the said Defendant is in fact the article so as aforesaid manufactured and sold by your Orators or how doth the said Defendant make out the contrary thereof   And whether your Orators said house or firm has not been for some years known by the name and description of Robert Warren of Number 30 Strand   And whether the Defendant has in fact now or has had within the last two years and when in particular and during what times or time in particular any and what house or premises or place for business belonging to or occupied or held by him at number 30 Hungerford Stairs Strand and how doth the said Defendant make out that he has   And whether such placards and bills or labels of the said Defendant or some or one and which of them are not or is not a close imitation of those of your Orators or how otherwise   And whether the said Defendant did not contrive and cause the same or some or one and which of them to be printed solely for the purpose of enabling him by reason of their very great similarity to those of your Orators to sell and dispose of his blacking as and for the blacking of your Orators or how otherwise   And whether such bills or labels of the said Defendant are not in fact so close an imitation or copy of those of your Orators that many persons who were desirous of purchasing your Orators blacking have been deceived or misled by them   And whether such persons or some and what persons have not actually purchased the blacking of the said Defendant intending to purchase and conceiving that they were purchasing your Orators said article or commodity or how otherwise   And whether very great loss and injury has not thereby been occasioned to your Orators or how otherwise

And whether many persons customers of your Orators and also many other persons have not been deceived or misled by such false and fraudulent representations of the said Defendant and his said travellers or agents that his house or business was a branch or part of your Orators said house or business or how otherwise   And whether such persons or some of them have not in consequence dealt with the said Defendant and purchased blacking of him to a large and what amount in value And whether such persons or some of them did not conceive and believe that they were dealing with your Orators said house or firm and were purchasing your Orators said blacking or how otherwise And whether your Orators have not thereby sustained great and what pecuniary loss and damage And whether the said Defendant ought not to account with your Orators for the profits made by him by such unfair and fraudulent means as aforesaid and to pay over such profits unto your Orators and if not why not

And that the said Defendant may answer the premises And that he and his travellers agents servants and workmen may be restrained by the order and injunction of this Honorable Court from representing that his house or business is a branch or part of the house or business of your Orators or in any way connected therewith or that he the said Defendant is in anyway connected with your Orators in their said trade or business And also from soliciting or taking or receiving any orders for Blacking as and for the house or firm of your Orators or as and for the house of Warren of the Strand And also from selling or exposing to sale any blacking as and for the blacking of your Orators and from using or employing the name of your Orators

And that the said Defendant may in like manner be restrained from circulating or using his said placards and handbills or labels or <u>any</u> of them and from copying or imitating your Orators said placards and bills or labels or any of them and from using any placards or bills or labels the same as those of your Orators or similar thereto or so nearly similar thereto that they may impose on and lead the public to a belief that they are your Orators

And that an account may be taken by and under the direction of this Honorable Court of the profits made by the said Defendant upon the blacking sold by him by such unfair and fraudulent means as aforesaid And that he may be decreed to pay such profits unto your Orators And that your Orators may have such further or other relief in the premises as the nature and circumstances of their case may require or to your Lordship may seem meet

May it please your Lordship the premises considered to grant unto your Orators not only His Majesty's Most Gracious Writ of Injunction to be directed to the said George Lamerte for the purposes aforesaid but also His Majesty's Most Gracious Writ or Writs of Subpoena issuing out of and under the Seal of this Honorable Court to be directed to the said

George Lamerte (and the rest of his confederates when discovered) thereby commanding him at a certain day and under a certain pain therein to be limited personally to be and appear before your Lordship in this Honorable Court   And then and there full true and perfect answer make to all and singular the premises and further to stand to perform and abide such order and Decree therein as to your Lordship shall seem meet   And your Orators shall every pray &c./-   A. Crombie.
James Harnett   Ref   Soer   29 Northumberland Street   Strand
Mills

The Answer of George Lamerte

Sworn at my House in the… Hospital in the County of Middlesex this
… day of February 1828 Before me Jam: C: Cox
Allen   16th Feby 1828

The Answer of George Lamerte the Defendant to the Bill of Complaint of Robert Warren and Benjamin Warren complainants

This Defendant now and at all times hereafter saving and reserving to himself all and all manner of benefit and advantage which can or may be had or taken to the said Bill of Complaint by way of exception or otherwise for answer thereunto or unto so much thereof as this Defendant is advised it is any way necessary or material for him to make answer unto answering says

the complainants on or about the seventeenth day of November One thousand eight hundred and twenty seven applied for and obtained an injunction in this cause and that such Injunction was upon the application of this Defendant on or about the twenty seventh day of November One thousand eight hundred and twenty seven dissolved

And this Defendant says that in order to obtain such Injunction and in order to dissolve such Injunction divers Affidavits were made and by means of some of such Affidavits this Defendant was for the first time made acquainted with many facts and circumstances which till then were unknown to this Defendant

however this Defendant says he has heard and believes that in or about the year One thousand seven hundred and ninety eight Jonathan Warren in the said Bill mentioned as a fictitious person commenced the Business of a Blacking Manufacturer and that he carried on such business in his own name and on his own account until the month of October One thousand eight hundred and twenty two when as hereinafter mentioned he sold such business to William Edward Woodd hereinafter mentioned

And this Defendant says he has heard and believes that the said Jonathan Warren was the Uncle of the said Complainants and that the Complainant Robert Warren commenced his business of a Blacking Manufacturer in or about the year One thousand eight hundred and five And this Defendant says he has heard and believes that in or about the month of March One thousand eight hundred and twenty one the said Jonathan Warren removed his Business of a Blacking Manufacturer to a House situate in Hungerford Stairs Strand and which House was in and before the month of October One thousand eight hundred and twenty two Numbered 30 but this Defendant says he has heard and believes that the said Number 30 was exchanged for the Number 25 which had been the previous Number of the said House however this Defendant says he was no party to such exchange of Number nor did this Defendant know thereof until long after such exchange had been made

And this Defendant says he has heard and believes that the said Jonathan Warren advertized his said Business for Sale some time in the year One thousand eight hundred and twenty two and that the said William Edward Woodd in or before the month of October One thousand eight hundred and twenty two purchased the good will of such business and the right to use the name of the said Jonathan Warren therein for a valuable consideration

And this Defendant says that after the said William Edward Woodd had so purchased the good will of the said trade and the right to use the name of the said Jonathan Warren he the said William Edward Woodd engaged this Defendant to assist in such Manufactory and business and when this Defendant was thus introduced into the said business he found the said Trade or Business settled and carried on at the said House in Hungerford Stairs aforesaid and which House was then Numbered 30 as aforesaid   And this Defendant found the said Jonathan Warren employed by the said William Edward Woodd to Manufacture such Blacking and this Defendant says when he so first entered into the employment of the said William Edward Woodd he was totally unacquainted with the art of manufacturing blacking but that this Defendant by the desire of the said William Edward Woodd paid most particular attention to the manufacture and used great exertions to obtain every information in his power as to the best mode of Manufacturing Blacking and constantly assisted the said Jonathan Warren in Manufacturing the Blacking manufactured on account of the said

William Edward Woodd and sold and sold [sic] by him under the name of the said Jonathan Warren   And this Defendant says the said Jonathan Warren always asserted that he was the original Inventor of the Blacking sold under the name of Warrens Blacking

And this Defendant says by diligent attention to the subject and constant study and by application of the Principles of Chemistry to the art this Defendant greatly improved upon the practice of the said Jonathan Warren and thereby extended the Sale of such Blacking which acquired a great and profitable reputation under the Name of Jonathan Warren or Warrens Blacking No 30 Hungerford Stairs Strand

And this Defendant says that the said Jonathan Warren died in or about the month of August One thousand eight hundred and twenty four and that this Defendant from the death of the said Jonathan Warren continued exclusively to Manufacture the Blacking sold under such name and description as aforesaid by the said William Edward Woodd until the month of October one thousand eight hundred and twenty four

and that in the month of January One thousand eight hundred and twenty five this Defendant commenced business on his own account in Partnership with Lewis Worms and in the hand Bills and Labels used by this defendant and the said Lewis Worms the Blacking manufactured and sold by them was described as made by the late Manufacturer to Jonathan Warren No 30 Hungerford Stairs Strand as this Defendant submits and insists is consistent with the facts of the Case and that he was well entitled so to describe the Blacking manufactured and sold by this Defendant

but this Defendant says it has always been an important object to this Defendant to connect his own name with such Blacking and at the same time to secure to himself the advantage which has arisen from the reputation of the Blacking manufactured by this Defendant for the said William Edward Woodd and sold by the said William Edward Woodd as Jonathan Warrens Blacking No. 30 Hungerford Stairs Strand

and therefore this Defendant has on all such hand Bills and Labels inserted his own name therein and described himself as this Defendant submits and insists he was late Manufacturer to Jonathan Warren   And this Defendant says that some time since the partnership between this Defendant and the said Lewis Worms was dissolved and this Defendant says that during such Copartnership the firm or style of such

Copartnership was "G Lamerte & Co." and since then this Defendant has used his own name only

and this Defendant says he sells by far the larger quantity of his blacking in the Country and upon Credit and that all bills of parcels delivered of such blacking have as this Defendant believes been written upon paper on which were engraved either the words and figures following that is to say "London Bot. of G. Lamerte & Co. Japan Blacking Manufacturers Whitechapel Road" or the words and figures following that is to say "London Bot. of G. Lamerte Japan Blacking Manufacturer 56 Mansell Street" and on such last mentioned Bills of parcels neither the name of Jonathan Warren nor the description No. 30 Hungerford Stairs Strand appears

And this Defendant says that on the direction Cards of the packages of Blacking so sold by this Defendant in the Country are printed the words and figures following that is to say "Keep this side up from the Warehouse of G. Lamerte & Co. proprietors of the Blacking made by the late Manufacturer to Jonathan Warren 107 Whitechapel Road London" and that on such direction Cards the description No 30 Hungerford Stairs Strand does not appear

And this Defendant says he believes that no person who has read all or any or either of the placards labels invoices and Cards used by this Defendant and his late partner or by this Defendant since the Dissolution of such Partnership could or have been deceived thereby or induced thereby to believe that this Defendant and his late partner or that this Defendant had or ever had any connection with the house concern or business of the Complainants but on the contrary that this Defendant and his late partner and this Defendant since the dissolution of such partnership traded and carried on business on their and his own account and not only unconnected with but in opposition to the complainants whose blacking is greatly inferior to that Manufactured by this Defendant

however this Defendant says that Hungerford Stairs aforesaid is close to the Shop of the Complainants and that the Complainants must have known and did as this Defendant believes well know that the Blacking sold by the said Jonathan Warren from the beginning of the year One thousand eight hundred and twenty one until October One thousand eight eight hundred and twenty two and by the said William Edward Woodd from October One thousand eight hundred and twenty two until October One thousand eight hundred and twenty four was sold under and by means of placards and labels describing the same as the blacking of or as blacking Manufactured by Jonathan Warren No. 30 Hungerford Stairs Strand and that the Complainants never in any way during such periods or any part thereof complained of such placards and labels

And this Defendant says he and his partner used during such their partnership and this Defendant has since the dissolution of such partnership used the same placards Cards hand Bills and Labels with the variation only that since the dissolution of the said Copartnership the "& Co" has been omitted therein and that the address or place of business of this Defendant has been changed and this Defendant says the Complainants must have known and did as this Defendant believes know of the use of such placards cards hand bills and labels by this Defendant and his said partner and by this Defendant since the dissolution of such Partnership ever since January One thousand eight hundred and twenty five and except by filing their present Bill of Complaint in the month of November One thousand eight eight hundred and twenty seven being a period of nearly three years they never complained thereof or objected thereto to this Defendant and the first knowledge which this defendant had of the Complainants questioning the right of this Defendant to use such placards cards hand Bills and Labels was when he was served with the order of the Injunction hereinbefore mentioned to have been granted and dissolved as aforesaid

And this Defendant says he has heard and believes that the Complainant Robert Warren did for about seventeen years prior to the year One thousand eight hundred and twenty two that is in or about the year One thousand eight hundred and five as is hereinbefore mentioned commence the Trade or business of a Blacking Manufacturer and that for the purpose of raising and establishing such business the Complainant Robert Warren was in the habit of advertizing in the Public Newspapers and of circulating placards and Bills but this Defendant says he has also been informed and believes that the said Jonathan Warren was in the habits of advertizing in the public Newspapers and of circulating hand bills and placards for the purpose of raising and establishing his Business of a Blacking Manufacturer

however this Defendant says he has heard and believes that the Complainant Robert Warren was also in the habit of Travelling or sending other persons to travel for him to most parts of England for the purpose of procuring Customers for the Article so manufactured by him but this Defendant says he does not know and is unable to set forth as to his belief or otherwise whether by the ways and means in the said Bill or any or what other ways and means or whether in fact the Complainant Robert Warren did succeed in raising and establishing long or how long prior to the said year One thousand eight hundred and twenty two a very large and extensive business or how otherwise or whether in having Customers in most Towns or other places in England

but this Defendant says he has heard and believes that the complainant Robert Warren by Puffs and otherwise made a great show of carrying on an extensive business however this Defendant says he has heard and believes that such business was carried on in the name of complainant Robert Warren alone but save from the complainants said Bill and the Affidavits filed in support thereof this Defendant says he does not know but has not been informed and is unable to set forth as to his belief or otherwise whether in or about the said year One thousand eight hundred and twenty two or at any other time or when the Complainant Robert Warren did take his Brother the Complainant Benjamin Warren into partnership with him or how otherwise or whether the Complainants have ever since carried on or do still carry on the said trade or business in Copartnership or how otherwise or whether for the reasons in the said Bill mentioned or any other or what reasons or whether in fact such business has notwithstanding such alledged copartnership continued to be carried on or is still carried on in the name of the Complainant Robert Warren alone but this Defendant says he believes such business is carried on in the name of the Complainant Robert Warren alone

however this Defendant says he does not know but he believes that for the purpose of carrying On such business as aforesaid the Complainants or the Complainant Robert Warren have or has continued and are or is still in the habit of circulating such Placards and hand bills or labels as in the said Bill Mentioned and that the Complainants or the Complainant Robert Warren have or has continued and are or is still in the habit of sending Travellers to receive orders from their or his customers residing in different parts of England

And this Defendant says he believes that with the exception of Blacking hawked about the Streets the Article so manufactured by the Complainants or by the Complainant Robert Warren and by other persons in the same Trade or business is sold by them in Bottles and also in Boxes or Jars however this Defendant says that the whole or nearly the whole of the persons engaged in the blacking Trade use similar bottles Boxes and Jars or nearly so and that the whole or nearly the whole of the persons engaged in the Blacking Trade use Placards and Labels very much resembling each other as the form color and disposition and the disposition of the printing although on inspection the differences are discovered and which consist in the true name and address being used and in the words printed being different as in the case between the placards and labels used by this Defendant and the Complainant Robert Warren or by the Complainants in the name of the Complainant Robert Warren

however this Defendant says though he does not know yet he believes that the Complainants or the Complainant Robert Warren with a view of distinguishing the Article so sold by them or him from that sold by others have been in the habit of pasting or affixing one of such hand bills or labels as in the said Bill mentioned on each of such bottles and Boxes or Jars

And this Defendant admits that he has as aforesaid but not otherwise for some period of time also carried on the said Trade or business of a Blacking Manufacturer and that about two years ago he began to Travel about the Country with a view of procuring orders for his Blacking And this Defendant says that while he was in the employment of the said William Edward Woodd as aforesaid he this Defendant became and was well known to most of the customers of the said William Edward Woodd as the Manufacturer with the assistance of the said Jonathan Warren of the Blacking sold by the said William Edward Woodd as Jonathan Warrens Blacking and as such Manufacturer this Defendant before he commenced business on his own account had acquired a name and reputation as a Manufacturer of Blacking but save as aforesaid this Defendant is unable to set forth as to his knowledge belief or otherwise whether he had at the time in the said Bill in that behalf mentioned acquired a name and reputation as a Manufacturer of Blacking or to set forth or discover in what manner in particular or in what place or places he had acquired such name and reputation

And this Defendant denies that the Complainants have lately discovered or that the fact is that this Defendant did for the purpose of procuring a Sale for his Blacking or for any other purpose begin either by himself or by means of Travellers or Agents employed by him for that purpose or any otherwise falsely and to the great loss and injury of the Complainants to represent or has represented to every or one of the Customers of Complainants and to the Public in general that his this Defendants House or business was a branch or part of the house or business of Robert Warren No 30 Strand

And this Defendant denies that he and to the best of his knowledge information and belief he denies that his said Travellers or Agents or any or either of them did ever represent that their style or form was George Lamerte Jonathan Warren & Co. or that the Warehouse for the Shipping and sending of Goods was No 30 Hungerford Stairs Strand or any otherwise than as aforesaid or that This Defendant or his said Travellers or Agents or any or either of them did accordingly or otherwise solicit or obtain orders for Blacking as or for the house of Robert Warren of the Strand or any otherwise than as aforesaid

And this Defendant says he does not know and cannot set forth as to his belief or otherwise whether the Article so as in the said Bill alledged to be manufactured by the Complainants was at the time in the said Bill mentioned well known by the description of the Blacking of Warren of the Strand or how otherwise however this Defendant says he believes that the Complainants or the Complainant Robert Warrens said House or firm was in fact and is now the only house of that name carrying on such a Trade or business as in the said Bill mentioned in the Strand and the Defendant denies that to aid and assist such pretended false and fraudulent representation as in the said Bill is untruly alledged this Defendant did print or cause to be printed and circulate placards and hand Bills of Labels in imitation of or similar to those of the Complainants or that he did paste or cause to be pasted one of such hand Bills or Labels on each of the Bottles and Boxes or Jars containing the Blacking or as aforesaid Manufactured by him Defendant or that he so did in order the more easily to pass off and sell the same to the Customers of the Complainants and the Public in general as and for the Article Manufactured by the Complainants or that by such pretended several false and fraudulent representation and contrivances of this Defendant as in the said Bill is falsely alledged many or any persons either Customers of the Complainants or of other persons who intended or were desirous to purchase the Complainants blacking have been led to purchase or have actually purchased the article manufactured by this Defendant or that such persons did at the time conceive that they were purchasing the Blacking of the Complainants or that by the means or in the manner aforesaid or by any such or the like means this Defendant has been enabled to sell or that he still sells a very great quantity of his Blacking and to a large amount in value as and for the Article manufactured by the Complainants or that the Complainants have thereby sustained great or any loss or injury in their alledged trade or business however this Defendant says he has pasted his own labels on his bottles Jars and Boxes but this Defendant says the same are are not imitation of the labels in the said Bill alledged to be the Labels of the Complainants and that on the contrary there is a material difference between the labels of this Defendant and those in the said Bill alledged to have been used by the Complainants

And this Defendant denies that the Complainants have by themselves and their Agents or any otherwise made such applications and requests to this Defendant as are in the said Bill in that behalf mentioned or any such or the like or any other applications and requests in respect of the several matters in the said Bill mentioned or any or either of them

And this Defendant denies that he has refused to comply with such pretended requests or that he threatens and intends or ever threatened or intended to continue the pretended false and fraudulent representations and practices as in the said Bill is untruly alledged unless he shall be restrained therefrom by the Injunction of this Honorable Court

but this Defendant says he insists he has a right to carry on his business as he has heretofore been accustomed and which he submits and insists he has a right to do

however this Defendant admits that he does now carry on such Trade or business as aforesaid by himself alone and that he does not now carry on such Trade or business in partnership with any other person or persons and that he this Defendant is not in partnership with or in any way connected with any person of the name of Jonathan Warren in his said Trade or business but this Defendant denies that the name of Jonathan Warren is a fictitious name or any otherwise than that when the Complainants filed their said Bill of Complaint and when the affidavits were made in support of it the Complainant well knew that such allegation was false and that the said Jonathan Warren instead of being a fictitious person was their own Uncle the Brother of their own Father and that they were personally acquainted with him and knew he had in his own person and for his own account and benefit carried on the business of a Blacking Manufacturer

And this Defendant denies that the said name of Jonathan Warren is merely made use of by this Defendant in order the more easily to sell and dispose of his Blacking as and for Article so as in the said Bill alledged to be manufactured by the Complainants or any otherwise than as aforesaid   And this Defendant says he has only used the said name of Jonathan Warren for the purpose and in manner as aforesaid

And this Defendant submits and insists that he ought not be restrained from using such name and that by reason of the facts and circumstances aforesaid however this Defendant admits that the house and premises in which the complainants or the Complainant Robert Warren carry or carries on their or his said Trade or business is situated in the Strand aforesaid and Numbered 30 and is not far distant from Hungerford Stairs Strand aforesaid but is near thereto and that the said No. 30 the Number of the Complainants or of the Complainant Robert Warrens said house and premises is printed on their or his said placards and Bills or labels in very large and conspicuous characters

however this Defendant says that in some of his hand Bills and Labels he has inserted the number 30 in the same or nearly the same size as the said Number 30 is printed in the placards or Bills of the Complainants or of the Complainant Robert Warren but this Defendant says that the Number 30 as inserted by this Defendant in his said placards hand bills and Labels is in many material particulars different from the number 30 printed by the Complainants or by the Complainant Robert Warren in their or his placards hand bills and labels or by reference of such placards hand bills and labels will fully appear but save as aforesaid this Defendant denies that he this Defendant has caused the said No 30 to be printed on his said placards or bills or labels in characters in the same size and appearance as those in which such Number is printed in the complainants or in the Complainant Robert Warrens said placards or Bills or labels but how such Characters differ in size or appearance from those of the Complainants or of the Complainant Robert Warren said placards Bills and Labels can only be correctly shewn by a comparison thereof and thereby this Defendant craves to refer thereto and to such comparison

however this Defendant denies that he has selected the No. 30 in consequence of such being the Number of the Complainants said house and premises or that he has selected the address of Hungerford Stairs Strand on account of its vicinity to the Complainants said house and premises in the Strand or that this Defendant selected such No. 30 or such address or either of them with the view of aiding and assisting his said pretended false and fraudulent representations or contrivances or any otherwise than that he never selected such number and address or either of them or that he selected such number and address or either of them with a view of inducing the public the more readily to believe that

210

the article sold by this Defendant was in fact the Article manufactured and sold by the Complainant but on the contrary this Defendant says he found such Number and address to be the number and address at which the said William Edward Woodd in the name of the said Jonathan Warren was carrying on the said business of a Blacking Manufacturer and instead of the name of Jonathan Warren or of such Number and address being fictitious the same were an existing name number and address when this Defendant first entered into the employment of the said William Edward Woodd as is hereinbefore mentioned however this Defendant admits that he this Defendant has not and in fact has not had within the last two years or at any other time any house or premises or place for business belonging to or occupied or held by him at Number 30 Hungerford Stairs Strand

And this Defendant says he has compared the placards or Bills and Labels used by this Defendant with those of the Complainants or of the Complainant Robert Warren and this Defendant to the best of his Judgment and belief denies that such placards or Bills or Labels of this Defendant or any or either of them are or is a close imitation of those of the Complainants or of the Complainant Robert Warren or any otherwise than that no such or other imitation exists

And this Defendant denies that he this Defendant did contrive or cause the same or any or either of them to be printed solely or at all for the purpose of enabling him this Defendant by reason of their pretended very great similarity to those of the Complainants or of the Complainant Robert Warren to sell and dispose of his Blacking as and for the Blacking of the Complainants or of the Complainant Robert Warren or any otherwise than as aforesaid

And this Defendant to the best of his knowledge information and belief denies that such Bills or Labels of this Defendant are in fact so close an imitation of Copy of those of the Complainants or of the Complainant Robert Warren that many or any persons or person who were or was desirous of purchasing the Complainants or the Complainant Robert Warrens Blacking have or has been deceived or misled by them or that any persons or person have or has actually purchased the Blacking of this Defendant intending to purchase and conceiving that they he or she were or was purchasing the Complainants or the Complainant Robert Warren's said article or commodity or any otherwise than as aforesaid or that a very great or any loss and Injury has thereby been occasioned to the Complainants or either of them or any otherwise than as aforesaid or that many or any persons or person customers of the complainants or of the Complainant Robert Warren or any other persons or person have or has been deceived or misled by such pretended false and fraudulent representations of this Defendant and his said Travellers and Agents that his house or business was a branch or part of the Complainants said house or business or any otherwise than that no such representations have been made by this Defendant nor as he believes by his Travellers and agents or any or either of them

And this Defendant denies that such pretended persons or any of them have in consequence dealt with this defendant and purchased Blacking of him to a large or any amount in value or that such pretended persons or any of them did conceive or believe that they were dealing with the Complainants or with the Complainant Robert Warren's said house or firm or were purchasing the Complainants or the Complainant Robert Warrens said Blacking or any otherwise than as aforesaid or that the Complainants have thereby sustained great pecuniary or any loss or damage or that this Defendant ought to account with Complainant for the pretended profit made by him by such pretended unfair and fraudulent means as in the said Bill are untruly alledged and to pay over such pretended profits to the Complainants

however this Defendant says that in consequence of the very great superiority of the Article or Blacking manufactured by this Defendant over that manufactured by the Complainants or the Complainant Robert Warren this Defendant believes that many persons who were customers of the Complainants or of the Complainant Robert Warren have intentionally become Customers of this Defendant

And this Defendant says he believes the present Bill of Complaint was filed and the said Injunction applied for merely for the purpose of putting off and advertizing the Blacking of the Complainants and by the interception which it caused to the trade of this Defendant to induce the Customers of this Defendant to leave him and deal with the Complainants and as Evidence of such fraudulent purpose on the part of the Complainants this Defendant says that as soon as the said Injunction was obtained they sent to and circulated amongst the Customers of this Defendant a printed Letter and notice in the words and figures following that is to say

"Blacking Manufactory 30 Strand London,
Sir, Being informed you have been selling and now have a quantity of the Counterfeit Article in imitation of the genuine Warrens Blacking made by me I beg to recommend the annexed Notice to your very serious

attention presuming you have been deceived by the close imitation and having no wish to proceed to extremities, without giving an opportunity for your immediately discontinuing a practice so injurious to my trade and reputation as a Blacking Manufacturer I have to request you will take the earliest means in your power to stop such proceedings. The most effectual will be to return the Spurious Blacking to the parties from whom you receive it. I shall feel further obliged by your favouring me with an order for a supply of the Genuine Blacking. A line by post will meet with immediate attention from,

Sir, your obedient Servant Robert Warren"

"Court of Chancery   An Injunction has this day been granted by the Lord Chancellor to restrain G. Lamerte from making or selling any Blacking with Labels in imitation of the genuine Warren's Blacking, which he has been in the habit of doing, by using the fictitious name of Jonathan Warren, and otherwise imitating the genuine Labels of Robert Warren No 30 Strand. It is therefore strongly recommended that those Shopkeepers or others who have any of the Counterfeit Blacking, as above described do return it to the parties from whom they received it, which they are justified in doing. By neglecting this Notice they will be liable to the heavy expences and penalties of a Suit in Chancery which will be immediately commenced against them. The genuine Blacking is signed "Robert Warren 30 Strand" on each Label all others are counterfeit and of very inferior quality

London 13ᵗʰ November 1827"

but for his greater certainty this Defendant craves to refer thereto   And this Defendant says that on the merits of the case being investigated the injunction which the complainants had obtained on an exparte application was dissolved on which occasion it was proved that the said Jonathan Warren was not a fictitious person but on the contrary that he was the Uncle of the Complainants and that he had carried on business at a House No 30 Hungerford Stairs Strand as is hereinbefore fully set forth   And this Defendant denies all and all manner of unlawful combination and confederacy in the said bill untruly alledged

Without that there is any other matter cause or thing in the Complainants said Bill of Complaint contained material or necessary for this Defendant to make answer unto and not herein and hereby well and sufficiently answered confessed and avoided traversed or denied or true to the knowledge or belief of this Defendant   All which matters and things the Defendant is ready and willing to aver maintain and prove as this honourable Court shall direct   And hereby prays to be hence dismissed with his reasonable costs and charges in this behalf most wrongfully sustained

[signed] Geo Lamerte   Daniel Wakefield

Chapter Ten

Affidavits in the case of Warren v Woodd

These documents are held at The National Archives at Kew in London, catalogued at reference C 31/448. They are contained in a box with affidavits from a great many other cases, all relating to the Michaelmas Term 1827, and dealing with Complainants whose names begin with the letters I-Z. Within the box they are maintained in first-letter order, but not all documents relating to the case of Warren v Woodd are kept together. The Affidavits were written by officers of the Court and signed by the witnesses. Paper about the size of A5 was used. I have arranged the transcripts that follow here in chronological order of the date they were originally written.

1 Robert Warren and Benjamin Warren, blacking manufacturers
2 Robert Ashdown, ex-traveller for Woodd and Pilcher
3 William Bean, shoemaker
4 Lucy Faulkner, shopkeeper
5 Wiliam Gooderham, labourer
6 James Harnett, solicitor
7 Michael Hughes, greengrocer
8 Thomas Lambley, labourer
9 Frederick Robinson, grocer and cheesemonger
10 John Henry Wencelin, foreman, Italian warehouse
11 Stephen Pilcher, blacking manufacturer
12 Elizabeth Warren, widow of Jonathan Warren
13 George Garey, plate powder manufacturer
14 Joseph Lampit, foreman to Woodd and Pilcher
15 William Langley, traveller for Woodd and Pilcher
16 William Whalley, traveller for Jonathan Warren, then Woodd and Pilcher
17 John Wright, carman for Woodd and Pilcher
18 Samuel Mann, rent collector and acting beadle
19 James Phillipps, custom house agent and lighterman
20 George Whitehead, grocer and cheesemonger
21 Valentine Thomas Coombes, solicitor's clerk
22 John Windsor Jones, grocer

23 Mary Warren, widow of Thomas Warren, and
     William Arundel, boot and shoe maker

[1. The affidavits of Robert Warren and Benjamin Warren]
In Chancery   Between Robert Warren and Benjamin Warren,
Plaintiffs and William Edward Woodd and Stephen Pilcher,
Defendants

Robert Warren and Benjamin Warren both of No. 30 Strand in the
County of Middlesex Blacking Manufacturers the above named Plaintiffs
in this Cause severally make Oath and Say   And first this Deponent
Robert Warren for himself Saith that Thomas Warren the Father of
these Deponents in or about the year One thousand seven hundred and
ninety five commenced the Business of a Blacking Manufacturer having
premises for that purpose in Saint Martin's Lane in the said County and
that the said Article of Blacking so manufactured by the said Thomas
Warren having got into great reputation and esteem with the Public he
the said Thomas Warren in his life time sold a large quantity thereof and
made a great profit thereby and that such Article was called by the said
Thomas Warren and was known to the Public by the name and
description of Warrens Japan Blacking and that the said Thomas Warren
continued to carry on such Trade as aforesaid up to and until the time of
his death and that upon his decease which took place in the year One
thousand eight hundred and five this Deponent Robert Warren
succeeded to his said Trade or Business and carried on the same in the
said premises in Saint Martin's Lane aforesaid until the year One
thousand eight hundred and sixteen And these Deponents also say that
the said Deponent Robert Warren for the purpose of encreasing and
extending the same and procuring a large Sale for the article so as
aforesaid manufactured by him was in the habit of advertising in the
Public Newspapers and of circulating Placards and Handbills and was
also in the habit of travelling or sending persons to travel for him to
most parts of England and that by the ways and means aforesaid this
Deponent Robert Warren at length succeeded in establishing a very large
and extensive business having Customers in most Towns in England and
that such Business was carried on in the name of him this Deponent
Robert Warren alone   – That in or about the said year One thousand
eight hundred and sixteen he this Deponent Robert Warren having
occasion by reason of the very great increase in his said Business for
larger premises than those occupied by him in Saint Martin's Lane
aforesaid he removed his said Trade or Business to the Premises now
occupied by him this Deponent and the said Benjamin Warren and
situate and being No. 30 in the Strand aforesaid and that in or about the
year One thousand eight hundred and twenty two he this Deponent

Robert Warren took his said Brother the above named Benjamin Warren into Partnership with him and that these Deponents have ever since carried on and do still carry on the said trade of business in Copartnership together but that such business having been established and carried on for many years as aforesaid first under the name of Thomas Warren the Father of these Deponents and afterwards more extensively under the name of this Deponent Robert Warren alone the Deponent Robert Warren did not like to change the name or style under which the same was conducted and that such business has therefore notwithstanding such Copartnership continued to be carried on and is still carried on in the name of Deponent Robert Warren alone - That for the purpose of keeping up and carrying on such extensive business they these Deponents Robert Warren and Benjamin Warren have continued and still are in the habit of circulating such Placards and Hand bills or Labels as aforesaid and also of sending Travellers to receive Orders from their Customers residing in the different parts of England and that the article so manufactured by them as aforesaid and by other persons in the same Trade or Business with these Deponents is sold by them in Bottles and also in Boxes or Jars and that with the view of distinguishing the Article so sold by them from that sold by others in the same trade or business with Deponents Deponents have been in the habit of pasting or affixing one of such Handbills or Labels as aforesaid on each of such Bottles and Boxes or Jars   And these Deponents also further say that William Edward Woodd and Stephen Pilcher the above named Defendants have for some time past carried on the Trade or Business of Blacking Manufacturers at No. 9 Noble Street Cheapside in the City of London and that the said Defendants as these Deponents have lately been informed and believe for the purpose of procuring a Sale for their Blacking have both by themselves and also by means of Travellers or Agents employed by them for that purpose falsely and to the great loss and injury of Deponents been represented to the Customers of these Deponents and to the Public in general that their the said Defendants House or Business was a Branch or part of the House or Business of Warren No. 30 Strand thereby meaning and intending the House or business of these Deponents and that their Warehouse for the shipping and sending off Goods was No. 30 Hungerford Stairs Strand And the said Defendants and their said Travellers or Agents as Deponents believe accordingly solicited and obtained Orders for Blacking as and for the House of Warren of the Strand Deponents said House or firm being thereby meant and intended or understood for Deponents say that the Article so as aforesaid manufactured by them was at that time well known by the description of the Blacking of Warren of the Strand and that Deponents said House or firm was in fact at that time and is now the only House of that name carrying on such Trade or Business as aforesaid in the Strand   And Deponents also say that to aid and assist such false and fraudulent representations as aforesaid the said Defendants also caused to be printed and circulated Placards and Handbills or labels in imitation of and similar to those used by these Deponents and that they also pasted one of such Handbills or labels on each of the Bottles and Boxes or Jars containing the Blacking so as aforesaid manufactured by them the said Defendants in order the more easily to pass off and sell the same to the Customers of these Deponents and the Public in general as and for the Article so as aforesaid manufactured by them these Deponents and Deponents also further say that by such several false and fraudulent representations and contrivances of the said Defendants as aforesaid many persons both Customers of Deponents and others who intended and were desirous to purchase Deponents Blacking have been as Deponents believe led to purchase and have actually purchased the Article so as aforesaid manufactured by the said Defendants conceiving that they were purchasing the Blacking of Deponents   And these Deponents further say that by the means and in the manner aforesaid the said Defendants have been enabled as Deponents believe to sell and have actually sold and do still sell a very great quantity of Blacking and to a large amount in value as and for the article so as aforesaid manufactured by Deponents and that these Deponents have thereby sustained great loss and injury in their said Trade or Business   And these Deponents believe that the said Defendants threaten and intend to continue such false and fraudulent representations and practises as aforesaid unless restrained therefrom And these Deponents further say that they believe there is no person in Partnership with the said Defendants or either of them of the name of Jonathan Warren and that the name Jonathan Warren is used for the purpose of enabling the said Defendants the more easily to sell and dispose of their Blacking under the name of Warrens Blacking   And this Deponent the said Robert Warren for himself saith that he believes that Jonathan Warren now deceased was some years afters this Deponent's said ffather had acquired a name and reputation as a Manufacturer of Blacking induced by the success of Deponent's said ffather also to commence the trade or business of a Blacking Manufacturer but that failing to establish himself in such trade or business he abandoned it and that Deponents having heard of the said Jonathan Warren they or one of them did in order to have a colourable pretext for using the name of Warren in their said trade or business and in their said placards and bills or labels take the said Jonathan Warren into their Service as a Workman or Labourer at a weekly salary and induced him in consideration thereof to permit them the said Defendants to use his name in the manner aforesaid and that the said Jonathan Warren soon afterwards departed this life

[nine blank lines]

That the said Defendants are not now nor ever were in partnership with any person of the name of Warren or save as aforesaid in any way connected with any person of that name in their said trade or business and therefore that the said name of Warren is made use of by the said Defendants in their said trade or business and in their said placards and bills or labels not fairly and bona fide but only colorably and fraudulently for the purpose of misleading the public and enabling them said

Defendants the more easily to sell and dispose of their blacking as and for the Article so as aforesaid manufactured by Deponents and that the said name of Warren is inserted by said Defendants in their said placards and bills or labels not fairly or bona fide but only for such fraudulent purpose as aforesaid and that the names of the said Defendants themselves do not appear at all in such placards and bills or labels and that the said Defendants ought therefore to be restrained from using such name   That the house and premises in which Deponents carry on their said trade or business is situated in the Strand aforesaid and numbered 30 and is in fact not far distant from Hungerford Stairs Strand aforesaid and that the said No 30 the No of their said house and premises is printed in the Centre of the said placards and bills or labels in very large and conspicuous characters and that the word Strand is printed towards the bottom of Deponents said placards and bills or labels also in large and conspicuous Characters   That said Defendants have caused the said No 30 to be printed in the centre of their said placards and bills or labels in Characters of the same size and as conspicuous as those in which such No is printed in said Deponents said placards and bills or labels and that they have also caused the address of Hungerford Stairs Strand to be printed towards the bottom of their said placards and bills or labels in large and conspicuous characters and that the said Defendants have selected that Number in consequence of such being the number of these Deponents said house and premises and that they have selected the address of Hungerford Stairs on account of its vicinity to these Deponents said house and premises in the Strand with the view of aiding and assisting their said false and fraudulent representations and contrivances and of inducing the public the more readily to believe that the Article So sold by the said Defendants is in fact the Article so as aforesaid manufactured by these Deponents for these Deponents say that the said house or firm has been for some years known by the name and description of Robert Warren No 30 Strand And that the said Defendants have in fact no house or premises or place for business belonging to or occupied of held by them at No 30

Hungerford Stairs Strand And that the Number of the house and premises in which the said Defendants carry on their said trade is Nobel Street aforesaid is No 9 and is not now nor ever was No 30 And although the Defendants pretend that their said placards and bills or labels are in other respects very unlike those of these Deponents yet Deponents say that if such placards and bills or labels are not precisely and in all respects similar to those used by these Deponents as aforesaid they are nevertheless a very close imitation thereof and that the said Defendants contrived and caused the same to be printed Solely for the purpose of enabling them by reason of their very great similarity to those of Deponents to sell and dispose of their blacking as and for the blacking of these Deponents And Deponents further say that such bills or labels of the said Defendants are in fact so close an imitation or copy of those of these Deponents that many persons who were desirous of purchasing these Deponents blacking have been as Deponents have heard and believe deceived or misled by them and have actually purchased the blacking of the said Defendants intending to purchase and conceiving that they were purchasing the blacking manufactured by Deponents And these Deponents also say that they have been informed and believe the same to be true that many persons have been imposed upon and prevailed upon to give orders for blacking to the agents or travellers of the said Defendants conceiving that they were giving orders for blacking to the agent or travellers of Deponents and that when the said Defendants had furnished their blacking the imposition was detected and in some instances their said blacking was refused to be received upon the ground of imposition and in other instances the fraud and imposition was not detected until it was too late and the money paid for the same And these deponents further say that by reason of the constant and daily frauds practised upon them by the said Defendants and their travellers and servants as aforesaid these Deponents have sustained and are daily sustaining very considerable loss and injury both in their good names and reputation as Blacking Manufacturers as aforesaid as well as loss by reason of such constant frauds

Robert Warren [signature]
Benjamin Warren [signature]
Sworn before me This Nineteenth Day of Nov. One Thousand Eight Hundred & Twenty Seven at the Public Office Southampton Buildings In the County of Middx by Both the Deponents
H Cross [signature]

[2. The affidavit of Robert Ashdown]
In Chancery   Between Robert Warren and Benjamin Warren,
Plaintiffs and William Edward Woodd and Stephen Pilcher,
Defendants

Robert Ashdown of No 32 Crooked Lane in the City of London late in the employment of the above named defendants as Travelling Clerk Maketh oath and saith that in or about the Month of August now last past this Defendant was employed by the above named Defendants to go about and collect orders for Blacking and was directed by them to distribute their Labels as "Warrens Blacking" to the various Shopkeepers and others buying and selling Blacking, that Deponent went to several persons and obtained Orders for Warrens Blacking and that many persons on giving to this Deponent such orders fancied they were ordering the Blacking of Robert Warren of No. 30 Strand, that Mrs Lawson of Coleman Street in the City of London Dealer in Oil and Colours about the beginning of the Month of October last gave this Deponent an order to send her Blacking to the amount of One Pound four shillings and that when this Deponent applied to the said Mrs Lawson to obtain the said Order for the said Blacking this Deponent did as he had been previously directed by the said Defendants represent that he applied for Warrens Blacking and this Deponent further saith that Mrs Lawson when she gave this Deponent the said Order for Blacking fancied and believed that this Deponent was one of Robert Warren's Travellers of No 30 Strand and in order to expedite the delivery of the said Order Deponent desired that it should be delivered without any loss of time and before any of the Plaintiff Robert Warren's Travellers called upon the said Mrs Lawson for fear they should stop the delivery thereof and which Blacking was accordingly on the same day or very soon afterwards delivered to the said Mrs Lawson and this Deponent also saith that the said Mrs Lawson was in the habit previously of dealing with the above named Plaintiffs for Goods in the way of the Business of Blacking Manufacturers and that when Deponent prevailed upon her to give Deponent the said Order for Blacking the said Mrs Lawson thought she was ordering the Blacking of the above named Plaintiffs and did not as Deponent believes find out the contrary thereof until some time after the same had been delivered and paid for   And this Deponent also saith that when the said Mrs Lawson had given this Deponent the said Order for Blacking this Deponent told the said Stephen Pilcher that he did not think the said Mrs Lawson would take in the said Blacking if she found out in time that the Blacking was not Robert Warrens Blacking of No. 30 Strand, in reply to which the said Stephen Pilcher said that he would send it in and take the chance of it   And this Deponent also saith that he applied to one Mr Smith an Oil and

Colourman in Fleet Market for an order for Robert Warrens Blacking of No 30 Strand amounting to the sum of One Pound and eight shillings and that this Deponent directed the Defendants Blacking to be sent to the said Mr Smith instead of the said Plaintiffs Blacking – that the said Defendants Blacking was taken to the said Mr Smith who is a keen sharp man and who carefully inspected the Label upon the said Blacking and finding that it was not Blacking from the Plaintiffs house of No. 30 in the Strand refused to take it in and the same was therefore returned to the above named Defendants that the said Defendants on finding that the said Mr Smith would not take in the said Blacking because it was not the Plaintiffs Blacking of the Strand, this Deponent went back to Mr Smith to endeavour to prevail upon him to take it in, but he refused to do so – alleging that it was nor from the right house and he would not therefore take it in, that Deponent then gave the order to the above named Plaintiffs who supplied the Blacking required by the said Mr Smith and the said Mr Smith received the same and paid for it – And this Deponent also saith that he obtained an order in like manner from Mr Povey a Boot and Shoe maker residing Old Kent Road to send him Robert Warrens Blacking to the amount of Twelve shillings and that this Deponent sent him the said Defendants Blacking in lieu thereof but Mr Povey detected the difference and refused to receive the said Defendants Blacking   And this Deponent lastly saith that it was a constant practice with this Deponent and the rest of the said Defendants Travellers where they had met with difficulties in obtaining orders for the Defendants Blacking to represent to persons that they were collecting Orders for Blacking for the house of the said Robert Warren of No. 30 Strand and take the chance of the same being taken in and that in many instances the Blacking so ordered had been taken in by several persons in mistake for Robert Warrens Blacking of the Strand the No. 30 and the name of Warren at the top of the Defendants Label upon each of his Bottles of Blacking operated in many instances as a powerful deception which was not detected until the Blacking had been taken in and paid for and in such cases it was not usual either for the said Defendant to take back their said Blacking so sold and delivered or return the money paid for the same   And this Deponent lastly saith that the said Defendants reside at No 9 in Noble Street Cheapside in the City of London   And that the number 30 put upon each of their said Bottles of Blacking is put thereon for the more easily passing the same off upon the public as and for the Blacking of Robert Warren of the Strand and that the said Defendants purposely keep their names from appearing upon their said Labels as it would in such case prevent so quick a sale of their said Blacking And that the said Defendants nor either of them have any house or place of Business at No. 30 Hungerford Stairs Strand nor do they reside there or

near it – but that their usual place of residence is No. 9 Noble Street aforesaid   And that they have no partner of the name of Jonathan Warren nor to the knowledge or belief of this Deponent ever had.
Robert Ashdown [signature]
Sworn at the public office Southampton Buildings Chancery Lane in the County of Middlesex this 19th. day of November 1827 before me.
H. Cross [signature]

[3. The Affidavit of William Bean]
In Chancery   Between Robert Warren and Benjamin Warren, Plaintiffs and William Edward Woodd and Stephen Pilcher, Defendants
William Bean of Dartford in the County of Kent Shoe Maker Maketh oath and saith that for the last Fifteen years this Deponent hath been in the constant habit of dealing with the above named Robert Warren as well when he resided in Saint Martins Lane in the County of Middlesex as also since he came to reside at No 30 in the Strand for Blacking and that he hath continued to deal with him and his Brother Benjamin Warren since their Partnership and this Deponent also saith that about the middle of September now last past one of the Travellers of the above named Defendants called upon this Deponent and asked Deponent if he wanted any Blacking and that he was one of Mr Robert Warren's Travellers of the Strand – that this Deponent told him that he was not then prepared to pay the small balance which Deponent then owed to the said Robert Warren and his Partner, that the said Traveller replied "Oh its no consequence we only want further orders" – that the said Traveller then pressed this Deponent to give a further Order for Blacking upon which this Deponent consented to give a further order for Goods amounting to little more than One pound And this Deponent further saith that about a week or ten days afterwards the said Defendants caused to be delivered to this Deponent a quantity of their Blacking as and for Robert Warrens Blacking of No. 30 Strand so packed up in a small Cask that this Deponent could not see what the said Cask contained until he had opened it that in the Evening of the day on which this Deponent received the said Cask he opened it and on looking at the name of 'Warren' at the Top of the said Label and the number 30 in the Centre thereof this Deponent thought it was the Blacking of the above named Plaintiffs of No 30 Strand and was not undeceived for a few days afterwards until the contrary was pointed out to this Deponent by this Deponents Wife   And this Deponent saith that if he had discovered the fraud so practised upon him he would not have taken in the said Blacking nor have paid the carriage of it which this Deponent did in ignorance of the fact that it was the said Defendants Blacking and not

the said Plaintiffs - And that his Deponent never had any dealings for Blacking with the said Defendants nor any other Blacking Manufacturer except the said Plaintiffs save as hereinbefore stated.

William Bean [signature]

Sworn at the Public Office Southampton Buildings Chancery Lane in the County of Middlesex this nineteenth day of November 1827 Before me

H Cross [signature]

[4. The affidavit of Lucy Faulkner]

In Chancery   Between Robert Warren and Benjamin Warren, Plaintiffs and William Edward Woodd and Stephen Pilcher, Defendants

Lucy Faulkner of No. 70 Ossulton Street Somers Town in the County of Middlesex Shopkeeper Maketh Oath and saith that for upwards of Seven Years now last past she this Deponent has dealt with the House of the above named Plaintiffs Robert Warren and Benjamin Warren since their Copartnership in their Trade or Business of Blacking Manufacturers that in the Month of September last a person called upon Deponent for orders for "Warrens Blacking" and represented that he had come from the Plaintiff's House No 30 in the Strand   that this Deponent being then in want of blacking gave him an Order to send her two dozen bottles of Blacking conceiving that she was giving an order for Warrens Blacking of No 30 in the Strand   that on the said day or very shortly afterwards a person called with two dozen bottles of Blacking and as this Deponent saw the name of Warren at the top of the label upon the said Bottles and also the No. 30 in the centre of the said label she believed that the said Plaintiffs had sent the said bottles of Blacking and was deceived by the name and No. 30 upon the Label pasted on the said Bottles and did not detect the fraud until afterwards one of the Travellers of the above named Plaintiffs applied to this Deponent for orders for Goods of the same description Deponent then for the first time found out that she had been imposed upon and that the said Defendants had sent this Deponent their Blacking as and for the Plaintiffs Blacking of No. 30 in the Strand and this Deponent upon the delivery of the said Defendants Blacking was induced and did pay for the same in the full belief that she was paying for the Blacking of the above named Plaintiffs of No. 30 in the Strand and not the Blacking of the said Defendants who live at No 9 Noble Street Cheapside in the City of London –

Lucy Faulkner [signature]

Sworn at the Public Office Southampton Buildings Chancery Lane in the County of Middlesex this 19th day of November 1827 before me

H Cross [signature]

[5. The affidavit of William Gooderham]
In Chancery   Between Robert Warren and Benjamin Warren,
Plaintiffs and William Edward Woodd and Stephen Pilcher,
Defendants

William Gooderham of No 2 Seymour Court Chandos Street in the County of Middlesex Labourer maketh oath and saith that he this Deponent did on Tuesday the thirteenth day of November instant go to the house or shop of the above named Defendants William Edward Woodd and Stephen Pilcher situate at No 9 Noble Street Cheapside in the City of London where he saw a person whom he this Deponent believes to be one of the said Defendants in the said Shop and asked for six bottles of Warrens Blacking That a Young Man in the said Shop sold this Deponent six bottles of blacking All alike three of which said Bottles with the labels pasted thereon respectively marked A.B.C now produced and shewn to this Deponent and that this Deponent paid four shillings for them and at the same time Deponent asked him if this (meaning the said six bottles of blacking then in his hands) was the Genuine Warrens Blacking of the Strand in Answer to which the said person replied Oh Yes   And this Deponent also saith that there appeared many Hundred bottles of Blacking similarly labelled in the said Defendants Shop exposed for Sale   And this Deponent also saith that on comparing the labels or placards on the said bottles of blacking so sold by the said Defendants Deponent with the labels or placards used upon the bottles of blacking usually sold by the above named Plaintiffs this Deponent conceives and believes that the labels of the said Defendants were made to imitate the labels or placards of the said Plaintiffs for the purpose of deceit particularly in the introduction of the name of Warren at the top of the said bottles and also the No 30 in the Centre   And this Deponent also saith that the three bottles of blacking with the labels or placards thereon placed respectively marked No 1   No 2   No 3   are bottles containing Blacking manufactured by the Plaintiffs and that the labels pasted upon the said bottles respectively are the said Plaintiffs labels and the same as those usually sold by them in the way of this aforesaid Trade or Business –
William Gooderham [signature]
Sworn at the Public Office Southampton Buildings Chancery Lane in the County of Middlesex this 19th day of November 1827 Before me
H Cross [signature]

[6. The affidavit of James Harnett]
In Chancery   Between Robert Warren and Benjamin Warren,
Plaintiffs and William Edward Woodd and Stephen Pilcher,
Defendants

James Harnett of Northumberland Street Strand in the County of Middlesex Solicitor for the Plaintiffs in the above named Cause Maketh Oath and saith that he did on the seventeenth day of November instant serve the above named Defendants with a Subpoena issuing out of and under the Seal of this Honourable Court by delivering to and leaving with the said Defendant Stephen Pilcher the body of the said Subpoena so under Seal as aforesaid and also delivering to and leaving with the said Defendant Stephen Pilcher a label of the said Subpoena the said Defendant William Edward Woodd being from home by which said Subpoena the said Defendants were directed to appear in this Honourable Court on the said seventeenth day of November instant at the suit of the Plaintiffs in this Cause as appeared by the label of the said Subpoena

James Harnett [signature]

Sworn at the Public Office Southampton Buildings Chancery Lane in the County of Middlesex this 19th day of Novr. 1827 before me

H Cross [signature]

[7. The affidavit of Michael Hughes]
In Chancery   Between Robert Warren and Benjamin Warren, Plaintiffs and William Edward Woodd and Stephen Pilcher, Defendants

Michael Hughes of No 14 Silver Street Golden Square in the County of Middlesex Green Grocer Maketh Oath and saith that about the middle of the Month of September now last past a person called upon this Deponent and asked if Deponent wanted any of Warrens Blacking – that Deponent gave him an Order to send him three dozen bottles of Warrens Blacking but instead of sending Deponent three dozen bottles of Warrens Blacking the above named Defendants sent Deponent four dozen bottles of their own blacking as and for Warrens Blacking of the Strand and that one of the same Bottles so sold and delivered to this Deponent is marked with the Letters W. and P. now produced and shewn to this Deponent   And this Deponent saith that he received the said Blacking believing that it was the Blacking of the above named Plaintiffs and in perfect ignorance that it was Blacking manufactured by the above named Defendants   And Deponent further saith that if he had been made acquainted with the fact that the Blacking so sold and delivered to this Deponent was the said Defendants Blacking he would not have received the same or permitted it to be taken in   And lastly this Deponent saith that the general appearance of the said Defendants bottles of Blacking with the labels thereon and the name of Warrens placed conspicuously at the top and the No. 30 also in the centre in imitation of the Plaintiffs bottles led this Deponent to a belief that he was dealing with the above named Plaintiffs and not the Defendants of whom this Deponent had no knowledge in the way of their Business or otherwise

X   The Mark of Michael Hughes   Witness David Thomas Harris

Sworn at the Public Office Southampton Buildings Chancery Lane in the County of Middlesex this 19th day of November 1827 before me by the Deponent Michael Hughes Witness to the Mark of the said Deponent being first sworn that he had truly distinctly and audibly read over the contents of this affidavit to the said Deponant and that he saw him make his Mark there to

H Cross [signature]

[8.   The affidavit of Thomas Lambley]
In Chancery   Between Robert Warren and Benjamin Warren, Plaintiffs and William Edward Woodd and Stephen Pilcher, Defendants

Thomas Lambley of No 2 Seymour Court Chandos Street Covent Garden in the County of Middlesex Labourer Maketh Oath and Saith that on Tuesday the thirteenth day of November instant he this Deponent went to the House or Shop of the above named Defendants situate and being No 9 Noble Street Cheapside in the City of London where he saw a person belonging to the said Defendants in their counting house and asked him for one dozen Bottles of Warrens Blacking That a Man in the said Defendants Shop gave this Deponent fourteen bottles of blacking all alike – three of which said bottles with the labels pasted thereon respectively are marked D. E. F now produced and shewn to this Deponent and that this Deponent paid four shillings for the said fourteen bottles and at the same time again asked the person whom he had seen in the said Counting house if this meaning the said fourteen bottles of blacking then in his hands was the same Blacking as sold for Warrens Blacking in the Strand in answer to which the said person in the said Counting house replied Oh yes exactly the same   And this Deponent also saith that there appeared to be several hundred bottles of Blacking similarly labelled in the said Defendants Shop exposed for Sale   And this Deponent also saith that on comparing the labels or placards on the said Bottles of Blacking so sold by the said Defendants to this Deponent with the labels or placards used upon the bottles of blacking usually sold by the above named Plaintiffs this Deponent conceives and believes that the labels of the said Defendants were made expressly to imitate the labels or placards of the said Plaintiffs for the purpose of deceit   And this Deponent also saith that the three bottles of blacking with the labels or placards thereon pasted and respectively marked No 4 No 5 No 6 are Bottles containing

Blacking manufactured by the Plaintiffs and that the labels pasted upon the said bottles respectively are the Plaintiffs labels and the same as those usually sold by them in the way of their said trade or business
Thomas Lambley [signature]
Sworn at the Public office Southampton Buildings Chancery Lane in the County of Middlesex this 19th day of November 1827 Before me
T Cross [signature]

[9. The affidavit of Frederick Robinson]
In Chancery   Between Robert Warren and Benjamin Warren, Plaintiffs and William Edward Woodd and Stephen Pilcher, Defendants

Frederick Robinson of No 23 Garden Row London Road in the County of Surrey Grocer and Cheesemonger Maketh Oath and saith that on or about the twentieth day of September a Traveller from the House of the above named Defendants called on this Deponent at his House in Garden Row aforesaid and asked this Deponent if he wanted any Blacking this Deponent said "Yes" and thereupon gave the said Traveller an order for one dozen Bottles of Warrens Blacking meaning the Blacking of the above named Plaintiffs of No. 30 Strand That instead of the said Defendants sending Deponent one dozen bottles of the Plaintiffs Blacking as Deponent ordered the said Defendants sent Deponent five dozens of the Defendants bottles of Blacking And this Deponent further saith that when he received the said bottles of Blacking from the said Defendants he was led by their Traveller to believe and this Deponent conceived that he was purchasing the Blacking manufactured by Robert Warren of No. 30 Strand and that when the bottles of Blacking were delivered with the labels on them they were so like the labels on the Bottles of Blacking usually sold by the said Plaintiffs that this Deponent was deceived by them and was not aware of the deception and fraud practised upon him by the said Defendants in sending to him this Deponents neighbourhood and to whom this Deponent had sold one of the said Defendants bottles of Blacking as and for the said Plaintiffs Blacking he'd pointed out to this Deponent the difference between them and this Deponent then for the first time discovered that he was imposed upon by the Traveller of the said Defendants
Frederick Robinson [signature]
Sworn at the Public Office Southampton Buildings Chancery Lane in the County of Middlesex this 19th. Day of November 1827 before me
H Cross [signature]

[10. The affidavit of John Henry Wencelin]

In Chancery Between Robert Warren and Benjamin Warren, Plaintiffs and William Edward Woodd and Stephen Pilcher, Defendants

John Henry Wencelin Foreman to Mrs. Ann Lawson of No 33 Coleman Street in the City of London Italian Warehouse keeper Maketh Oath and saith that in the Month of October now last past a person called at No 33 Coleman Street aforesaid and enquired of Deponent if Deponent wanted any of Warrens Blacking that Deponent said Yes we want some small bottles and thereupon gave him an order for three dozen of small and one dozen large bottles of Warrens Blacking (meaning Warrens Blacking of No 30 Strand) that the next day or the day afterwards a person called upon Deponent and delivered three dozens of small and one dozen of large Bottles of Blacking which the Carter who delivered it put on the floor that this Deponent counted the Bottles saw the No 30 upon the labels thought they came from the Plaintiffs Warehouse at No. 30 in the Strand and under that impression Deponent paid for them and was not undeceived for three or four days afterwards until a person pointed out the difference between the said Plaintiffs labels and the said Defendants and then this Deponent found out the imposition when in fact it was too late for the said Blacking had been paid for on delivery
John Thomas Wencelin [signature]
Sworn at the Public Office Southampton Buildings Chancery Lane in the County of Middlesex this 19th day of Novr. 1827 before me
H Cross [signature]

[11. The affidavit of Stephen Pilcher]

In Chancery Between Robert Warren and Benjamin Warren, plaintiffs and William Edward Woodd and Stephen Pilcher, Defendants

Stephen Pilcher of No 9 Noble Street Cheapside in the City of London Blacking Manufacturer one of the above named Defendants maketh Oath and Saith That in the year One thousand eight hundred and twenty four he this Deponent entered into Copartnership with the other Defendant William Edward Woodd in the manufacturing of Blacking under the name of Jonathan Warren's Blacking and that he hath always been informed and verily believes that the said Jonathan Warren was the Original Manufacturer of the Blacking known by the name of Warren's Blacking And Deponent Saith that he was also informed that the said Jonathan Warren carried on the Business of a Blacking Manufacturer in great Suffolk Street and at No 30 Hungerford Stairs Strand from the year One thousand seven hundred and ninety five until the year One thousand eight hundred and twenty two when he parted with his

Business to the other Defendant William Edward Woodd. And this Deponent has been informed and verily believes that the said Jonathan Warren for the purpose of increasing the Sale of his said Blacking advertised the Sale thereof in the public papers and by circulating placards and Hand Bills and that he was in the habit of employing Travellers and sending persons to travel for him through England Scotland and Ireland and that of necessity the same must have been known to Thomas Warren the Father of the said plaintiffs from the commencement of the business as aforesaid to his death and to the said plaintiffs themselves and that he verily believes the said Thomas Warren never pretended to have any right to prevent or hinder the said Jonathan Warren from so doing But on the contrary at intervals when friendly and upon good terms they have aided and assisted each other in the Business of Blacking Manufacturers. And Deponent hath also been informed and verily believes that the said Jonathan Warren obtained a very extensive Sale for the said Article of Blacking and which was known to the World as Warren's Blacking or Jonathan Warren's Blacking the public calling it Warren's Blacking but the said Jonathan Warren always describing and studiously trying to inform the Public of his Christian Name and representing his Article of Blacking as Jonathan Warrens Blacking and of the original Manufacture. And this Deponent further saith That he hath been informed and verily believes the said Jonathan Warren entered into an Engagement with the said other Defendant William Edward Woodd whereby he authorized him to make and vend the Article of Blacking in his the said Jonathan Warren's name and for that purpose he entered into a written Agreement on or about the eighth day of November One thousand eight hundred and twenty two and that in pursuance of such Agreement the said William Edward Woodd manufactured and vended blacking at No 30 Hungerford Stairs aforesaid in the name of the said Jonathan Warren from that period down to August one thousand eight hundred and twenty four or thereabouts when he removed to Chandos Street near Covent Garden And this Deponent Saith that on the first of December One thousand eight hundred and twenty four he this Deponent entered into Copartnership with the said William Edward Woodd in the manufacturing of Blacking under and in pursuance of the said last mentioned Agreement And that they continued so to do until the latter end of the same month of December One thousand eight hundred and twenty four when they removed to No 9 Noble Street aforesaid in consequence of the House in which they resided in Chandos Street being a Subject of litigation and being so compelled to remove they were induced to take a House in the City the better to enable them to execute the extensive Orders which they obtained from their City Connexions for foreign Shipments and that they have continued to Manufacture Blacking there from that period until the time of receiving a Notice of the Injunction of this Honorable Court And this Deponent Saith that they have used the copies of the Labels now produced and shewn to him at the time of swearing this his Affidavit marked with the Letters A and D and no others excepting similar Labels varying in size And this Deponent Saith he hath been informed and verily believes the said Jonathan Warren used the label or Copies thereof now produced at the time of swearing this his Affidavit marked with the Letter C And this Deponent further Saith he verily believes the said Jonathan Warren was the first manufacturer of Blacking of that Name and that his Blacking was known to the Public as Warren's Blacking before his Brother Thomas Warren the Father of the said Plaintiffs commenced the Manufacturing of a similar Article and that although he the said Thomas Warren used the name of Warren's Blacking to deceive the Public and to mislead them into a belief that it was an Article manufactured by the said Jonathan Warren and from the period of his the said Thomas Warren's commencing the manufacturing of blacking it has always been the aim of the said Jonathan Warren and of the said William Edward Woodd And this Deponent to make the distinction between Jonathan Warren's Manufacture and the manufacture of his Brother Thomas Warren and of the said plaintiffs. And this Deponent Saith that it has been more especially the study of this Deponent and the said William Edward Woodd because of the facility which the said Plaintiffs and their Father have had of imposing upon the Public by reason of their Surname And this Deponent further Saith that he and his said Copartner have been in the habit of sending out Travellers and other persons to procure Orders for Blacking and that they having succeeded to the Business of the said Jonathan Warren as aforesaid have succeeded to the Accounts of his Customers and obtained accounts from Houses in almost every part of England Scotland and Ireland and thereby continued to make a most extensive Sale And this Deponent further Saith he admits that the said Jonathan Warren and since his Decease the said William Edward Woodd and this Deponent have sold Blacking as Jonathan Warren's Blacking And this Deponent humbly Submits that he and the said William Edward Woodd had a right so do to under and in pursuance of their aforesaid Agreement with the said Jonathan Warren And this Deponent positively Saith that he did not nor to the best of his belief did his said Copartner William Edward Woodd eve authorize or direct any Traveller Agent or Servant in their employ to represent that their said Manufactory at No 9 Noble Street was a branch of the Manufactory of the said Plaintiffs nor does this Deponent believe that any Traveller Agent or Servant in their employ ever represented or stated any thing to the same or the like effect except

as after mentioned by the said Robert Ashdown   And this Deponent
further Saith that the said William Edward Woodd upon his purchasing
the Business and permission to use the recipe and name of the said
Jonathan Warren used copies of the Labels marked with the Letter D
on the liquid blacking and paste blacking and similar Labels were
formerly used by the said Jonathan Warren   And this Deponent further
saith that the said plaintiffs at the time of his entering into the Business
used similar Labels to those used by the said Jonathan Warren and
afterwards by the said William Edward Woodd   And this Deponent
with the exception of the name "Jonathan Warren " and "30 Hungerford
Stairs Strand" the said Plaintiffs used the words "Robert Warren" and
"30 Strand"   And this Deponent further saith that at the time this
Deponent and the said William Edward Woodd removed their said
Manufactory to No 9 Noble Street aforesaid they at a very great expence
altered their said labels to the labels marked with the Letters A and B
And this Deponent further saith that immediately upon the alteration of
the labels of Deponent and the said William Edward Woodd the said
Plaintiffs altered their labels to the labels marked with the Letter E   And
this Deponent further saith that in or about the Month of August now
last past this Deponent and the said William Edward Woodd employed
Robert Ashdown as their Travelling Clerk to collect orders for Blacking
and to distribute their labels for the Sale of Jonathan Warren's Blacking
but this Deponent positively saith that neither he or his said Copartner
William Edward Woodd to tbe best of his belief ever directed or
authorized the said Robert Ashdown to represent that the said Blacking
was Blacking manufactured by the said Plaintiff Robert Warren or that
the said Blacking was the Blacking of "Warren of N0. 30 Strand" and
that if the said Robert Ashdown did ever represent the said Blacking to
be the Blacking Manufactured by the said Robert Warren it was without
the knowledge or direction of this Deponent and his said Copartner
And this Deponent further saith that he recollects the said Robert
Ashdown informed this Deponent that he had received an Order for
Blacking from Mr. Smith of Fleet Street that this Deponents carman
delivered the said Blacking so ordered to the said Mr. Smith who when
the Carman was about delivering the goods informed him that he had
given the order for the Plaintiffs Blacking and the same was immediately
taken back the Carman not pretending or attempting to represent the
Blacking as of the Plaintiffs but on the contrary distinctly as of
Defendants Manufacture   And this Deponent also saith that the said
Carman in this and every other instance took the Bill of Parcels with the
names of Defendants as the Vendors of the Article and received general
directions to state the difference between the Blacking of this Deponents
and his said partner and the Blacking of the said Plaintiffs which this

Deponent verily believes the said Carman always to have done as occasions required   And this Deponent was not aware either that he had ordered the Blacking of the Plaintiffs or that the said Robert Ashdown made any representations to induce the said Mr. Smith to believe that he was ordering the Plaintiffs Blacking   And Deponent saith he verily believes if he made any such representations it was to answer his own purposes and in collusion with the Plaintiffs   And this Deponent further saith that it was not the constant practice of the said Travellers of this Deponents said House to represent that they were collecting orders for the House of Warren of No 30 Strand and to take the chance of such Blacking being taken in by their several Customers and Dealers   And in no instance does he recollect it to have happened that any Blacking was returned after the same had been delivered and paid for   And this Deponent further saith he is informed and verily believes that the said Robert Ashdown was while he soliciting orders for Deponent and his partner and is now in the employ of the said Plaintiffs and that he artfully and with the privity and by the direction and in collusion with the Plaintiffs got into the employ of this Deponent and his said co-partner for the purpose of assisting the plaintiffs in their sale of Blacking and to send the Blacking sold by this Deponent and his said Partner as the Blacking of the said Plaintiffs to enable them the said Plaintiffs to apply to this Honorable Court to restrain this Deponent and his said Partner from carrying on their Business and to give publicity to the World of that fact which must have a tendency of stopping for a short period at least the whole of their Business and of doing them irreparable injury for this Deponent positively saith that he never in any manner authorized the said Robert Ashdown to represent the Blacking sold by this Deponent and his said partner as the Blacking of the said Plaintiffs   And this Deponent saith that he recollects the said Robert Ashdown upon One occasion artfully representing to this Deponent that if he went to the customers and dealers and stated that he sold the blacking of Warren of the Strand that it would increase their sale upon which this Deponent informed him that he must not upon any account make such representations that the Blacking sold by them was of the Original manufacture and if truly stated to the public would command a more extensive sale than the Blacking manufactured by the Plaintiffs And this Deponent saith that the said Robert Ashdown upon one occasion recommended to this Deponent to have a label printed in imitation of the label used by the Plaintiffs which he this Deponent declined doing   And this Deponent saith the said other Defendant is at present in Ireland attending to Business there

Stephen Pilcher [signature]   Sworn at the Public Office
Southampton Buildings in the County of Middlesex this 23d. day of
November 1827 before me   J S Doodswell [signature]

[12. The affidavit of Elizabeth Warren]
*In Chancery.   Between Robert Warren and Benjamin Warren
Plaintiffs and William Edward Woodd and Stephen Pilcher
Defendants*

Elizabeth Warren of No 5 Paradise Street Grays Inn Road in the County
of Middlesex widow maketh Oath and Saith that Jonathan Warren
formerly of Suffolk Street in the Strand in the said County of Middlesex
commenced the Business of Blacking Manufacturer for some years
previous to this defendants marriage with the said Jonathan Warren and
continued to carry on that Business from that period until the year one
thousand eight hundred and twenty Two   And this deponent Saith that
she intermarried with the said Jonathan Warren about twenty Six years
ago that Thomas Warren the Brother of her said husband and the Father
of the said plaintiffs formerly carried on the Business of a Boot Maker
in Saint Martins Lane in the said County and some time previous to this
deponents said Marriage entered into an agreement with the said
Thomas Warren deceased to admit him into partnership in the Business
of a Blacking Manufacturer which he was then carrying on and that they
continued together for a very short period not exceeding a Month to the
best of deponents recollection and belief but that the said Jonathan
Warren in faith of such Agreement for Copartnership instructed the said
Thomas Warren in the Manufacturing of Blacking according to the
recipe used by her said husband and which had at that time become an
Article of great consumption and bore every prospect of becoming a
Blacking better fitted for the Market both in the home and Foreign
Trade than any other Article Manufactured and that when the said
Thomas Warren had acquired that skill to enable him to Manufacture so
Superior an Article he broke his Agreement with a pretext of returning
to his former business and giving up the Blacking Business but
Deponent Saith he shortly after commenced the Business of Blacking
Manufacturer in Opposition to her said husband and from that Period
down to the present there has been a Spirit of competition between the
two Concerns   And this deponent further Saith that during this long
period of Competition the said Thomas Warren and afterwards his Son
the said Plaintiff Robert Warren have taken advantage of her said
husbands Business and of the Sirname of Warren and of Selling his
Blacking as Warrens Blacking very much to the injury of her said
husband and of Soliciting Orders under this advantage of the established
Customers of her husband   And this Deponent further Saith that it was

the practice of her husband to have large Placards for the purpose of advertising his blacking and to these Placards the names and residences of Customers and dealers who would sell the Blacking Manufactured by her husband and that the names and residences of such Customers and Dealers were printed on a small Slip of paper and such placards and slips of Paper were placed near the fire in the dwelling house of her said husband for the purpose of drying previous to distribution and the family of this deponent and the said Thomas Warren and his family were in the habit of visiting as relatives And this deponent Saith that she has heard her husband complain of loosing Customers and Dealers and upon inquiries has discovered that the said Thomas Warren and afterwards the said plaintiff Robert Warren have by the means of the names and residences of the said Customers and Dealers so printed and exhibited as aforesaid obtained the means of Applying to them and selling their Blacking as Warrens Blacking to such Customers and Dealers who at the time supposed they were buying the said Jonathan Warrens Blacking And this deponent further Saith that from the time of Thomas Warrens commencing the Manufacturing of Blacking as aforesaid to the period of his death and from that Period to the present time it has been notorious to the said Thomas Warren and the said Plaintiffs respectively that the said Jonathan Warren continued in the Business of Blacking Manufacturer to the year one thousand eight hundred and twenty two and that during the whole of that period they were opposed in Business to the said Thomas Warren and the said Plaintiffs and the placards and labels used by the said Jonathan Warren during that period were publicly issued And this deponent verily believes from the circumstances of their being so opposed that every label and placard used by the said Jonathan Warren and since that period by the said defendants was immediately upon its being used known to the said Thomas Warren and the said plaintiffs respectively and that their Attention as opposition Manufacturers would in the ordinary course of their Business be directed to discover the labels and placards so used by them And this deponent positively Saith that so far from the said Jonathan Warren during the time of his carrying on Business as aforesaid and the said defendants from that period respectively down to the present period ever Soliciting orders or selling their Blacking as an Article Manufactured by the said Thomas Warren and the said Plaintiffs that it was the invariable and studious practice of her said husband and as she verily believes of the said Defendants to give Public Notice and to cause to be known that the Blacking Manufactured by her said husband and the said Defendants was not the Blacking Manufactured by the said Thomas Warren and by the said plaintiffs and that the Blacking so Manufactured by her said husband and the said defendants was

Manufactured According to the Original recipe and the Public and their Customers and Dealers were cautioned against receiving the Article Manufactured by the said Thomas Warren and the said Plaintiffs as the Article Manufactured by the said Jonathan Warren under the name of Warrens Blacking And this deponent Saith she verily believes that such practice was well known to the said Thomas Warren and the said Plaintiffs and this deponent further Saith that the said Jonathan Warren carried on the Business of Blacking Manufacturer in Great Suffolk Street aforesaid from his commencing that Business until the same Street was pulled down for the Improvements in that neighbourhood and he then removed his Business to Hungerford Stairs Strand where the said Business was carried on until the eight Day of November in the year one thousand eight hundred and Twenty two when the said Jonathan Warren entered into an agreement with the above named defendant William Edward Woodd whereby after reciting that the said Jonathan Warren had for many years carried on the business of Manufacturing of Blacking Accordingly to an Original recipe in his possession and the said William Edward Woodd being desirous to take up the Business of the said Manufactory had contracted with the said Jonathan Warren to pay him the sum therein mentioned at the time therein also mentioned on being permitted to use the name of the said Jonathan Warren in the said Business And the said Jonathan Warren for the consideration in the said agreement mentioned agreed with the said William Edward Woodd to permit and suffer him the said William Edward Woodd to use the name of him the said Jonathan Warren in his lables and advertisements and that he the said Jonathan Warren should not carry on the Business of the said Manufactory on his own Account but for the sole use and benefit of the said William Edward Woodd provided that in case the said Jonathan Warren should depart this life pending the said agreement leaving Elizabeth Warren his widow him surviving that then and in such case he the said William Edward Woodd for the Considerations aforesaid agreed to pay to the said Elizabeth Warren the sum therein mentioned and at the time therein specified provided Also and it was agreed that in case the said William Edward Woodd should after the decease of the said Jonathan Warren relinquish and give up the said concern that he the said William Edward Woodd should upon such relinquishment give unto the said Elizabeth Warren three Months Notice previous thereto Signed by the said Jonathan Warren and William Edward Woodd and witnessed by William Glendon and Thomas Gully And this deponent Saith that in pursuance of the said Agreement the said William Edward Woodd continued to carry on the said Business until the year one thousand eight hundred and twenty four when he

admitted the other defendant Stephen Pilcher into Copartnership and the same Business has been by them carried on up to the present period E Warren [signature]
Sworn at the Public Office Southampton Buildings Chancery Lane in the County of Middlesex this 23d. day of November 1827 before me.
J S Dowdeswell [signature]

[13. The affidavit of George Garey]
In Chancery   Between Robert Warren and Benjamin Warren, Plaintiffs and William Edward Woodd and Stephen Pilcher, Defendants
George Garey of No. 1 Barlow Street Great Marylebone Street in the County of Middlesex Plate Powder Manufacturer maketh Oath and Saith that he was intimately acquainted with Jonathan Warren deceased for some years previous to his commencing the Business of a Blacking Manufacturer that the said Jonathan Warren in the year one thousand seven hundred and ninety five commenced making Blacking and this Deponent was in the habit at that time of assisting the said Jonathan Warren by informing him what this deponent had discovered in the Manufacturing the said Article of Blacking and the said Jonathan Warren was also at that time in the habit of informing this Deponent of his discoveries   And this Deponent further Saith that Shortly after the above discoveries had been compleated the said Jonathan Warren commenced Manufacturing and Selling the said Article of Blacking for his own benefit and that the said Jonathan Warren first commenced such Sale in Suffolk Street Charing Cross in the said County of Middlesex and afterwards removed his Manufactory of Blacking to Hungerford Stairs in the Strand where the Sale of his said Blacking became very extensive and his name became publickly known as the Manufacturer of Warrens Liquid and paste Blacking and this Deponent further Saith that for several years after the said Jonathan Warren so commenced Business as aforesaid there was not to the best of this Deponents remembrance and belief any other person of the Sirname of Warren who Manufactured Blacking and this deponent further Saith that the said Jonathan Warren carried on his said Business of Manufacturing Blacking from his Commencement in Suffolk Street until the year one thousand eight hundred and twenty Two when he disposed of the same to the above named Defendants as this deponent hath been informed and believes but the said Jonathan Warren never to the best of this deponents belief abandoned such Business during the period before mentioned   And this Deponent hath heard and believes it to be true that many years ago and Several years after the said commencement of the said Jonathan Warren, Thomas Warren the Father of the said Plaintiffs and who has been

engaged with the said Jonathan Warren in the Manufacturing of Blacking quarrelled with him and that the said Thomas Warren was afterwards asked by some person if he knew the said Jonathan Warrens Secret of Blacking making and if he did the said person would advance him the said Thomas Warren money to commence and carry on the Business of Blacking Manufacturing.- George Garvey [signature]
Sworn at the Public Offices in Southampton Buildings in the County of Middlesex this 23d. day of November 1827 before me
G Wilson [signature]

[14. The affidavit of Joseph Lampit]
In Chancery *Between Robert Warren and Benjamin Warren, Plaintiffs and William Edward Woodd and Stephen Pilcher, Defendants*
Joseph Lampit of No 4 Fox Court Long Lane West Smithfield in the County of Middlesex Foreman to Messrs William Edward Woodd and Stephen Pilcher the above named Defendants maketh Oath and Saith that he has been in the Employ of the said defendants for the last three years or thereabouts   And this deponent further Saith that during such the period of his Employ with the said defendants he never was directed or authorized by either of the said defendants to use the name of Robert Warren or Warren of 30 Strand on any Occasion whatever and deponent positively Saith that during such his Employ with the said Defendants he never on any one Occasion used those words in the Sale of the said defendants Blacking altho' the deponent Saith that during the last twelve months and particularly while Robert Ashdown was in the Employ of the said Defendants Several genteel dressed persons have called at the Warehouse of the said defendants in Noble Street in the City of London and Asked this Deponent if the Blacking Sold by the defendants was Robert Warrens Blacking or if Messrs Woodd and Pilcher meaning the said defendants had any connection with Robert Warren of the Strand to which this Deponent replied it was not Robert Warrens Blacking but that it was Jonathan Warrens Blacking and that the said Defendants had no connexion whatsoever with Robert Warren of the Strand   And this Deponent further Saith that some short time since a person who said his name was Jones called at the warehouse of the said defendants aforesaid and Asked for half a dozen of Blacking at four shillings which this defendant served the said Mr Jones with who put them into a hand Basket and deponent thereupon Asked him If he should put some straw between them to prevent Accident but the said Mr Jones declined this deponents offer and immediately placed his handkerchief between the said Bottles of Blacking to prevent as he informed this deponent the lables on the said Bottles from being rubbed   And this deponent further

238

Saith that the said Mr Jones immediately after being Served by this deponent as aforesaid went into the Counting house where the said defendant Stephen Pilcher then was that the said Stephen Pilcher gave to the said Mr Jones a Bill of Parcels as this Deponent understood but to the best of this deponents Recollection and belief the said Mr Jones never Asked the said Stephen Pilcher or this deponent whether the said Blacking was the Blacking of "Robert Warren" or Warren of 30 Strand or of any Other persons but immediately upon his leaving the Counting house of said defendants this deponent opened the Door of the Warehouse for the said Mr Jones who did not make any remark whatever in this Deponents hearing   And this deponent further Saith that he hath been lately informed and verily believes that while the said Robert Ashdown was in the Employ of the said defendants he was also taking Orders for the Plaintiffs /-

Joseph Lampit [signature]

Sworn at the Public Office Southampton Buildings in the County of Middlesex this 23d day of November 1827 before me –

J S Dowdeswell [signature]

[15. The affidavit of William Langley]

In Chancery   Between Robert Warren and Banjamin Warren, Plaintiffs and William Edward Woodd and Stephen Pilcher, Defendants

William Langley of No. 32 Crooked Lane in the City of London Traveller for the house of Messrs Woodd and Pilcher of No 9 Noble Street Cheapside in the City of London Blacking Manufacturers the above named Defendants maketh Oath and saith that he hath been for some time past in the imploy of the above named Defendants as their Traveller for the purpose of taking Orders for the Sale of Jonathan Warrens Blacking   And this Deponent further saith that if any of the Customers or Dealers of the said Defendants asked this Deponent what Warrens Blacking it was he always explained to them it was "Jonathan Warrens Blacking" and that the said Jonathan Warren was the Original Manufacturer   And this Deponent further saith that the said Defendants gave this Deponent positive direction to sell their Blacking as the Blacking of "Jonathan Warrens" and not as the Blacking of "Robert Warren" or "Warren of 30 Strand"   And this Deponent positively saith that during the time he has been in the imploy of the said Defendants he never represented the said Blacking to be the Blacking of "Robert Warren" or "Warren of 30 Strand" but this Deponent always represented the same to be the Blacking of "Jonathan Warren" and if any further questions were asked him by any persons for whom he sold it he replied for Messrs Woodd & Pilcher (meaning the said Defendants)

And this Deponent further saith he hath been frequently informed by Robert Ashdown who was also a Traveller for the house of the said Defendants and who lodges in the same House as this Deponent that he the said Robert Ashdown had taken Orders for Blacking both for the house of the said Defendants   And for the house of Robert Warren from One and the same person   And this Deponent further saith that in One particular instance the said Robert Ashdown informed this Deponent he had taken an Order for One poundsworth of Blacking for the house of Defts and had afterwards taken the same Order to the House of the Plaintiffs for them to Execute, that the Blacking was sent by the said Defendants and taken in by the Party who ordered it, and that Blacking was sent by the said Plaintiffs Robert Warren but it was returned in consequence of the Order being compleated by the Defendants

Wm Langley [signature]

Sworn at the Public Office in Southampton Buildings in the County of Middlesex this 23d day of November 1827 before me

J S Dowdeswell [signature]

[16. The affidavit of William Whalley]

In Chancery   Between Robert Warren and Benjamin Warren, Plaintiffs and William Edward Woodd and Stephen Pilcher, Defendants

William Whalley of No 4 Kings Row Pentonville in the County of Middlesex Traveller to the above named Defendants Maketh Oath and Saith that he Travelled for the late Mr Jonathan Warren Blacking Manufacturer from the year one thousand eight hundred and Seven until the year one thousand eight hundred and twenty Two when he disposed of his Business to the defendant William Edward Woodd and Since the year one thousand eight hundred and twenty Two to the present time this deponent has travelled for the said defendants William Edward Woodd and Stephen Pilcher   And this deponent further Saith that Since the said year one thousand eight hundred and seven until the present time he hath Sold Blacking for the said Jonathan Warren and Also for the said Defendants   And this deponent further Saith that during the time aforesaid he never represented to any person that he was Selling the Blacking of Robert Warren or Warren of 30 Strand and if any Customer or Dealer asked these questions he invariably replied no he was Selling the Blacking of Jonathan Warren the Original Manufacturer   And this deponent further Saith that the said defendants never Authorized him to Sell their Blacking as Robert Warren or Warren of 30 Strand nor was it the constant practice of the Travellers or Servants of the said defendants to the best of his information and belief to represent the said defendants

Blacking in any such Manner   And this deponent further Saith that the said Jonathan Warren informed him and he always understood and believed that he was the Original Inventor and proprietor of Warrens Blacking   And this deponent also particularly Saith that during the fifteen years he so Travelled for the said Jonathan Warren as aforesaid the said Jonathan Warren never Abandoned his Business in any manner whatever or left the same until he disposed of the same to the said defendant William Edward Woodd as aforesaid and this deponent further Saith that the said Jonathan Warren informed this deponent that he had taught the said Plaintiff Robert Warren the art of Blacking Manufacturing and that he the said Jonathan Warren was very sorry that he had done so

William Whalley [signature]

Sworn at the Public Office Southampton Buildings in the County of Middlesex this 23 day of November 1827 before me

J E Dowdeswell [signature]

[17. The affidavit of John Wright]
In Chancery   Between Robert Warren and Benjamin Warren,
Plaintiffs and William Edward Woodd and Stephen Pilcher,
Defendants

John Wright of Brewers Yard West Smithfield in the County of Middlesex Carman in the Employ of the above named defendants maketh Oath and Saith that since he has been in employ of the said Defendants he never was directed or Authorized by the said defendants to use the names of Robert Warren or Warren of 30 Strand in the delivery of Blacking to any of their Customers or Dealers   And

this Deponent also Saith that he never left any Blacking with any Person as being the Blacking of Robert Warren or Warren of 30 Strand during the time he has been in the Employ of the said defendants and this Deponent further Saith that while Robert Ashdown was in the Employ of Defendant he has been Asked by many persons whether the Blacking he was about to deliver was the Blacking of Robert Warren or Warren of 30 Strand but this deponent on such Occasions Replied it was Jonathan Warrens Blacking and explained to them the said Jonathan Warren was the Original Manufacturer   And this deponent further Saith on such Occasions he hath Shewn the Placards of the said defendants to such persons and explained to them that it was Jonathan Warrens Blacking and if they did not take such Blacking in it was his usual practice to write on the Bills of parcels that such persons wanted Robert Warrens Blacking and to return them to the said Defendants   And this deponent further Saith that some short time since this defendant delivered some Blacking at the house of Mrs Lawson in Coleman Street in the City of

London which Blacking was taken in by Mrs Lawsons Foreman that this deponent gave the said foreman the Bill of Parcels of the said Defendants in which their names as the Sellers of the Blacking is printed in large letters for the said Blacking and the said foreman after looking at it said it was right and desired this deponent to bring the Blacking in that this deponent took the Blacking into the Shop and put it on the floor and asked the said foreman to look at it and see if it was right which the said foreman did and afterwards took the Bill of parcels into the parlor and brought out the money and the Bill and this deponent gave a receipt on the Bill of its being paid that after the said Foreman had paid deponent he took up one of the Bottles and made some remark about Woodd and Pilcher and asked deponent who Woodd and Pilcher were that deponent told him they were the propriators of Jonathan Warrens Blacking that the said foreman asked what had become of Mr Jonathan Warren and this deponent Informed him the said foreman that Jonathan Warren was dead to which the said foreman replied he knew Jonathan Warren very well and had sold his Blacking before that time   And this deponent further Saith that he has been lately informed and verily believes that while the said Robert Ashdown was in the Employ of the said Defendants he was also taking Orders for the said Plaintiffs /-

John Wright [signature]

Sworn at the Public Office Southampton Buildings Chancery Lane in the County of Middlesex this 23 day of November 1827 before me

J E Dowdeswell [signature]

[18. The affidavit of Samuel Mann]
In Chancery   Between Robert Warren and Benjamin Warren, Plaintiffs and William Edward Woodd and Stephen Pilcher, Defendants

Samuel Mann of Hungerford Street Strand in the Parish of Saint Martin in the fields in the County of Middlesex the acting Beadle of the said Parish Maketh Oath and Saith that he this Deponent hath been for many Years Collector of the Rents of the Estate of the Reverend Henry Wise of Offchurch in the County of Warwick Clerk which Estate is situated in Hungerford Market Hungerford Street little Hungerford Street and various other places adjoining thereto and that on the ninth day of February in the Year One thousand eight hundred and twenty one Jonathan Warren named in the Pleadings in this Cause applied to this Deponent to take a Lease of a House situate and being in Little Hungerford Street Hungerford Market that this Deponent required a reference as to Character of the said Jonathan Warren who referred Deponent to a Baker in Whitcomb Street that this Deponent made enquiries and at last let to the said Jonathan Warren a House situate and

being in little Hungerford Street for one Year at the Yearly Rent of Sixty
Pounds that soon after the said Jonathan Warren took the said House he
put up a large number thirty precisely in imitation of the Number Thirty
then used by the above named Plaintiffs   And this Deponent also
further saith that he has been from the Year One thousand eight
hundred and eighteen to the year One thousand eight hundred and
twenty six in the habit of Collecting the Rents of the said Hungerford
Estate and that during the whole of that period and for many years
before and up to the present time there were not nor are there in fact
more than twelve houses in Little Hungerford Street where the said
Jonathan Warren resided   And this Deponent further saith that neither
of them had any such number as that of thirty until the said Jonathan
Warren came to reside there And this Deponent also saith that he
remembers that Robert Warren came to reside at Number Thirty in the
Strand some time in or about the year One thousand Eight Hundred and
sixteen and that shortly afterwards he put in front of his House in large
projecting letters the name of Warrens Blacking Warehouse 30 – and
also Robert Warren and that the said name of Robert Warren and
Number have continued there from that to the present time
Saml Mann [signature]
Sworn at the Public office Southampton Buildings Chancery Lane this
Twenty sixth day of November One thousand Eight Hundred and
Twenty seven Before me
T: P Stratford [signature]

[19. The affidavit of James Phillipps]
In Chancery   Between Robert Warren and Benjamin Warren,
Plaintiffs and William Edward Woodd and Stephen Pilcher,
Defendants
James Phillipps of Little Hungerford Street Strand in the County of
Middlesex Custom House Agent and Lighterman Maketh Oath and Saith
that this Deponent and this Deponents Father in his life time have
resided nearly Thirty years in little Hungerford Street Strand   And that
he this Deponent has been in the Constant habit of Shipping and
Transmitting Goods consisting of Blacking Manufactured by the above
named Plaintiffs to various parts of England Ireland and Scotland and
this Deponent further saith that little Hungerford Street is but a short
street and only contains twelve houses and that there is not any house in
the said Street having the number Thirty upon it   And this Deponent
also saith that he well remembers the above named Plaintiff Robert
Warren when he resided in Saint Martins Lane and carried on Business
there that his business became and was extremely extensive and that his
premises in Saint Martins Lane were too small to enable him to carry on

his business there that in or about the Year One thousand eight hundred and sixteen the said Robert Warren removed to Number thirty in the strand and that shortly after his so doing the name of Robert Warren and Number thirty Strand were placed in very large projecting Letters and figures in front of his House and that he was also in the constant habit of advertising his Blacking as Robert Warrens Blacking Number Thirty Strand   And this Deponent also saith he remembers that about Five Years after the said Robert Warren had been established as a Blacking Manufacturer at Number Thirty Strand Jonathan Warren came to reside in Little Hungerford Street aforesaid and shortly afterwards put up His name and a large number thirty precisely in imitation of the Plaintiffs Robert Warrens number Thirty and in other respects as regards their name similarly done and gave little Hungerford Street the appellation of Hungerford Stairs which name the Place never had before or since   And this Deponent also saith that the true number of the House in which the said Jonathan Warren resided was number six and not number Thirty
James Phillipps [signature]
Sworn at the Public office Southampton Buildings Chancery Lane in the County of Middlesex this Twenty six day of Novr. 1827 Before me
T. P Stratford [signature]

[20. The affidavit of George Whitehead]
In Chancery   Between Robert Warren and Benjamin Warren, Plaintiffs and William Edward Woodd and Stephen Pilcher, Defendants
George Whitehead of No. 37 Wardour Street in the Parish of Saint Ann Soho in the County of Middlesex Grocer and Cheese monger Maketh Oath and saith that in the Month of August one thousand eight hundred and twenty four this Deponent was applied to by a Traveller of the above named Defendants who called at the house of this Deponent and asked him Deponent if he was in want of any of Warrens Blacking that this Deponent has been for many years in the habit of dealing with the House of Robert Warren of No 30 in the Strand for Blacking and that when the said Traveller called upon this Deponent for orders for Blacking this Deponent was in want of a few dozens of bottles of Blacking and that believing that the said person had applied from the House of Robert Warren of the Strand aforesaid this Deponent gave him an Order for two dozens bottles of Blacking and a day or two afterwards the said Blacking was left at this Deponents House and he this Deponent paid for the same conceiving that he was paying for the Blacking of the said Plaintiffs   And this Deponent further saith that the general appearance of the bottles and the labels upon them were so similar to those used by Robert Warren of the Strand that this Deponent at first

did not discover that the said bottles of Blacking were not the bottles of Blacking of the said Robert Warren but on closer looking into them found that they were the Blacking of the above named Defendants who were at that time and still are perfect strangers to this Deponent this Deponent never having bought any Blacking either before or since of them the said Defendants but on the contrary give particular directions that no more of the same Blacking of the said Defendants should be taken in

George Whitehead [signature]

Sworn at the Public Office Southampton Buildings Chancery Lane in the County of Middlesex this 26th. Day of Novr. 1827 before me

T: P Stratford [signature]

[21. The affidavit of Valentine Thomas Coombes]

In Chancery   Between Robert Warren and Benjamin Warren, Plaintiffs and William Edward Woodd and Stephen Pilcher, Defendants

Valentine Thomas Coombes Clerk to James Boxer of Furnivals Inn in the County of Middlesex Gentleman maketh Oath and saith that he this Deponent hath been this morning and taken a view of the Premises occupied by Mr Robert Warren in which said Premises the Business of a Blacking Manufacturer appears to be carried on and on the front of which said Premises there appears in large figures "30"   And this Deponent further saith the said Premises are situate between the houses numbered "28" and "31"   And this Deponent further saith that from the observations he so made he verily believes that the said Premises now occupied by the Blacking Manufactory was formerly two houses and that they were numbered "29" and "30" but for for what purpose they are now numbered "30" only this Deponent cannot say

Valentine Thomas Coombes [signature]

Sworn at the Public Office Southampton Buildings in the County of Middlesex this 27 day of November 1827 before me

R H Eden [signature]

[22. The affidavit of John Windsor Jones]

In Chancery   Between Robert Warren and Benjamin Warren, Plaintiffs and William Edward Woodd and Stephen Pilcher, Defendants

John Windsor Jones of No 48 James Street Manchester Square in the Parish of Saint Marylebone in the County of Middlesex Grocer Maketh Oath and saith that about the middle of the Month of October last he this Deponent was applied to by one George Langley a Traveller from the House of the above named Defendants who asked this Deponent if he wanted any of Warrens Blacking to which Deponent replied that he did and desired him to send one dozen of small bottles as he this Deponent wished to get rid of his Stock of large Bottles which he had then in hand and at the same time showed the said Traveller the same large Bottles which were Bottles containing Blacking of Robert Warren No. 30 Strand that on the following day he this Deponent received fourteen bottles of Blacking from the same Defendants and this Deponent sent to the said Defendants the empty Bottles which had contained the Blacking of Robert Warren of No 30 in the Strand with whom this Deponent was in the constant habit of dealing for Blacking And this Deponent saith that he had no knowledge whatever of the above named Defendants and that when he gave their Traveller an order for Blacking he thought he was ordering the Plaintiffs Blacking and was not undeceived some time after the same had been received   And this Deponent afterwards saw the said Traveller who again applied to the Defendant   for further orders for Blacking and this Deponent remonstrated with him upon the impropriety of applying to Deponent for orders for Warrens Blacking of No 30 Strand and sending Deponent Blacking manufactured by the said Defendants of whom this Deponent had no dealings or knowledge   And this Deponent also saith that seeing the name of Warren at the top of the said Bottles and the No. 30 in the centre corresponding with the Blacking manufactured by the said Plaintiffs this Deponent was induced and did receive the same in perfect ignorance and with a full belief that it was Robert Warrens Blacking of No. 30 Strand

John Windsor Jones [signature]

Sworn at the Public Office Southampton Buildings Chancery Lane in the County of Middlesex this 26th day of November 1827 before me

T P Stratford [signature]

[23. The affidavits of Mary Warren and William Arundel]
In Chancery   Between Robert Warren and Benjamin Warren, Plaintiffs and William Edward Woodd and Stephen Pilcher, Defendants

Mary Warren of No. 30 Strand in the County of Middlesex Widow the Mother of the above named Plaintiffs and William Arundel formerly of No 469 in the Strand but now of High Street Marylebone in the same County Boot and Shoe Maker severally make Oath and say and first this Deponent Mary Warren for herself saith that it is not true as stated in the Affidavit of Elizabeth Warren made on the twenty third day of November instant and filed in this Cause in this Honorable Court that Thomas Warren ever entered into an Agreement with Jonathan Warren to admit him Into partnership in the business of a Blacking manufacturer nor did they ever carry on together the said business for a short or any other period and that if any such Agreement had ever been entered into this Deponent must have been aware of that circumstance nor did the said Jonathan Warren ever instruct the said Thomas Warren in the Art of making Blacking but on the contrary thereof the said Thomas Warren carried on the business of a Blacking manufacturer from about the year One thousand seven hundred and ninety five in Saint Martins Lane where he continued until the time of his death which took place in the year one thousand eight hundred and five and that from the said year one thousand eight hundred and five to the year one thousand eight hundred and sixteen the said Robert Warren carried on the business of a Blacking manufacturer in Saint Martins Lane until he found that his premises were too small he took the House No. 30 in the Strand in which he has ever since carried on his said business   And this Deponent the said William Arundel for himself saith that he was intimately and confidentially acquainted with the said Thomas Warren and Jonathan Warren for upwards of Forty years and that if any Partnership or Agreement for a partnership in the way or business of Blacking makers or manufacturers had been entered into or even contemplated between them Deponent must have known that fact   And this Deponent also Saith that the said Jonathan Warren began in a very small way the business of a Blacking maker at No. 18 in Suffolk Street Haymarket and removed from thence to No. 6 Little Hungerford Street in Hungerford Market where he carried on the business in a very small way – in fact in a perfect Chandler Shop style compared to the extensive and general manner in which the said Robert Warren carried on his business of a Wholesale and Retail Blacking manufacturer   And this Deponent also Saith that about Two years after the said Robert Warren had taken the House No. 30 in the Strand this Deponent had a conversation with the said Jonathan Warren who informed this Deponent that from the quantity of Vinegar Treacle and other Articles which Robert Warren was in the habit of purchasing for his business of a Blacking manufacturer he was carrying on a most extensive business and would certainly make a rapid fortune – while on the other hand the business which he the said Jonathan Warren was doing was scarcely sufficient to pay his rent and expences and the said Jonathan Warren seemed to lament that his business was not in as flourishing a condition as the business of the said Robert Warren   And this Deponent also Saith that the No. 30 put by Jonathan Warren on his house in Little Hungerford Street aforesaid was as Deponent verily believes put up in fraud and with a view to lead the Public to a belief that his house formed a part of the house or business of the said Robert Warren of No. 30 Strand the No. 30 being put up to imitate the No. 30 upon the house of Robert Warren as nearly as possible and that he the said Jonathan Warren did not in point of fact come to reside to Little Hungerford Street aforesaid for five years or thereabouts after the sd. Robert Warren had taken his said house and premises No. 30 Strand aforesaid And this Deponent lastly saith that during all the years that this Deponent was acquainted with the said Jonathan Warren he was as Deponent verily believes a Man always in very needy and distressed circumstances and was as Deponent hath been informed and also believes a considerable time a Prisoner in White Cross Street Prison and also a Prisoner in the Fleet Prison for Debt

Mary Warren [signature]

Wm. Arundel [signature]

Sworn at the public Office Southampton Buildings Chancery Lane in the County of Middlesex this 25th day of November 1827 by both Deponents Before me

J. S. Harvey [signature]

Old Bailey embezzlement trial of Thomas Gore, employee of Abraham Lamert

COPELAND, MAYOR. CENTRAL CRIMINAL COURT. MINUTES OF EVIDENCE, Taken in Short-hand. BY HENRY BUCKLER.
VOLUME IV. SESSION VII. TO SESSION XII.
LONDON: GEORGE HEBERT, CHEAPSIDE. WILLIAM TYLER, PRINTER, BOLT-COURT, FLEET-STREET. 1836.

NEW COURT, *Wednesday, May* 18, 1836. *Fifth Jury, before Mr. Common Sergeant.* **Reference Number:** t18360509-1335

1335. THOMAS GORE was indicted for embezzlement
MESSRS. BODKIN *and* CHAMBERS *conducted the Prosecution.*
ELIZABETH LAMERT:- I am the widow of Dr. Abraham Lamert, who carried on business at No. 10, Church-street, Spitalfields. He was a patent medicine vender—the prisoner came into his employ about four years since—he was clerk and assistant—he was authorized to receive money for medicines that were sold, and to make proper entries of them in the book—there was a day-book kept to enter money received from customers for goods sent out, or medicines sold—this is the book (*looking at one*) in which I have always seen the accounts entered—my husband died on the 4th of March, 1836—on the 19th of May, 1835, I left London, and joined him in Dublin, and continued with him until his death—I am his administratrix—the prisoner has not accounted to me, independently of the day book, for 5s., 3d., received from Zaccheus Hunter, on the 9th of July, 1835; nor for 8s. 9d. received from Alfred Willoughby, on the 22nd of August, 1835—he has never accounted for or paid me the sum of 10s., received on the 19th of October, from Mr. James Knight—two days before my husband's death I authorized my son, Joseph Lamert to obtain the prisoner's account from him.
Cross-examined by MR. PHILLIPS.
Question: This is the book in which the accounts were kept, and in which you have always seen the accounts entered?
Answer: It is the book that was given to me by my son since I returned home—it is the book that was taken from the prisoner when I

authorized my son to take the books from him—it is the book I was to have had the accounts kept in, after my departure from London.

Question: Is your first answer a true one, that this is the book in which you have always seen the accounts entered?

Answer: That is the book that was given to the prisoner to keep his accounts in after my departure—I might certainly have said that I saw it—that book was given to keep accounts in after my departure from London—I could not swear that I saw accounts entered in it, because it was given to keep the accounts in after I left London—I could have no motive in swearing it—there has been an examination before the Court of Bankruptcy with respect to my husband's effects, and the prisoner was examined as a witness—My husband became a bankrupt in November 1834—I remember after Gore's giving his evidence his being sent with a messenger to take possession of some secreted goods, of which he had made a discovery—they were my son's—this might have been a fortnight or three weeks before he was apprehended—I think it was as long as that—after Gore's evidence there was a writ for 55l. issued against my son Samuel, at the instance of the assignees—I saw Samuel a fortnight ago—he is travelling—I do not know where he is—he set out after Gore's evidence—I do not know anything about the writ—I have heard of it—he set out after the information I had about the writ—I got this book from my son, Joseph Lamert—I put the greatest confidence in my sons, both before and after my husband's death.

Question: Upon your oath, with respect to those sons, did you not invoke your vengeance, and God Almighty's vengeance upon their heads?

Answer: I do not recollect that I have—I cannot swear that I have not—no recollection. I received a letter from the prisoner at the bar, (indeed, more than one or two), saying that my sons were the greatest enemies I had, and he so set the mind of the father and against them, that I believe I replied with irritated feeling, being incensed at such disobedient conduct—all the letters I had at my husband's death, I delivered over to my sons—I had destroyed several—the prisoner wrote me a letter, saying that one son would take the bed from under me, and the other acted very badly; and the letter I wrote denouncing my children, was in consequence of a letter of Gore's—I am the mother of these sons—the letter I received was in great cause the reason of my writing as I did; and it was in consequence of my eldest son getting married and his father being too ill to come to his marriage, which was one cause of setting me against him—Mr. Gore's letter and my son's marriage, and little family affairs, was the cause of my being alienated from my sons—the two brothers were not friends for some time—it was not to prejudice the

Jury that I said it was Gore's letter that alienated me from my sons.

Question: Is not the cause still kept back purposely by you from the Jury?

Answer: The prisoner's letter and my son's marriage without the consent of his father, and little family matters were the cause of it—there might be other causes with the father—to the best of my belief these are the causes with myself.

Question: Was it not in consequence of a letter from your son, Samuel Lamert, written with his own hand to you to Dublin, that you did it? *A.* Indeed it was not—I do not recollect ever receiving such a letter.

Question: Then if you wrote to Gore that you had received a letter from your son Samuel, and that while breath remained in your frame the character of its contents would never be erased from your memory—is that true?

Answer: Well, I did—I do not know whether the sight of my own letter has brought it to my remembrance—I did write that letter (*looking at it*)—I heard at the Magistrate's of letters being burnt belonging to Gore—I heard Joseph swear before the Magistrate that he burnt some—I was not paying any attention to what he said—I cannot tell what letters my son said he burnt—I did not think this letter was burnt, when I said I was paying no attention—I cannot tell what letters were burnt—I did not hear from Joseph that he had burnt some letters I had written to Gore— I heard Joseph say he had burnt some letters in Gore's possession, but I do not know what they were—that was before Gore was taken into custody—he did not tell me he had burnt papers as well as letters—he said they were letters from patients to his father, and different things, and as there was going to be a sale on the premises, he thought they had better be burnt—I cannot tell when I wrote the letter to Gore, denouncing my children—it was in August, I believe.

Question: Was it not what you considered the base conduct of Samuel, in a letter from himself, that caused you to write that letter?

Answer: I do not recollect any letter from him—I know the letter from the prisoner was the great means—Samuel's letter and the prisoner's together might have caused my denouncing him—I do not recollect the contents of my son's letter now.

Question: Did you ever say, that while breath animated your frame the character of Samuel's letter would never be erased—that to all the world you would show the infamous manner in which he threatened to reduce to the street his unfortunate parents—but that you never would acknowledge yourself a parent to such an unnatural fiend—did you forget that?

Amswer: No.

Question: Did you say to Gore "He says, if I do not remit 10l. or 15l. by return of post, that without any further notice, he will sell off all our furniture to pay himself?—did you forget that?

Answer: No, I did not—I acknowledge having received a letter from my son—my sons were continually threatening to sell me up, if I did not repay the money we owed—Samuel threatened to come to the house and take the property by force, and sell it—both might have done so—I say Samuel, I did not mean to exclude Joseph—they might have both done it—I do not know—I did give Gore directions, if he dared to enter his father's house, or to touch any article, to eject him by law immediately. Dr. Lamert's affairs were in a very bad state—I do not know that Miss Blits, the housekeeper, was obliged to pawn her clothes, to support the current expenses of the household—she showed me the duplicates, but she did not say it was to pay the household expenses—I do not know whether it was for the household expenses or herself—I never told the prisoner to keep money which he had received to pay up the arrears of his salary, which the embarrassed state of the firm would not enable me to do—it might be so, but I do not remember it—all monies that he was authorized to receive in the shop business, he was desired by my late husband to enter in the book—he always wrote that he did not get money enough to pay up the arrears of his salary—I have sent him money, not to pay other persons but I have to pay Miss Blits— I have not written to the prisoner to shut up the house, and to sell the things, that I recollect—the furniture was to be left in the house—the furniture was not mine—I do not know of his removing any property—I do not know whether it was the custom of my husband and the prisoner to put down on bits of paper, the sums they received in town and country, and at certain chronological times to enter them in the book—I travelled with my husband, he kept a book, but he put down person's names and residences on papers—he might have put down sums he received also—I cannot swear that he did not.

Question: Was there nothing removed before the bankruptcy from your husband's house?

Answer: Ten or eleven months ago, Dr. Lamert gave to his son ten or twelve very old chairs, a table, and a few little things; these things were seized at my son's house; and the gentleman of the Court came down, and went through all our house—a great many things were pointed out by Mr. Gore that did not belong to us—on looking over the inventory, they were all there—they came back and searched my trunk—the prisoner said I had a box of jewels; and all they found in my trunk, was a little locket and some seals—Gore has been three or four years in the employment of my husband—these letters are all in my own hand-writing (*looking at them.*)

MR. BODKIN.

Question: You have been asked whether the bankruptcy did not take place in November, 1834?

Answer: Yes; it was; and in February, 1835, that my husband obtained his certificate—I do not know whether the furniture was removed before the certificate was obtained—I was summoned to attend the Bankruptcy Court some time in March last, about the 23rd—Gore appeared as a witness, and I was summoned to answer it—my husband died on the 4th of March, and I had returned home about three days before I was summoned—it was alleged that things had been removed before the bankruptcy, and Gore was examined as a witness on that occasion—he had remained in our service from November, 1834, to March, 1836, without saying any thing about it—on my return from Liverpool, I and my son expressed great surprise at the small returns said to have been made by the business—Gore represented, from time to time, that they were not sufficient to pay his wages—when I returned I think they were sufficient—Mr. Isaacs, who had been clerk to my husband many years, attended to the business.

Cross-examined by MR. CLARKSON

Question: There is a charge of 5s. 3*d.* from Zaccheus Hunter; was that mentioned before the Magistrate?

Answer: Yes, it was all stated—the prisoner was not with me in Dublin on the 7th of July—I think he left on the 1st.

MR. BODKIN

Question: Was there a house full of furniture at the time of the bankruptcy?

Answer: Yes, very elegant furniture—my son Samuel bought and paid for it, at the value which it came to, by the person sent down by the court to value it—it was valued. I think, as 198*l.*—there were eight old chairs, a table, and a pair of bed-steps, given by my husband to one of my sons—these were the things that were seized as the property of the creditors after my examination—they sold for 5*l.* for 5*l.* 14*s*—I never was acquainted that there was a writ out against my son, till I heard Gore say so at the office at Lambeth-street—we never knew it till that moment—I cannot say whether the early part of this book had been torn out—it looks like it—this book was for the prisoner to enter what he received from customers after I left London in May—there is nothing in this letter that has the slightest reference to these sums of money.

MR. CLARKSON

Question: Did you not on the 2nd of February last, receive from the prisoner an account of the sums paid and received?

Answer: I do not recollect it—I cannot swear whether I have such an account to the 2nd of February or have not.

COURT

Question: Or any time this year?

Answer: Not to my recollection.

Question: Had he any authority to pay himself his wages from the time you went to Ireland?

Answer: Not that I recollect.

JOSEPH LAMERT:- I am son of the last witness. In March last I received instructions from my mother to go to the prisoner—I went about the 2nd or 3rd of March—my mother was at Liverpool, with my father—I told the prisoners I had instruction to receive all books and papers, and that my father was dangerously ill—I requested him to give up the books and papers—amongst others I got this book—the prisoner came in, and asked me what authority I had to take it—I told him I had authority and showed him a letter written by an assistant of my father, I believe, and signed by my mother—I have not that letter, nor I cannot tell what has become of it—it was addressed to my brother and myself— I told the prisoner I had taken the books by the authority contained in that letter, and asked whether this book was correct, as it appeared only to he made up to the 2nd of February—he said, "There are only a dozen of pills to go down, and I belive that will make it correct, " or something to that effect—that was all he said—I have looked through the book—it begins on the 23rd of May—there is no entry of either of these sums in it.

Cross-examined by MR. CLARKSON

Question: Can you tell me where your brother Samuel is?

Answer: He is in the country—I believe in Liverpool—I am not positive—he went away about three weeks or a month ago—I do not know whether it was before or after the prisoner was taken—it might have been within a week of it—I do not live at my mother's—I have an establishment of my own—my brother's is in Drury-lane—that has closed—he is on his travels—he has been away about three weeks—he has been about three or four years in business, and about twelve months in Drury-lane—I am a chemist and druggist, in the Minories.

Question: Shortly before the 2nd of last February had you been upon good or best terms with your father and mother?

Answer: I cannot exactly say—we were not ill friends—there was a sort of coolness between me, and my friends, and parents, but not ill terms— I do no know that I did allege that they owed me money—I think they did—I have a doubt about it—I do not recollect writing for the money—I will not swear I did not—I did not write continually, to dun them for it—it was a month before the 2nd of February that I wrote—I did not write that I and my brother would go to my father's and mother's house, and threaten to sell it up—I never knew of any thing of the kind.

Question: Upon your oath, did you not go to the house of your father and mother, at a time when you were quarrelling and complaining of each other?

Answer: I was at their house—I did not think it required their consent—I had not been forbidden the house—they had not complained to me of my unfilial conduct towards them—I never heard from the prisoner that I was described in my mother's letter as that wicked young man who would be subject to a higher power than theirs for my unfilial conduct to them—I never heard it from Gore, nor from any other source—I had not reason to believe that my father and mother were bitterly incensed against me—there was a coolness arising from money lent—it might be about 50*l.* or 60*l.*—but between relations, having lent money, I thought I ought to be paid it—the money was lent at various times before and after the bankruptcy—I cannot tell for what purpose—I believe my brother bought the furniture of the assignees—I went to the house on the 3rd of March, and found Miss Blits and the servant—I took a variety of letters out of a closet—I did not take a 50*l.* bill of exchange, to my knowledge—I took a variety of papers—it is impossible for me to tell you any particular items—having taken so many I cannot tell you whether I have taken that bill—there were one or two of the prisoner's memorandums—I will not swear there were not twenty—I burnt one or two letters of the prisoner's—I did not burn any memorandums, nor a bill for 50*l.*—I did not find a bill for 50*l.*, receipted—all the papers were burnt—they were confidential letters, addressed to my father in business, of old dates—there were some letters addressed to the prisoner by my mother—I examined some—I scanned over them—I will not swear I examined them all—I do not recollect that the prisoner came in and said, upon finding his papers being burned, "Now I have nothing to say, now I am ruined"—I cannot swear he did not—I did not say, when I burnt his papers, "Now he will have nothing to shew"—he asked me whether I had burnt his letters, or any letters—I said there were a variety of memorandums, which could be of no use, as we were going to have a sale—I did not run out of the house with the letters in my hand, pursued by the prisoner—my brother did not take them—I swear they were never removed from the house.

Question: When you found the prisoner had arrived, you having got there in his absence, did you forbid the servant to let him come in?

Answer: No—I do not think I did—I will swear I did not, nor did my brother in my presence—I do not know the name of the servant—I did not cram the papers into my hat first—I do not know whether I took the bill amongst two or three hundred papers of no earthly use in keeping.

MR. BODKIN

Question: You say they were letters from patients?

Answer: Yes—four-fifths of them were confidential letters—I looked at the letters from my mother—I am confident they did not allude to this case—I took no letters that were not referable to his business as a servant—I took no private papers of the prisoner's—I looked at the two letters my mother sent—they did not refer to monies he had received in business—at that time I was not aware of any deficiencies on his part, nor had I looked at the books.

MR. CLARKSON

Question: Did these letters from your mother contain two or three sides?

Answer: They contained two or three.

RICHARD MACLEAN: I was porter to the late Mr. Lamert for eighteen years—it was my business to carry out medicines ordered from him to the customers—Mr. Hunter lives in Blackfriar's-road—on the 7th of January, 1835, I received 5*s.* 3*d.* or 5*s.* 6*d.* from him—I paid it over Mr. Gore when I got home—I took a bill and receipt which the prisoner gave me—on the 19th of October I received 10*s.* from James Knight, and gave it to the prisoner—he gave me 6*d.* for my trouble.

Cross-examined by MR. CLARKSON

Question: Did Rebecca Blits live in the house?

Answer: Yes—I always gave the money to Mr. Gore—I have never paid money to Blits—I cannot tell the day I paid it to the prisoner—what I received from Hunter I received in July—I remember my master's bankruptcy—I lent a hand in removing the goods—I cannot say when it was—whether it was within a week of the bankruptcy—it was within a week—there were some chairs and boxes, and a trunk—Mr. Gore gave them to me—I think my master and mistress were there—I think Mrs. Lamert packed the trunk—the fenders and tables and chairs were removed to Charlotte-street just by where Samuel lives—I went with them with: cart—I cannot say to whose house it was—it was in the afternoon—I cannot say whether it was winter or summer—it was rather dark.

MR. BODKIN

Question: Were these the things that were afterwards sold for 5*l.*?

Answer: No; I do not know that they were sold—I cannot say how much they were worth—I was employed by Mr. Gore.

ZACCHEUS HUNTER: I live in Webber-row, Blackfriars. I do not know Mr. Lamert's porter—I did not pay this 5*s.* 3*d.*—I have got a receipt—my petty cash-keeper is not here.

ELIZABETH LAMERT: I do not believe this receipt to be the prisoner's handwriting.

ALFRED WILLOUGHBY: I have a receipt for 8*s.* 9*d.* paid to the account of Mr. Lamert on the 22nd of August, 1835—I did not pay it myself.

ELIZABETH LAMERT: This is the prisoner's writing "8*s.* 9*d.*, received T.G." as he usually used to receipt the bills.

Cross-examined by MR. PHILLIPS

Question: At the date of that Miss Blits was living in your husband's house?

Answer: I believe she was.

JAMES KNIGHT: I live in King-street, Blackfriars—I remember a sum of 10*s.* being paid to the porter of Mr. Lamert—this is the receipt taken at the time, I believe.

ELIZABETH LAMERT: This is Gore's writing.

Prisoner's Defence: The real object of this prosecution against me is for the express purpose of invalidating evidence given by me, and to be given by me before the Commissioners of Bankruptcy—a quantity of jewels and valuable things were secreted by me under the direction of the bankrupt, and the prosecutrix in particular—a fellow clerk gave notice, and I was summoned to give evidence, and when upon my oath was obliged to give conscientious evidence which was the means of recovering these goods and jewellery and other things, and it is to be proved whether my evidence will enable the Commissioners to get a sum of 55*l.* obtained by Samuel Lamert—it will be proved that Joseph and Samuel Lamert came to the house during my absence—that they had gone over the house, and Joseph had put my letters, correspondence, and accounts into his hat—I went to the cupboard where they had been kept, and they had taken my papers, and left Rebecca Blit's paper which were close to the side of mine—Mr. Lamert has stated that he had authority from his mother—I knew he had not—he produced a letter from Mr. Issacs I said I would not attend to that: but the moment they produced their mother's written authority, I said I would go into the account with them—I went to the closet and missed my accounts; Joseph Lamert was down in the water-closet with them in his hat reading them—I went and told him they were of the greatest possible importance to me, and one bill of 50*l.* I had paid only a few days before—he stated they were in a little box sealed up—I ran to the box and cut the string—they were not there—I ran back and told him, and insisted upon having my letters—the two brothers went out with my letters in their hats—I followed them out thinking to go to the magistrate for advice—I overtook them and passed them both—I turned my head and they had returned to the house—I went to the house and rang four times, and not being answered, I jumped over the kitchen rails, and got in at the kitchen window, the servants said they had orders not to open the door till the letters were burnt; and Joseph Lamert took me to the ashes and showed me the ashes of the letters, and he said to Rebecca, "You are a witness that I burnt them."

NOT GUILTY .

Reference Number: t18360509-1336

1336. THOMAS GORE was again indicted for embezzlement.

MR. BODKIN *conducted the prosecution.*

JOSEPH LAMERT: I left town for Liverpool, my father being ill, on Friday evening, the 4th of March—before I left I saw the prisoner in the afternoon, between two and three o'clock—I said, "Is there any thing to go down; have you had any orders?"—he said there was only a doze of pills to go down, and there were no orders—I left town—I afterwards saw the prisoner on the 15th or 16th of March—I had told him to put down upon paper any orders he might have had during my absence, and them I asked him if he had any orders—he said, "Nothing, except the dozen of pills"—he has never accounted for 6*l.* received from George Jones, assistant to Mr. Sutton, of Bow Church-yard.

ELIZABETH LAMERT: My husband died on the 4th of March, at Liverpool—the prisoner has not accounted for 6*l.*, received on the 4th of March, from Messrs. Sutton.

Cross-examined by MR. PHILLIPS

Question: You have had a Mr. Issacs in your employ since your husband's death?

Answer: Yes; and he was with us a long time before.

Question: Has not the prisoner, since your husband's death, come to you to account for certain sums received, and you refused to hear him, because Mr. Issacs was not at home?

Answer: Never; the prisoner called at the house but did not say it was to settle accounts—I have refused to see him, because my son told me, that when he gave him the bills, he said he had accounted for every thing but one dozen of pills—I refused to see him—I never received a message that he wanted to account with me—he called twice at the house—I do not know what he called for—he said he wished to see me—he told his message to Mr. Issacs in the back parlour, and Miss Blits brought it to me—I said I would see him some other time—I do not recollect that she said he wanted to see me for the purpose of settling his accounts, but I will not swear that she did not—my husband died at a quarter before four in the morning, on the 4th of March—my son Joseph gave me this book about the 15th or 16th, when I returned—the prisoner has had no opportunity of looking at it since.

GEORGE JONES: I was assistant to Messrs. Sutton, of Bow church-yard, in March last—when we want goods, we sent a written order by one of our men—I put a paper out in front warehouse on the 3rd of March, and I believe we did receive some goods from Mr. Lamert—I do not know—I paid for them on the 4th of March, to the prisoner, and have his receipt for them—6*l.* was the money paid, for six dozen of Scarlett Pills.

Cross-examined by MR. PHILLIPS

Question: What time did you pay it?

Answer: I cannot say; I believe it was after twelve o'clock.

Witness for the Defence.

REBECCA BLITS: I remember hearing of Mr. Lamert's death—I was the housekeeper when Mrs. Lamert went to see her husband—I was there before his death a long time—I remember, after the 4th of March, Mr. Lamert sending me for the prisoner—I went to him, and he came—she sent for the express purpose of settling with Mr. Gore—he came at the time Mr. Issacs happened to be at home—I told Mrs. Lamert he was come, in obedience to her direction—she said she could not see him then.

MR. BODKIN

Question: I believe you are on very intimate terms with the prisoner?

Answer: No—I never quarrelled with him—I was very friendly with him—I lived in the house with him when Mr. and Mrs. Lamert went away—I was then on friendly terms, but not more than before.

NOT GUILTY.

There were two other indictments, on which no evidence was offered.

Henry Worms' first trial at The Old Bailey

The Proceedings of the Old Bailey, London's Central Criminal Court, 1674 to 1913
HENRY WORMS, SOLOMON WORMS, Theft, receiving, 22nd October 1823.
Reference Number: t18231022-124
SEVENTH DAY, WEDNESDAY, OCTOBER 29.
Middlesex Cases, First Jury, Before Mr. Common Sergeant.
1425. HENRY WORMS and SOLOMON WORMS were indicted for feloniously receiving two iron weights, the goods of Samuel Bye, they well knowing the same to have been stolen.
SAMUEL BYE: I am a green-grocer, and live in Beauchamp-street, Brooke's-market. On the 14th of October, two weights were stolen from my shop, after seven o'clock in the evening. I found them next morning, in Worms' back premises - they keep a marine store shop, in Fox's-court; about a hundred yards from my house. I called on them, and asked if they had lately bought two weights - the prisoner Henry said, we have not; the son said, "We have, father," and fetched them out - the boy who took them received 3 1/2d. a piece for them; they are worth 2s. 3d. each. The boy who took the weights is named Ballard. I told the prisoners they ought to know better than to purchase such things of a boy. The father said to the son, "If you have bought them, fetch them;" the son said, "You gave me 2d. to help pay for the last weight I bought" - he did not deny it at the time, but he did at Hatton-garden. Ballard said he received 2d. from the elder prisoner.
Cross-examined by MR. ANDREWS.
Question: Did Ballard go with you to Worms's shop –
Answer: Yes; he said he took one at a time, and another afterwards, that the younger prisoner gave him 3 1/2d. each for them, and that the son got 2d. from the father, in part payment for one. I do not know whether the weights are standard - I have not had them tried since they were stolen. The younger prisoner said his father was not at home at the time.
GEORGE BALLARD: I first took one weight to Fox's-court to sell; I took it out of Bye's shop. I saw young Worms, who gave me 3 1/2d. for it. He asked if I had anything else to sell; I said, Yes, and he said, "Go and fetch it." When I brought the second weight, he said he had only 1 1/2d., and went to his father for 2d. to make up the sum.

Cross-examined.

Question: Was the father present –

Answer: Yes, he was in the shop when the son asked for the halfpence to pay for the second weight; he was not there when I took the first. It is a large shop, and he was attending to his business: it was between eight and nine o'clock in the evening. Old Worms took the 2d. out of his pocket.

SAMUEL BYE: Ballard told me that young Worms asked his father for some halfpence - I know nothing farther about it myself. I heard the son say, "Father, we bought the weights last night." The ring only is wrought iron.

MATTHIAS WELDEN: I am a constable. The weights were given to me by Mr. Bye. The father surrendered at the office.

THOMAS ENNIS: I am a shoemaker, and live in Brook's-market. I saw Ballard, who said he should like these weights. I said, "Do not take them, for if you do, I'll tell Mr. Bye."

The prisoners called the following witnesses.

ANN EDWARD: I am servant at the Rose, public-house, Hatton-wall. On the evening of last Tuesday fortnight, the elder prisoner was at our house; he had two glasses of gin and water, a pint of half and half, and two pipes of tobacco. I am sure he was there after nine o'clock that evening, because I take out my beer exactly at nine, and I found him there when I returned - I believe he had been there a length of time, but I cannot say. He was taken to Hatton-garden Office next morning, and I was sent over as a witness.

SARAH WORMS: I am daughter to the elder prisoner. I was at home yesterday fortnight. I do not remember the boy Ballard coming there on that day - I was at home from five to ten o'clock in the evening; I remember lending my brother 2d. to pay for something. It was long before nine o'clock.

LEWIS WORMS: I am brother to the last witness. I went home about half-past eight o'clock; I do not live at my father's. I was told he was at the Rose - I did not leave the house till the watchman cried nine o'clock, when my father had not returned.

- DUNN: I live in Fox's-court, and know the prisoners. Sometimes I go to the Rose - I was there on the night in question, and saw the prisoner there.

NOT GUILTY.

Henry Worms' second trial at The Old Bailey

The Proceedings of the Old Bailey, London's Central Criminal Court, 1674 to 1913
JOHN MORIARTY, HENRY WORMS, MORRIS WORMS, Theft, grand larceny, Theft, receiving, 13th January 1825.
Reference Number: t18250113-200
Before Mr. Recorder
381. JOHN MORIARTY was indicted for stealing, on the 23d of December, a quart pot, value 18d. , the goods of William Winder; and HENRY WORMS and MORRIS WORMS were indicted for feloniously receiving the same, well knowing it to have been stolen.
WILLIAM WINDER: I keep the Fox and Peacock, public-house, Gray's Inn-lane. On the 23d of December, between 4 and 5 o'clock, the prisoner Moriarty came to my house for a pint of porter, which I served him with; he took that away, and came again for another pint of beer, which I served him in a quart pot. I asked him for the other pint pot, which he did not bring back. I said "Where is that pot, you have taken it away." He said he had not. He then came a third time, for half a pint of beer, and I said "You have taken that quart away." He said he had not. I served him with half a pint in another quart pot, he took that into the tap-room - I do not know where he had taken the others. He drank that porter. A person said to me "That man has taken the pot away." I have known him for these two years - he has frequented the house occasionally. I went to his house, in Fox-court, immediately, but the house was in darkness, and I did not go in. I came back for a candle to go to his house, but I thought I would go to Henry Worms's shop, which is a marine store shop, about sixty yards from my house, in Fox-court. I went towards the shop, and saw Moriarty standing there, shaking hands with Henry Worms, and heard Worms say to him, "I will make it all right." They could not see me. I then went into the shop, and told Moriarty they had got my pot. They said they had not got it. I told Worms I would search the place - and he said I should not do it. Morris Worms was then behind his father, and he took up the pot and ran to another shop, where they melt the mettle. I attempted to run after him, and the father stopped me, and said I should not go. I pushed him aside, and followed the boy, and saw him throw the pot under the grate - I

took it up, it had my name and sign on it. I took Henry Worms out of the shop, and gave charge of him and Morris. I then went to search for Moriarty, who had left the shop, and found him sitting in my tap-room. I went for a constable, and gave him in charge. I have not found the other quart pot, or the pint. I then took Mr. Mayo to the house where Worms was in charge, and we went down to his shop - we found a very large fire, three melting pans, and some pewter, which had been very lately melted, in the pans.

Cross-examined by MR. ANDREWS.

Question: How many pots were missing?

Answer: Three, in less than two hours. I did not see any of them taken - I did not look in at Worms's window. I looked down a passage leading to his house. I could not see what was passing in the shop, but I saw Moriarty inside - the door was open - there was a light in the shop; I could not see who Moriarty was with, but when I went in I saw old Worms, he had his hat on, but he had not just come in, or I should have seen him - he told me he had just come in, and knew nothing about the matter. It is a private house, the shop lies back - there is a board up, with "Dealer in Marine Stores" on it; there is a back-room, which I call the other shop, where they do their business. Worms did not buy his beer of me, nor did any person in his house. The pot was found in the first room. Henry Worms stood before me, and Morris behind him - I saw Morris take it into the back-room, and put it under the grate - I heard him take it up from the counter. I took Morris because he had the pot in his hand, and the father, because I saw him shake hands with Moriarty. The pot was very good, I gave 1s. 6d. for it: when I exchange my old pots for new, I am allowed a half in exchange - in the state it was then in it was worth more than 1s.

JOHN GODWIN: I am a currier, and was in Mr. Winder's house on the 23d of December. I saw Moriarty there about half-past six o'clock - the gas was alight - he called for a pint of beer - I cannot say whether he drank it or not. I saw him take a quart pot off the table and put it under his blue jacket; he then left the room: I told the pot-boy of it, and Mr. Winder went after him. In four or five minutes Moriarty returned again; he had left the room before - when he returned he was taken. I am certain of his person.

MATHIAS WELDEN: I am a constable of St. Andrew, Holborn. On the 23d of December, soon after six o'clock, Mr. Winder sent for me. I went into Fox-court, and saw a number of persons at Worms's door. Mr. Winder was there, and gave charge of Worms and his son, for receiving a pot, which he delivered into my hands. He said he had lost three within two hours, and if I went into Worms's premises he was convinced I should find the others. I went into the shop, down the open passage, and at the further end of the shop there was a strong fire, and three melting pans by the side of the fire; one, if not two of them, had pewter in them; which appeared to me to be recently melted, and felt very warm. I took the prisoners into an adjoining house till they were taken before a Magistrate. It is a marine store shop - no one can avoid seeing the name of Winder upon the pot, and the sign of the house. Here is the pot in the state in which I received it.

Cross-examined.

Question: Are you the person who Mr. Winder desired to break some metal which you found there, and which was not pewter:?

Answer: Unquestionably - it is what is called type metal, but I have no hesitation in swearing that the metal in the pans was pewter - it is my firm belief. I heard old Worms say that he knew nothing of the matter - he had but just come in, and if any one was to blame it was not him.

Prisoner WORMS, SEN.

Question: Did not a woman in the house tell you I had but just come in?

Answer: I have no recollection of that. I heard you tell the boy to say nothing but the truth, and that repeatedly.

THOMAS THOMPSON: I am a Bow-street patrol. I was desired to take charge of Moriarty - I asked him where the pot was - he said he had sold it to a Jew, for 4d., pointing towards Fox-court; I do not know any other Jew, but the prisoners, keeping a shop there. I found 2 1/2d. on his person.

(Property produced and sworn to.)

HENRY WORMS'S Defence: I was at the White Hart tavern, in Tower-street, at four o'clock - I had a ticket to go to the play that night, in Wych-street, Strand. I have some persons here with whom I had been in company till half-past five o'clock; I went home, and found Moriarty drunk, in the shop, and making a great noise - I said, "Go away, I want to go out, and if there is anything wrong come in the morning, and I will set it right" - he said he would not go; I said, "I will shake hands with you." The boy has always been cautioned by me not to buy goods when I am out.

MORRIS WORMS'S Defence: I was in doors, sitting by the five - a man came in, and threw the pot under the fire; I said I would not buy it, and he swore, and said, "I will leave it" - I said, "You must not leave it:" he swore again and said he would hit me on my head; he was going out of the shop and met my father, who had just that moment come in.

LEWIS WORMS: I am the prisoner's son. I went to my father's house, on the day in question, about ten minutes before six o'clock; my father was not at home. I went to Baldwin's-gardens, and was detained there about five minutes - when I got home to my house, in Cloth-fair, my sister told me what had happened - there was some type-metal in my father's house, but it was not pewter - there was no melted pewter, and when I was there, there was a fire; it is the room in which my father eats, drinks and sleeps. I had called to borrow some money - there were two melting pans, and one ladle there - I did not examine the metal, but I sat so close, I could see that it was not pewter - I believe there was an ingot there - Winder was not there. I had a watch in my pocket, and I looked at it a few minutes afterwards, because I was under the necessity of parting with it, in Baldwin's-gardens; it was then about six o'clock - it is a good watch, and keeps time very correctly - I did not see the constable at my father's house, I cannot swear that there was no pewter there when he was there.

WILLIAM HENRY RAWLINGS: I know Mr. Worms, Sen. I was in his company, on Thursday the 23d of December, from about half-past four o'clock, to a quarter past five, or thereabouts. I parted with him, at the White Hart, in Tower-street - it would take a man pretty near half an hour to get from Tower-street, to where he lives - a Mr. Rochester pulled out his watch, and said it was half-past five - Worms had then part of a glass of gin and water, standing before him, and Rochester would not let him go, till he had drank it.

JOSEPH STOREY: I was at the public-house, in Tower-street, and saw Worms there, drinking some gin and water - I heard nothing said about time; but I left the house at five o'clock.

Three witnesses deposed to the good character of Worms, and three to that Moriarty.

HENRY WORMS - GUILTY. Aged 57.

Transported for Fourteen Years.

MORRIS WORMS - GUILTY. Aged 14.

Judgment Respited.

JOHN MORIARTY - GUILTY. Aged 38.

Confined Three Months.

A day at Day and Martins, from *The Penny Magazine*, December 1842[113]

GAY, the author of the well-known Fables, published, somewhat above a century ago, a lively work under the title of 'Trivia, or the Art of Walking the Streets of London;' in which he thus addresses the *"shoe blacks,"* an important fraternity at that time:-

"Go, thrive: at some frequented corner stand;
This brush I give thee, grasp it in thy hand;
Temper the foot within this vase of oil,
And let the little tripod aid thy toil;
On this methinks I see the walking crew,
At thy request, support the miry shoe;
The foot grows black that was with dirt embrown'd,
And in thy pocket jingling halfpence sound.
The Goddess* plunges swift beneath the flood,
And dashes all around her showers of mud:
The youth straight chose his post; the labour ply'd
Where branching streets from Charing Cross divide
His treble voice resounds along the Mews,
And Whitehall echoes – 'Clean your Honour's Shoes.'"
* Gay gives to the shoe-black a mythological descent from the Goddess of Mud.

One of the early numbers of Mr. Knight's 'London,' wherein the above lines are cited, thus records a modern revolution in the black-ball world:- "In one of the many courts on the north side of Fleet Street, might be seen, somewhere about the year 1820, the *last of the shoe-blacks*. One would think that he deemed himself dedicated to his profession by Nature, for he was a negro. At the earliest dawn he crept forth from his neighbouring lodging, and planted his tripod on the quiet pavement, where he patiently stood till noon was past. He was a short, large-headed

---

113 The Penny Magazine of the Society for the Diffusion of Useful Knowledge. New Series, Charles Knight & Co., 1842.

son of Africa, subject, as it would appear, to considerable variations of spirits, alternating between depression and excitement, as the gains of the day presented to him the chance of having a few pence to recreate himself, beyond what he should carry home to his wife and children. For he had a wife and children, this last representative of a falling trade; and two or three little woolly-headed *decrotteurs* nestled around him when he was idle, or assisted in taking off the roughest of the dirt when he had more than one client. He watched, ·with a melancholy eye, the gradual improvement of the streets; for during some twenty or thirty years he had beheld all the world combining to ruin him. He saw the foot-pavements widening; the large flag-stones carefully laid down; the loose and broken piece, which discharged a slushy shower on the unwary foot, instantly removed: he saw the kennels diligently cleansed, and the drains widened: he saw experiment upon experiment made in the repair of the carriage-way, and the holes, which were to him as the 'old familiar faces' which he loved, filled up with a haste that appeared quite unnecessary, if not insulting."

We may picture to ourselves an old gentleman of the last century, with his foot upon a stool, reaping the lustrous fruits of the shoe-black's labours; and we may fancy we hear him cry – "Clean your Honour's Shoes!" But (to quote from the same work) "The cry is no more heard. The pavements of Whitehall are more evenly laid than the ancient marble courts of York Place, where Wolsey held his state, and Henry revelled; and they are far cleaner, even in the most inauspicious weather, than the old floor beneath the rushes. Broad as the footways are, as the broadest of the entire original streets, the mightiest of paving-stones is not large enough for the comforts of the walker; and a pavement without a joint is sought for in the new concrete of asphaltum. Where the streets which run off from the great thoroughfares are narrow, the *trottoir* is widened at the expense of the carriage-road; and one cart only can pass at a time, so that we walk fearless of wheels. If we would cross a road, there is a public servant, ever assiduous, because the measure of his usefulness is that of his reward, who removes every particle of dirt from before our steps. No filth encumbers the kennels; no spout discharges the shower in a torrent from the house-top. We pass quietly onwards from the Horse Guards to the India House without being jostled off the curb-stone, though we have no protecting posts to sustain us; and we perceive why the last of the shoe-blacks vanished from our view about the time when we first noticed his active brothers at every corner of Paris – a city then somewhat more filthy than the London of the days of Anne." (*London*, chap. ii., 'Clean your Honour's Shoes,' p.18.)

But if this be so – if the streets be so 'incomparably cleaner now than they were a century ago (and no one can doubt it), what must become of the blacking-makers? The shoe-blacks of old became street-sweepers by degrees, from utter want of custom; and it might be feared that the vendors of the "incomparable jet" – the "easy-shining" composition which produces "the most brilliant lustre ever beheld," and will "keep good in any climate" – would likewise be driven to seek another source of employment. By no means. The blacking-makers are more important personages now than ever they were; they surprise us with magnificent buildings – more like mansions than factories – and with horses and waggons, travellers and agents, and all the commercial machinery incident to a large branch of manufacture. What sort of blacking the Londoners used a century ago, or who were the persons by whom it was made, we do not know; but if the streets are less miry than they were then, and yet blacking be more generally used by all classes, we arrive at a sort of logical deduction, that we are a more cleanly people than our ancestors – that the boots and shoes of 1842 are more resplendent than those of 1742. A city clerk or a London tradesman, instead of applying to the shoe-black at the corner of a court, and staying there until "the foot grows black that was with dirt embrown'd," now has the mirror-like polish imparted to his boots before he leaves his home: he does not leave his door in search of an agent of cleanliness, for every house has now such an agent within.

We are not about to instruct the reader how to make a bottle of blacking; but we hope to convey a slight idea of the large and remarkable extent of the arrangements involved in the manufacture, as carried on by a celebrated London firm. If anyone were to picture to himself a dark and dirty room, containing a few tubs and coppers, and half a dozen men mixing up and bottling a black liquid – their faces and garments vying with the tubs and floor in blackness (and such a picture is not unlikely to be formed), he would be somewhat surprised at witnessing, as we have recently done, the scene presented at "Day and Martin's" factory in Holborn. Whether we regard this establishment in respect to its elegant exterior, the large and lofty packing-warehouse which forms its main apartment, the ranks and files and tiers of bottles in the 'filling rooms,' or the general economy which pervades the manufacture of a commodity apparently so humble as backing, there is much to admire, and, perhaps we might say, much more from which instruction might be reaped; for the division of labour, and the apportionment of duty, so that every man may be ready to do the work at the moment when the work is ready for him, and have just as much to do as will occupy his whole working-day, are features of factory-economy in which much ingenuity and calculation are called for.

All the world has heard of "Day and Martin". The two names are so associated that we can hardly conceive a Day without a Martin, or a

Martin without a Day; and that either Day or Martin should ever die, or be succeeded by others, seems a kind of commercial impossibility – a thing not to be thought of. "Day and Martin" it has been for forty years, and "Day and Martin" it will probably be for forty years to come, or perhaps till blacking itself shall be no more. To "Day and Martin's," then, the reader's attention is directed.

Those who knew High Holborn a dozen years ago may perhaps remember the former premises occupied by this firm: unimportant and inelegant, they called for no admiration without, and probably possessed little symmetry of arrangement within. Since then, however, the whole of the premises have been built on a scale of great magnificence. On the north side of Holborn, between Red Lion Street and Kingsgate Street, a frontage of about ninety feet shows the façade of the new building. As all the manufacture is carried on in the rear of the premises, the front buildings are leased off to other parties, with the exception of the central portion, which pertains to the factory. From the arched entrance, the premises extend to a distance of upwards of two hundred feet northward, to a street running parallel with Holborn; and the working parts of the factory are nearly a hundred feet in width. The site on which the factory stands affords an instructive example of the value imparted by manufacturing premises to the land on which they are situated. This site, and a considerable portion of ground near it, was purchased many years ago, by the parish authorities of St. Clement Danes, for a sum of one hundred pounds, which was put into the poor-box by some benevolent person. The rack-rent of this same portion of ground now amounts to four thousand pounds per annum, and will probably go on increasing in value!

On entering from Holborn, we come first to a range of offices and counting-houses, lying on the right hand side of the main archway or entrance. The polished mahogany desks and cases of these offices are the scene of book-keeping operations of the customary kind, and do not call for notice here. At the north end, the wide entrance passage terminates in a large arched window, between twenty and thirty feet in height, a door in the lower part of which leads to the 'warehouse,' the central portion of the whole establishment. This warehouse has a striking effect, both from its wide and lofty dimensions, and from the busy operations of which it is the theatre. Its area is perhaps not much less than a hundred feet square; and its general arrangement will be better understood if we divide it into three portions, a centre and two sides, running parallel from north to south. The central portion is open from the ground to the iron roof, a height of probably fifty feet. It is lighted by about a dozen sky lights in the roof, and by an ornamental kind of window, or glazed scroll-work, extending along both sides between the walls and the roof. This central area is separated from the side aisles (if we may so term them) by arches and piers of brickwork, beyond which are these side warehouses, lighted only from the central skylight and windows.

The northern end of the warehouse presents, in the lower part, an arched entrance to another warehouse or store-room beyond, and at the upper part, doors and windows belonging to the 'tun-room,' or manufactory in which the blacking is made. Two light and elegant iron staircases lead from the floor of the warehouse to the level of this upper room, one on each side. The side warehouses or aisles are not above half the height of the central portion; for they have over them two very long rooms or galleries called 'filling-rooms.' Four openings furnish communication between these filling-rooms and the warehouse, two on each side; that is, one opening to each, in communication with the iron staircase, and one by which crates are hauled up to, or lowered from, the filling-room. If the side of each filling-room were thrown open, the whole would bear some resemblance to the form of a church; there would be a nave, or middle aisle, two side aisles, and two galleries over the latter.

This warehouse, from morning till night, is a continued scene of bustle and activity. It is the part of the premises in which the finished commodity is packed for London shopkeepers, for country trade, or for foreign shipment. Packers and porters and coopers occupy the greater part of the central area. The coopers are making or altering and adjusting the casks in which the bottles are generally packed; for many of the casks are made here from the rough staves, and all are fitted to the wants of the packers. The packers are in all sorts of attitudes, according to the state of the cask which is being filled: some are bending over the cask, to put in the lower layer of bottles; some, by having nearly filled a cask, are enabled to stand either more erect at their work; one man has got his foot in a cask, pressing down the straw; another, with a stick in his hand, is thrusting straw between the bottles; some are closing in the casks; and the porters are arranging the filled casks ready for removal from the factory. At night, both the filling-rooms and the warehouse are lighted with gas, by branches ranged along the centre.

The side warehouses, or those portions which are separated from the centre by the arches and piers, are crammed with enormous piles of stores, pertaining to some branch or other of the manufacture. Casks ranged by scores and by hundreds; staves and hoops for the use of the coopers; crates of empty stone bottles; huge bags of corks or bungs, containing a hundred gross or more in each bag; boxes for packing 'paste-blacking,' -these are some of the multitudinous stores here deposited. An underground furnace and boiler, under each of the galleries, furnish hot water for heating the whole premises; and subterraneous communication is kept open from one side of the building to the other. Under the right hand gallery is deposited a kind of fire-escape, consisting of a series of ladders capable of sliding, telescope-like, to a height of a hundred feet; by which any part of the walls or roof may be reached from below, either for cleaning or repairing, or any more urgent purpose. Near the south-eastern corner of the warehouse are several rooms devoted to the labels, papers, and wrappers, to which we shall allude further by and by; and over some of these rooms is a very large reservoir, from which an abundant supply of water can be obtained in case of emergency.

Before ascending the two dozen steps which lead up to the galleries, we will follow out the lower range to its northern termination. An archway leads from the large warehouse to a smaller store-room filled with stores like the other. The western exhibits rows and piles of casks heaped up to the ceiling; while crates are here and there deposited, containing bottles afterwards to be filled, each crate holding about a hundred dozens. At the eastern side of this store-room is a kind of washing-house, where old and used bottles are cleansed before being employed again. Everyone who is learned in the matter of domestic perquisites knows that old blacking-bottles, like old things of many other kinds, can find a market: the manufacturer would probably be quite as well pleased to use new bottles altogether, and save himself the trouble of washing old ones; but whenever this washing is necessary, it is effected in the washing-house. - Coppers, and tubs, and brushes, sloppiness below, and steam above, all indicate the somewhat dirty occupation of bottle-washing; while near at hand are the crates into which the cleansed bottles are put.

In this part of the factory is also a furnace and the necessary apparatus for preparing the red-wax with which the corks of blacking-bottles are sealed. Those who know anything of the nature of sealing wax, whether the finer kinds for sealing letters, or the courser kinds for sealing bottles, need hardly be told that 'wax' is altogether a misnomer, for there is no wax in it. It is a compound of several resinous substances, coloured by some one among the numerous mineral colours. In the finer qualities, gum-lac is the principal resin, spirit of wine the principal solvent, and vermilion the chief colouring substance. Among manufacturers, however, common resin and spirits of turpentine and Venetian red, or some analogous materials, are sufficiently good for the materials of 'bottle-wax.' In this part of the factory bags and boxes and tubs of the ingredients are disposed conveniently for the manufacture, and a particular kind of furnace is provided for melting them. This furnace is deeply imbedded in brickwork, and situated in a recess quite secluded from any other part: it has also a very heavy iron shutter which can be drawn down in front of it in an instant, and thus render the occurrence of an accident from fire scarcely possible. The melted ingredients, when thoroughly mixed, are poured into vessels to cool, thence to be removed and re-melted in a way of which we shall speak hereafter.

Proceeding still farther northward, we come to a pair of folding-gates, which open into the last portion of this range. We here find the cart and

Packing warehouse

waggon house, where the carts and waggons are kept which convey the manufactured article to the London dealers, the coach, waggon, canal, and railway offices, and the docks and shipping wharfs. On each side are stables for the horses, over which are corn and hay lofts. This brings us to the extremity of the range, to which an entrance is obtained by folding-gates from a small street beyond.

Let us now return to the great warehouse, and ascend one of the iron staircases to the upper range of buildings. Having surmounted this stair and reached a platform which crosses the northern end of the warehouse at a height of above twenty feet from the ground, we obtain a bird's-eye view of the operations below; and a busy scene it is. The coopers and packers are distributed about the whole area below; crates of empty bottles are being hauled up, and other crates of filled bottles are being lowered. Opposite, at the southern end, a large clock meets the eye; and through the large arched window we catch a glimpse of bustling Holborn.

Filling   **Sealing**

Labelling   **Packing**

Passing from this platform or passage into one of the galleries, or 'filling-rooms,' we find doors leading into the northern range of upper rooms, comprising those in which the manufacture is principally conducted. One of these, used as a store-room, opens upon the street behind, from which tubs, and butts, and casks of ingredients are hauled up and stowed round the room. The vinegar comes in casks of sixty gallons each, the oil in larger casks, the 'ivory-black' or other kinds of black in casks containing nearly a ton each, and the remaining ingredients in packages and casks of various kinds, according to their quality.

From the store-room the ingredients are brought into the 'tun-room,' or manufactory, the least attractive but the most important place in the establishment. It is singularly occupied. Nearly a hundred tubs, each capable of containing about a hundred gallons, are ranged from end to end of the room in regular rows. Each tub is supported on a separate stand, or trestle, half a yard in height; and each one is capable of being moved by a couple of men at a certain stage in the manufacture. The tubs are all more or less filled with blacking, according to the hour of the day when they are seen. A few of them are filled with blacking of a stiffer or thicker consistence. The room also contains other vessels and apparatus connected with the manufacture.

On either side of this room are smaller rooms, in which subsidiary portions of the manufacture are carried on. In one are the vessels and arrangements for filling pots and tin cases with paste-blacking; and round this room are stored in immense number cylindrical packets, each containing a dozen tin-boxes, intended for the use of the army. A soldier is not provided with any too much room for his implements and appurtenances, and a bottle of liquid-blacking would be rather a burden to him. Yet, as the soldier's boots or shoes must to some extent emulate the brightness and glitter of the boots of those who pay for battles instead of fighting them, a portable blacking apparatus is provided. The blacking, instead of being liquid, is made into stiff paste, and in that state is put into circular tin-boxes, about three inches in diameter, and half or three-quarters of an inch thick. What becomes of the tin-boxes when emptied – whether they are applied to any useful purpose, or whether, like the millions of pins made every year, they go no one knows whither – we cannot say.

From this room we proceed to the western gallery, or 'filling-room,' a room in which bottles certainly have the ascendant; for what with hauling up and opening crates, and disposing bottles on benches, and filling, and corking, and sealing, and labelling, and storing on shelves, it is certainly the busiest 'bottle department' we have seen. The arrangement of this room is well adapted to facilitate the rapid progress of the manufacture. It is about ninety feet in length, and perhaps one-third as broad. Along the middle extends a double row of shelves or stands, three or four in height, each shelf being calculated to hold bottles. Along the eastern and western walls are similar tiers of shelves or stands adapted for similar purposes. In the two avenues which separate these series of shelves are broad benches, fitted for holding the bottles during the processes of filling, corking, sealing, pasting, &c. At about the middle of its length is a door or opening in the east side, which places the filling-room in communication with the warehouse below. A crane is fixed immediately outside this opening, by which crates of empty bottles are drawn up from the warehouse, and baskets of filled bottles lowered from the filling-room. The tiers of shelves in the room are fixtures; but the benches are provided with castors or wheels, by which they may be moved from place to place, according as convenience may require. The room is lighted by ten or a dozen sky lights in the daytime, and by gas at night, or rather in the evening. According to the time of the day when the filling-room is visited, will be the nature of the operations witnessed; but at all hours, from an early time in the morning till eight in the evening, men and boys are actively engaged in the operations which intervene between the making and the packing of the ingredient.

The western filling-room communicates with two of the manufacturing rooms and also with the iron platform stretching across the northern end of the warehouse. We will therefore pass along this platform and visit the eastern filling-room, which resembles the other in its main features. There are ranges of shelves for bottles, disposed one above another, and in parallel ranges; but the eastern half of the room is somewhat differently occupied. Here the shelves, instead of being occupied by bottles, contain trays filled with blacking of a different kind, placed there to cool and solidify. The benches, too, and the operations of the workmen, are adapted to the preparation of paste-blacking rather than that of a liquid kind. All the shelves in the two filling-houses are capable of containing six or seven thousand dozens of bottles; and as these bottles seldom remain many days on the shelves before they are packed, an incessant interchange is going on – from the manufactory to the filling-room, from thence to the warehouse, and from thence to the purchaser. The odour of the filling-rooms, as well as of those more immediately pertaining to the manufacture gives to the visitor unmistakable evidence that vinegar is one, and a principle one, of the ingredients employed.

We have now made a tour of the rooms of this remarkable establishment, and may next endeavour to give a slight outline of the modes of proceeding in the course of the manufacture. There is, to be sure, nothing very elaborate, no complicated machinery, no array of engines and machines for making the commodity produced; but still there are some manipulations which strike a stranger as being not a little curious, illustrating as they do the dexterity which is acquired by long practice in some one particular department of labour. This dexterity of hand (which, by the way, is exactly expressed by the French word "legerdemain," although we usually attach a conjuring meaning to this term) is most frequently exhibited in branches of manufacture where machinery has not been extensively introduced, and is often more interesting to a looker-on than the complicated action of an elaborate machine.

There are many ingredients employed in the making of blacking, each manufacturer having a recipe of his own. If therefore, the reader should look out for an exposition of the whole affair, the names and proportions of the ingredients, the temperature of mixture, and so on, we shall not be able to furnish these details; for – to use an expression which Scott puts into the mouth of one of his characters, in relation to a very different subject – "we cannot, if we would; and we ought not, if we could." Let it suffice for our present object to know that ivory-black or some similar substance constitutes the principal colouring-material, and that vinegar and oil are the two principal liquids.

At five o'clock in the morning, winter and summer, the manufacture of each day's quantum of blacking commences. The work is not extended from day to day, one portion of the manufacturing processes being effected on one day and the remainder on another; but each day's labours are complete in themselves, so that a 'day' at a blacking-factory is a tolerably uniform day. The 'tun-room' or that part of this establishment which is called the 'manufactory,' is the scene of operations in the first instance. The mixing-vessels are ranged in rank and file over the greater portion of the room. A stirring or mixing apparatus is ingeniously contrived so as to be applicable to all the vessels, one after another, and is worked through the medium of a shaft descending to a room below, where the moving power is applied. The oil, the black, the vinegar, and the other ingredients are brought from the adjacent store-room, and are mixed and worked up in the requisite proportions; the temperature, the stirring, and the general order of processes being of course dependent on the system of manufacture which the firm pursues.

While the manufacture of the commodity is being thus carried on in the northern part of the premises, the other workmen, in the 'filling-rooms' and warehouse, are preparing for the bottling arrangements. The bottles employed, as most persons are probably aware, are made of brown glazed earthenware: they have very wide mouths, and are made of three different sizes, calculated to hold a pint, two-thirds of a pint, and one-third of a pint each. They are principally made at the Derbyshire potteries, and are brought to London packed with straw in large crates, each crate containing on an average about a hundred dozen bottles, and weighing half a ton. The crates are first deposited on the floor of the warehouse, and are thence hoisted up to the filling-rooms by means of the large cranes seen In our frontispiece. When a crate is deposited In the filling-room, it is at once opened, and the bottles passed on with great quickness from hand to hand, and laid in regular rows on the broad benches near the centre of the room.

When the bottles are all thus arranged, and the blacking is in a prepared state, the latter is brought out of the tun-room or manufactory by several men, each tub or vessel being brought on the stand or frame by which it is supported. These vessels, to a considerable number, are then placed at equal distances near the bench which contains the empty bottles; and the process of filling then begins. Each vessel is attended by a man and a boy, the latter of whom continually stirs the blacking till the whole of it is bottled. The man stands by the side of the vessel with his left hand next to the bench of empty bottles; and in his right hand he holds a measure, or small can. Taking up a bottle in his left hand, he fills it with blacking by means of his measure; the size of the measure, and the quantity of blacking which he collects in it at each dipping into the vessel, being so adjusted to the size of the bottles as to expedite the process as much as possible. The laying-down of the filled bottle and the taking up of an empty one are but the work of a moment; every little circumstance being pre-arranged which could in any way facilitate it.

It might at first thought be supposed that this process would be effected more quickly if the liquid were drawn out of a large vessel at once into the bottles by means of a cock or valve. But there are doubtless good reasons for adopting the opposite course. It may be that a sediment would fall to the bottom of the vessel, or that the liquid would flow from the cock too rapidly to enable the filling of each bottle to be adjusted to the required point; for the quantity poured into each bottle is very exact. But be this as it may, the filling is effected by hand; several open vessels being ranged along the filling-room, and each one being attended by a man and a boy, whom we may perhaps term a 'filler' and a 'stirrer'.

The corking of the bottles is the next process. We have said that, in the warehouse beneath, the corks are stored in bags or sacks containing a hundred gross (fourteen or fifteen thousand) each. These bags are opened, and the corks are sorted into different parcels, according to the sizes of the bottles for which they may be adapted. They are then conveyed to the 'filling-rooms,' and the process of corking commences. A man, provided with an ample supply of corks, proceeds along the range of benches on which the filled bottles are placed, putting a cork into the mouth of each bottle, but without staying to fix or drive it in.

Another man, provided with a wooden mallet, immediately follows him,and forces the corks so far into the bottles, that the upper surface of each shall be level with the top of the bottle, a succession of smart blows being given to one cork after another. All this progresses with very great quickness, the bottle being ranged with such regularity as to afford every facility for the operation. Of the thousands of bottles which are filled every day, all are corked in this way, by a sufficient number of men, each pair taking one bench or range of benches.

The bottles are filled, and the corks are adjusted in their places; but sufficient has not yet been done to secure the blacking in its 'prison-house'. When a cork is so large as those here employed, the escape of the liquid contained in the bottle can scarcely be avoided unless some cement covers the whole surface of the cork and mouth of the bottle. A course kind of sealing wax, as we have before observed, is used for this purpose, and is of course applied in a melted state. In some of the upper rooms of the factory are several portable stoves for melting the wax. These consist of tripods, supporting a brazier or pan for containing ignited charcoal; and immediately above the brazier is a kind of bowl or ladle for containing the sealing wax. This substance, after being prepared, as was before alluded to, in the lower part of the factory, is taken up in lumps, an melted in these bowls or ladles. When melted, it has a cream like consistence, and presents the well known red colour. This apparatus being ready, and placed close beside the ranges of filled bottles, a workman proceeds to seal the corks. He has no brush, no ladle, no contrivance for pouring the wax on the cork, but, holding the bottle upside down, he just immerses the corked surface in the liquid wax. practice has enabled the men to effect the dipping so exactly, that the wax rarely comes over the sides of the bottle. The apparently simple matter of reversing the bottle again, without scattering the wax, or causing it to flow over the sides of the bottle, is effected by a peculiar movement of the wrist and hand, impossible to describe and difficult to imitate. Many of our manufactures present analogous instances, in which a process is effected quite as much by the muscular movement of the hand as a whole, as by the delicate agency of the fingers. For instance, 'imitation' or 'mock pearls' are made by blowing glass beads so that each bead shall be hollow and shall have two holes in the exterior; then a liquid, made of a pearl-like powder obtained from the scales of fish, is dexterously blown into the hollow of the bead through a tube; and by a peculiar twisting of the hand, this single drop of liquid is made to diffuse itself over the internal surface of the bead, without having more or less than just enough to cover the whole. Again, in type-founding, when the melted type-metal has been forced into the mould, the caster throws up his left hand with a peculiar motion, giving it a kind of jerk at the same time with his right, by which the liquid metal is forced or shaken into all the minute interstices of the mould. Instances of this kind might be adduced in great number; and among them is this one of sealing the filled bottles. The celerity, too, with which this is effected is not less note-worthy than the neatness; for a man can seal one hundred dozens of bottles in an hour, or twenty in a minute.

The sealing, as well as the filling and corking, is effected in the two 'filling-room'; and so is likewise the next process, which is perhaps the most remarkable to a stranger of all which the factory presents, from the astonishing rapidity with which it is effected, – we allude to the pasting of the labels on the bottles. But before speaking of this process, it will be desirable to pay a little attention to the labels themselves, the complexity of which has doubtless puzzled many persons.

Those who have not watched the proceedings of the last few years in respect of colour-printing, can perhaps scarcely conceive how the printing of these blacking labels can be effected. If we examine one of "Day and Martin's" labels, we see that nearly the whole of the ground consists of a kind of lace-work,red on white paper, the meshes or interstices being probably about one-twentieth of an inch in diameter. This ground-work, occupying about sixteen square inches, is diversified by several compartments printed in black ink; one, for instance, containing a view of the front façade of the factory; another, the name of the firm; a third, the retail price of the commodity contained in the bottle; a fourth; the number of the house, curiously bedecked with a double enunciation of the name of the firm; and two others containing remarks and directions to the purchaser. All these are printed with black ink on the white paper, no red lace-work being here seen. Above these are letters printed in black and white on a wavy or undulating ground of black, red, and white; while at the top are black letters, and at the bottom letters in white, red, and black, printed on, or at least interspersed among, the lace-work ground itself. All this relates to the labels for the liquid blacking contained in bottles; and the circular labels for paste blacking are on the same principle, though different in detail.

Now it may naturally be asked by those to whom the subject is new, how these various devices, and these differently coloured inks, can be imprinted on one piece of paper without confusion or distortion. Without going into any description of the various modes by which printing in diverse colours is now effected, we will attempt a brief sketch of the contrivance by which these labels are produced. One of the rooms in the factory is a printing-room, in which is contained a beautiful machine, invented by Mr. E. Cowper, of King's College, who was the original patentee of the machine by which this Magazine is printed. It is a cylinder printing-machine, specially adapted for printing many-coloured devices, such as those on these labels. There is one cylinder for printing all the red portion, and another for printing the black. Eight labels are printed at once, but it will simplify the description if we speak only of one. In the first place a stereotype plate is arranged for receiving the device of the black portion of the label; and another, exactly the same size, for the red portion. These plates, for the liquid blacking, measure rather less than five inches by four; and on the surface is depicted, in relief, all the letters and ornaments, which are afterwards inked and printed; the plates being prepared, we believe, by a combined process of casting, stamping, and modelling. The plates are so exactly adjusted, that every raised part in one of them shall coincide with a depressed part in the other, and vice versa. This is in fact precisely the same principle as that on which the several blocks for printing floor-cloths are adjusted, as described in one of our recent Supplements. The nature of the adjustment might be instructively shown by printing a label by hand with the two plates; although, of course, this would never do in practice. We might take one of the plates, carefully ink its surface either by an inking-ball or an inking roller, and then impress it on a piece of damp paper. Then (supposing the first inking to have been black) if we ink the second plate with red, and print the paper a second time, the clearness or confusion of the resulting device would correctly measure the degree of accuracy with which the one impression was superposed on the other. It would be seen how very small a deviation from exactness in the adjustment of the second plate would be sufficient to give a distorted appearance to the label.

If the printing-machine were adapted for flat printing, these prepared plates might be adjusted to a flat bed or support. But a cylinder-machine is employed, in which both the plates lie on the surface of cylinders. Here, however, a difficulty at once occurs. If flat plate be placed on a curved surface, it is easy to see that they cannot conform to the curvature of that surface; and the mode of contact between the plates and a sheet of paper to be printed would be wholly incompatible with the object in view. The means had therefore to be devised of curving the plates without disturbing the device on their surfaces; and this has been effected. Eight plates, all exactly alike, are bent in conformity with the curvature of the cylinders, and are then fixed to the surface of one of the cylinders by means of delicate adjusting mechanism. Eight other plates, all alike, but differing from the former, are similarly fitted to the surface of the other cylinder. These two cylinders are so adjusted in the machine as to rotate in contact, or nearly in contact, with a third, round which a sheet of paper may be made to travel. An inking apparatus for black ink is placed near one cylinder at one end of the machine; another apparatus for red ink is fixed near the other cylinder at the other end; and when the machine is at work, if a sheet of damp paper be placed at one end, it is drawn into the machine, carried over and under various rollers, and made to pass under the two cylinders. Meanwhile, by various rollers and other connecting mechanism, the eight plates on the one cylinder become coated or charged on the projecting parts with black ink, and those on the other with red; and matters are so adjusted, that exactly when the paper comes near the black-inked cylinder, the plates are ready to print; and immediately after the paper has received its black impress, it is caught by the other cylinder and printed with the red portion of the device. As may be readily supposed, the most scrupulous exactness of adjustment is necessary, in order to ensure the juxtaposition of the red and black portion of the device at the proper places. By means of adjusting-screws, the printing-plates can be shifted to so minute a distance as the two-hundredth of an inch, in order to bring the 'register,' or superposition of device, at the proper points. One grain of ink only is used to print eight labels. The circular labels for the paste-blacking tin boxes, as well as the square ones for the bottles, are printed at this press. The demand is so large and so constant, that the machine is nearly always at work; and when the sheets of labels are printed, boys are employed to cut the separate labels from them.

These are the labels, then, which we are now to see pasted on the bottles. One man or boy can paste as many labels as two others can attach to the bottles, so that they work together in groups of three. On the bench is placed on the one side a large tub of paste, and on the other a ranged series of filled and sealed bottles. A heap of labels is laid down face downwards, and the paster pastes them one by one with a brush. The dexterity in this simple act is not in the pasting, but in a peculiar final touch with the brush, by which the pasted label is jerked off the heap, and caught in the left hand. So rapidly is this effected, that one man will paste a label, jerk it off the heap, catch it in his left hand, and lay it on one side, nearly two thousand times in an hour; for one man can thus paste a hundred and sixty dozen labels in this time. As fast as the labels are pasted, the other two workmen attach them to the bottles. Each one takes a bottle in his left hand, and a pasted label in his right, and attaches the one to the other by two or three touches which the eye can scarcely follow. To a spectator it seems that almost before the bottle is taken fairly into the hand, it is laid down again, properly labelled. Let any uninitiated person endeavour thus to secure sixteen labels per minute to as many bottles, and see what progress he will make.

The labelling of the bottles is the last process which is effected in the filling-room. All the bottles, after having been labelled, are ranged on the systems of shelves in the filling-rooms, and there kept till the paste is properly hardened. They are then put into a basket, and lowered from the filling-room to the warehouse by the aid of one of the cranes. Here they pass into the hands of the packers and coopers. The general mode of sending out the bottles from the factory is in casks, containing from three to a hundred dozens. The casks are prepared by the coopers to the proper dimensions, and the packers proceed with their work. This like many other apparently simple operations require tact and judgement. The packer first ranges a circle of bottles around the inner surface of the cask, then encircles a wisp of straw within this ring of bottles, and then arranges a smaller ring. In this way he proceeds till one tier is filled; and by the aid of a stick or wedge he inserts straw and extra bottles wherever there is room for one or another, until at length the whole are jammed immoveably together. A second tier of bottles is then built up, separated from a lower one by a layer of straw; and this is in a similar manner hardened and compressed till nothing can shake about or become displaced. So on to the top of the cask, which is finally topped with straw, and the head fastened in, ready for marking and carting.

Such is the career of a bottle of blacking, before it leaves the hands of the manufacturer. But there are one or two other forms of blacking which we may briefly notice, in illustration of the arrangements of this factory.

We have before said that in one of the rooms of the factory small tin boxes are piled in great number, and that these contain, or are destined to contain, paste-blacking for the use of the army. Whether any particular ingredients are used in this composition, different from or in addition to those which compose liquid blacking, we do not know; but the consistence to which it is mixed is much stiffer. The paste-blacking, when fully prepared, is contained in a large vessel or tub, round which two or more boys place themselves, each one provided with a small scoop or ladle, shaped like a spoon, with the handle affixed to one side instead of one end. Tin boxes are close at hand, which the boys take one by one, and fill with the thick paste-like blacking. All the boxes, as they are filled, are ranged in rows in the filling-room, where they remain till the blacking has solidified, and assumed a stiff clayey consistence. Then, tin covers are put on them, and they are packed in dozens, and wrapped in paper. They reach the soldiers, we believe, through the medium of the army clothiers.

There is another kind of paste-blacking which is sold in little wide-mouthed stone pots, something like crucibles. This is nearly the same in quality as the soldiers' blacking; while the pots are of the same character, as to material, as the bottles. The paste-blacking is laded into them by the same simple apparatus as into the tin boxes; and is then allowed to stand aside to solidify; after which the mouths of the pots are well secured with paper.

Another form of blacking, different from all the others, remains yet to be noticed. This is a kind which is stiffer than liquid or bottle blacking, but thinner than the other kinds: it is in fact a soft paste. Its mode of being packed into a saleable form, after the manufacture is finished, is very different from the other instances. Shallow moulds or trays are provided about half a yard long, two-thirds as wide, and half an inch or so in depth. Into these moulds the paste-blacking is poured or laded from a large vessel; and the moulds are then put by on shelves to cool and solidify. One side of the eastern filling-room contains a very large number of these moulds, standing by till their contained blacking has become cool. When this cooling is effected, each tray or mould is laid flat on a bench, and one of the edges or ledges is removed, so as to enable a knife to be passed under the solidified blacking, as a means of loosening it from the bed of the mould. The whole sheet of blacking, if we may so term it, is then cut up into six dozen rectangular pieces, twelve in length and six in width, by a convenient kind of knife; and the cakes are then in the shape in which they are sold. But they are too soft to be left without a covering; while, on the other hand, they require neither bottles, pots, nor tin boxes. Pieces of paper, first printed with the name of the manufacturer, &c., are well saturated with oil, and when dry, are fit to be used as wrappers to the small cakes of blacking. The papers are laid flat on a bench, one cake is put into each, and by one of those neat and expeditious manipulations which so many other parts the factory exhibit, the cakes are wrapped-up, each in its oiled paper. Then, in order to sell these cakes to the dealers in a form fit to be handled, small wooden boxes are provided, each capable of holding a certain number, packed neatly one upon another.

Thus have we rapidly sketched the chief manufacturing features of the place, so far as is necessary for the present object; and have to acknowledge the courtesy of the proprietors in furnishing the facilities for so doing. Every day, we have said, witnesses a pretty, regular and uniform series of operations. The actual manufacture takes place at an early hour in the morning; while the bottling, corking, sealing, labelling, moulding, and wrapping cake-blacking, bottle-washing, &c., occupy the remaining hours of the day in the upper and hinder rooms. The packing in the warehouse is so arranged as to enable the waggons and carts to be dispatched with one cargo to the various dealers, wharfs, docks, &c., in different parts of town, at a pretty early hour in the morning; and with another cargo at a later period of the day. Taken altogether, it must be owned that a day at "Day and Martin's" is an early day, and a long day, and a busy day.

Newspaper reports from the Chancery Court

The Standard[114]

"COURT OF CHANCERY. – This day. Warren's Blacking.

Mr Sugden brought forward a motion to dissolve the injunction which had been granted some days since to an ex parte application made by this celebrated manufacturer of blacking in the Strand.

Mr Horne opposed the motion going forward at present; it was only this moment he had got his brief, and he had not had time to read the affidavits.

Mr Sugden could not consent to have this injunction hanging over his client's head, as he was prevented from the prosecution of his business, and if it continued he would be ruined.

The Lord Chancellor then said the case must proceed.

Mr Sugden commenced his motion for the dissolution of the injunction. He read the affidavits on which the injunction had been granted, which stated that Mr Lamert, against whom it had been given, had not such a person as Jonathan Warren in partnership with him, that he had frequently sold his blacking to the customers of Mr. Warren in the Strand, and that there was not to the deponent's (Warren's) knowledge and belief any such person in existence as Jonathan Warren; that the placards used by Lamert were similar to those of the deponent, who had, it was stated in the affidavit, chosen his situation at 30, Hungerford-stairs, from its vicinity to the house of the deponent. Some of the depositions were those of a servant discharged for improper conduct from the employment of the defendant. He (Mr Sugden) did not wish to defeat Mr Horne in the defenceless state he had described himself to be in, but justice required that he should go on.

Mr Horne. – Do anything you please, but do not bedaub me with your blacking. (Laughter)

Mr Sugden continued. – He would show from the affidavits made in his case, that the "real Simon Pure" was Jonathan Warren, uncle of Robert Warren, who had resided a number of years at 30, Hungerford-stairs; that his client was the successor of this Jonathan Warren, who had instructed him in the art and mystery of blacking manufacture.

---

[114] *The Standard*, Tuesday November 27th 1827

Mr Sugden then read his affidavits, which state that Jonathan Warren was the original inventor of the japan blacking; and that he removed in 1821 to Hungerford-stairs, where he carried on his business until October 1822, when he sold it to a person named Woods; the latter being allowed to use the name of Jonathan Warren, an agreement to which effect had been made between them; that at the time stated, the defendant was taken into the business by Woods, and instructed in the art by Jonathan Warren; that the plaintiff, since this injunction was obtained, had defaced from the defendant's house the No. 30, and painted No. 6, in lieu thereof. Thus, like a skilful general, he proceeds to the enemy's camp, and after an inspection of the outworks commences his attack by disfiguring the ground. There were several other affidavits, which were read at length.

[Mr Sugden] handed up the placards to the court; it was plain from its appearance that no deception was intended. The name of "G. Lamerte an Co." was on it, and the place where they resided.

The Lord Chancellor. – The name of "Jonathan" is as large as that of "Warren," and there appears no intention to pass it off for that of "George Warren." From your affidavits there can be no doubt that you have a right to make use of the name of Jonathan Warren.

Mr Sugden called the attention of the court to another part of the case of considerable importance. The object of the plaintiff was to ruin the defendant in his business; and how does he effect this? He sent advertisements to the John Bull and other papers relative to this injunction, in which the plaintiff had stated that Mr Lamerte had made use of the fictitious name of J. Warren; that all persons who had bought of defendant are authorized to send them back to him, and it contained a threat that unless they did so, they would be visited with the pains of a suit in Chancery. This was the greatest abuse of an order under the Great Seal that he had ever heard of.

Mr Horne wondered how these facts, of which he knew nothing, could be introduced into the present motion.

The Lord Chancellor. – If it can be traced to the plaintiff, it is undoubtedly very improper conduct.

Mr Sugden. – They had made application to the editor of the John Bull, for the authority on which he had inserted the advertisement, and his reply was, that it had been paid for by Robert Warren, who had requested that it might be inserted. Circular letters had also been sent throughout England, Ireland, and Wales, to the customers of his client, advising them to send back the blacking they had had from him, and holding out something like a threat if they did not. The consequences had been, that from the improper use made of this injunction, the defendant had been nigh ruined in his business.

Mr Horne supported the injunction. The conduct of the other side had been a system of ingenious, but fraudulent contrivances to palm off on the public as theirs a spurious and inferior quality of blacking. His client had conducted his business openly before the public at a place where he had an unquestionable right to do so, at No. 30, Strand. – A person had thought proper to impose on the public Lamert's blacking as that of Warren. The quality of the material made no part of the case; for if it were so good, it required no indirect mode of puffing it off. Good wine needed no bush. In the placard used by the defendant, the words "Warren's blacking" were so large that he who runs might read; while the intervening words "original liquid japan," were small and illegible from any distance. The figures "30 and Strand" were also large, while those "Hungerford stairs" were in small characters. In Hungerford stairs there were only 12 houses, and no number 30. In point of fact there was no Warren's blacking connected with any 30 except that of his client in the Strand. His only object was to deceive the public at the expense of the person selling them. The defendant in fact had no house occupied by him at 30, Hungerford-stairs, Strand, and this place, which was represented as a magazine of blacking, did not contain a single pot.

The Lord Chancellor. – If there be two persons named Jonathan and Robert Warren, blacking-manufacturers, it is too much to say that each of them have not a right to placard "Warren's Blacking"; and if Lamerte had purchased the original property of Jonathan, living at 30, Hungerford-stairs, Strand, has he not a right still, though the business be carried to another part of the town, to retain the original designation for the purpose of identity? The only point then to which you can direct your objections is the original assumption by Jonathan of the number 30. Under these circumstances it was too much to call for this injunction to be maintained."

The Morning Chronicle[115]
"COURT OF CHANCERY. Injunction. Warren v Lamert.
This was the case in which the plaintiff, the celebrated blacking maker, of No.30, in the Strand, had obtained an injunction to restrain the defendant from issuing placards, and using jars for the sale of his blacking, similar to those of the plaintiff. In the plaintiff's affidavit on which the injunction was granted, he swore that no other person of his name resided in the Strand; that no such person existed as Jonathan Warren, with whom the defendant pretended that he was in partnership; and that the defendant's placards and jars so nearly resembled the

---

[115] *The Morning Chronicle*, Wednesday 28th November 1827

plaintiff's, that the difference could only be discerned on close inspection.

This morning Mr Sugden stated, that he was instructed to move for the dissolution of the injunction.

Mr Horne, for the plaintiff, objected to hearing his Learned Friend this day, in consequence of the lateness of the notice.

The Lord Chancellor observed that this day had been appointed for the hearing of appeals.

Mr Sugden regretted that he was compelled by the urgency of the case to exercise his undoubted right of moving that the injunction be dissolved, as every moment of its existence was ruinous to his client. For the same reason, he could not accommodate his Learned Friend by consenting to postpone the motion. He then stated, that it appeared from the affidavits filed by the defendant, that a person named Jonathan Warren, the plaintiff's uncle, had, in the 1798, discovered, or claimed to have discovered, the composition called "Warren's Liquid Blacking," which he, for many years afterwards, manufactured and sold, at a house near Hungerford-stairs, in the Strand, and known there as No. 30. On the side of the house facing the river, the words "Warren's, 30, Blacking Warehouse," were painted in large black letters upon a white ground, and this inscription remained there until last week, when the plaintiff's solicitor prevailed on the occupier of the house to suffer it to be effaced. It appeared further, that Jonathan Warren carried on business on his own account alone until the year 1821, when he took a person named Wood into partnership; after which the partners used the words "Warren's Blacking" in their labels and jars, as Warren himself had done before. In that year Jonathan Warren died, and his surviving partner induced the defendant to join him in partnership, for the purpose of carrying on the business of blacking makers, and they had continued to use the same labels and placards as during the lifetime of Warren, which the Learned Counsel contended they had a perfect and unquestionable right to do. He then adverted to what he deemed very reprehensible conduct on the part of the plaintiff since he had obtained the injunction. By means of advertisements in the public papers, and by written applications to persons previously in the habit of dealing with the defendant, threatening them that he would file bills in Chancery against them, unless they relinquished the sale of the defendant's blacking; the plaintiff had succeeded in alarming them to such an extent that the defendant's business was reduced almost to nothing, and he himself brought to the verge of ruin. Under all the circumstances, the Learned Counsel submitted that he had made a good case for desisting this injunction.

Mr Wakefield followed on the same side. – Mr Horne, on the other side, contended that no court of justice could sanction the defendant's conduct, which was evidently fraudulent. By close imitations of the plaintiff's placards and jars, he had endeavoured to impose on the public an article made by himself as that of the plaintiff. He had copied the leading words of the placards and labels, so as to give them the appearance of the plaintiff's, and substituted his own name and residence in characters so small that they could hardly be perceived. As to the statement respecting Jonathan Warren's house, it was evidently unfounded. There were only twelve houses in Hungerford-stairs, and consequently there could be any No. 30. The reason for using the detached words, "Warren's Blacking," "No. 30," and "Strand," was manifestly to delude the public into the belief, when they were purchasing the defendant's blacking, that they were buying the plaintiff's. The Lord Chancellor asked whether, if a person of that name opened a shop for the sale of blacking made by himself, he had not a right to put up over his door "Warren's Blacking," without any reference to any other person of that name who might also sell blacking?

Mr Horne did not complain of the use of the words "Warren's Blacking," but of the attempt to identify the plaintiff's article with that of the defendant, by setting forth the "No. 30," and the word "Strand," so as to deceive any casual observer.

The Lord Chancellor: It appears he had a connection with No. 30, Hungerford-stairs.

Mr Horne: But not with "No. 30, Strand."

The Lord Chancellor said, it was clear that if Jonathan Warren had originally a right to use the name and description he had assumed, the defendant, deriving from Warren through Wood, had equally a right to the use of them, in order to keep up and identify the character of the article, no matter to what part of the town he might have removed his residence.

Mr Horne stated, that if time were afforded him, he would give a complete answer to every part of the defendant's allegations. A suit was now pending between Wood and the defendant, in which the former allegation denied the right of the latter to use the words "Warren's Blacking;" a further proof of the fraudulent intention of the defendant was to be found in the fact, that when the plaintiff changed the colour of his placards and labels, the defendant immediately afterwards made the same change in his.

The Lord Chancellor, in giving judgment, remarked, that the matters complained of had been going on for six or seven years, and animadverted strongly on the use of such terms as "lately" and "some time since" in affidavits referring to events so long gone by. It was impossible, certainly, to look at the placards and other papers issued by the defendant, without seeing that they imitated those of the plaintiff so nearly that the difference could not be detected without a very close scrutiny. As, however, these practices were of such long standing, his Lordship saw no sufficient reason for maintaining the injunction. The plaintiff had his remedy at law, and it was evident from his delay in bringing the case before the Court that the prompt interference of an injunction was unnecessary. But considering the character of the defendant's papers, the injunction must be dissolved without costs.

His Lordship observed afterwards, that the plaintiff's conduct, in regard to the advertisements he had issued and the letters he had written since he had obtained the injunction, was highly exceptionable."

The Morning Chronicle[116]
"VICE-CHANCELLOR'S COURT. – Wednesday. Warren v. Wood and Pilcher or Pitcher. – This was a motion to dissolve an exparte injunction granted a few days ago, against the defendants.

It appeared from the affidavits filed by the defendants, that a Mr Jonathan Warren, about the year 1795, began to turn his attention to the science of making a s superior composition for blacking, and that after great perseverance and infinite chemical research, he succeeded, by the aid of the talents of one of his neighbours, in discovering that famous composition, now sold under the name of Warren's Blacking. Shortly after the discovery was made perfect, Jonathan Warren took into partnership a brother, named Thomas Warren, the father of those gentlemen who now carry on the business at No. 30, Strand, and the plaintiffs in the present suit. Thomas Warren having by the means afforded to him as a partner, become possessed of his brother's secret in the manufacture of the blacking, thought it would be more condusive to his interests to dissolve the connection subsisting with Jonathan Warren, the original inventor, and to commence business for himself. Jonathan Warren occupied a house, No. 30, Hungerford-street, and his brother Thomas took a house No. 30, in the Strand; and from this resemblance in the numbers arose the greater portions of the dissensions and rivalries which have since taken place between the houses. In the year 1822, Jonathan Warren sold his business to the defendant Wood, who, in the year 1824, took Pilcher into partnership, and removed his residence from Hungerford-street. Still, however, retaining the celebrated number 30, and vending his composition as Warren's Patent Blacking.

Mr Heald, for the defendants, having stated these facts to be contained in the affidavits put in by them, in answer to the claim for an injunction,

[116] *The Morning Chronicle*, Thursday 29th November 1827

observed, that the father of the plaintiffs had evidently been himself the first infringer of the title of his brother. Whatever the Court of Chancery might have thought fit to do then, if it had been applied to, was not, however, a question to be agitated now; but he apprehended, at all events, that no injunction like the present could be supported against the defendants at the present time.

Mr Horne, for the plaintiffs, denied the truth of the statements contained in the defendant's affidavits. The fact was that Thomas Warren and his representatives, the plaintiffs, carried on business in St. Martin's-lane up to the year 1816, when they removed to the Strand. Jonathan Warren, on the contrary, did not occupy the house in Hungerford Stairs until the year 1821; and it was impossible that he, or any other person, could say his house was properly called No. 30, for there were not eleven houses in the place. The Learned Gentleman was proceeding to comment upon the conduct of the defendants, in using the No. 30 upon their labels, when –

The Vice-Chancellor begged to be informed at what time the plaintiff's first discovered this improper use of their name and number.

Mr Horne being unable to state the precise time from any thing which appeared in the affidavits –

His Honour declared that he must dissolve the injunction. The plaintiffs had allowed this use of their name and label to continue so long, that they could nor fairly make it a matter of complaint now. He might, however, have come to a different conclusion, if they had made their application at an earlier period.

Mr Heald applied to have the injunction dismissed with costs.

His Honour refused allowing any costs in the cause."

An excerpt from *Green Leaves* by John Harrison Stonehouse

Green leaves: new chapters in the life of Charles Dickens, by John Harrison Stonehouse; revised and enlarged edition. The Piccadilly Fountain Press, 1931. An extract from Chapter IV: Dickens's contemplated autobiography

The reference to Holcroft's *Memoirs* is a more interesting and more important one; for the book exercised a considerable influence on Dickens. The *Memoirs* were published in three volumes, in 1816; the first seventeen chapters only were written by Holcroft himself; the rest of the book being compiled from his Journals, by William Hazlitt, who writes in his Introduction: 'Few lives have been marked with more striking changes; and no one possessed the qualities necessary for describing them with characteristic liveliness in a greater degree than he did.'

Describing his early life, Holcroft himself writes: 'When I was about six years old, the scene suddenly changed, a long train of increasing hardships began, and I have no doubt my sufferings were rendered more severe from a consciousness of the little I had suffered till then. This may therefore be properly considered as the first remarkable era in my life.

'How far the state of my father's affairs might contribute to the steps he took, is more than I can now tell; but on a sudden the house-keeping broke up .... What became of his effects, in what manner they were sold, and of every circumstance of that kind, I am totally ignorant. My father was very fond, and not a little vain of me. He delighted to show how much I was superior to other children.'

Holcroft relates how on one occasion he was even sent out to beg from house to house; he relates:

'Young as I was, I had a considerable readiness in making out a story, and on this day, my little inventive faculties shone forth with much brilliancy. I told one story at one house, another at another, and continued to vary my tale just as the suggestions arose: the consequence of which was that I moved the good country people exceeding.'

This reminds us of David Copperfield, who, on being asked a good many questions, 'To all of which, that I might commit nobody, I invented, I am afraid, appropriate answers.' *(David Copperfield,* chap. xi.)

On his return to his parents with the farthings and scraps he had collected, young Holcroft repeated the stories he had invented, when his father, struck with remorse, decided that he should 'never go on such errands again'. By the emphatic manner in which he stated this to his wife, it would appear that she was the prime mover in the degrading errand on which the boy had been sent. Here again, we are reminded of the fact that it was Dickens's mother who was keen on his being sent back to the blacking-factory. Holcroft then goes on to say, 'How fortunate for me in this respect that I had such a father! He was driven by extreme poverty, restless anxiety, and a brain too prone to sanguine expectations, into many absurdities, which were but the harbingers of fresh misfortunes: but he had as much integrity and honesty of heart as perhaps any man in the kingdom, who had no greater advantages.' Later on he elaborates his description of his father in words which might well be descriptive of Mr. Micawber. 'The habit that became most rooted in, and most fatal to my father, was a fickleness of disposition, a thorough persuasion, after he had tried one means of providing for himself and family for a certain time, that he had discovered another far more profitable and secure. Steadiness of pursuit was a virtue at which he could never arrive: and I believe few men in the kingdom had in the course of their lives been the hucksters of so many small wares.'

Compare this with Dickens's account of his father as quoted by Forster: 'I know my father to be as kind-hearted and generous a man as ever lived in the world. Everything that I can remember of his conduct to his wife, or children, or friends, in sickness or affliction, is beyond praise .... But in the ease of his temper, and the straitness of his means, he appeared to have utterly lost at this time the idea of educating me at all, and to have utterly put from him the notion that I had any claim upon him, in that regard whatever.' (Forster, vol 1, p.18) And later on he said 'The longer I live, the better man I think him'. (Forster, vol 3, p11)

Holcroft wrote, 'I loved my father, and knew his intentions were honest: but almost from infancy, I was aware they were not wise.' (Holcroft's *Memoirs*, vol. 1, p. 150)

Somewhat later on, Holcroft relates that his father employs him as drover, when 'The bad nourishment I met with, the cold and wretched manner in which I was clothed, and the excessive weariness I endured in following these animals day after day, and being obliged to drive creatures perhaps more weary than myself, were miseries much too great, and loaded my little heart with sorrows far too pungent ever to be forgotten.' He goes on to tell us that in bringing the result of his labours to his father, 'I could not help secretly accusing him of insensibility, though that was the very reverse of his character.' This is just the manner in which Dickens ever found excuses for his father's neglect.

The story of David Copperfield's adventure with the too friendly waiter at Yarmouth, who ate up his dinner, is evidently founded on the following childish experience of Holcroft's: he had been left by his father on one occasion at a village three miles from Haslem, in care of an old woman who kept a lodging-house, when two Irishmen arrived, who for food had provided a halfpenny roll between them – 'my good dame they noticed to be mashing up a plentiful supper of new milk and potatoes for me, a dish in which their hearts delighted. Whether it was contrivance, accident, or according to rule, I cannot say; we did not, however, sup in the presence of the old woman, but in the room in which we all three slept. No sooner were we there, and I had begun in imagination to devour my delicate mashed potatoes, than the Irishmen came up to me, pulled my cheeks, told me what a pretty little boy I was, asked me my name, inquired who took care of me, and to what county I was going; and swore by the holy father they never in all their lives saw so meek a looking boy, and so compliant and good-tempered. "Do now," said one of them, "let me taste of your mashed potatoes!" "Aye, and me, too," said the other; "I *warrand* you don't much care about them! We now are a *dale* more used to them in Ireland: I'm sure you'll be very glad to make an exchange. Here now, here is a very fine halfpenny roll, which is very nice *ating*, and which to be sure we bought for our own supper. To be sure we would be fond enough of it, but we don't care about trifles; and as we have been used to *ate* potatoes all the days of our lives, and you English all like bread, why if you *plase*, my sweet compliable *fillow*, we will just make a bit of a swap, and so we shall all *ate* our suppers heartily." The action followed the word; they took my potatoes and gave me the dry roll: while I, totally disconcerted, said not a word, but quietly submitted, though I thoroughly regretted the dainty supper I had lost, and saw them devour it with an aching heart.'

Note: the various references to Holcroft's *Memoirs* all occur in the first seventeen chapters of vol. 1.

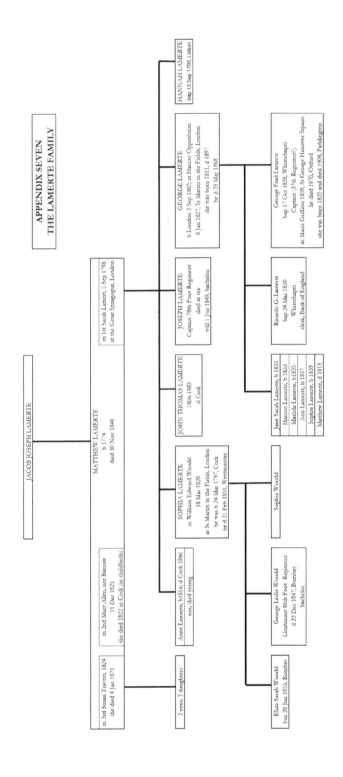

294

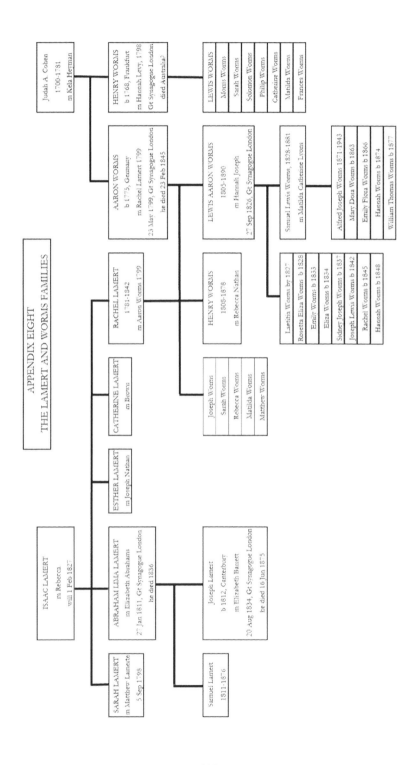

APPENDIX EIGHT
THE LAMERT AND WORMS FAMILIES

Judah A. Cohen
1700-1781
m Kela Herman

HENRY WORMS
b 1768, Frankfurt
m Hannah Levy, 1798
Gt Synagogue London
died Australia?

LEWIS WORMS
Morris Worms
Sarah Worms
Solomon Worms
Philip Worms
Catherine Worms
Matilda Worms
Frances Worms

AARON WORMS
b 1775, Germany
m Rachel Lamert 1799
23 May 1799, Gt Synagogue London
he died 23 Feb 1845

LEWIS AARON WORMS
1805-1890
m Hannah Joseph
27 Sep 1826 Gt Synagogue London

Samuel Lewis Worms, 1828-1881
m Matilda Catherine Lyons

Alfred Joseph Worms 1871-1943
Mary Dora Worms b 1863
Emily Flora Worms b 1866
Hannah Worms b 1874
William Thomas Worms b 1877

Laetitia Worms br 1827
Rosetta Eliza Worms b 1828
Emily Worms b 1833
Eliza Worms b 1834
Sidney Joseph Worms b 1837
Joseph Lewis Worms b 1842
Rachel Worms b 1845
Hannah Worms b 1848

RACHEL LAMERT
1781-1842
m Aaron Worms 1799

HENRY WORMS
1808-1878
m Rebecca Nathan

Joseph Worms
Sarah Worms
Rebecca Worms
Matilda Worms
Matthew Worms

CATHERINE LAMERT
m Brown

ESTHER LAMERT
m Joseph Nathan

ISAAC LAMERT
m Rebecca
will 1 Feb 1827

ABRAHAM LIMA LAMERT
m Elizabeth Abrahams
27 Jan 1811, Gt Synagogue London
he died 1836

SARAH LAMERT
m Matthew Lamette
5 Sep 1798

Joseph Lamert
b 1812, Canterbury
m Elizabeth Barrett
20 Aug 1834, Gt Synagogue London
he died 16 Jun 1875

Samuel Lamert
1811-1876

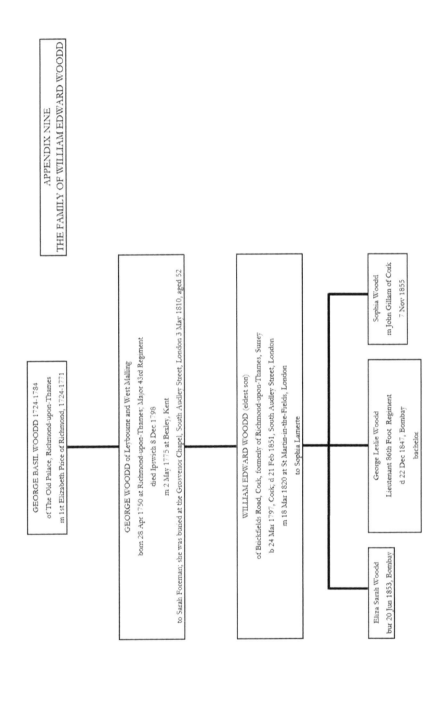

APPENDIX NINE
THE FAMILY OF WILLIAM EDWARD WOODD

GEORGE BASIL WOODD 1724-1784
of The Old Palace, Richmond-upon-Thames
m 1st Elizabeth Price of Richmond, 1724-1771

GEORGE WOODD of Leybourne and West Malling
born 28 Apr 1750 at Richmond-upon-Thames; Major 43rd Regiment
died Ipswich 8 Dec 1798
m 2 May 1775 at Bexley, Kent
to Sarah Foreman; she was buried at the Grosvenor Chapel, South Audley Street, London 3 Mar 1810, aged 52

WILLIAM EDWARD WOODD (eldest son)
of Brickfields Road, Cork, formerly of Richmond-upon-Thames, Surrey
b 24 Mar 1797, Cork; d 21 Feb 1851, South Audley Street, London
m 18 Mar 1820 at St Martin-in-the-Fields, London
to Sophia Lamerte

Eliza Sarah Woodd
bur 20 Jun 1853, Bombay

George Leslie Woodd
Lieutenant 86th Foot Regiment
d 22 Dec 1847, Bombay
bachelor

Sophia Woodd
m John Gillam of Cork
7 Nov 1855

Bibliography

Documentary Sources

The National Archives

Admiralty: Service Records, Registers, Returns and Certificates; Certificates and other papers submitted by applicants to the Charity. Ref ADM 6/352/37, ff157-162.

Court of Chancery: Records of Equity Side: the Six Clerks: Affidavits, Michaelmas Term 1827, box I-Z: Affidavits in the case of Warren v Woodd. Ref C 31/448

Court of Chancery: Records of Equity Side: the Six Clerks: Affidavits, Michaelmas Term 1827, box I-Z: Affidavits in the case of Warren v Lamerte Ref C 31/448

Court of Chancery: Six Clerks Office: Pleadings 1801-1842: Woodd v Lamerte. Ref C 13/865/12

Court of Chancery: Six Clerks Office: Pleadings 1801-1842: Warren v Lamerte. Ref C 13/909/36

Court of Chancery: Six Clerks Office: Pleadings 1801-1842: Warren v Woodd. Ref C 13/1500/110

Court of Chancery: Entry books of Decrees and Orders: Woodd v Lamerte. Ref C 33/759/1416

Court of Chancery: Entry books of Decrees and Orders: Warren v Lamerte. Ref C 33/770/6

Court of Chancery: Entry books of Decrees and Orders: Warren v Woodd. Ref C 33/770/42

Court of Chancery: Entry books of Decrees and Orders: Warren v Lamerte. Ref C 33/770/96

Court of Chancery: Masters reports and certificates: covering "W" names for 1827. C 38/1385

Records of the Prerogative Court of Canterbury: Will Registers: The will of Abraham Lamert. Ref Prob 11/1860.

Records of the Prerogative Court of Canterbury: Will Registers: The will of Isaac Lamert. Ref Prob 11/1721.

Records of the Prerogative Court of Canterbury: Will Registers: The will of Joseph Richard Lamert. Ref Prob 11/2095.

Records of the Prerogative Court of Canterbury: Will Registers: The will of Robert Warren. Ref Prob 11/2089.

Secondary sources

Allen, Michael   *Charles Dickens' Childhood*. Macmillan, 1988.

Burke's Irish Family Records.

Carlton, William J.   "The deed in *David Copperfield*", *The Dickensian*, June 1952.

Carlton, William J. In the blacking warehouse, *The Dickensian*, Winter 1964.

Carlton, William J. "Mr Blackmore engages an office boy", *The Dickensian*, September 1952.

Delavoye, Alex M. *Records of the 90th Regiment, Perthshire Light Infantry, with roll of officers from 1795 to 1880.* Richardson & Co., 1880.

Dickens, Charles "The haunted house", *All the Year Round*, Christmas 1859; reprinted in *Christmas Stories*.

Dickens, Charles *The letters of Charles Dickens.* The Pilgrim edition. Oxford University Press, 12 vols, 1965-2002.

Fessler, A. "Leaflets on the treatment of venereal diseases of the early nineteenth century", in *The British Journal of Venereal Diseases*, June 1946.

Forster, John The life of Charles Dickens. Chapman & Hall, 3 vols, 1872-1874.

Hart, H. G. *The New Annual Army List*, with an index, corrected to 7th February 1840. John Murray, 1840.

Horwood, Richard *Map of London, Westminster & Southwark, shewing every house, 1792-9.* Motco, 2006. ISBN 978-0-9545080-7-4 (CD)

The Household Narrative of current events (for the year 1851,) being a supplement to Household Words, conducted by Charles Dickens. London, 1851

James, William *The Naval History of Great Britain from the declaration of war by France in 1793 to the accession of George IV.* R. Bentley, 6 vols, 1837.

Litvack, Leon "Dickens, Australia and Magwitch, Part II: The search for *le cas Magwitch*", in *The Dickensian*, Summer 1999.

The London Medical and Physical Journal, vol 12, June-December 1804; vol 13, January-June 1805.

Mayhew, Henry *London labour and the London poor...* ; Griffin, Bohn, 1861.

Pedigrees and memorials of the family of Woodd, formerly of Shinewood, Salop, and Brize Norton, Oxfordshire; now of Conyngham Hall, co. York, and Hampstead, Middlesex, and of the family of Jupp of London and Wandsworth. Privately Printed, London: Mitchell and Hughes, 24 Wardour Street, Soho, W. 1875.

The Penny Magazine of the Society for the Diffusion of Useful Knowledge. New Series, Charles Knight & Co., 1842.

Slater, Michael, ed. *The Dent Uniform edition of Dickens' Journalism, vol 1: Sketches by Boz and other early papers 1833-39*, edited by Michael Slater. Dent, 1994.

Slater, Michael, ed. *The Dent Uniform edition of Dickens' journalism, volume 2: The amusements of the people and other papers*, edited by Michael Slater. Dent, 1996.

Slater, Michael, ed. *The Dent Uniform edition of Dickens' journalism, volume 3: 'Gone astray' and other papers from Household Words 1851-59*; edited by Michael Slater, Dent, 1998.

Stonehouse, John Harrison *Green leaves: new chapters in the life of Charles Dickens*, Piccadilly Fountain Press, rev ed, 1931.

Tallis, John   *London Street Views*, 1838-1840. The London Topographical Society, 2002.

Thornbury, Walter   *London recollected: its history, lore and legend*, Vol 2, The Alderman Press, 1985, p552. Originally published as *Old and New London*.

Internet sources

Antiquarian Booksellers' Association. Newsletter   "The ancestors of Laurence Worms: the true story of how I am related to Dickens (but not in a good way)". abainternational.com

Archives Office of Tasmania   Alphabetical record book of convicts arriving in Van Dieman's Land.   tas.gov.au

British Library Nineteenth Century Newspapers   Gale Cengage Learning newspapers.bl.uk/blcs/

Eastern Michigan University, The Adelphi Theatre Project. emich.edu/English/Adelphi_calendar

Hathi Trust Digital Library babel.hathitrust.org

The Internet Archive archive.org

The London Gazette london-gazette.co.uk

The Napoleon Series The Peninsula Roll-Call, compiled by Lionel S. Challis. napoleon-series.org/ research/biographies/ GreatBritain/Challis/ c_ChallisIntro.html

National Library of Australia   Trove: newspapers and more. trove.nla.gov.au/newspaper

Bankingletters.co.uk

Oxford Dictionary of National Biography   oxforddnb.com

Sun Fire Insurance Company   records held at the City of London's Guildhall Library; database accessed through nationalarchives.gov.uk/a2a/

The Times Digital Archive   archive.timesonline.co.uk

Picture credits

(**frontis**) Little Charles Dickens at the blacking warehouse, by Fred Barnard; from *Charles Dickens: extra number of The Bookman*, 1914. (**page 26**) Fox Court, detail from *Richard Horwood's map of London, Westminster & Southwark "Find your way round London in 1799"*, Motco Enterprises Limited, 2006. Ref: www.motco.com (**page 27**) The thieves' kitchen, from *London labour and the London poor...* by Henry Mayhew; Griffin, Bohn, 1861. (**page 30**) Tom-all-alone's by Hablot K. Browne, from *Bleak House*, Chapman & Hall, 1853. (**page 37**) Fagin, by George Cruikshank, from *Oliver Twist*, Richard Bentley, 2nd edition, 1839. (**page 42**) Stone bottles from Warren's Blacking: Michael Allen. (**page 45**) Robert Warren's Blacking in the Strand, a detail from *John Tallis's London Street Views, 1838-1840*, The London Topographical Society, 2002. (**page 46**) Detail from *Richard Horwood's map of London, Westminster & Southwark "Find your way round London in 1799"*, Motco Enterprises Limited, 2006. Ref: www.motco.com (**page 46**) Hungerford Market by Thomas H. Shepherd; from *London and its environs in the nineteenth century...* by Thomas H. Shepherd, Jones & Co., 1829. (**pages 52-54**) Robert Warren placards: Bodleian Library, University of Oxford: John Johnson Collection: Boots and Shoes 1 (28a); Boots and Shoes 1 (28c); Oil and Candles 1 (23); Oil and Candles 1 (27b); Oil and Candles 1 (24a); Oil and Candles 1 (24b); Oil and Candles 1 (27a); Oil and Candles 1 (26a); Oil and Candles 1 (24c). (**page 55**) Robert Warren farthing tokens: Michael Allen. (**page 55**) Street advertising: a sketch by George Scharf. (**pages 58-59**) Blacking labels; Bodleian Library, University of Oxford: John Johnson Collection: Labels 1 (16); Labels 1 (11b); Labels 1 (9a); Labels 1 (14). (**page 64**) Location of 3 Chandos Street; detail from *Richard Horwood's map of London, Westminster & Southwark "Find your way round London in 1799"*, Motco Enterprises Limited, 2006. Ref: www.motco.com (**page 65**) Map showing the three locations of Warren's Blacking: detail from *Richard Horwood's map of London, Westminster & Southwark "Find your way round London in 1799"*, Motco Enterprises Limited, 2006. Ref: www.motco.com (**page 66**) The blacking warehouse, 3 Chandos Street, Covent Garden, from a photo by T.W. Tyrrell; from *Charles Dickens: extra number of The Bookman*, 1914. (**page 75**) Robert Warren, from one of his own tokens: Michael Allen. (**page 80**) The Court of Chancery as drawn by Augustus Pugin and Thomas Rowlandson for *Ackermann's Microcosm of London*, 1808-11: Wikimedia. (**page 85**) View of Hungerford Stairs, near the market, 1822, by George Harley; City of London, Collage record no, 21243. (**page 98**) View of Adelphi Theatre, Strand, Westminster; City of London, Collage record no. 28464.. (**page 99**) Interior view of the Sans Pareil Theatre during a performance, 1816, by George Jones; City Of London, Collage record no. 22941. (**page 272**) Robert Warren's packing warehouse, from *The Penny Magazine of the Society for the Diffusion of Useful Knowledge*. New Series, Charles Knight & Co., 1842.. (**page 273**) Robert Warren's: filling, sealing, labelling and packing, from *The Penny Magazine of the Society for the Diffusion of Useful Knowledge*. New Series, Charles Knight & Co., 1842.

All reasonable efforts have been made to trace those with rights in the illustrations used in this book. If any further rights are brought to the attention of the author he will be pleased to recognise them in future editions or printings.

Index

Adelaide, Australia   36
Adelphi Theatre Project   4,101
Adelphi Theatre, London   4,98-103, **98,99**
advertising   16-20,42,43,47,49-56,**52-55**,60,69,72,81,83,88,109,120,132, 137,152,177-181,186,190,195,205, 212,216,230,235,236,244
affidavits, Warren v Lamerte   151-189
affidavits, Warren v Woodd   215-248
agents   see travellers
Aldgate, City of London   8,22,24,179, 187
All the Year Round   92
All the Year Round offices   13
Allen, Mary   5,6,8,9,11,12
Allen, Michael: *Charles Dickens' childhood*   5n,6n,12n,92,94,95
Allen, Thomas   5
American War of Independence   48
Andrews, Mr, barrister   260,263
Antiquarian Booksellers' Association Newsletter   25n,36n
army regiments
  37th Regiment of Foot   103-4
  43rd Regiment of Foot   48
  50th Foot (West Kent)   7
  78th Regiment of Foot   104
  86th Regiment of Foot   105
  90th Regiment of Light Infantry   7
  Ceylon Rifle Regiment   104
Artful Dodger (*Oliver Twist*)   37
Arundel, William, boot & shoe maker   43-4,246-8
Ashburton, Devon   51
Ashdown, Robert, traveller   63,221-3, 232-3,238-40,241-2
Australia   33-37,69,105-6
Bagstock, Major (*Dombey and son*)   8-9
Bakers Row, Whitechapel   160
Ballard, George   32,260-1
Balm of Life   17
Balm of Zura   19-20
Bank of England   49,61,97
bank shares   96-7
bankruptcy   21,24,25,43,44,97,250, 252-57
Barber and his brothers   101
Barlow Street, St Marylebone   237
Barnard, Fred   **frontis**

barristers   3,75-7,80-3,249-65,284-90
Barrow family   4
Barrow, Charles   5
Barrow, Mary   see Allen, Mary
Barrow, Thomas Culliford   13
Bayham Street, Camden Town   14-15,49,84-5,92-4,98,103
Beadle, St Martin in the Fields Parish   44,187,242
Beauchamp Street, Holborn   32,260
Bedford Street, Covent Garden   67, 87
Bexley, Kent   48
Bishopsgate, London   24,106
Black Prince Road, Kennington   13
Blackfriars   256-7
Blackfriars Road   256
blacking factory, work processes   67-70,86-7,91,266-283
Blits, Rebecca   252,255-9
Bloomsbury   87,90,92-4,96,103
Bodkin, Mr, barrister   249-59
Bodleian Library, John Johnson Collection   4,**52-54,58-59**
Bombay, India   104-5
Bonny, Jane   9
boot and shoe trade   23,24,41,105, 106,132,222,223,234,246,261
Boswell Street, Bloomsbury   96
bottles for blacking   **42**,51,56,68-9,73, 77,91,110,111,113-5,117,121-5, 128-30,134,140-1,143-6,152-3,156-60,163-4,176-7,182,188-9,191-2, 196-7,206-9,217-8,222,224-9,238, 242,244-6,268,270-1,273-9,281-3
Bounderby, Josiah (*Hard Times*)   56
Bow Churchyard   258-9
Bow Street Court   25
Boxer, James, solicitor   145,245
Brazil   5
Brewers Yard, Smithfield   241
Brickfields Road, Cork   105
Brighton, Sussex   96
Brighton, Tasmania   35
Bristol, Somerset   19-21
Bristol, William   28
British Journal of Venereal diseases   18n
Brodum, Doctor William   17
Brooke's Market, Holborn   260
Brown, Catherine   see Catherine Lamert
Brown, Hablot K.   29,31
Buckingham Street, Strand   92,96

301

Winder, William   262-5
Wise, Henry   44,187,242
Wood, John, clicker   78-9,166-7,170
Woodd family   4,47-9,105,296
Woodd v Lamerte
   court case 72-4
   Answer   130-150
   Complaint   107-130
Woodd, Basil George   48
Woodd, Eliza Sarah   105
Woodd, George   48
Woodd, George Basil   48
Woodd, George Leslie   105
Woodd, Rev. Basil   48n
Woodd, Sophia   see Sophia Lamerte
Woodd, William Edward   8,40,47-
   50,62-3,69-74,79-83,88-90,105,
   throughout 107-248,284-290
Wordsworth, William   51
Worms family   3,35,105-6,295
Worms, Aaron   22-5,105-6
Worms, Alfred Joseph   106
Worms, Catherine   106
Worms, Charles Frederick   106
Worms, Ethel Lane   106
Worms, Frances   106
Worms, Henry (brother of Aaron)
   24-37,105,260-1,262-5
Worms, Henry (son of Aaron)   22
Worms, Henry William   106
Worms, Joseph   106
Worms, Laurence   25n,36
Worms, Lewis (brother of Aaron) 105
Worms, Lewis Aaron   23-4,63,72-4,
   97,106,107-150,160-1,162-4,176,
   179,181-4,203,261,264
Worms, Lewis Henry   35,36,105-6
Worms, Matilda   106
Worms, Matilda   106
Worms, Matthew   106
Worms, Matthew Aaron   105
Worms, Morris   32-3,106,262-5
Worms, Philip   106
Worms, Rebecca   106
Worms, Rosetta   106
Worms, Samuel Lewis   106
Worms, Sarah   32,106,261
Worms, Solomon   32,106,260-1
Worms, Sophia   105
Worship Street, Shoreditch   143
Wright, John, carman   91,241-2
Wych Street, Strand   264
Yates, Frederick   100,101,103

310

Made in the USA
Charleston, SC
23 August 2012